Shojo Beat

# OTOMEN

Story & Art by
**Aya Kanno**

Volume
**SEVENTEEN**

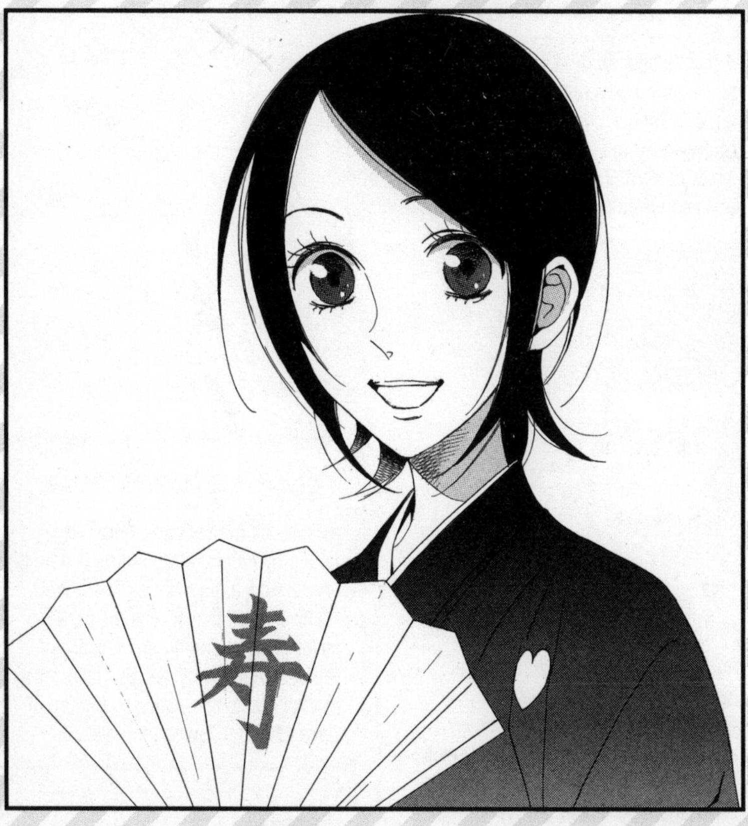
寿

# OTOMEN Characters & Story

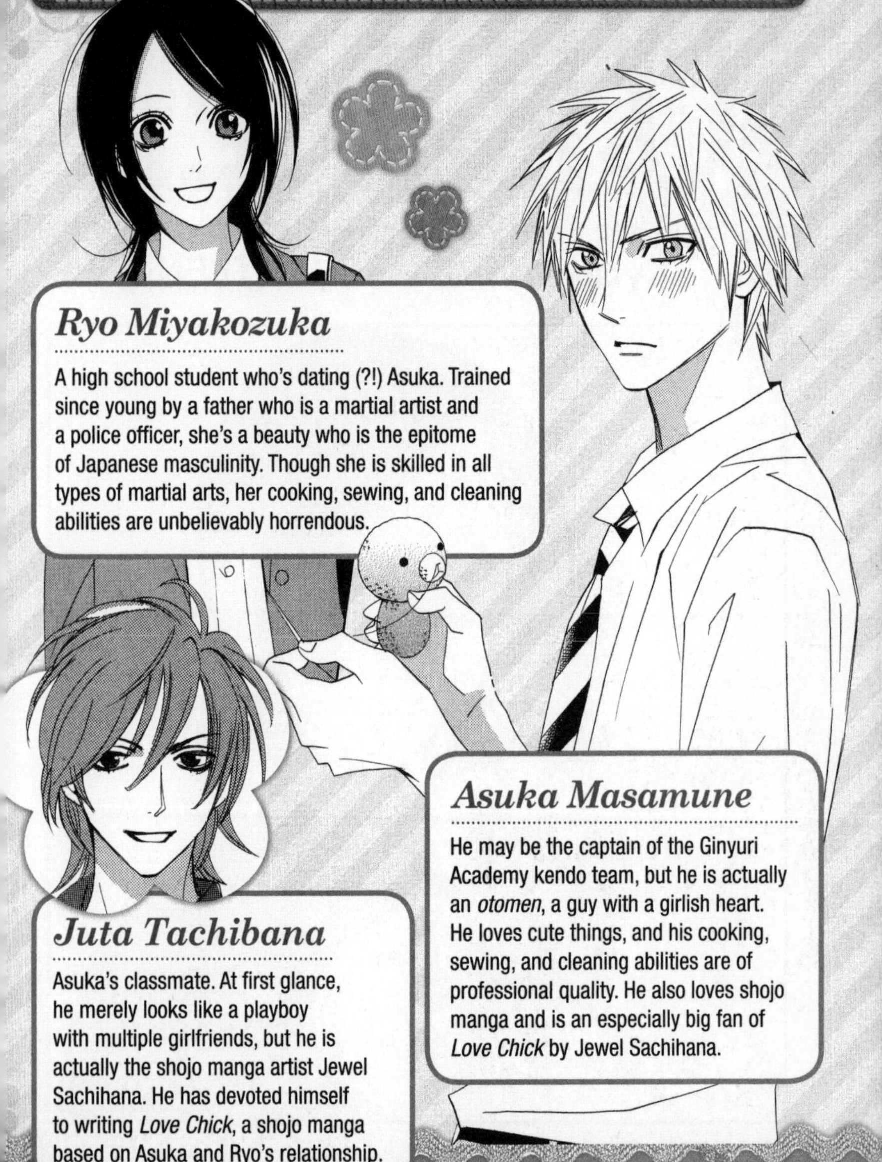

## *Ryo Miyakozuka*

A high school student who's dating (?!) Asuka. Trained since young by a father who is a martial artist and a police officer, she's a beauty who is the epitome of Japanese masculinity. Though she is skilled in all types of martial arts, her cooking, sewing, and cleaning abilities are unbelievably horrendous.

## *Asuka Masamune*

He may be the captain of the Ginyuri Academy kendo team, but he is actually an *otomen*, a guy with a girlish heart. He loves cute things, and his cooking, sewing, and cleaning abilities are of professional quality. He also loves shojo manga and is an especially big fan of *Love Chick* by Jewel Sachihana.

## *Juta Tachibana*

Asuka's classmate. At first glance, he merely looks like a playboy with multiple girlfriends, but he is actually the shojo manga artist Jewel Sachihana. He has devoted himself to writing *Love Chick*, a shojo manga based on Asuka and Ryo's relationship.

# STORY

While on stage at the school festival, Asuka confesses his feelings for Ryo, who accepts him for being an otomen. Asuka's mother Kiyomi sees this and discovers his secret. Kiyomi believes that it is Ryo, Asuka's friends, and shojo manga that have turned her son into an otomen. She secretly does things to make Tonomine, Kitora, and the Kameishi brothers distance themselves from Asuka. Furthermore, she buys out a publishing company and has *Love Chick* canceled!

KIYOMI MASAMUNE

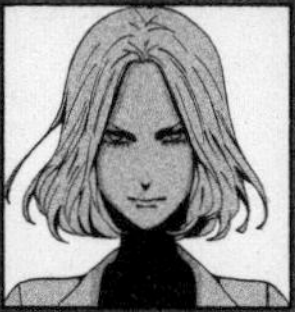

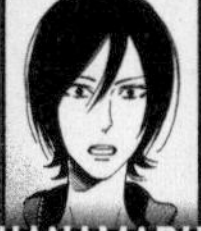

HANAMARU KAMEISHI (JOJI)

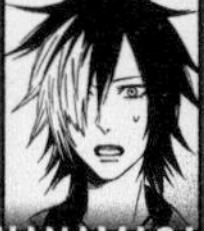

HANAMASA KAMEISHI

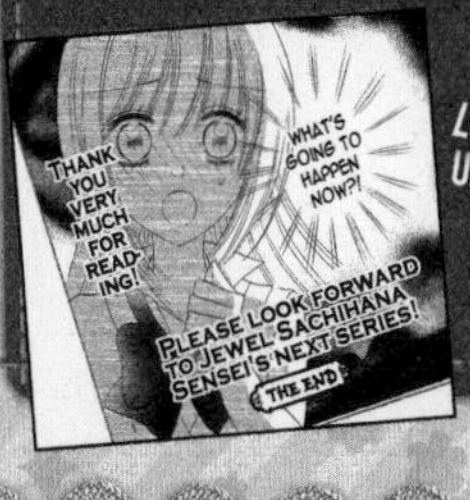
THANK YOU VERY MUCH FOR READING!
WHAT'S GOING TO HAPPEN NOW?!
PLEASE LOOK FORWARD TO JEWEL SACHIHANA SENSEI'S NEXT SERIES!
THE END

*LOVE CHICK'S* UNEXPECTED FINALE?!

# OTHER OTOMEN

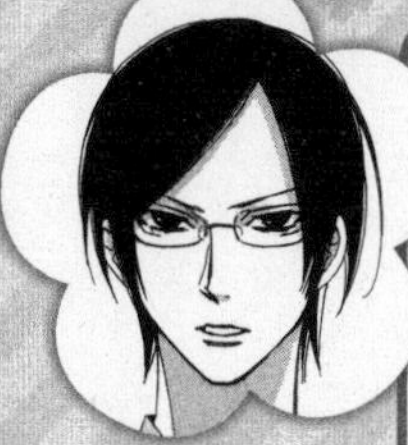

## *Hajime Tonomine*

The captain of the Kinbara High School kendo team, he considers Asuka his sworn rival. He is actually an *otomen* who is good with cosmetics.

## *Yamato Ariake*

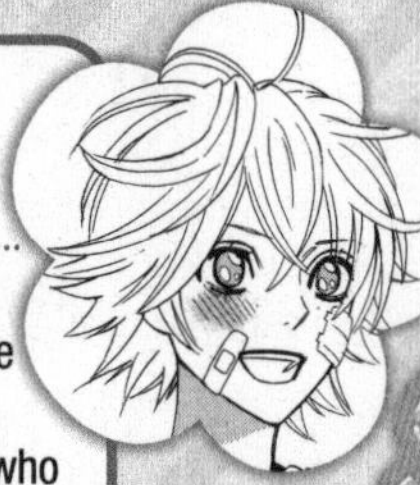

He is younger than Asuka and looks like a cute girl. He is a delusional *otomen* who admires manliness.

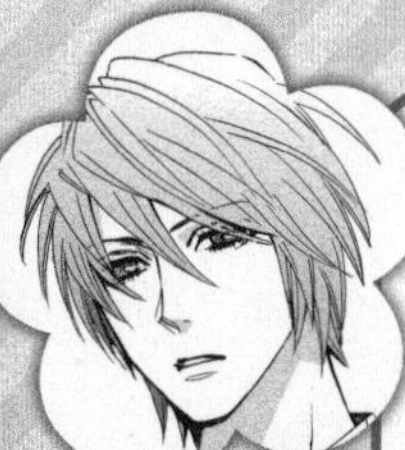

## *Kitora Kurokawa*

Asuka's classmate. A man who is captivated by the beauty of flowers. He is an obsessed *otomen* who wants to cover the world in flowers.

# OTOMEN
*volume 17*
## CONTENTS

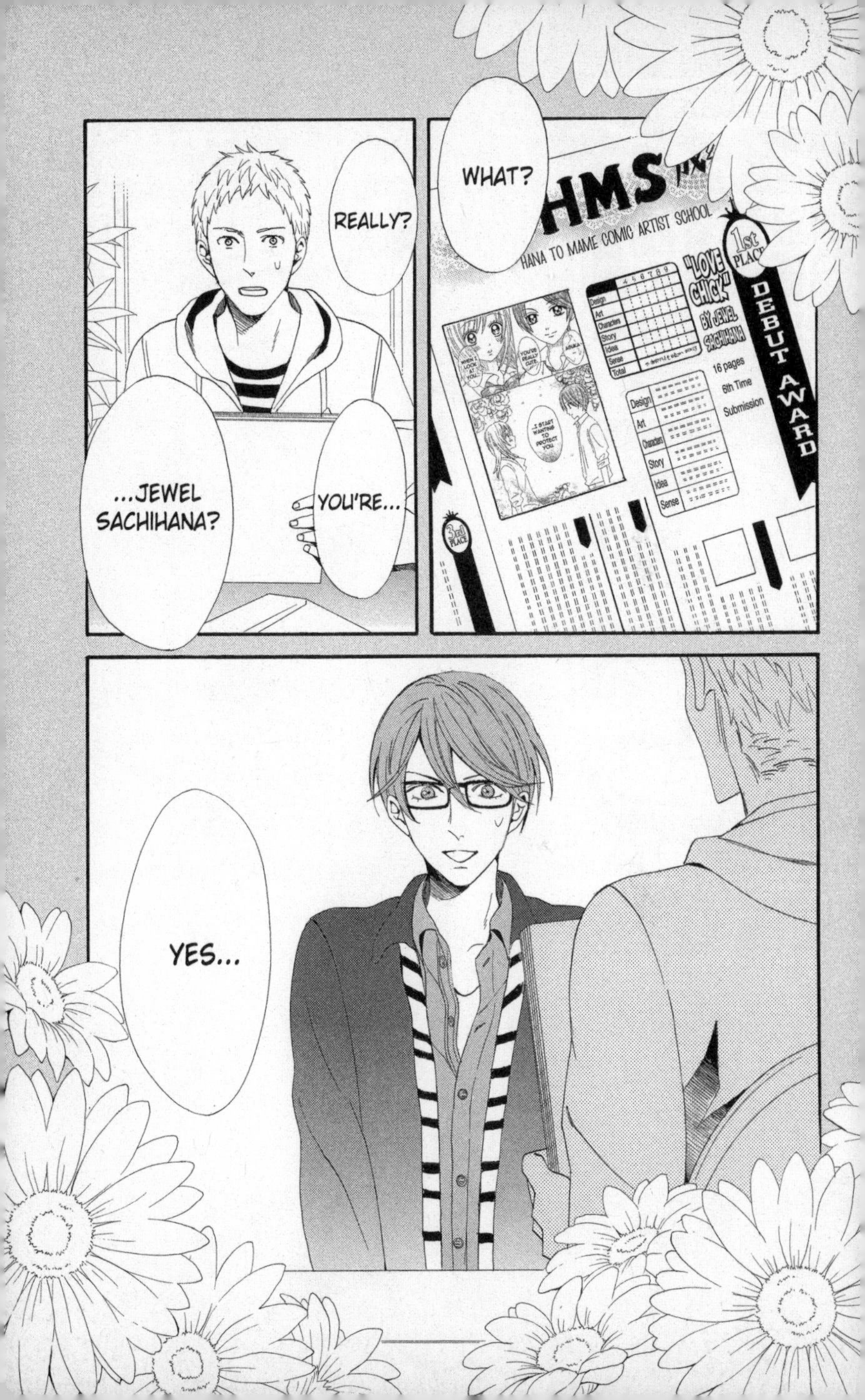
WHAT?
HMS
HANA TO MAME COMIC ARTIST SCHOOL
1st PLACE
DEBUT AWARD
"LOVE CHICK" BY JEWEL SACHIHANA
Design
Art
Characters
Story
Idea
Sense
Total
16 pages
6th Time
Submission
3rd PLACE
REALLY?
YOU'RE...
...JEWEL SACHIHANA?
YES...

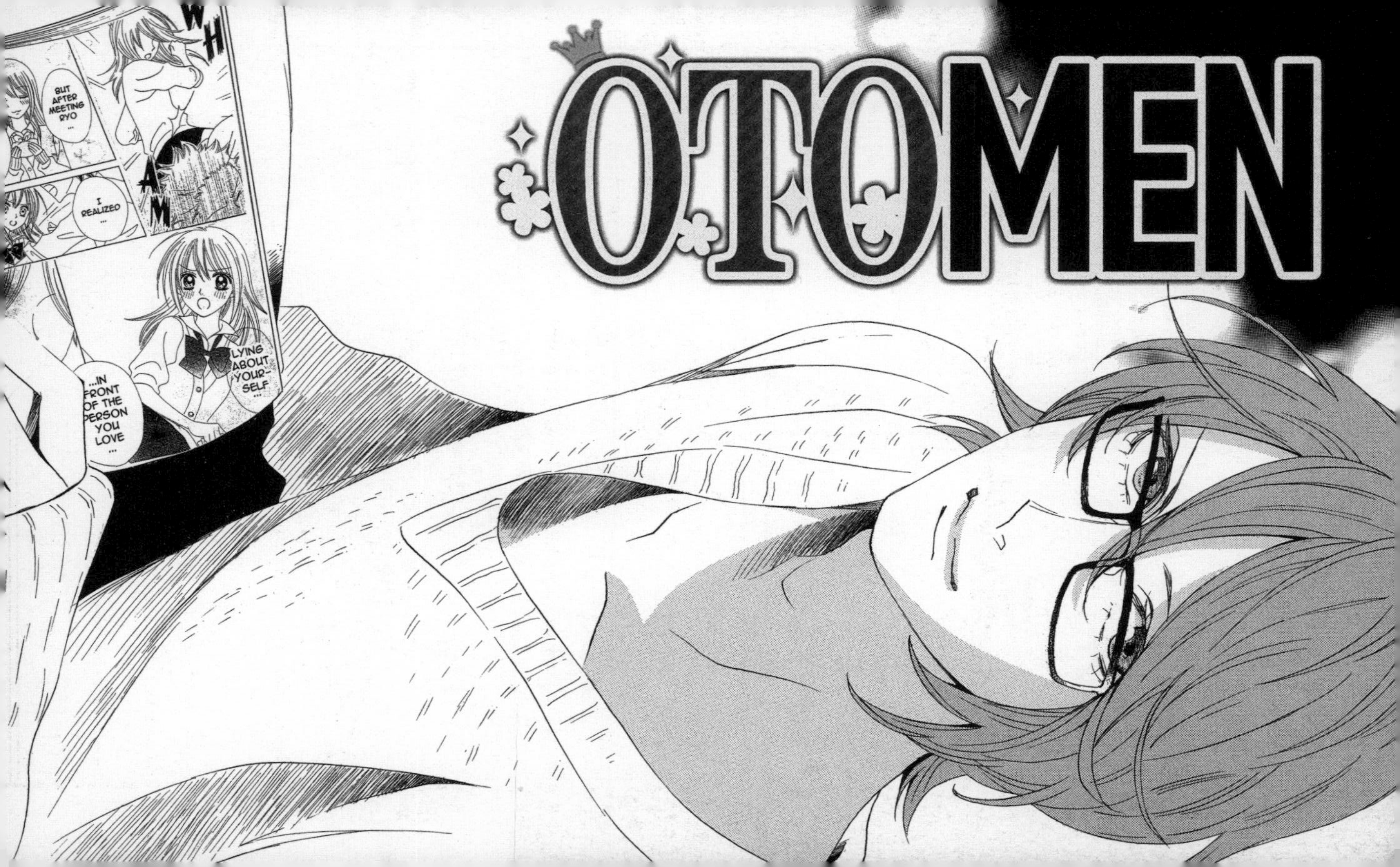
OTOMEN
WHAM
BUT AFTER MEETING RYO...
I REALIZED...
LYING ABOUT YOURSELF...
...IN FRONT OF THE PERSON YOU LOVE...

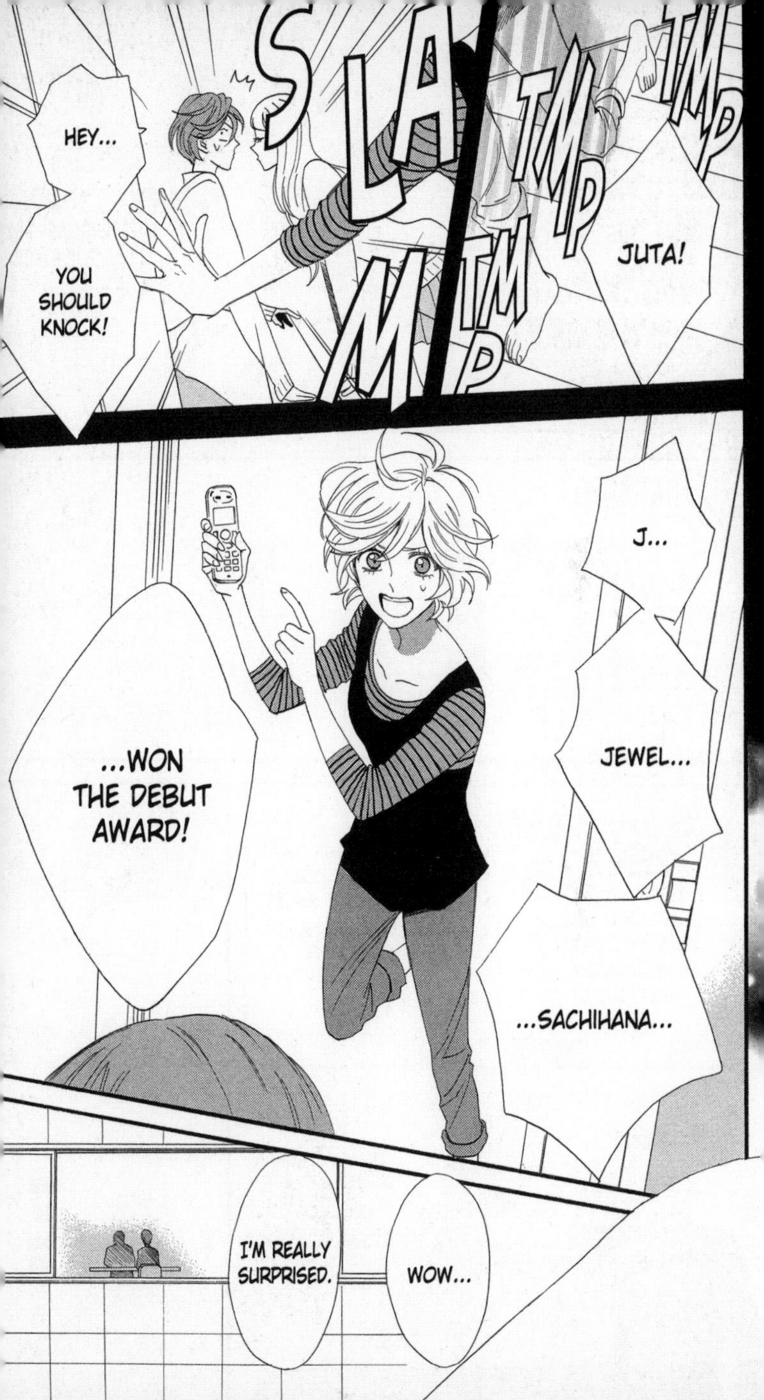
TMP
TMP
TMP
TMP
JUTA!
SLAM
HEY...
YOU SHOULD KNOCK!
J...
JEWEL...
...SACHIHANA...
...WON THE DEBUT AWARD!
WOW...
I'M REALLY SURPRISED.

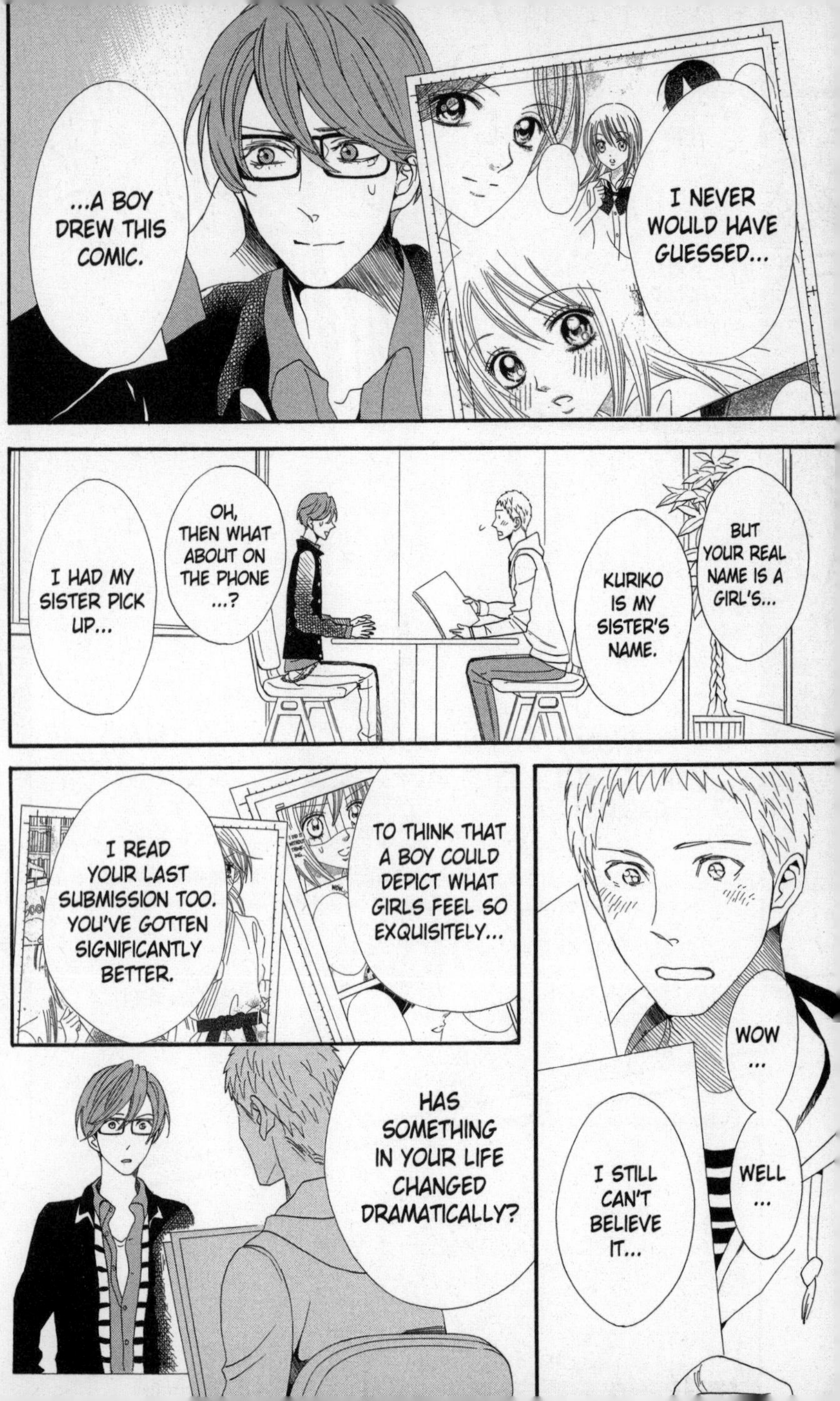
I NEVER WOULD HAVE GUESSED...
...A BOY DREW THIS COMIC.
BUT YOUR REAL NAME IS A GIRL'S...
KURIKO IS MY SISTER'S NAME.
OH, THEN WHAT ABOUT ON THE PHONE ...?
I HAD MY SISTER PICK UP...
WOW ...
WELL ...
I STILL CAN'T BELIEVE IT...
TO THINK THAT A BOY COULD DEPICT WHAT GIRLS FEEL SO EXQUISITELY...
I READ YOUR LAST SUBMISSION TOO. YOU'VE GOTTEN SIGNIFICANTLY BETTER.
HAS SOMETHING IN YOUR LIFE CHANGED DRAMATICALLY?

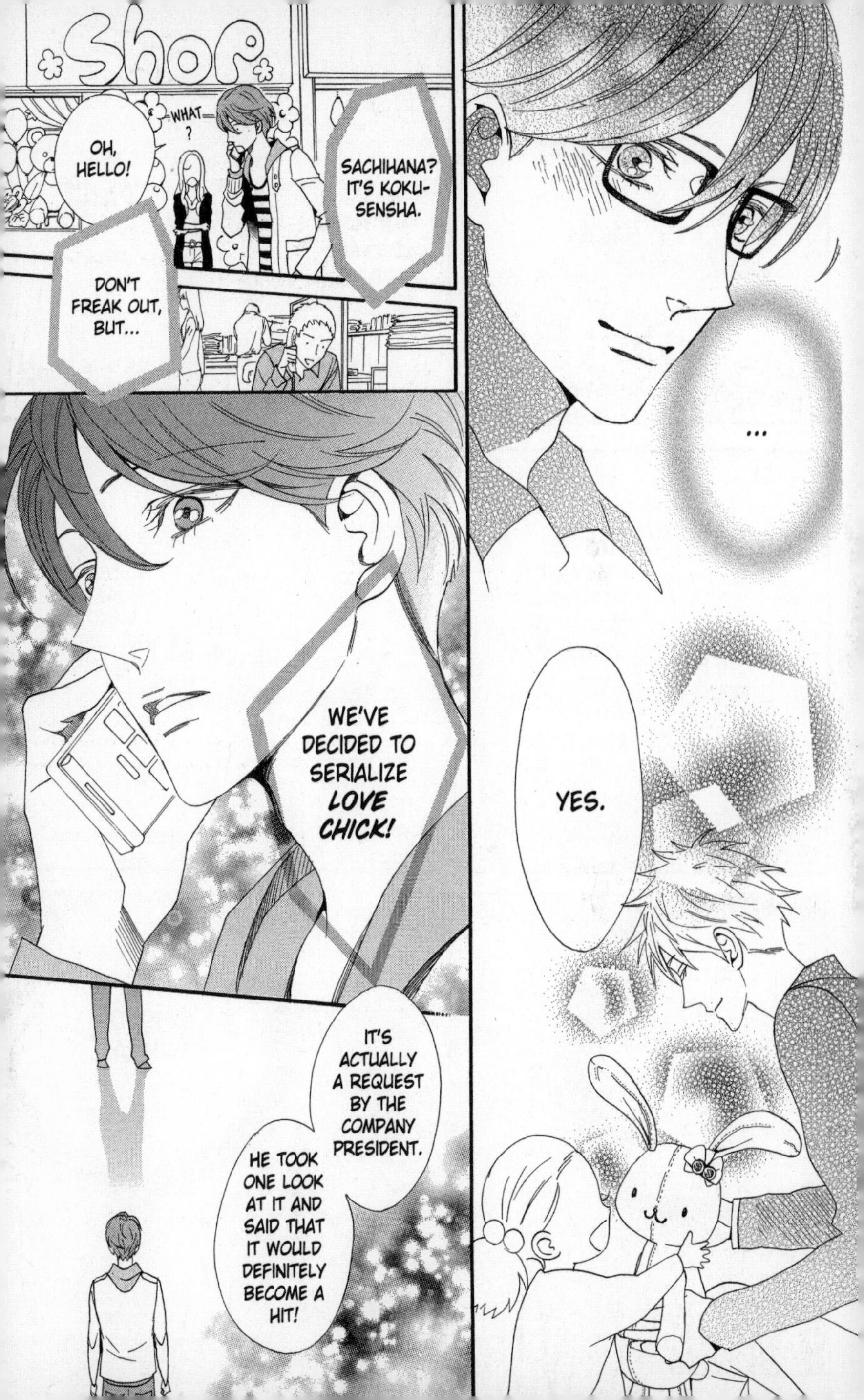
...
YES.
SACHIHANA? IT'S KOKU-SENSHA.
OH, HELLO!
WHAT?
DON'T FREAK OUT, BUT...
WE'VE DECIDED TO SERIALIZE *LOVE CHICK!*
IT'S ACTUALLY A REQUEST BY THE COMPANY PRESIDENT.
HE TOOK ONE LOOK AT IT AND SAID THAT IT WOULD DEFINITELY BECOME A HIT!

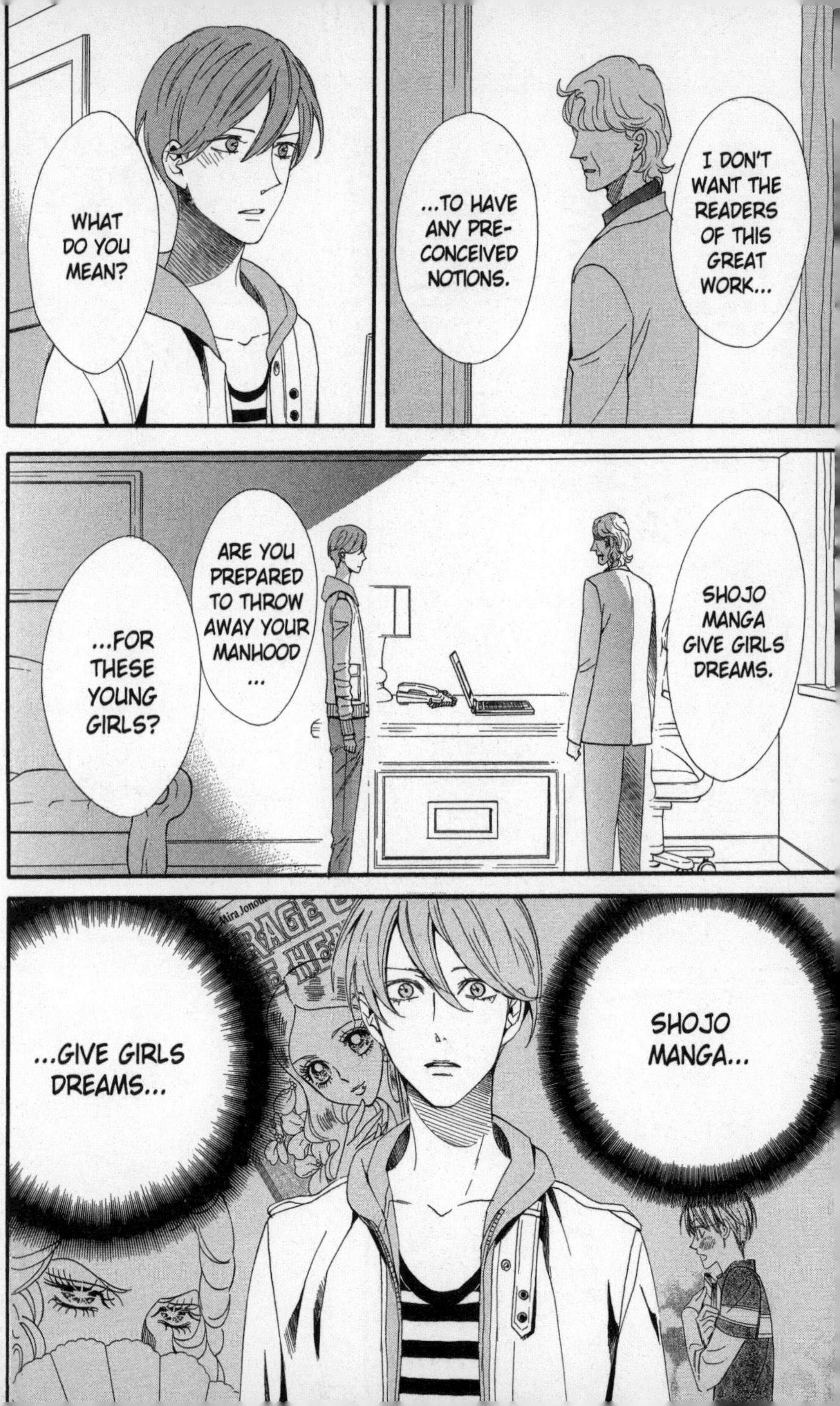
I DON'T WANT THE READERS OF THIS GREAT WORK...
...TO HAVE ANY PRE-CONCEIVED NOTIONS.
WHAT DO YOU MEAN?
SHOJO MANGA GIVE GIRLS DREAMS.
ARE YOU PREPARED TO THROW AWAY YOUR MANHOOD...
...FOR THESE YOUNG GIRLS?
SHOJO MANGA...
...GIVE GIRLS DREAMS...

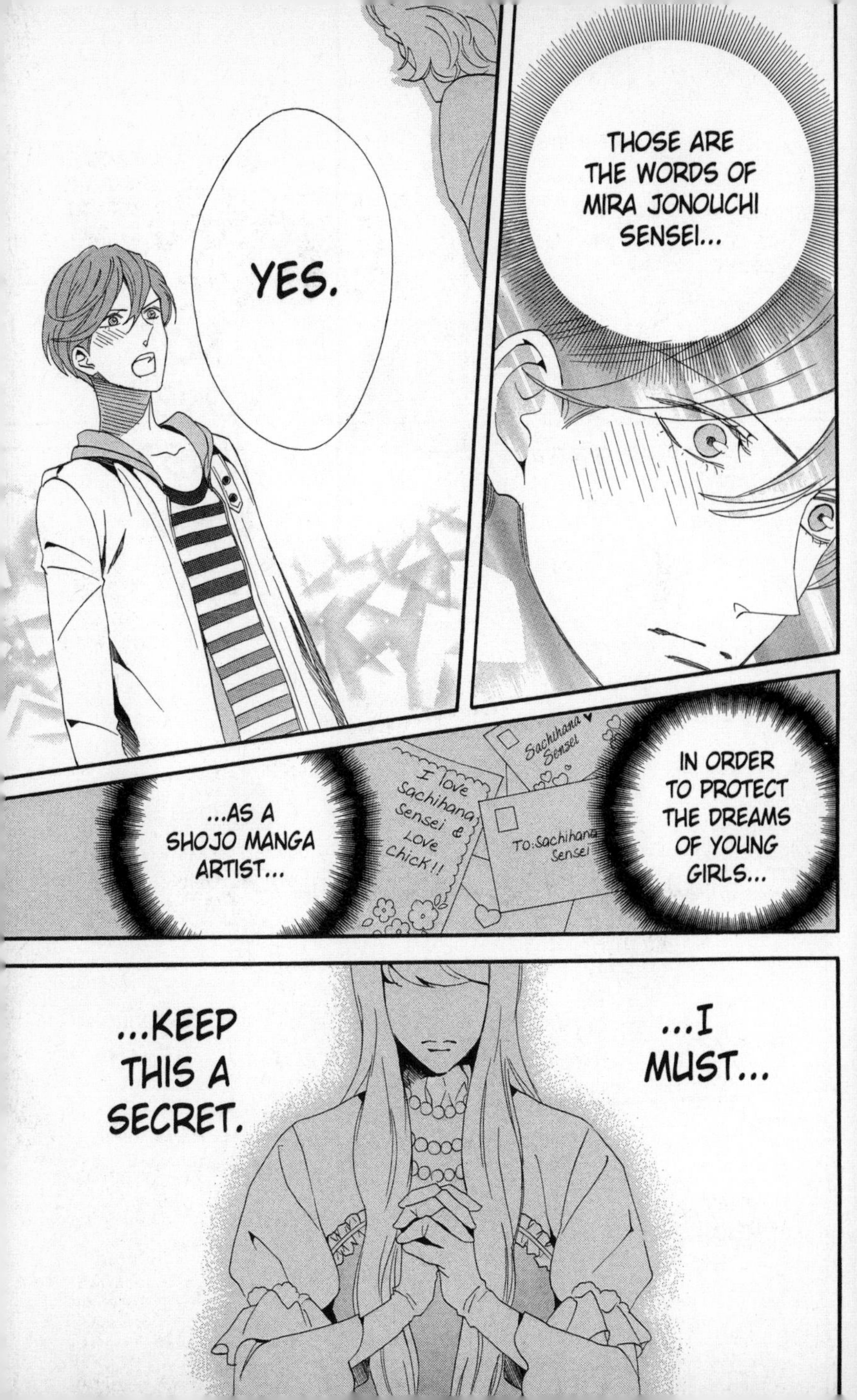
THOSE ARE THE WORDS OF MIRA JONOUCHI SENSEI...
YES.
IN ORDER TO PROTECT THE DREAMS OF YOUNG GIRLS...
Sachihana Sensei
To: Sachihana Sensei
I love Sachihana Sensei & Love Chick!!
...AS A SHOJO MANGA ARTIST...
...I MUST...
...KEEP THIS A SECRET.

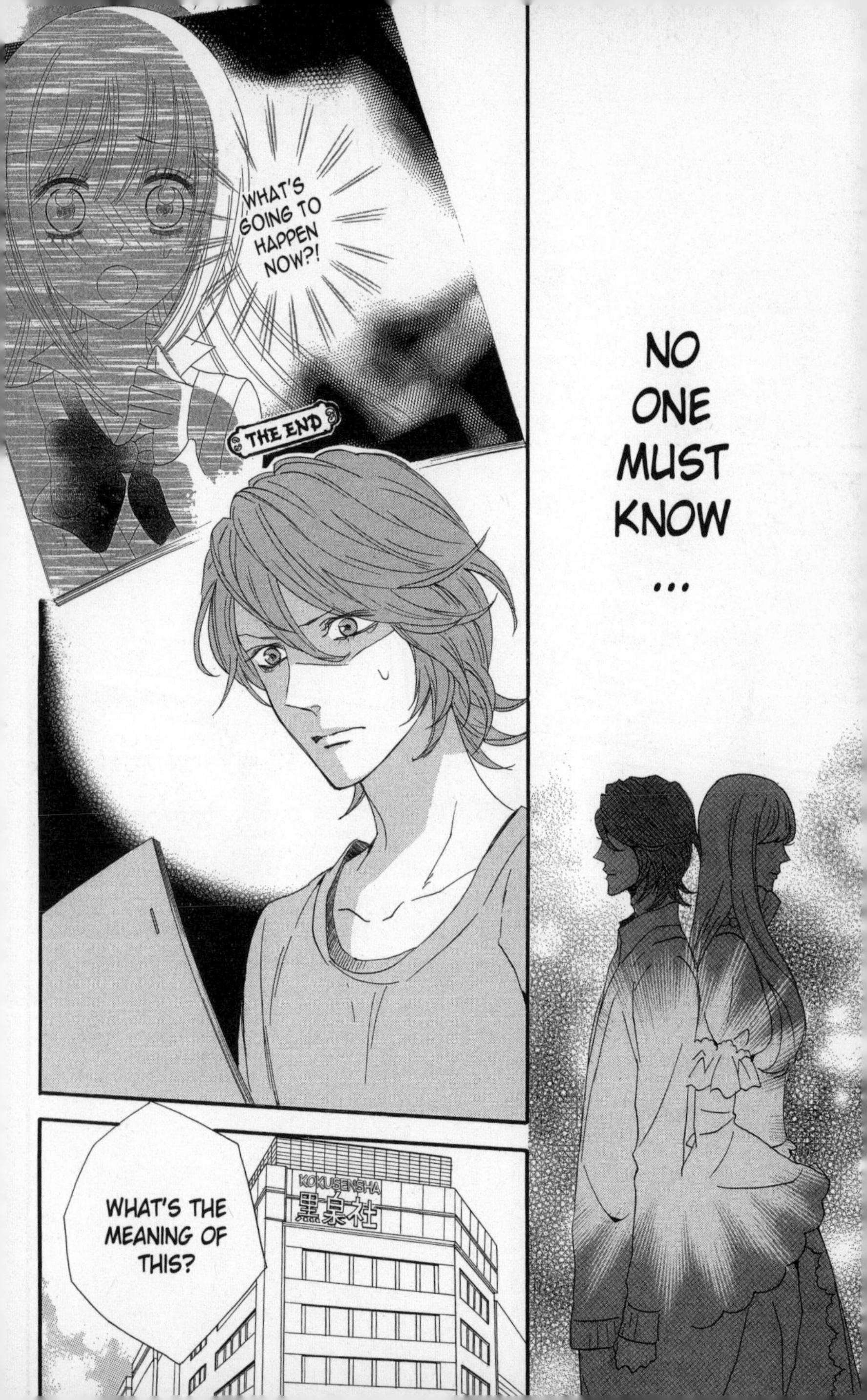
NO ONE MUST KNOW ...
WHAT'S GOING TO HAPPEN NOW?!
THE END
WHAT'S THE MEANING OF THIS?
KOKUSENSHA
黒泉社

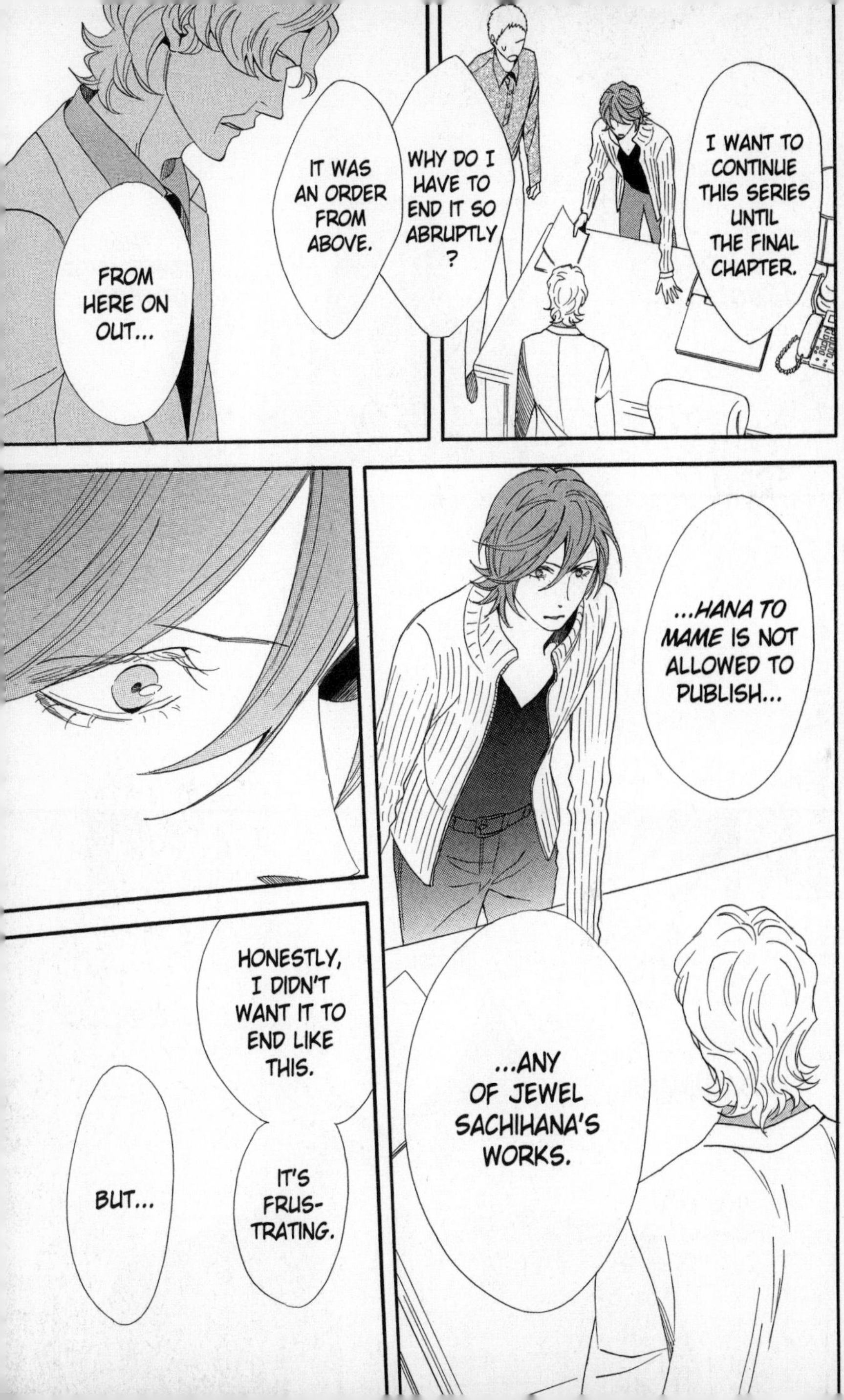
I WANT TO CONTINUE THIS SERIES UNTIL THE FINAL CHAPTER.
WHY DO I HAVE TO END IT SO ABRUPTLY?
IT WAS AN ORDER FROM ABOVE.
FROM HERE ON OUT...
...*HANA TO MAME* IS NOT ALLOWED TO PUBLISH...
...ANY OF JEWEL SACHIHANA'S WORKS.
HONESTLY, I DIDN'T WANT IT TO END LIKE THIS.
IT'S FRUS-TRATING.
BUT...

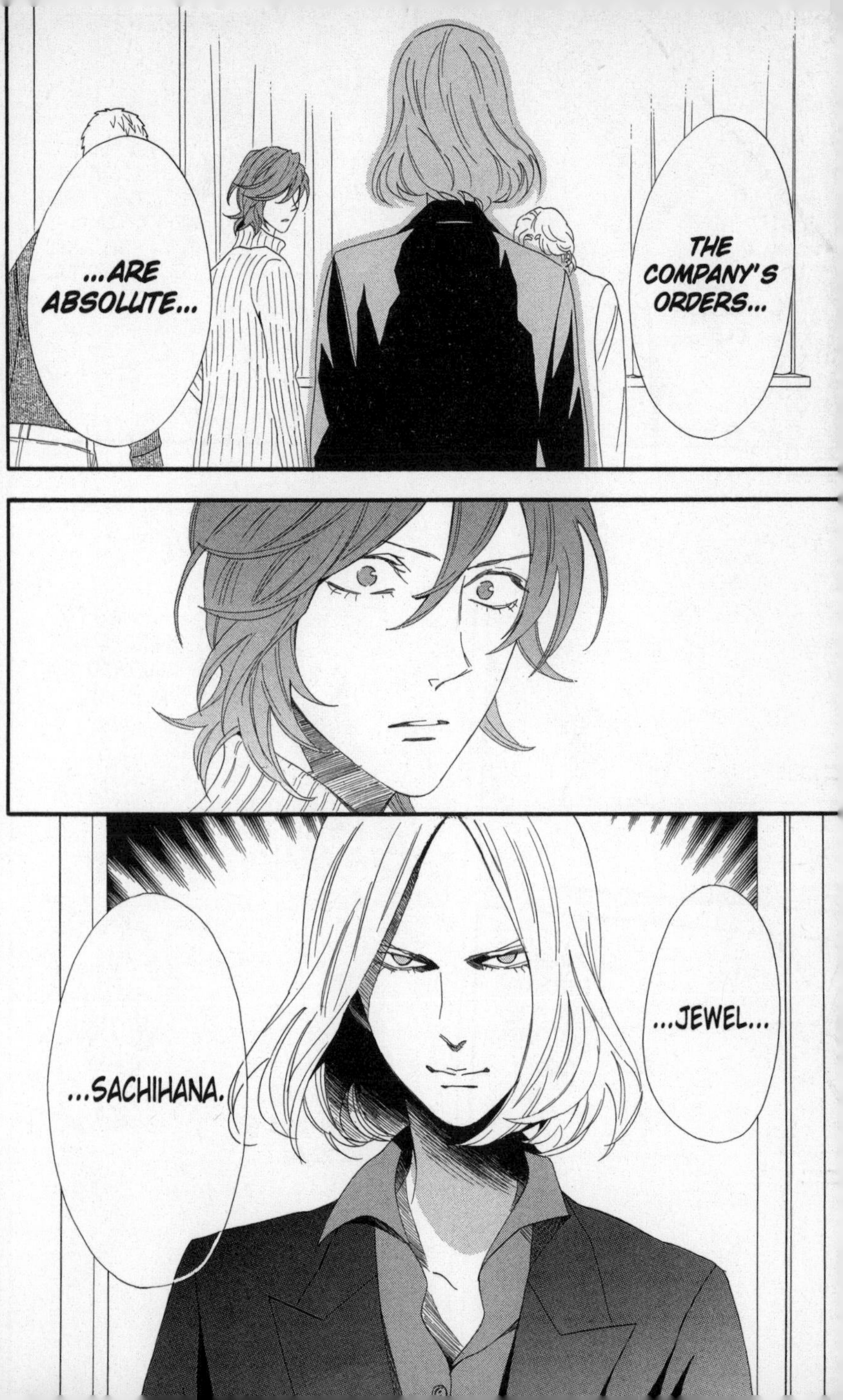
THE COMPANY'S ORDERS...
...ARE ABSOLUTE...
...JEWEL...
...SACHIHANA.

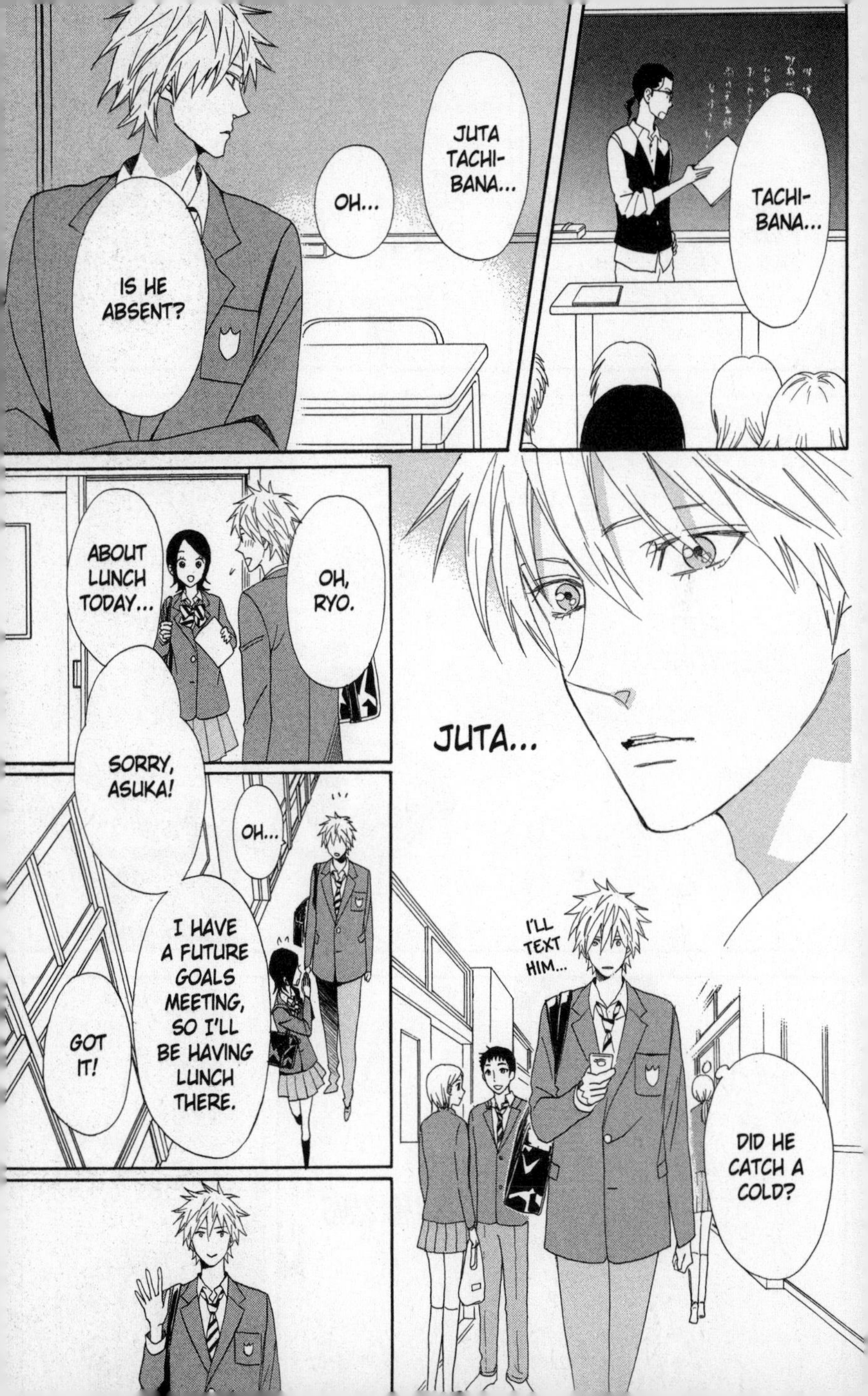
TACHI-BANA...
JUTA TACHI-BANA...
OH...
IS HE ABSENT?
JUTA...
DID HE CATCH A COLD?
I'LL TEXT HIM...
OH, RYO.
ABOUT LUNCH TODAY...
SORRY, ASUKA!
OH...
I HAVE A FUTURE GOALS MEETING, SO I'LL BE HAVING LUNCH THERE.
GOT IT!

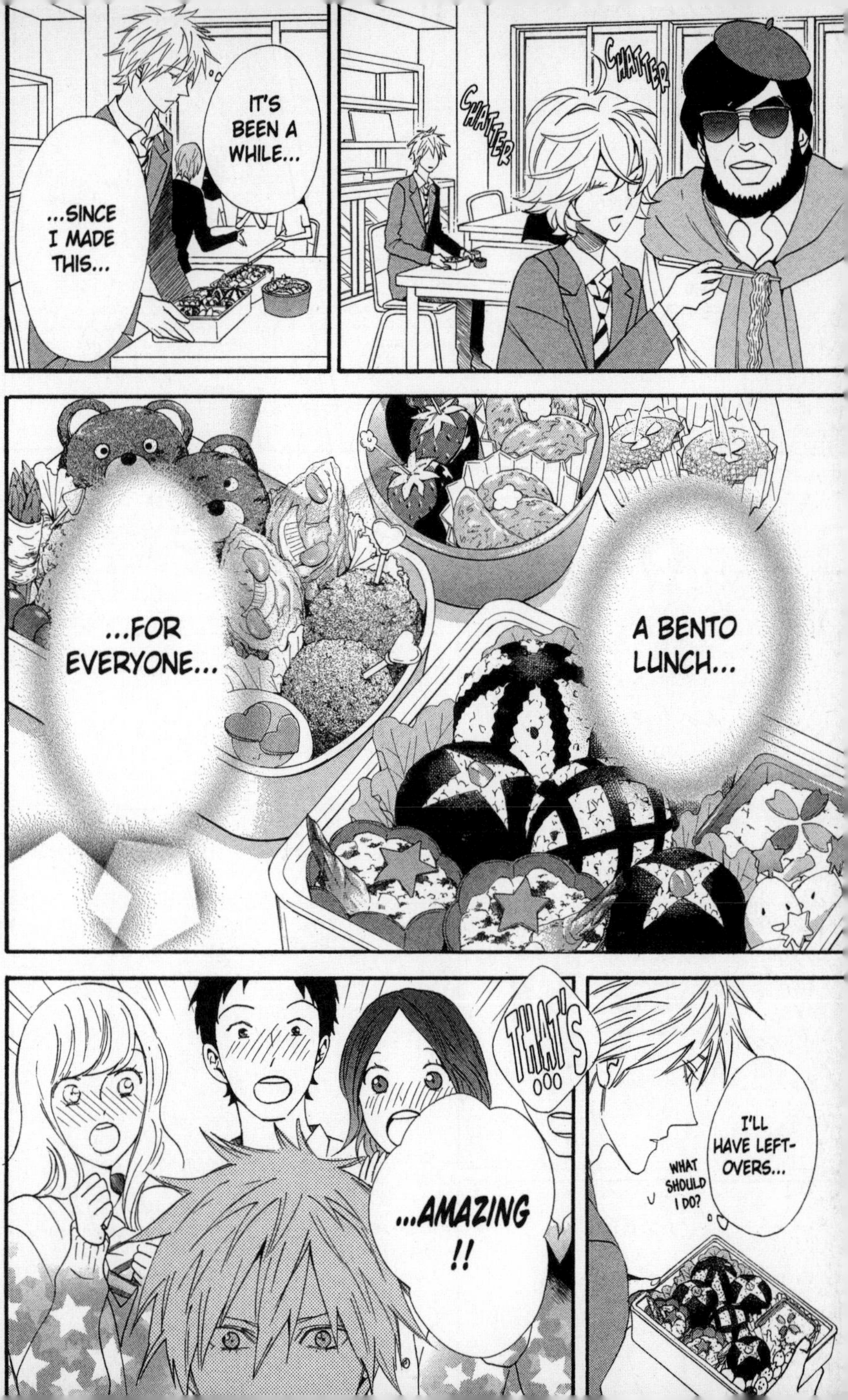
CHATTER
CHATTER
IT'S BEEN A WHILE...
...SINCE I MADE THIS...
A BENTO LUNCH...
...FOR EVERYONE...
I'LL HAVE LEFT-OVERS...
WHAT SHOULD I DO?
THAT'S
...AMAZING!!

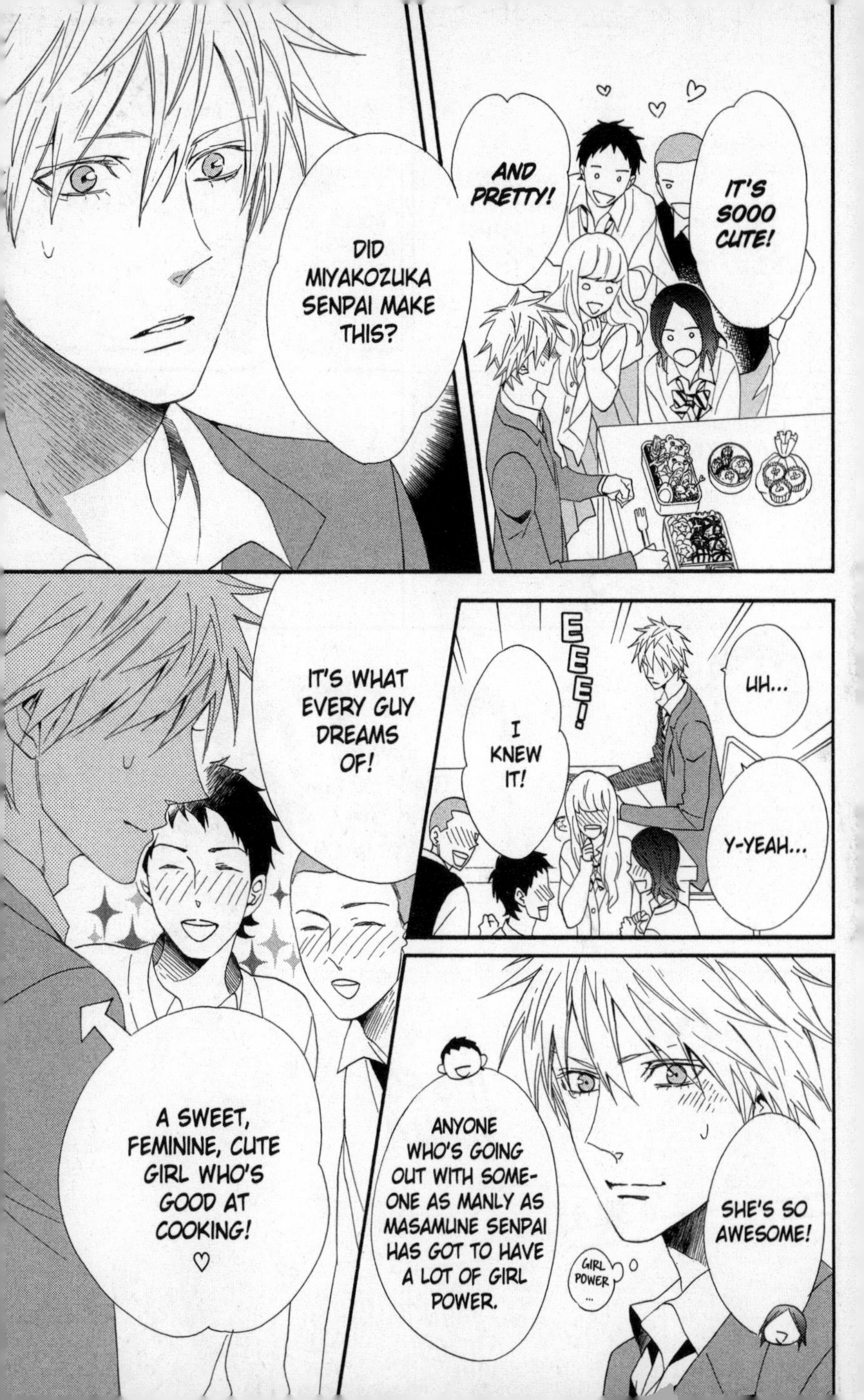
IT'S SOOO CUTE!
AND PRETTY!
DID MIYAKOZUKA SENPAI MAKE THIS?
UH...
Y-YEAH...
EEE!
I KNEW IT!
SHE'S SO AWESOME!
ANYONE WHO'S GOING OUT WITH SOME-ONE AS MANLY AS MASAMUNE SENPAI HAS GOT TO HAVE A LOT OF GIRL POWER.
GIRL POWER ...
IT'S WHAT EVERY GUY DREAMS OF!
A SWEET, FEMININE, CUTE GIRL WHO'S GOOD AT COOKING! ♡

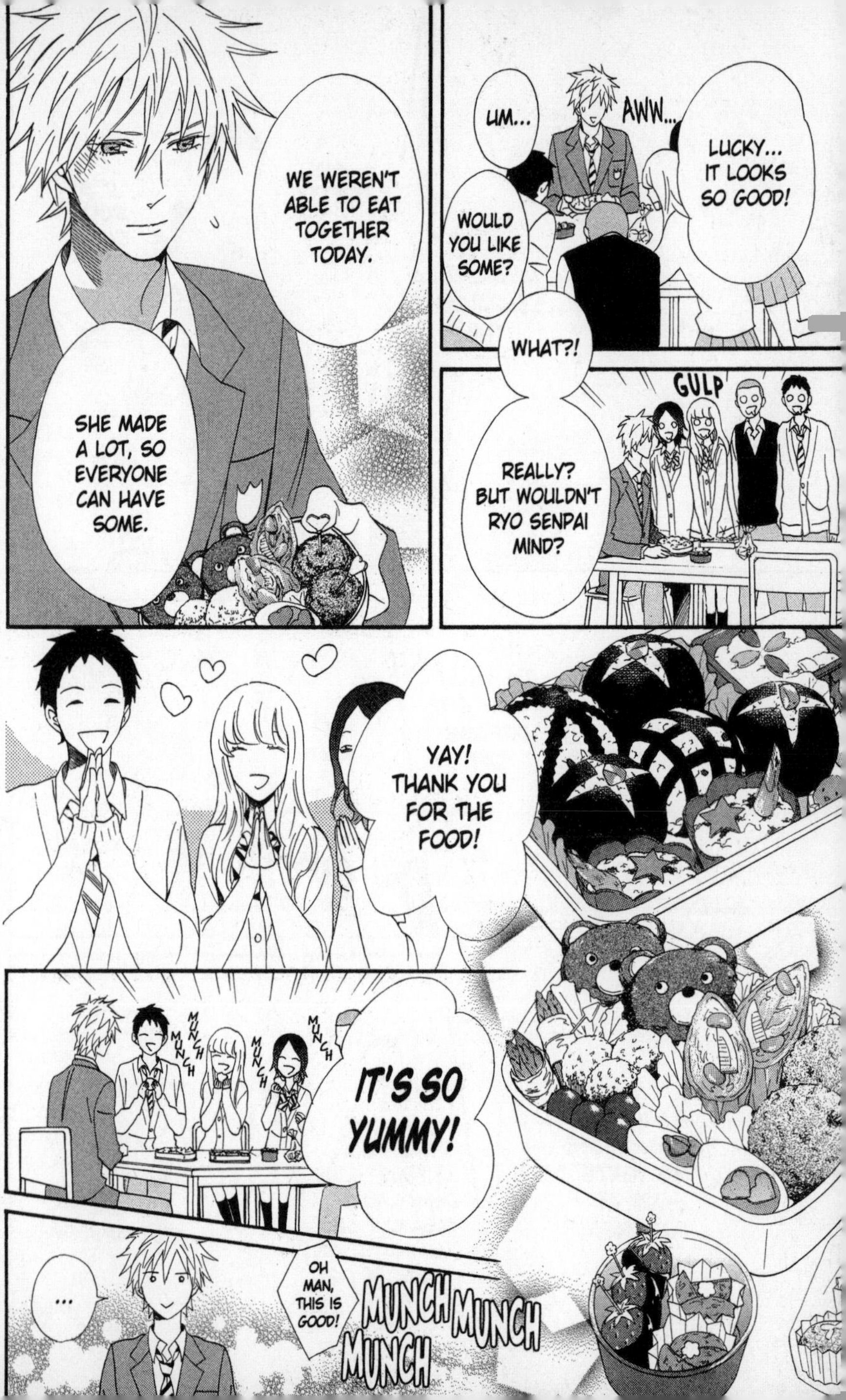

LUCKY... IT LOOKS SO GOOD!
AWW...
UM...
WOULD YOU LIKE SOME?
WHAT?!
GULP
REALLY? BUT WOULDN'T RYO SENPAI MIND?
WE WEREN'T ABLE TO EAT TOGETHER TODAY.
SHE MADE A LOT, SO EVERYONE CAN HAVE SOME.
YAY! THANK YOU FOR THE FOOD!
IT'S SO YUMMY!
MUNCH
MUNCH
MUNCH
MUNCH
MUNCH
MUNCH MUNCH
MUNCH
OH MAN, THIS IS GOOD!
...

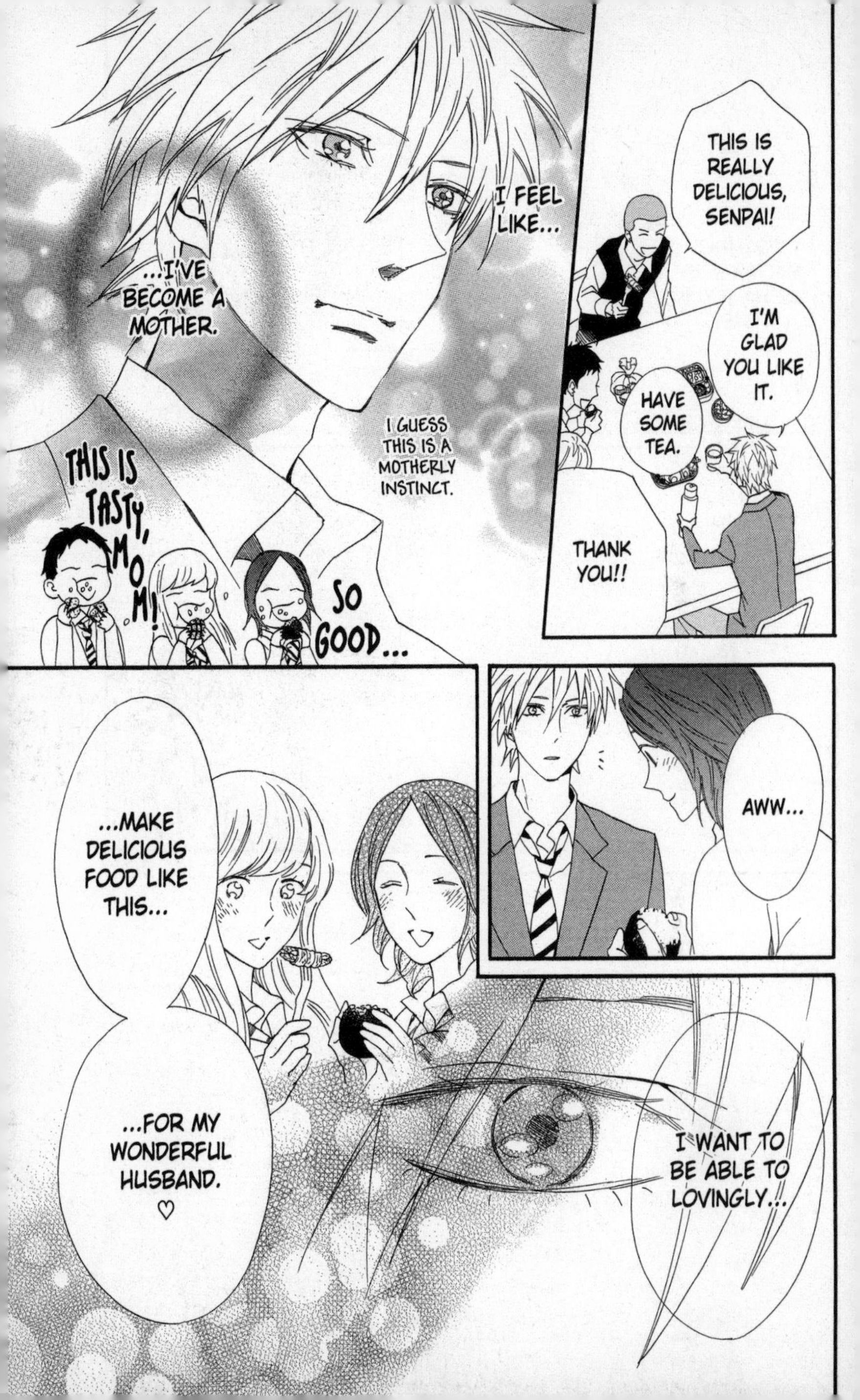
THIS IS REALLY DELICIOUS, SENPAI!
I'M GLAD YOU LIKE IT.
HAVE SOME TEA.
THANK YOU!!
I FEEL LIKE...
...I'VE BECOME A MOTHER.
I GUESS THIS IS A MOTHERLY INSTINCT.
THIS IS TASTY, MOM!
SO GOOD...
AWW...
I WANT TO BE ABLE TO LOVINGLY...
...MAKE DELICIOUS FOOD LIKE THIS...
...FOR MY WONDERFUL HUSBAND. ♡

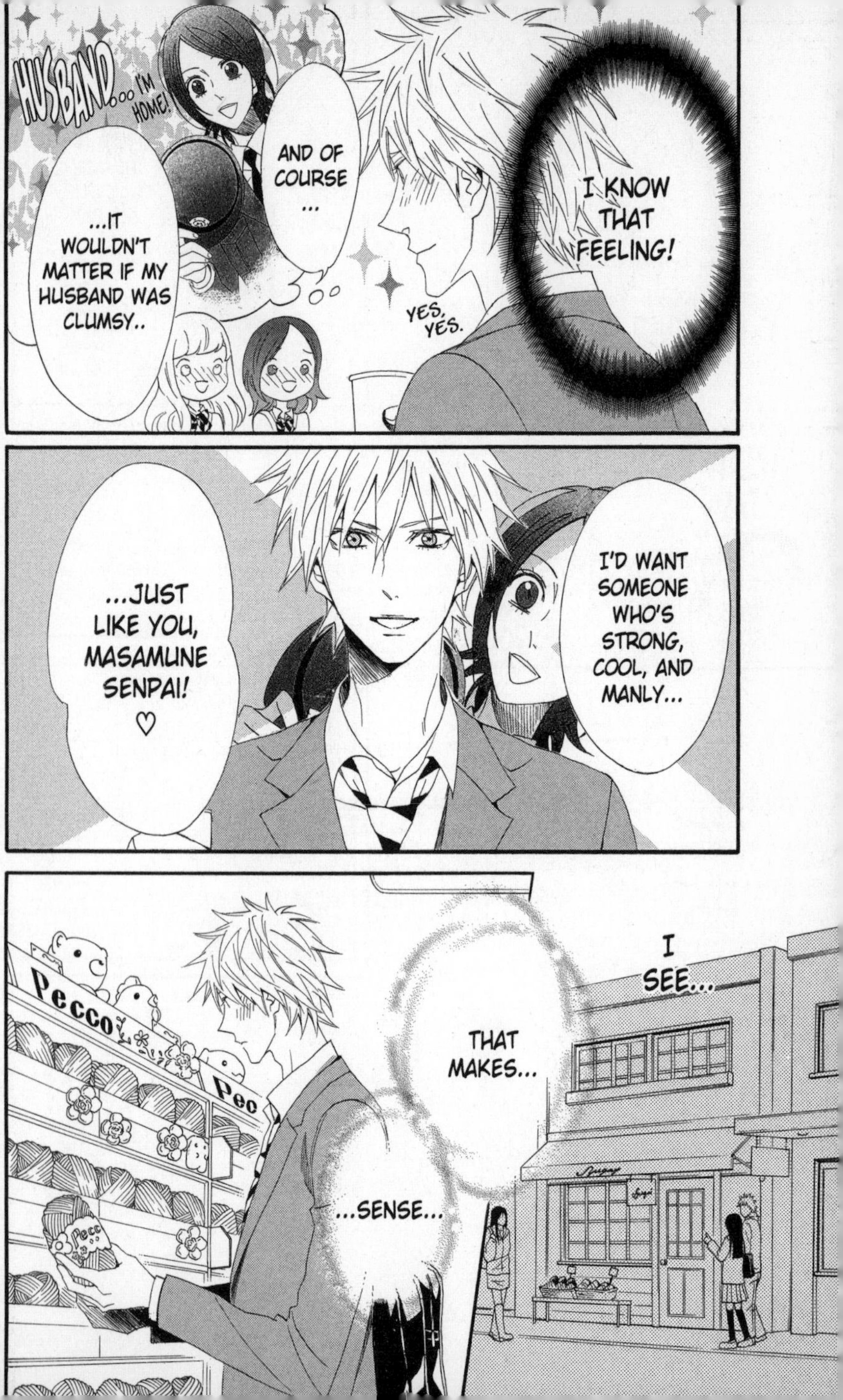
I KNOW THAT FEELING!
AND OF COURSE...
...IT WOULDN'T MATTER IF MY HUSBAND WAS CLUMSY..
HUSBAND... I'M HOME!
YES, YES.
I'D WANT SOMEONE WHO'S STRONG, COOL, AND MANLY...
...JUST LIKE YOU, MASAMUNE SENPAI! ♡
I SEE...
THAT MAKES...
...SENSE...
Pecco
Pec

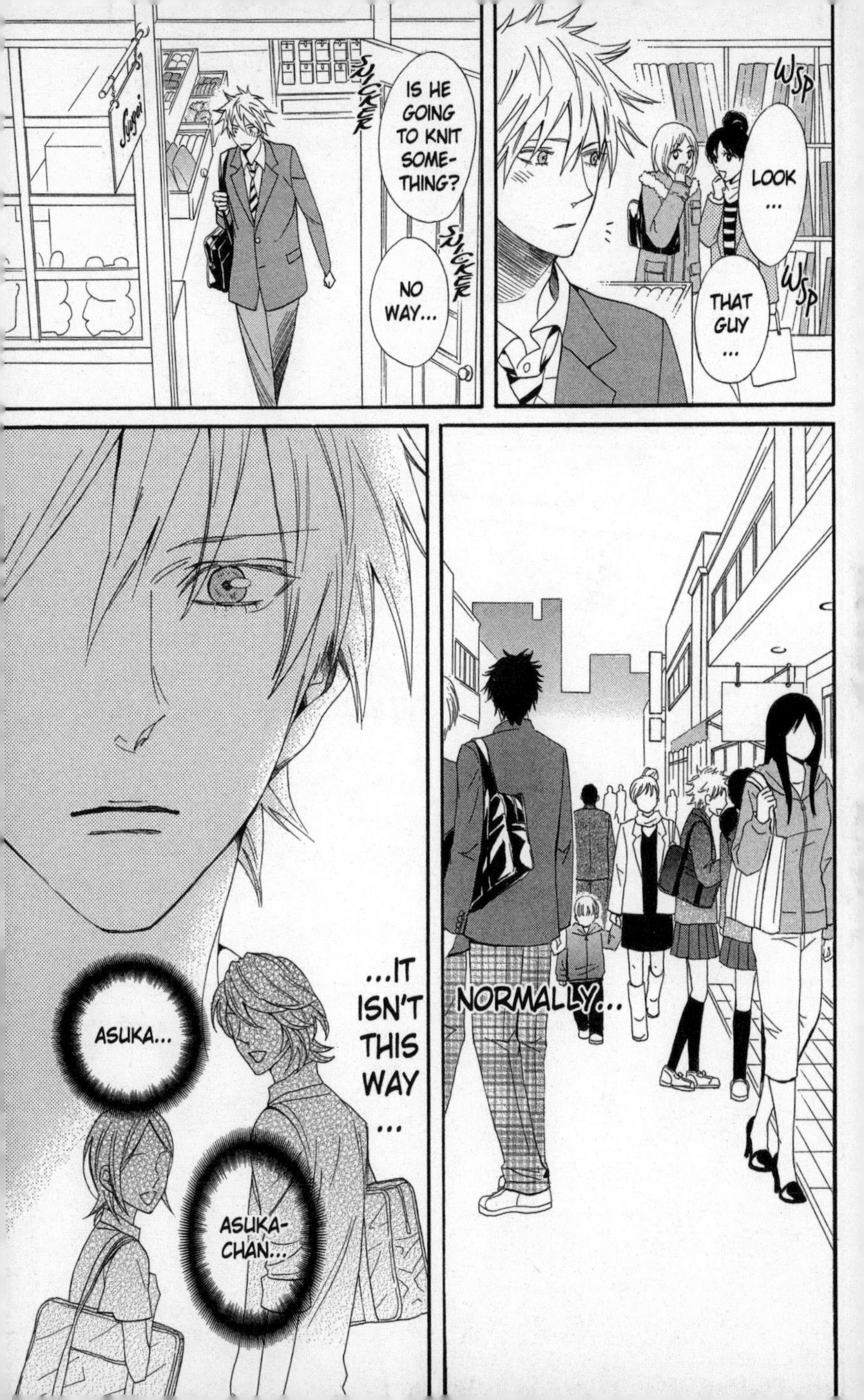

WSP
LOOK ...
THAT GUY ...
WSP
SNICKER
IS HE GOING TO KNIT SOMETHING?
SNICKER
NO WAY...
NORMALLY...
...IT ISN'T THIS WAY ...
ASUKA...
ASUKA-CHAN...

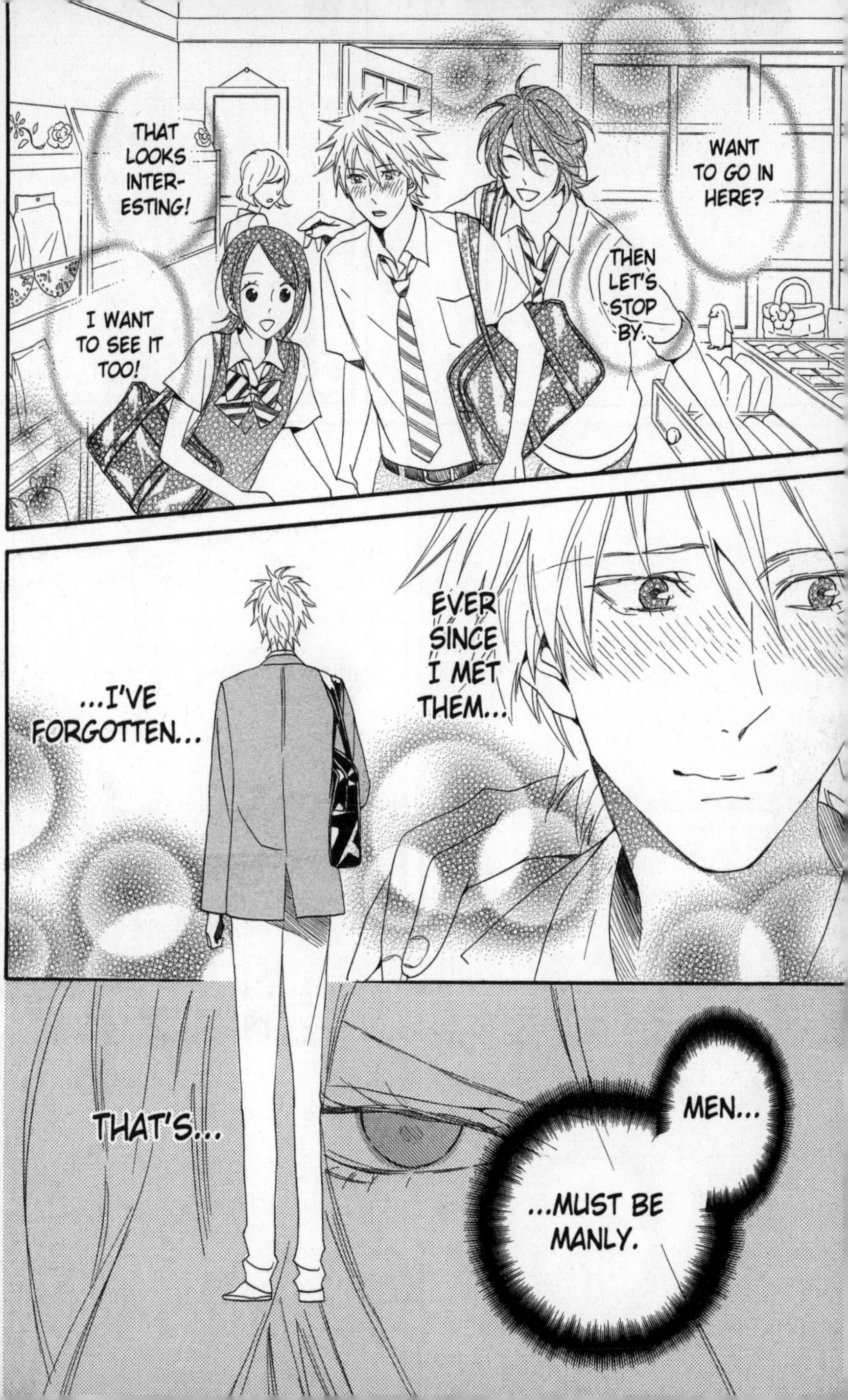
WANT TO GO IN HERE?
THEN LET'S STOP BY.
THAT LOOKS INTER-ESTING!
I WANT TO SEE IT TOO!
EVER SINCE I MET THEM...
...I'VE FORGOTTEN...
THAT'S...
MEN...
...MUST BE MANLY.

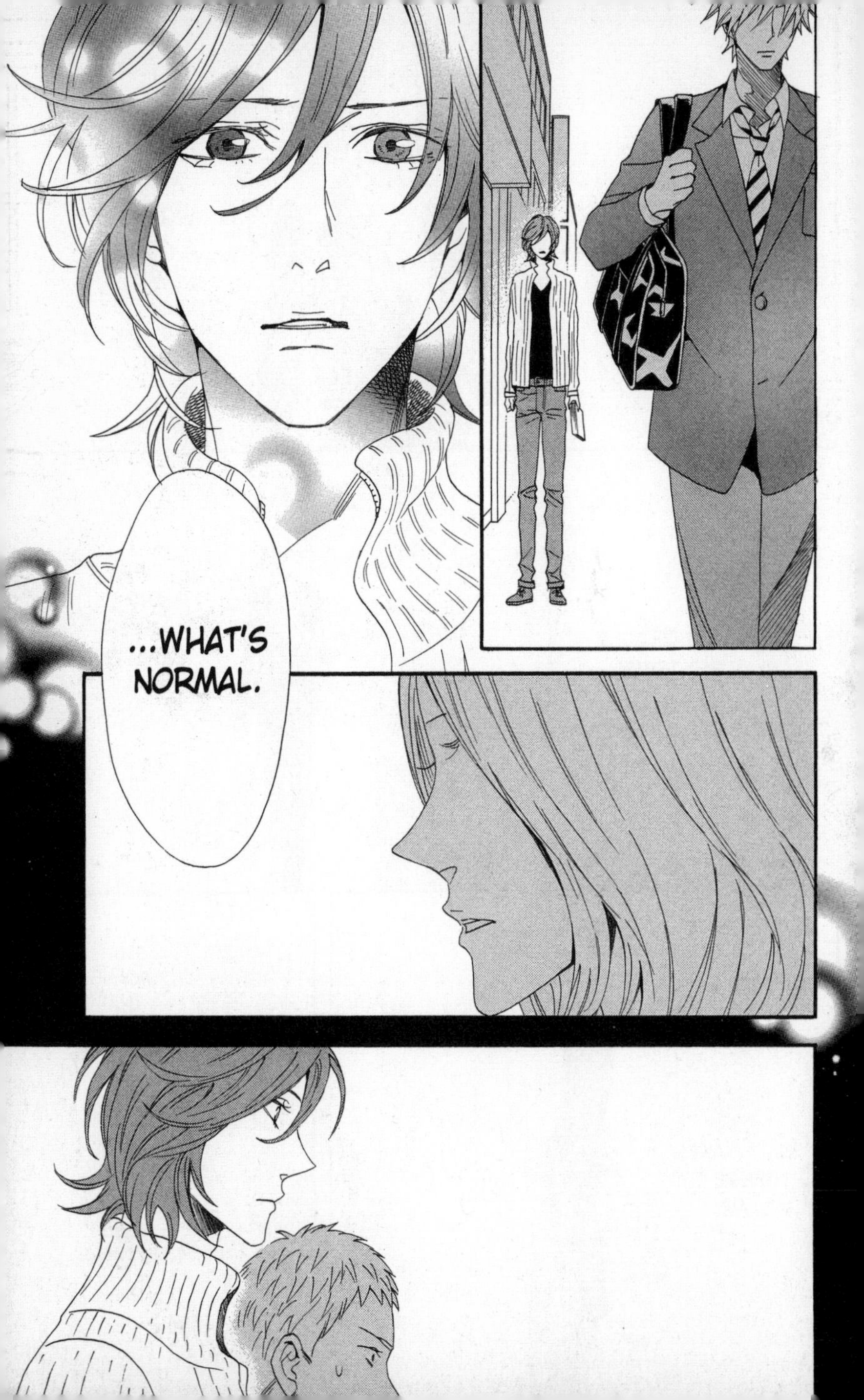
...WHAT'S NORMAL.

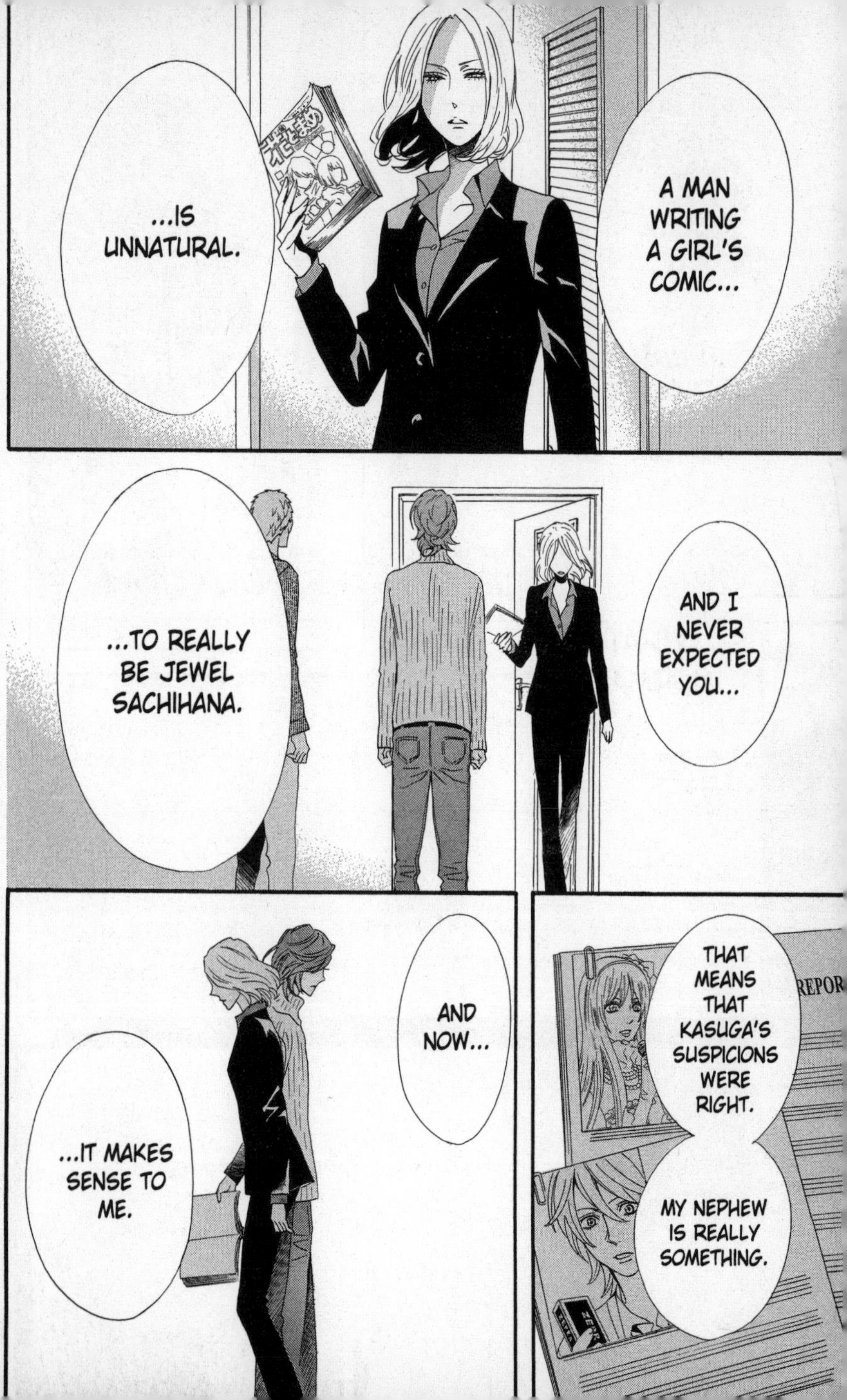
A MAN WRITING A GIRL'S COMIC...
...IS UNNATURAL.
AND I NEVER EXPECTED YOU...
...TO REALLY BE JEWEL SACHIHANA.
THAT MEANS THAT KASUGA'S SUSPICIONS WERE RIGHT.
MY NEPHEW IS REALLY SOMETHING.
AND NOW...
...IT MAKES SENSE TO ME.

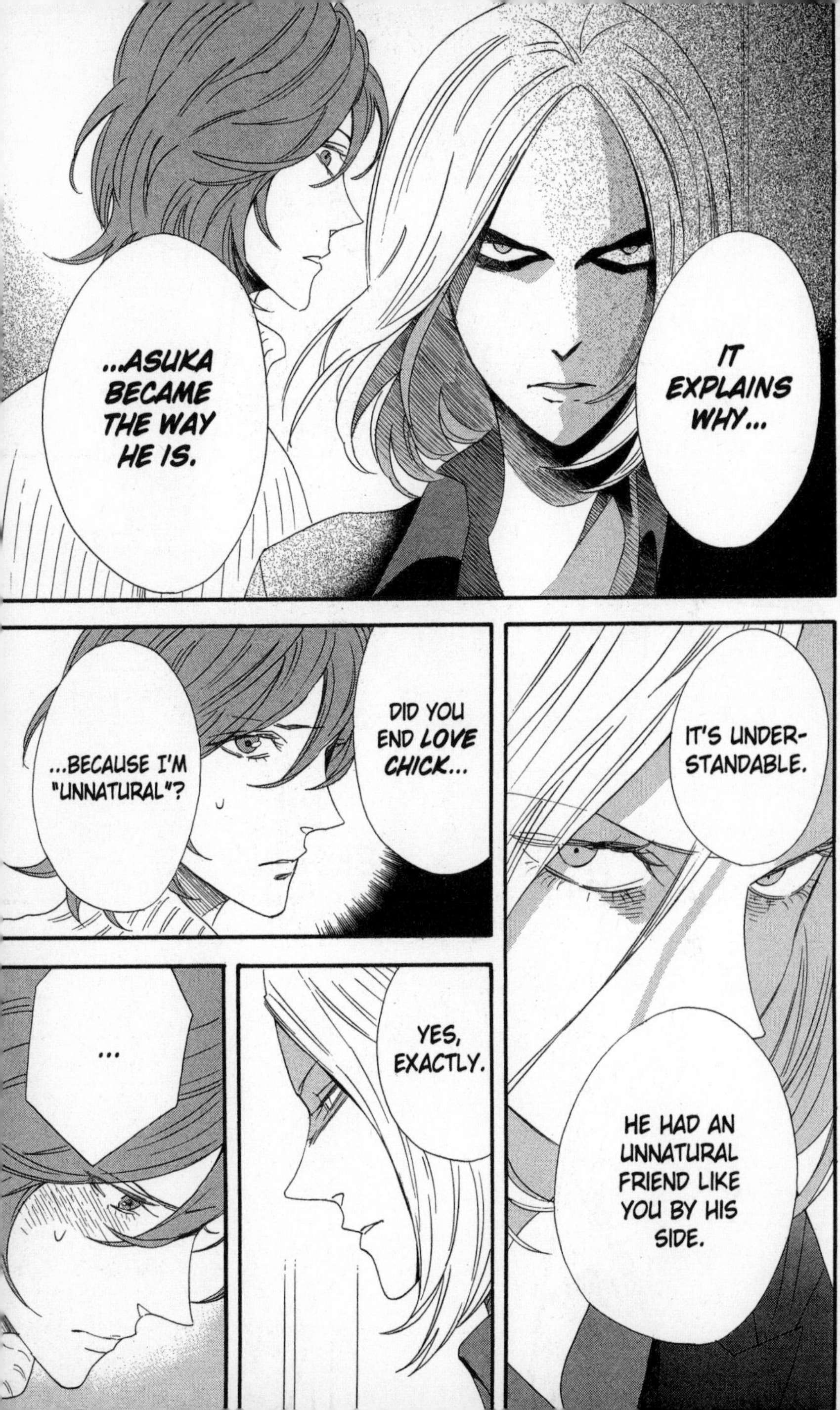
IT EXPLAINS WHY...
...ASUKA BECAME THE WAY HE IS.
IT'S UNDER-STANDABLE.
HE HAD AN UNNATURAL FRIEND LIKE YOU BY HIS SIDE.
DID YOU END *LOVE CHICK*...
...BECAUSE I'M "UNNATURAL"?
YES, EXACTLY.
...

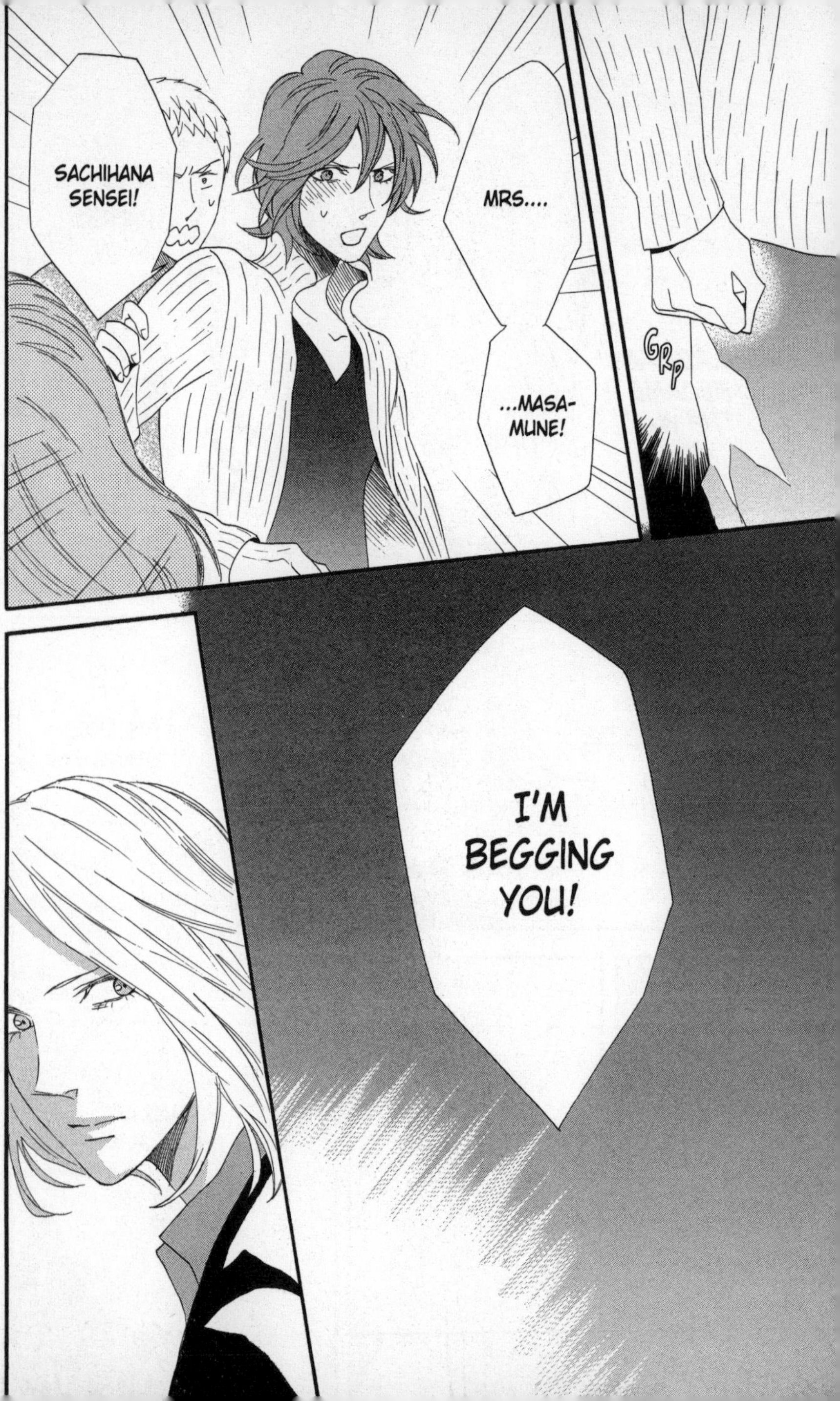
GRP
MRS....
...MASA-MUNE!
SACHIHANA SENSEI!
I'M BEGGING YOU!

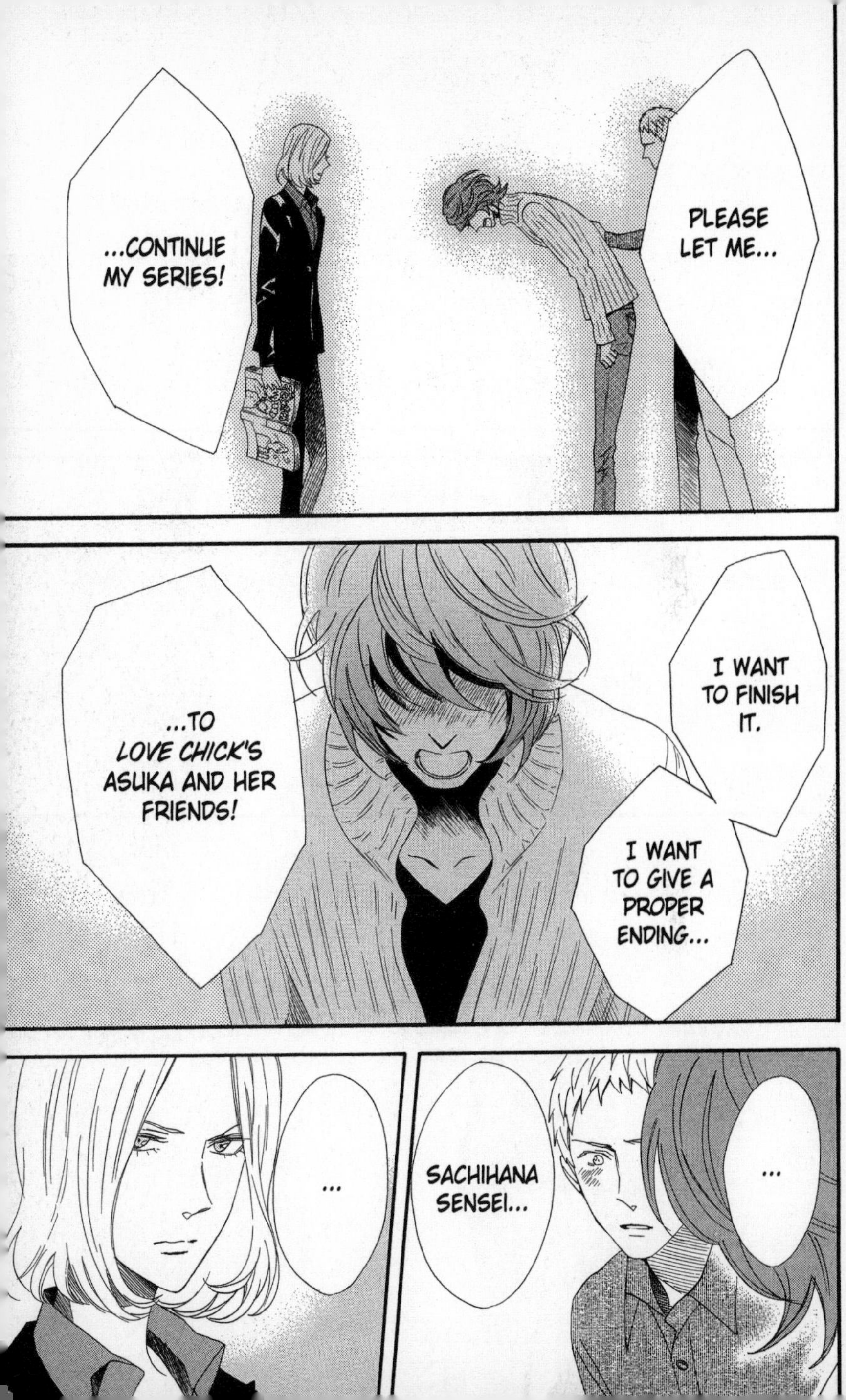
PLEASE LET ME...
...CONTINUE MY SERIES!
I WANT TO FINISH IT.
I WANT TO GIVE A PROPER ENDING...
...TO LOVE CHICK'S ASUKA AND HER FRIENDS!
...
SACHIHANA SENSEI...
...

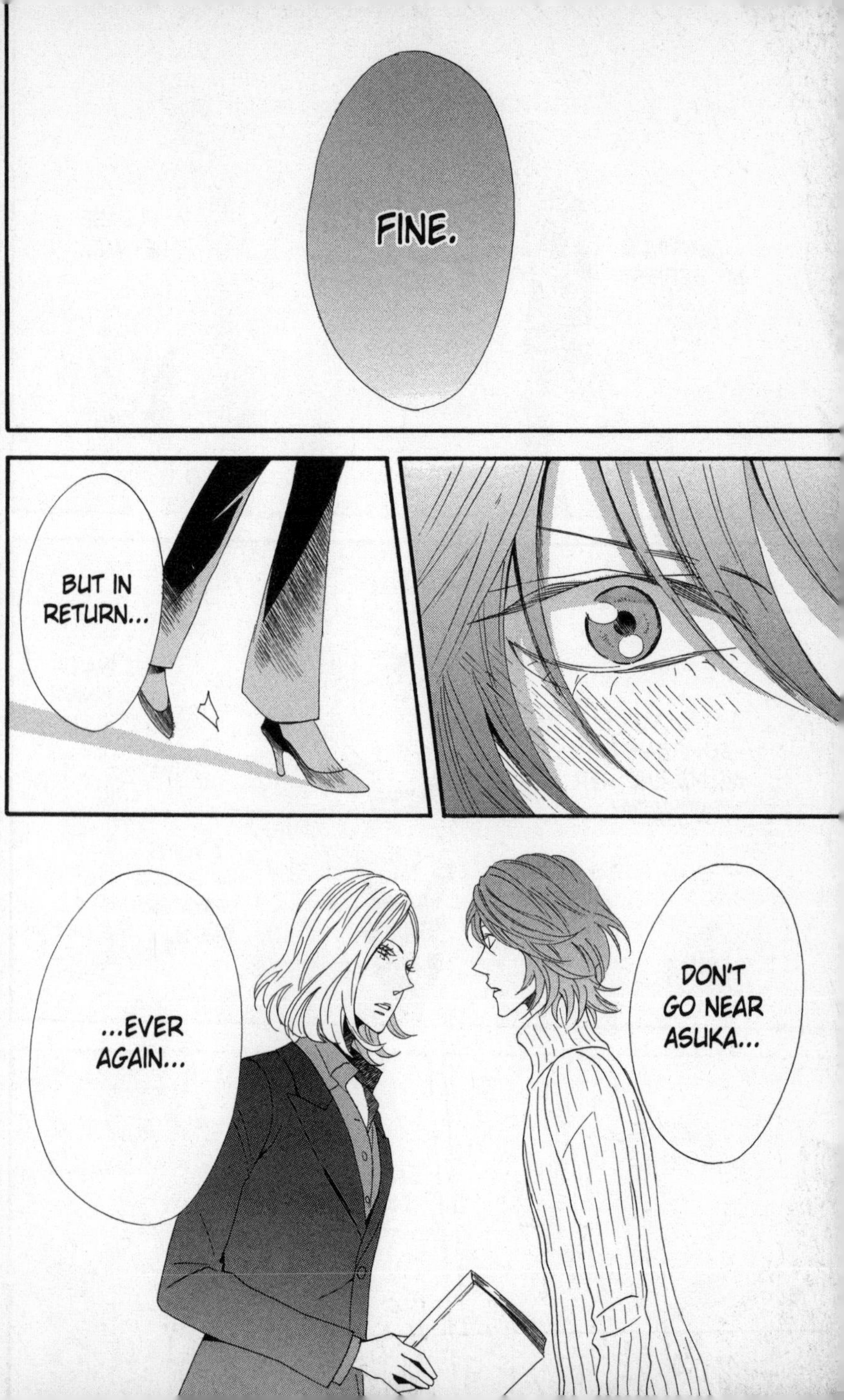
FINE.
BUT IN RETURN...
DON'T GO NEAR ASUKA...
...EVER AGAIN...

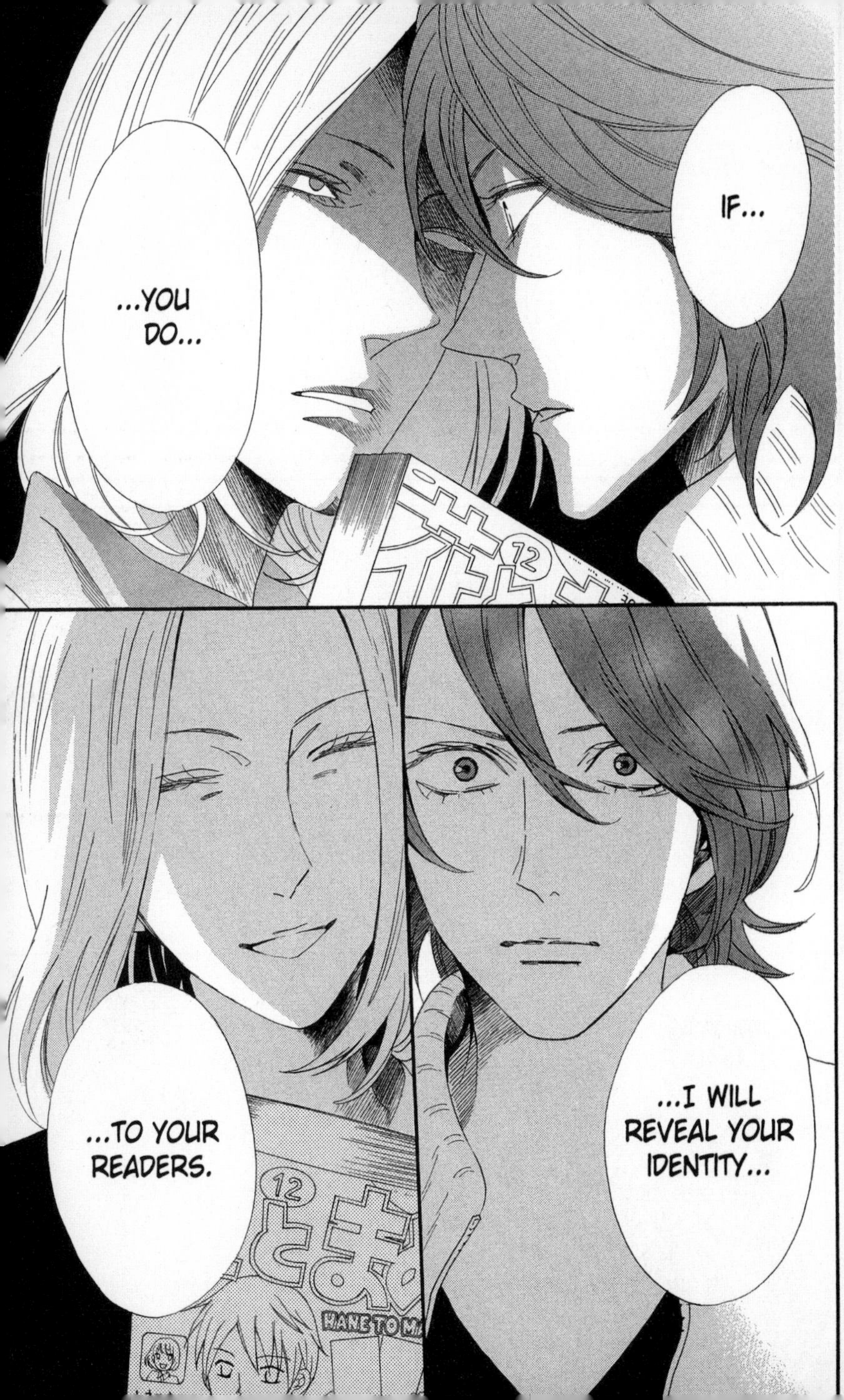
IF...
...YOU DO...
...I WILL REVEAL YOUR IDENTITY...
...TO YOUR READERS.

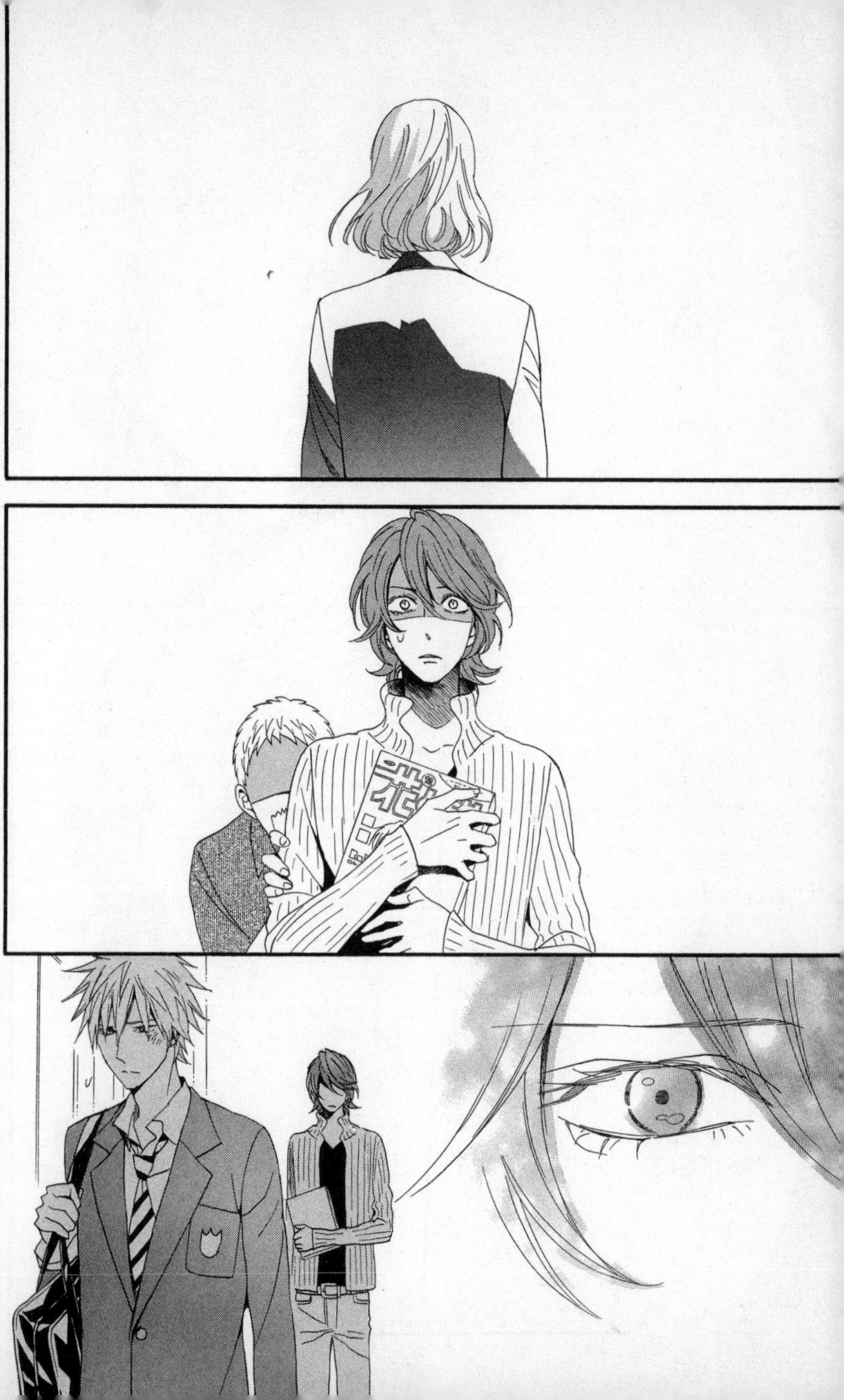

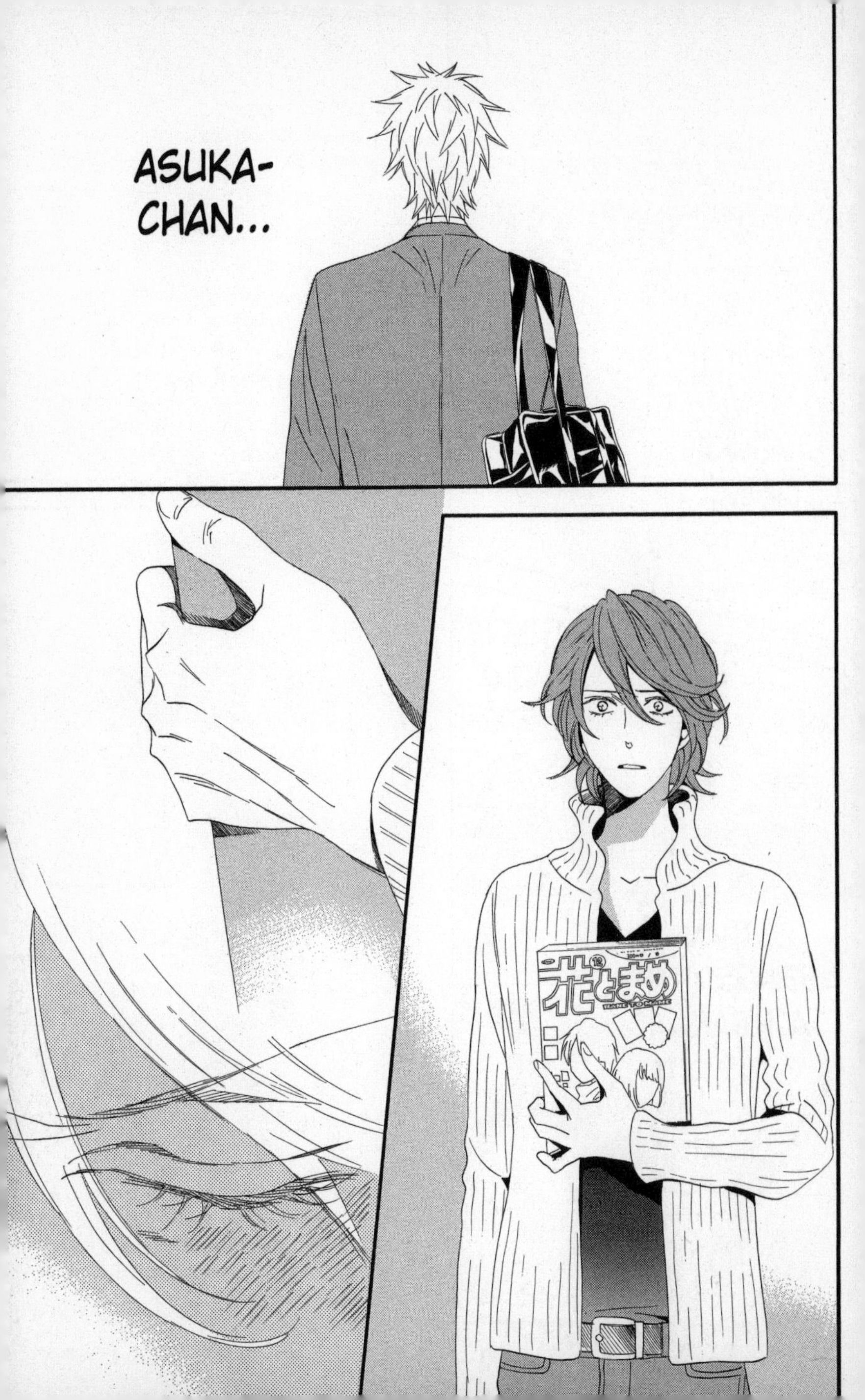
ASUKA-CHAN...
花とまめ

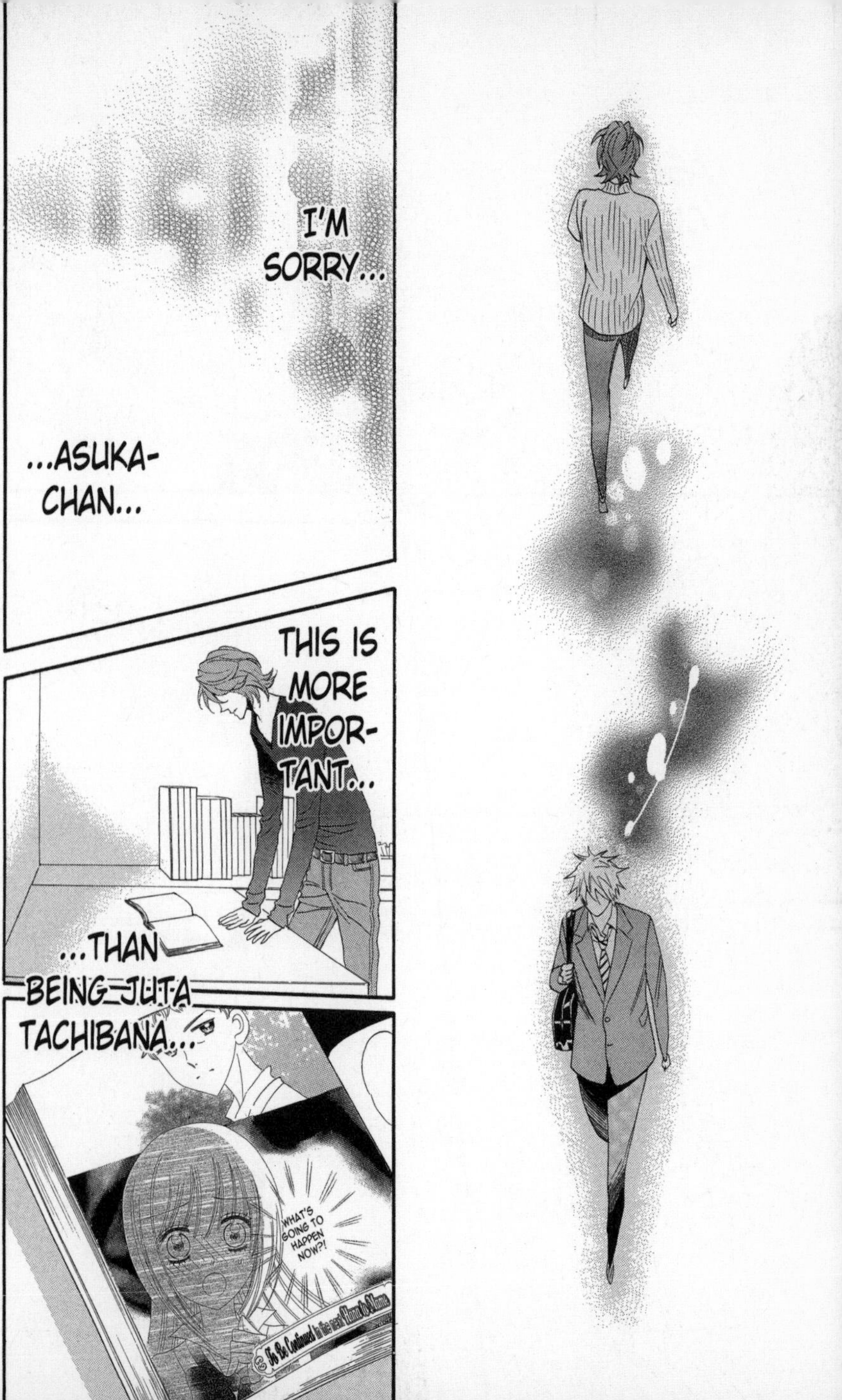
I'M SORRY...
...ASUKA-CHAN...
THIS IS MORE IMPORTANT...
...THAN BEING JUTA TACHIBANA...
WHAT'S GOING TO HAPPEN NOW?!
To Be Continued in the next Hana to Yume

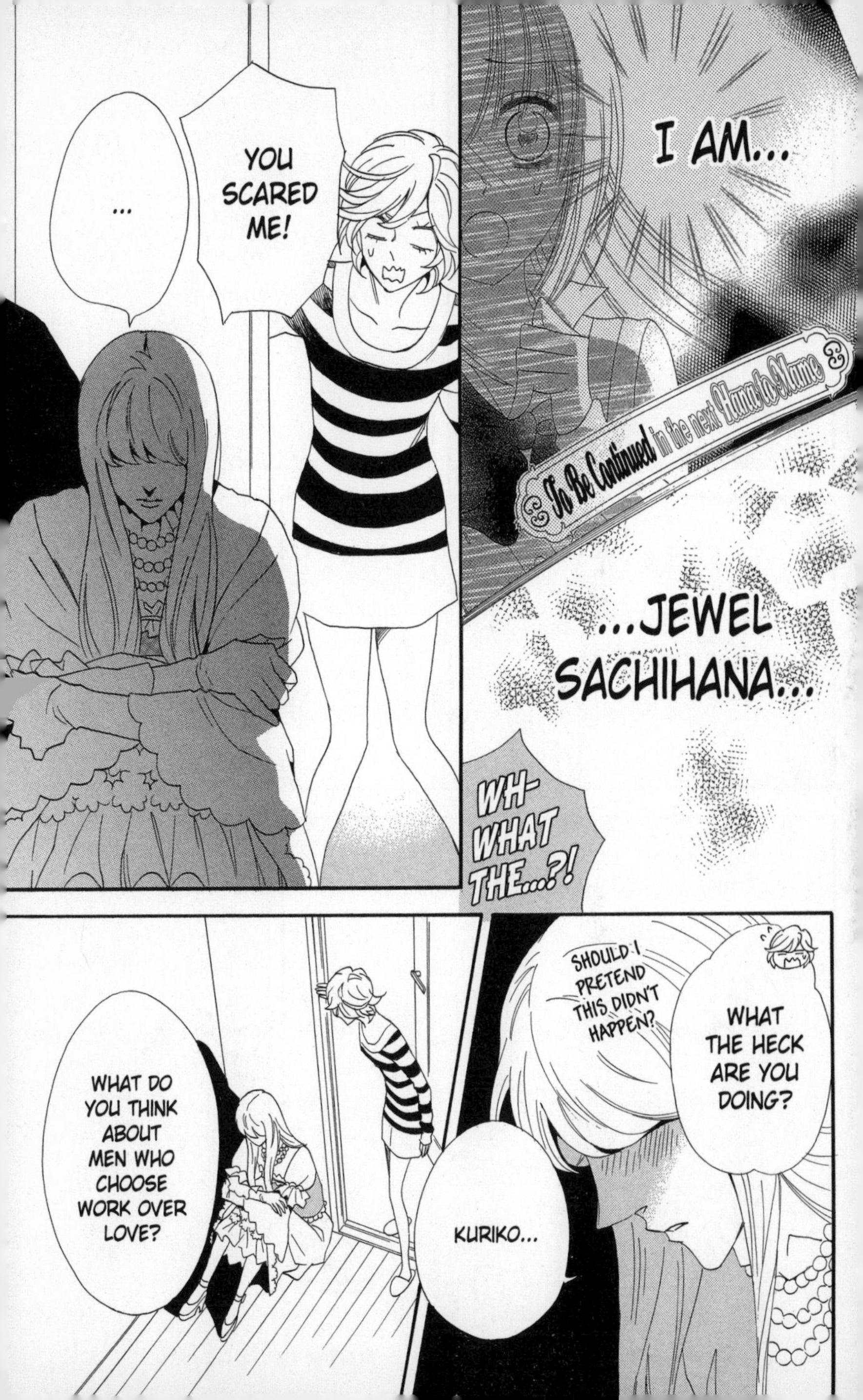
I AM...
To Be Continued in the next Hana to Yume
...JEWEL SACHIHANA...
WH-WHAT THE...?!
YOU SCARED ME!
...
WHAT THE HECK ARE YOU DOING?
SHOULD I PRETEND THIS DIDN'T HAPPEN?
KURIKO...
WHAT DO YOU THINK ABOUT MEN WHO CHOOSE WORK OVER LOVE?

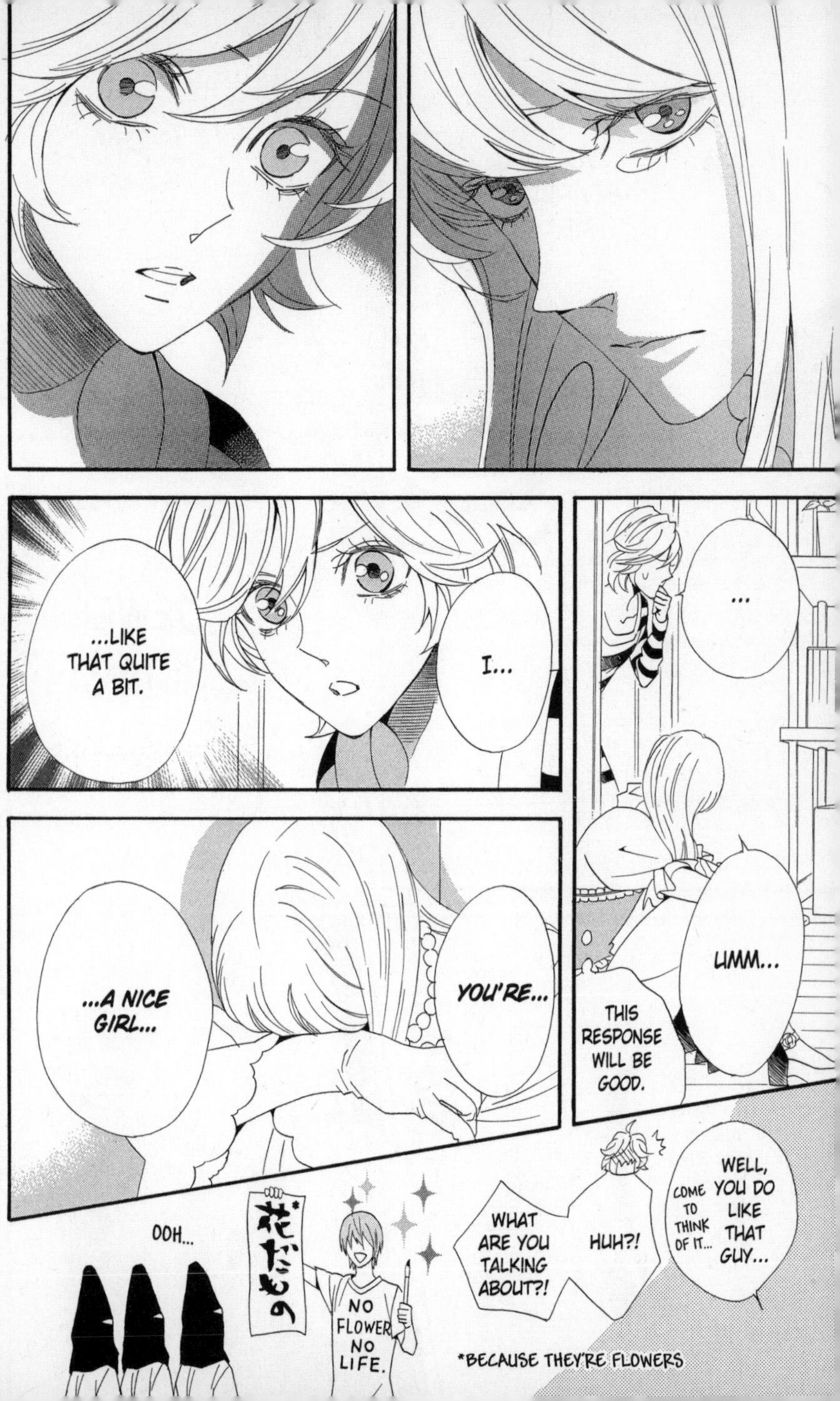
...
UMM...
THIS RESPONSE WILL BE GOOD.
I...
...LIKE THAT QUITE A BIT.
YOU'RE...
...A NICE GIRL...
WELL, YOU DO LIKE THAT GUY...
COME TO THINK OF IT...
HUH?!
WHAT ARE YOU TALKING ABOUT?!
花だもの*
NO FLOWER NO LIFE.
OOH...
*BECAUSE THEY'RE FLOWERS

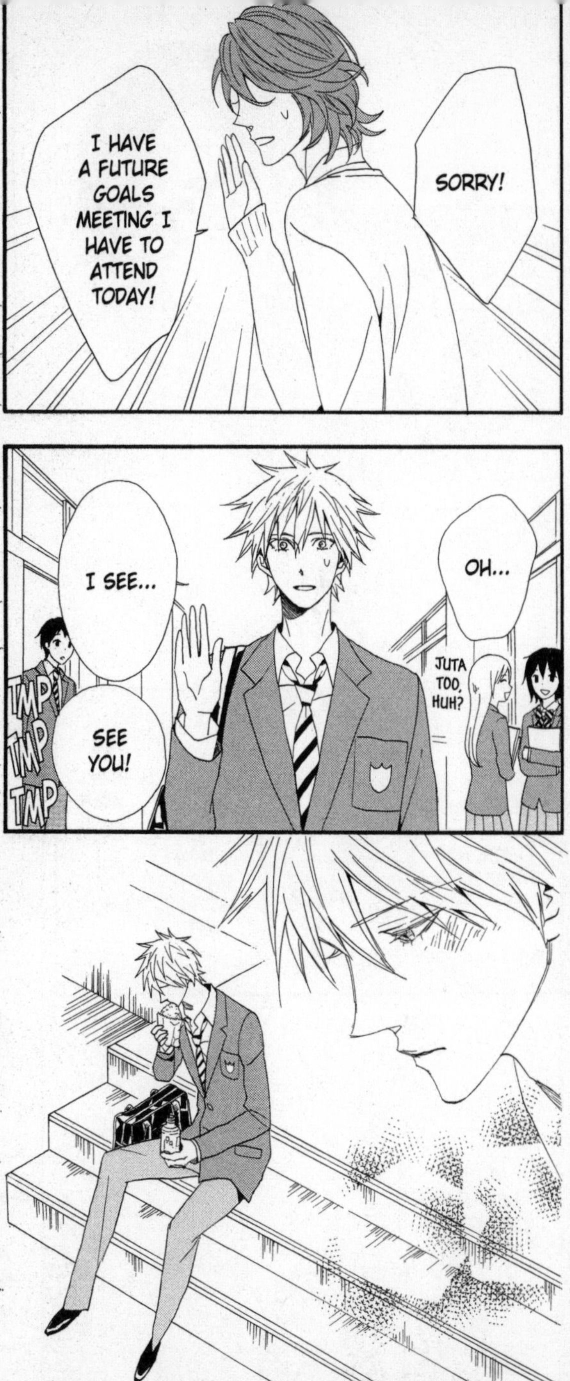
SORRY!
I HAVE A FUTURE GOALS MEETING I HAVE TO ATTEND TODAY!
OH...
JUTA TOO, HUH?
I SEE...
SEE YOU!
TMP TMP TMP

**This is volume 17.**

*Otomen* ends at volume 18.

I want to devote the remaining segments I have here to talk about the main characters.

Please stay with us until volume 18.

Aya Kanno

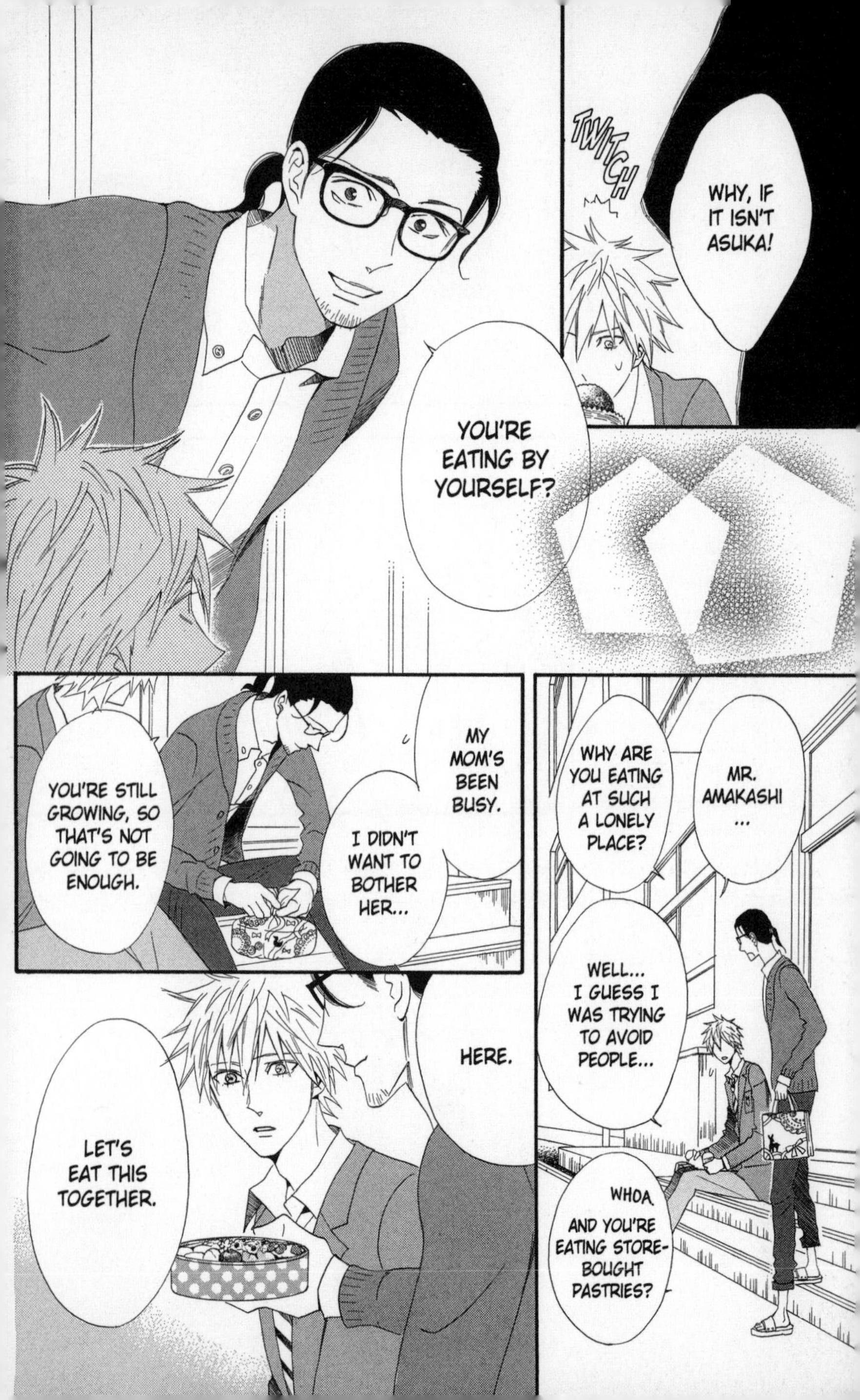
TWITCH
WHY, IF IT ISN'T ASUKA!
YOU'RE EATING BY YOURSELF?
MR. AMAKASHI ...
WHY ARE YOU EATING AT SUCH A LONELY PLACE?
WELL... I GUESS I WAS TRYING TO AVOID PEOPLE...
WHOA AND YOU'RE EATING STORE-BOUGHT PASTRIES?
MY MOM'S BEEN BUSY.
I DIDN'T WANT TO BOTHER HER...
YOU'RE STILL GROWING, SO THAT'S NOT GOING TO BE ENOUGH.
HERE.
LET'S EAT THIS TOGETHER.

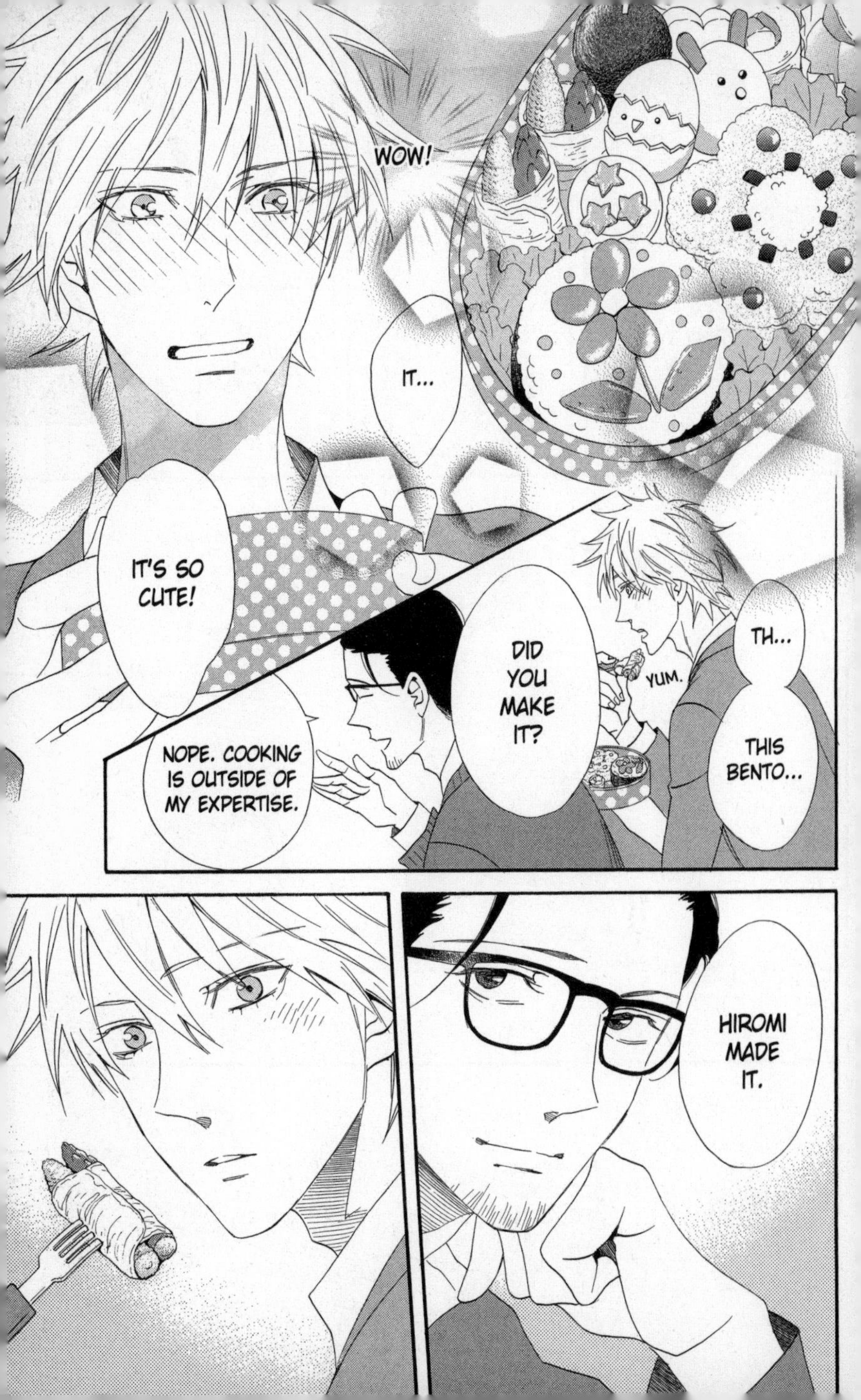
WOW!
IT...
IT'S SO CUTE!
TH...
THIS BENTO...
YUM.
DID YOU MAKE IT?
NOPE. COOKING IS OUTSIDE OF MY EXPERTISE.
HIROMI MADE IT.

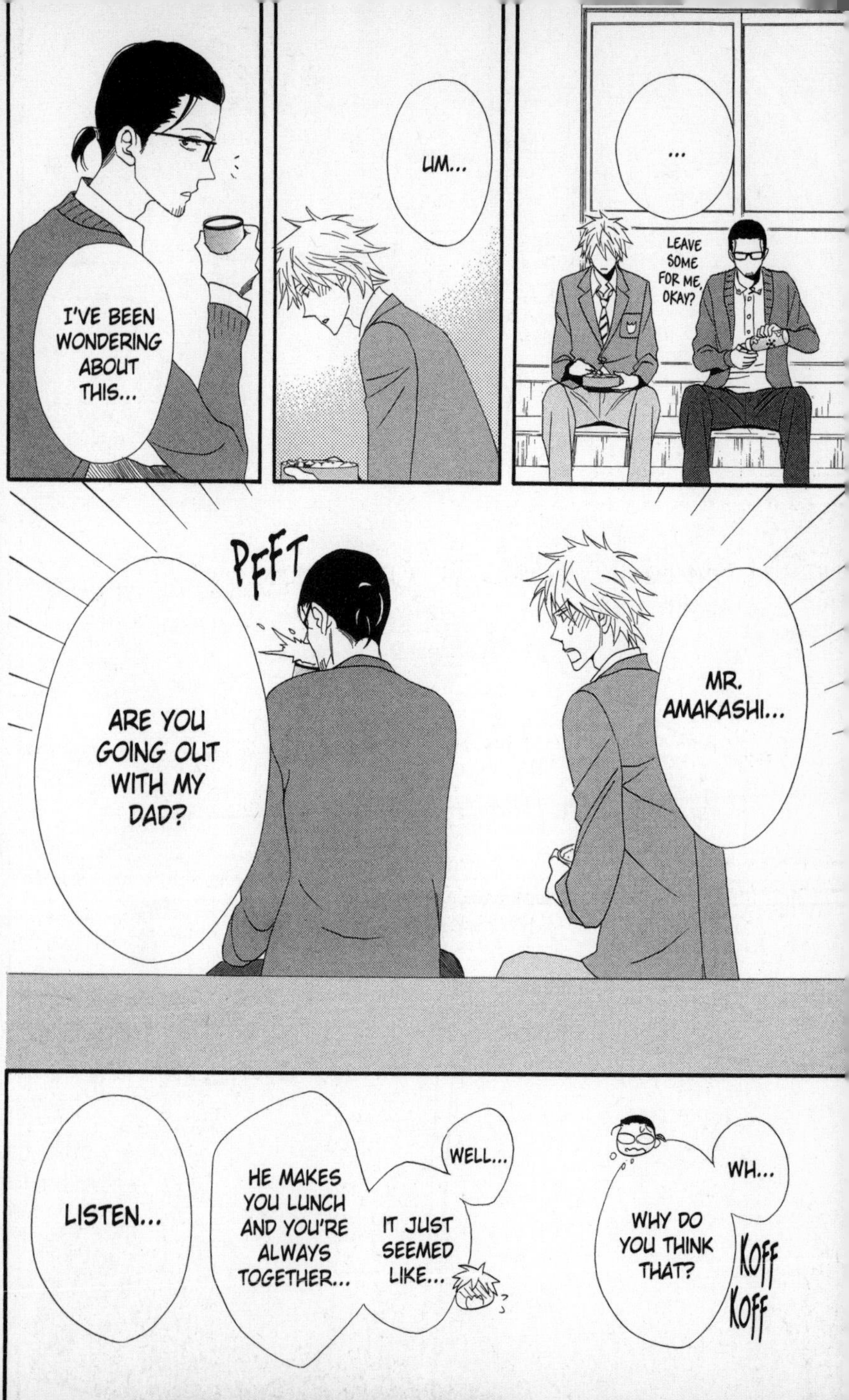
...
LEAVE SOME FOR ME, OKAY?
UM...
I'VE BEEN WONDERING ABOUT THIS...
MR. AMAKASHI...
PFFT
ARE YOU GOING OUT WITH MY DAD?
WH...
WHY DO YOU THINK THAT?
KOFF KOFF
WELL...
IT JUST SEEMED LIKE...
HE MAKES YOU LUNCH AND YOU'RE ALWAYS TOGETHER...
LISTEN...

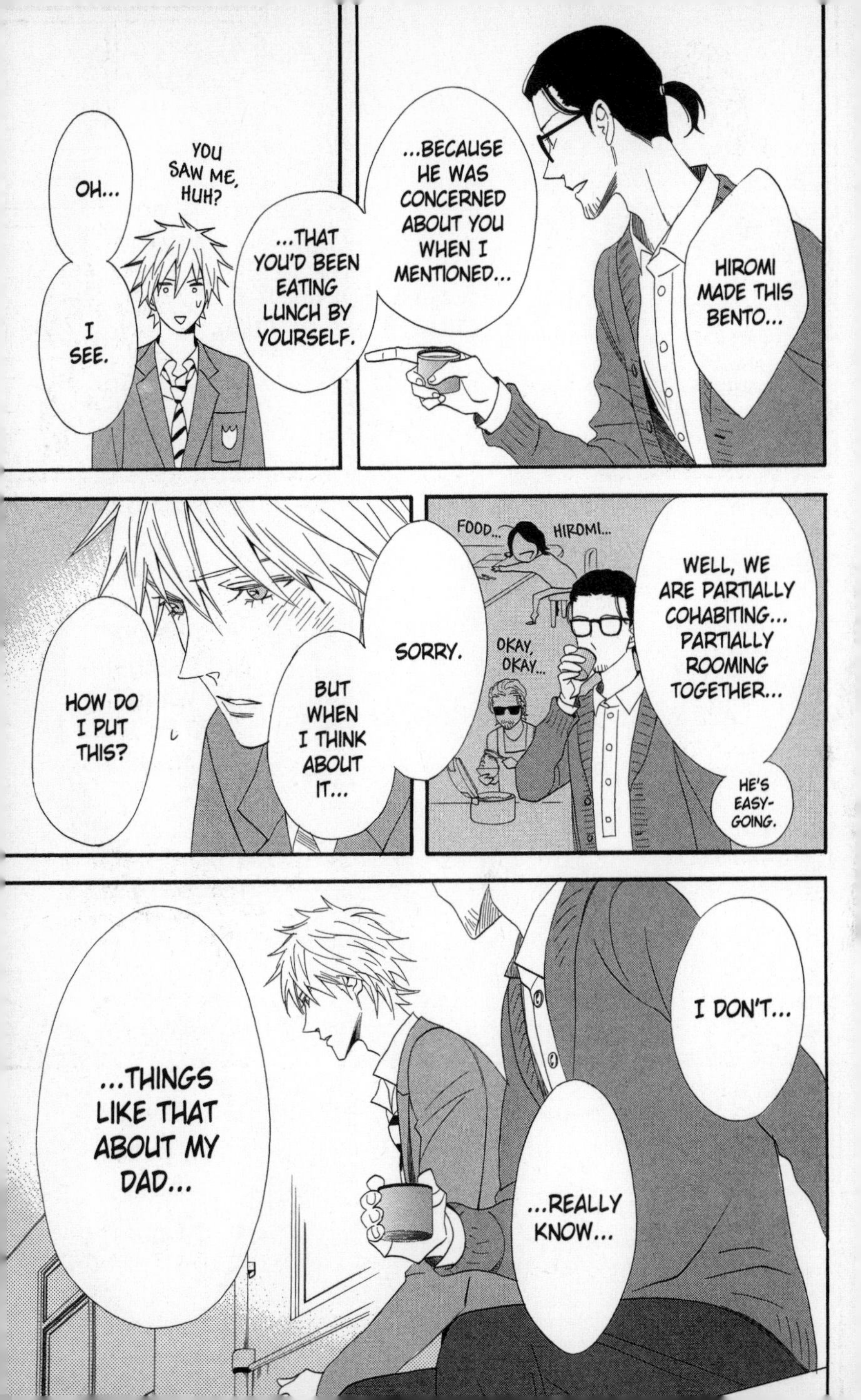
HIROMI MADE THIS BENTO...
...BECAUSE HE WAS CONCERNED ABOUT YOU WHEN I MENTIONED...
...THAT YOU'D BEEN EATING LUNCH BY YOURSELF.
YOU SAW ME, HUH?
OH...
I SEE.
WELL, WE ARE PARTIALLY COHABITING... PARTIALLY ROOMING TOGETHER...
FOOD...
HIROMI...
OKAY, OKAY...
HE'S EASY-GOING.
SORRY.
BUT WHEN I THINK ABOUT IT...
HOW DO I PUT THIS?
I DON'T...
...REALLY KNOW...
...THINGS LIKE THAT ABOUT MY DAD...

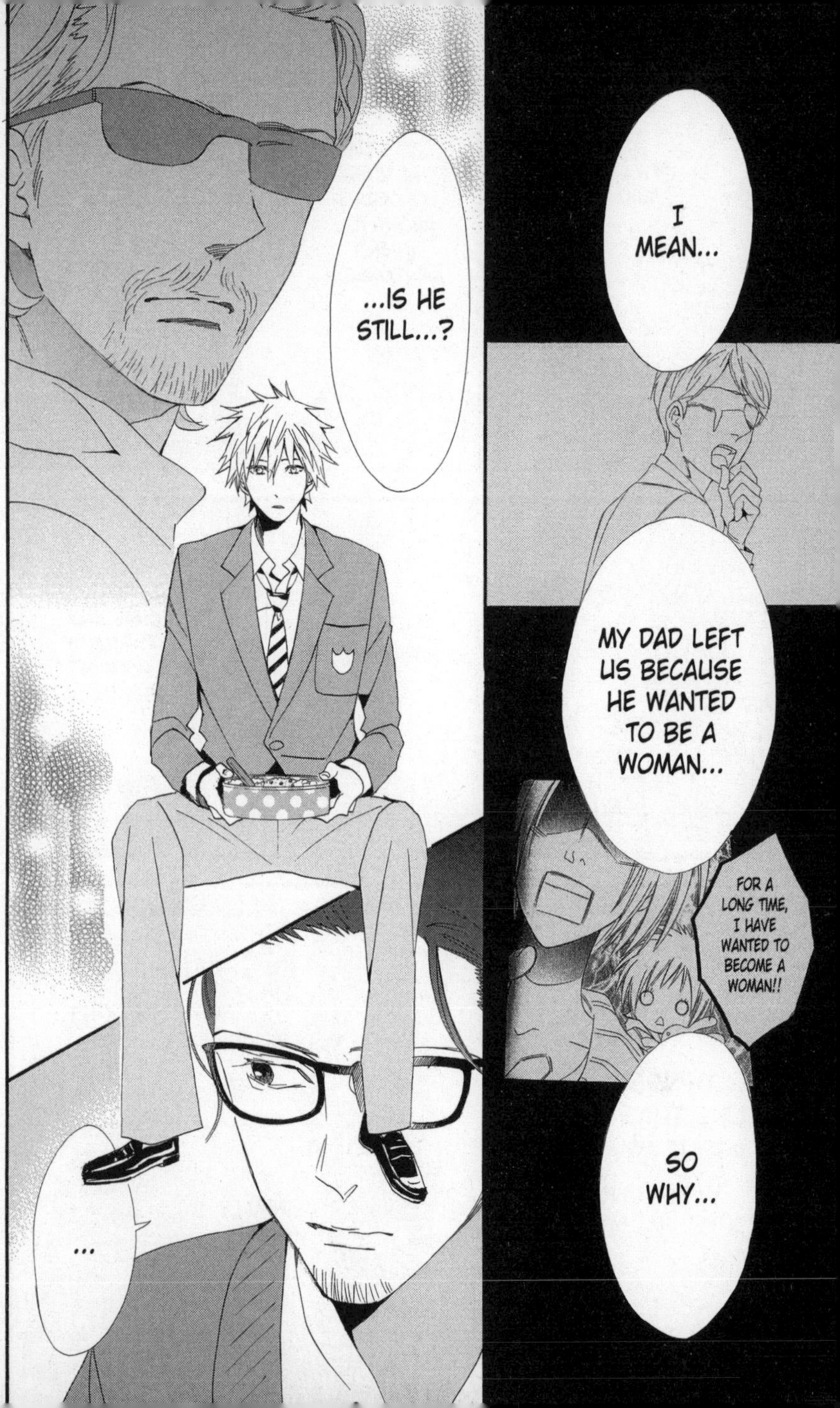
I MEAN...
MY DAD LEFT US BECAUSE HE WANTED TO BE A WOMAN...
FOR A LONG TIME, I HAVE WANTED TO BECOME A WOMAN!!
SO WHY...
...IS HE STILL...?
...

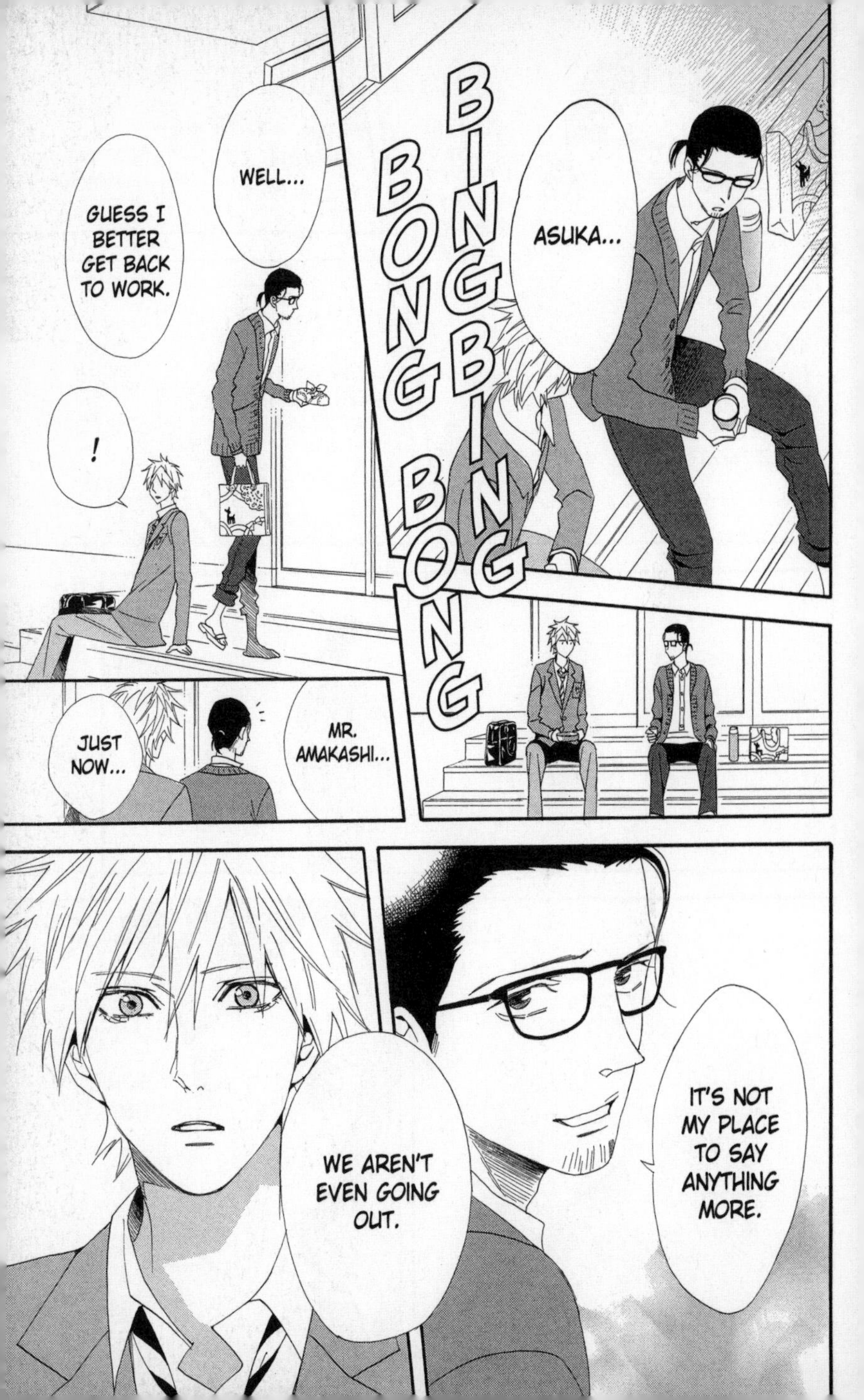
ASUKA...
BING BONG BING BONG
WELL...
GUESS I BETTER GET BACK TO WORK.
!
MR. AMAKASHI...
JUST NOW...
IT'S NOT MY PLACE TO SAY ANYTHING MORE.
WE AREN'T EVEN GOING OUT.

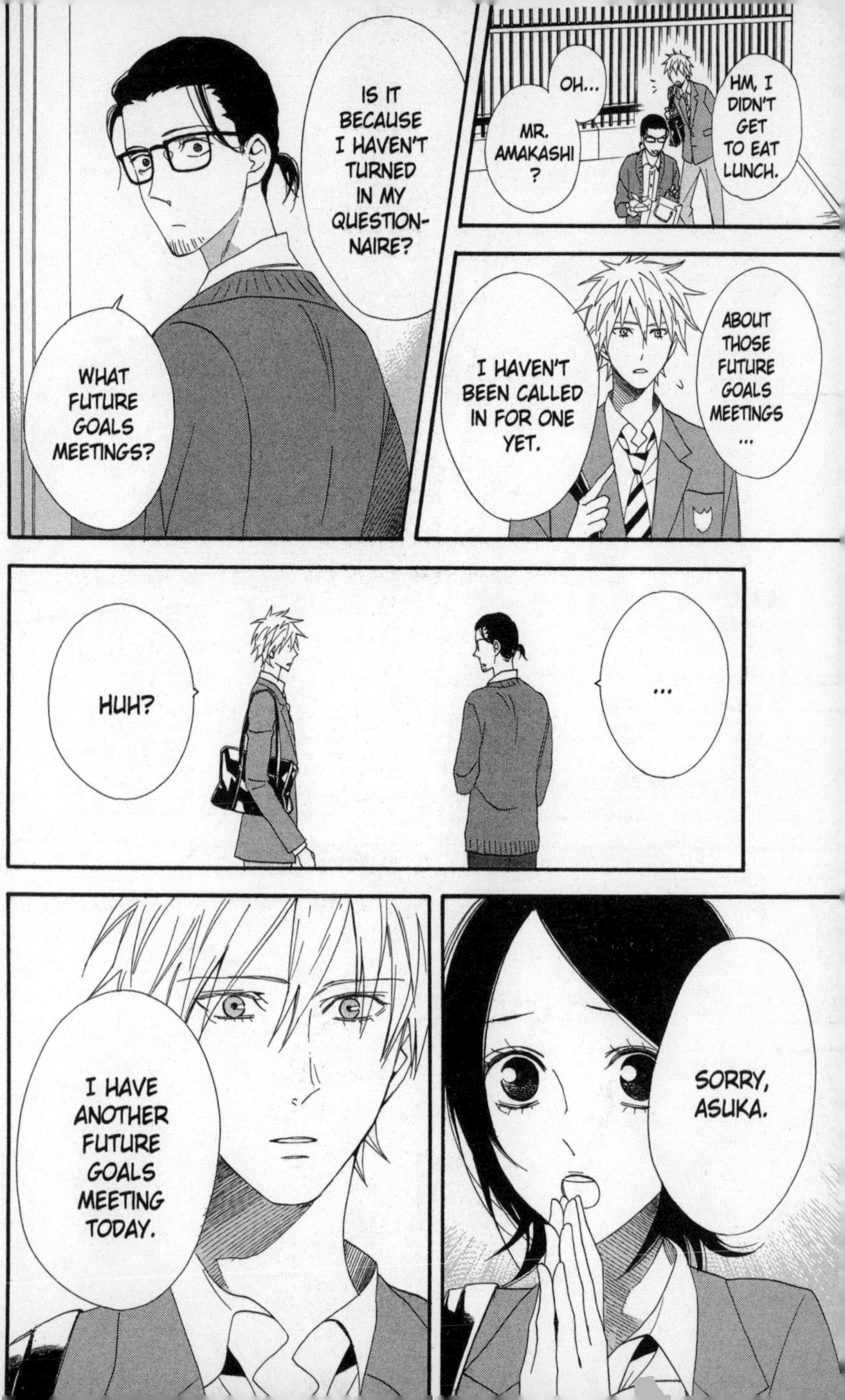
HM, I DIDN'T GET TO EAT LUNCH.
OH...
MR. AMAKASHI?
ABOUT THOSE FUTURE GOALS MEETINGS...
I HAVEN'T BEEN CALLED IN FOR ONE YET.
IS IT BECAUSE I HAVEN'T TURNED IN MY QUESTION-NAIRE?
WHAT FUTURE GOALS MEETINGS?
...
HUH?
SORRY, ASUKA.
I HAVE ANOTHER FUTURE GOALS MEETING TODAY.

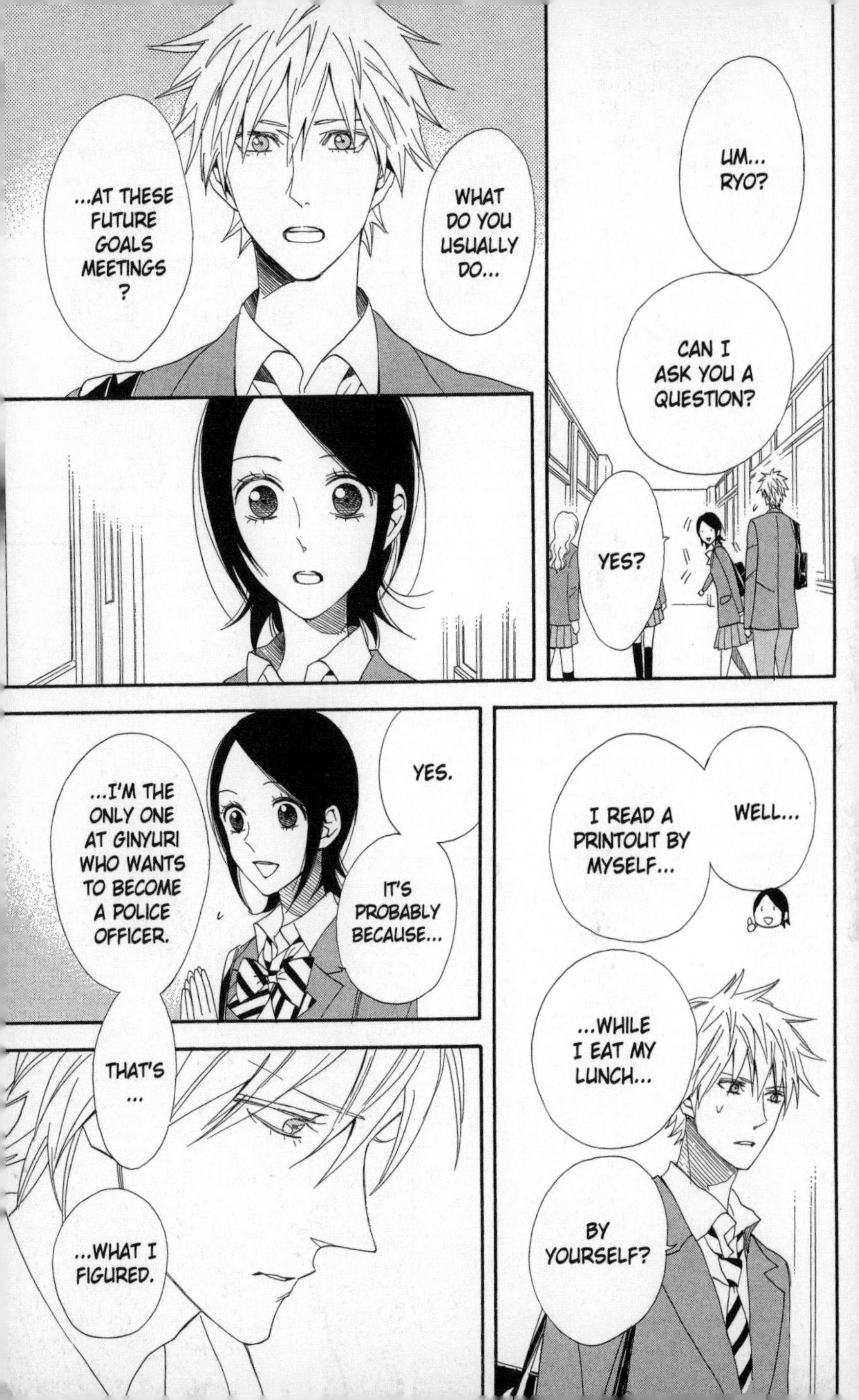
UM... RYO?
CAN I ASK YOU A QUESTION?
YES?
WHAT DO YOU USUALLY DO...
...AT THESE FUTURE GOALS MEETINGS ?
WELL...
I READ A PRINTOUT BY MYSELF...
...WHILE I EAT MY LUNCH...
BY YOURSELF?
YES.
IT'S PROBABLY BECAUSE...
...I'M THE ONLY ONE AT GINYURI WHO WANTS TO BECOME A POLICE OFFICER.
THAT'S ...
...WHAT I FIGURED.

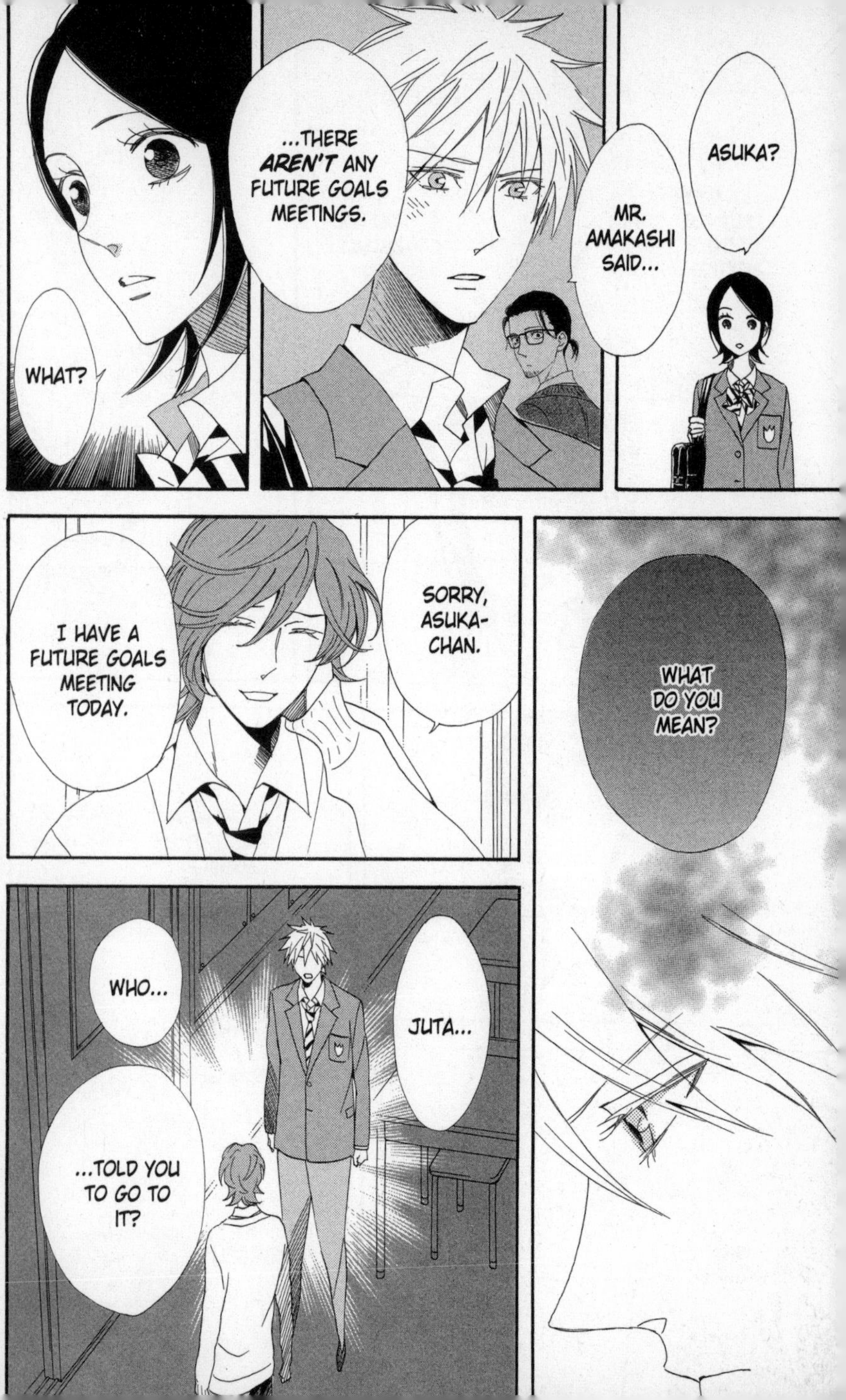
ASUKA?
MR. AMAKASHI SAID...
...THERE AREN'T ANY FUTURE GOALS MEETINGS.
WHAT?
WHAT DO YOU MEAN?
SORRY, ASUKA-CHAN.
I HAVE A FUTURE GOALS MEETING TODAY.
JUTA...
WHO...
...TOLD YOU TO GO TO IT?

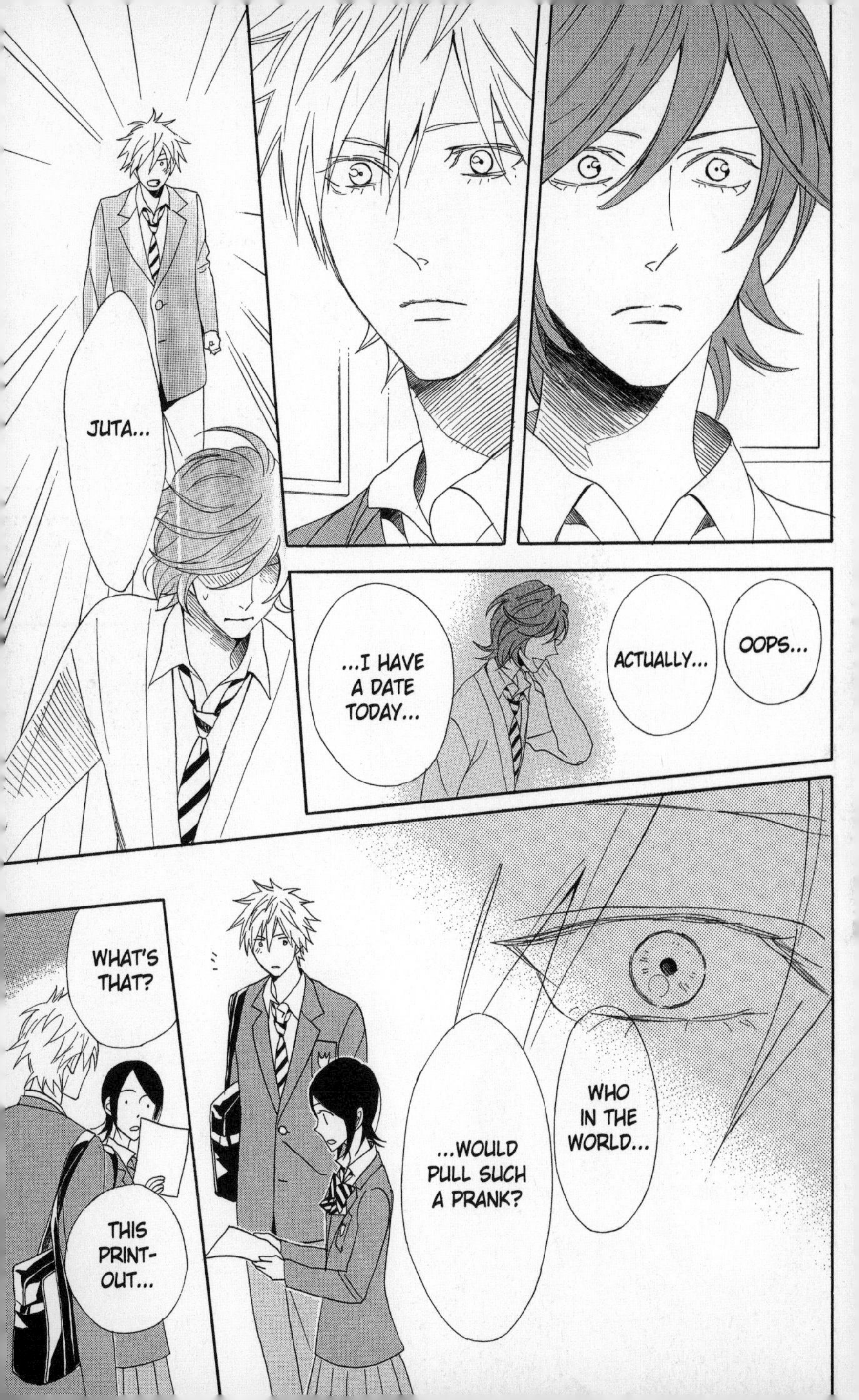
OOPS...
ACTUALLY...
...I HAVE A DATE TODAY...
JUTA...
WHO IN THE WORLD...
...WOULD PULL SUCH A PRANK?
WHAT'S THAT?
THIS PRINT-OUT...

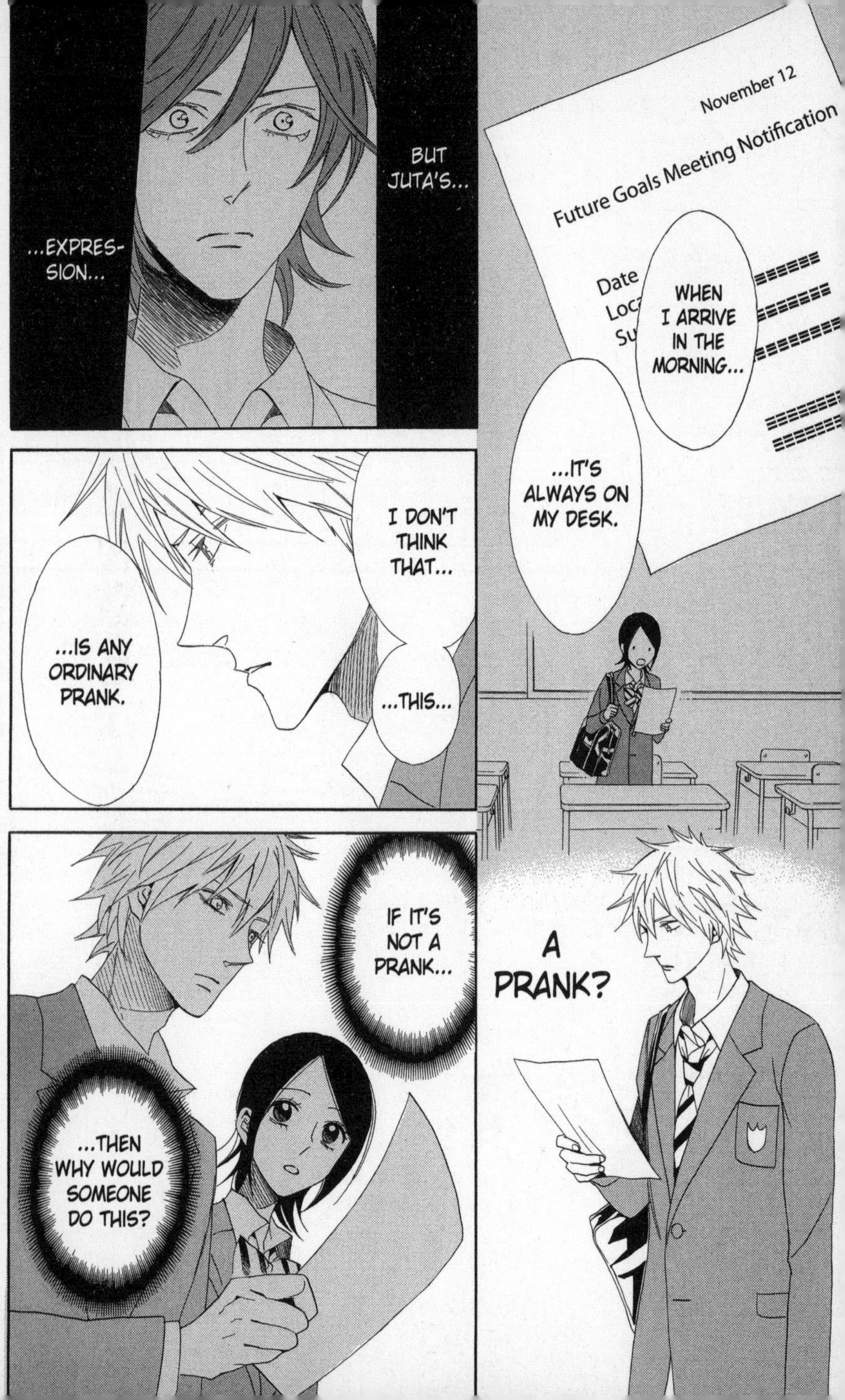
November 12
Future Goals Meeting Notification
Date
WHEN I ARRIVE IN THE MORNING...
...IT'S ALWAYS ON MY DESK.
A PRANK?
BUT JUTA'S...
...EXPRES-SION...
I DON'T THINK THAT...
...THIS...
...IS ANY ORDINARY PRANK.
IF IT'S NOT A PRANK...
...THEN WHY WOULD SOMEONE DO THIS?

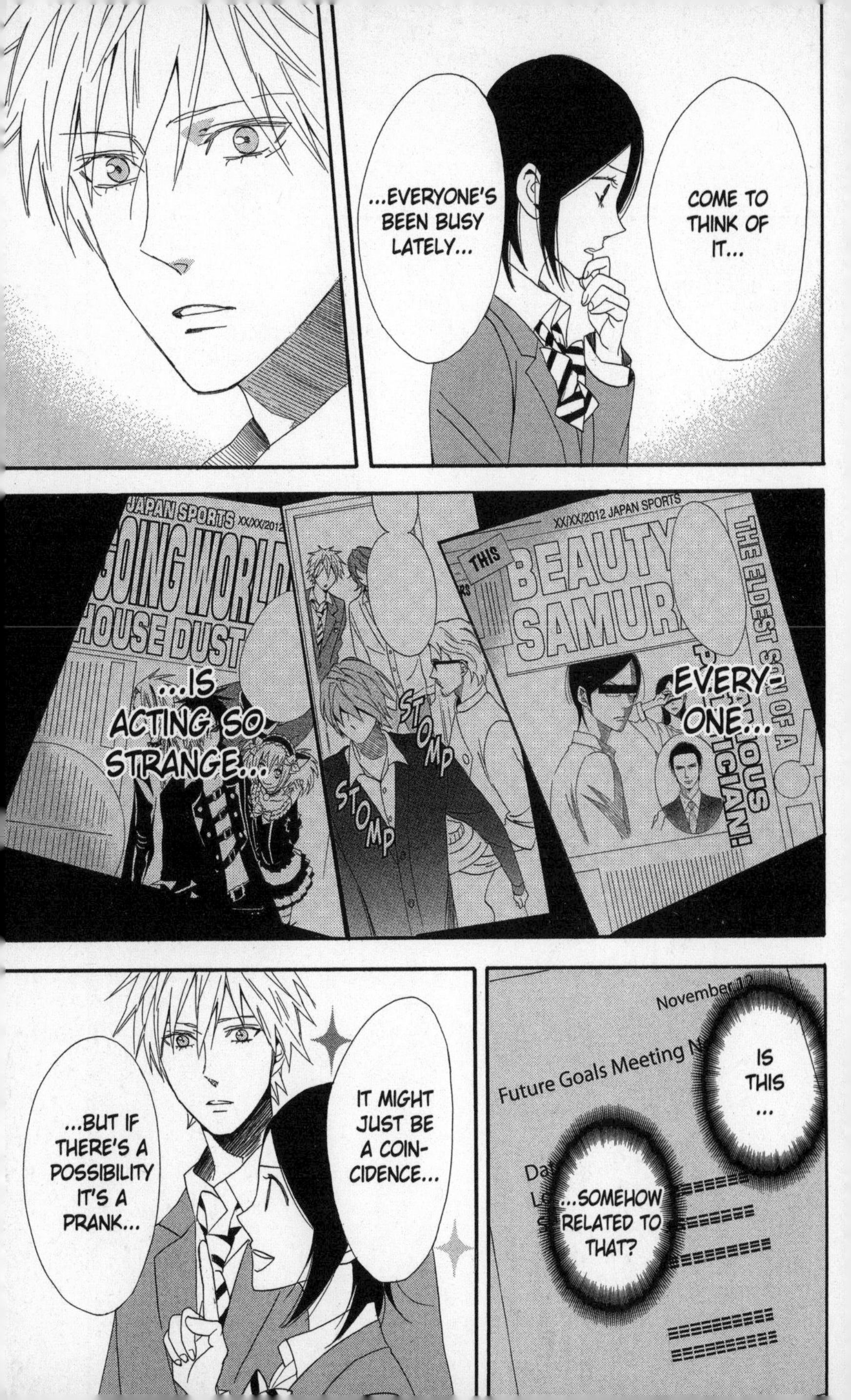
COME TO THINK OF IT...
...EVERYONE'S BEEN BUSY LATELY...
XX/XX/2012 JAPAN SPORTS
THIS
BEAUTY
EVERY-ONE...
STOMP
STOMP
JAPAN SPORTS XX/XX/2012
HOUSE DUST
...IS ACTING SO STRANGE...
November 12
Future Goals Meeting
IS THIS ...
...SOMEHOW RELATED TO THAT?
IT MIGHT JUST BE A COIN-CIDENCE...
...BUT IF THERE'S A POSSIBILITY IT'S A PRANK...

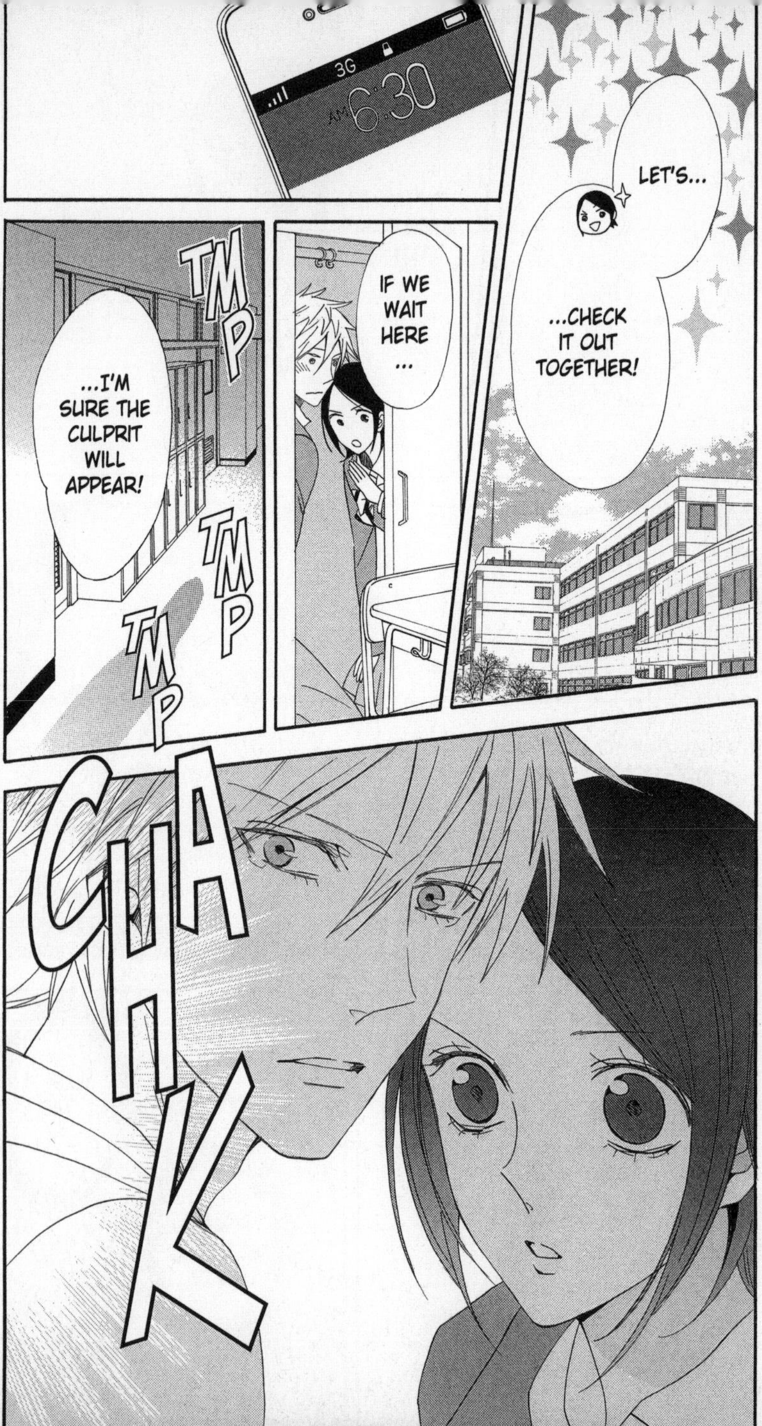
LET'S...
...CHECK IT OUT TOGETHER!
3G
AM 6:30
IF WE WAIT HERE ...
...I'M SURE THE CULPRIT WILL APPEAR!
TMP
TMP
TMP
CHAK

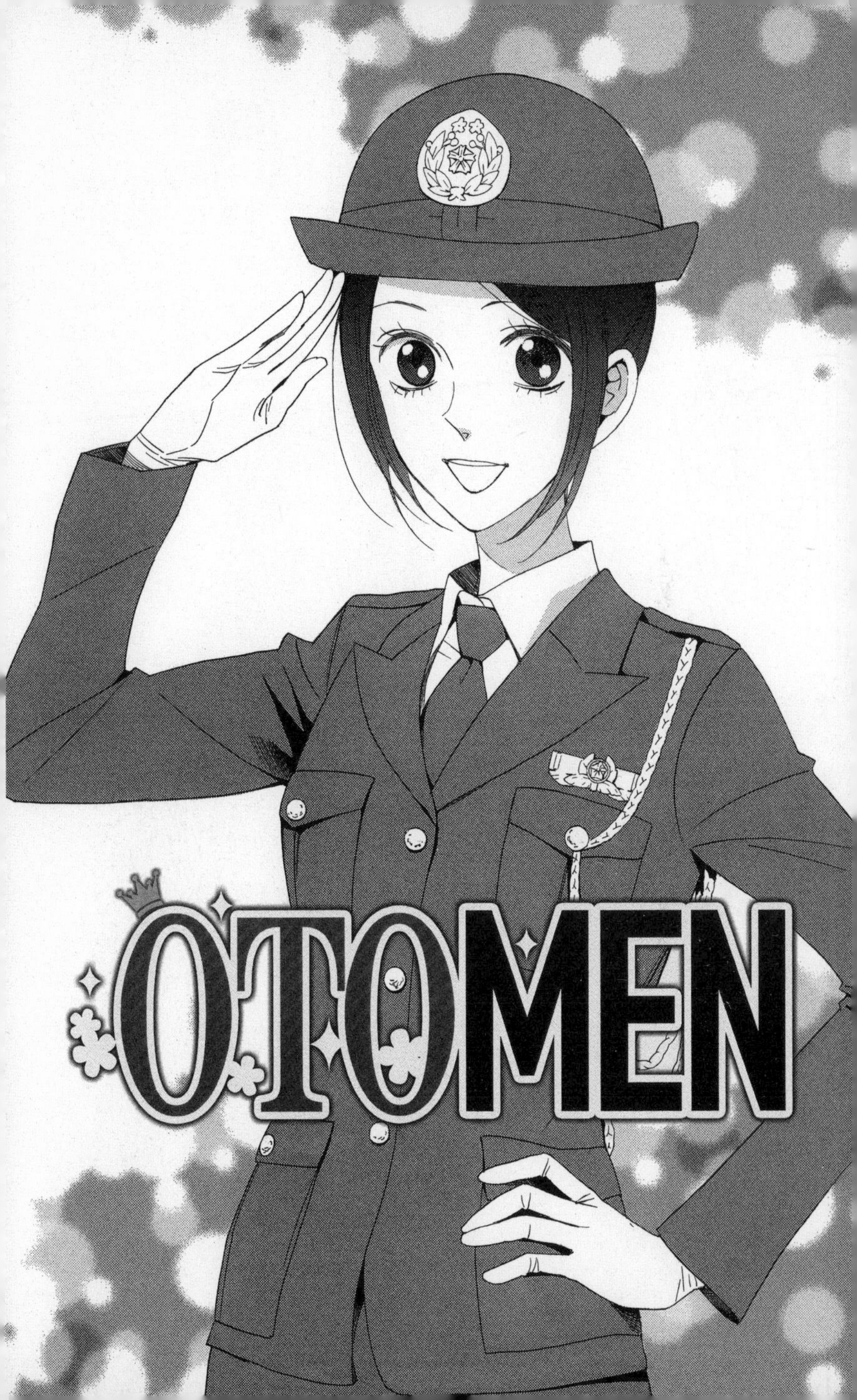
OTOMEN

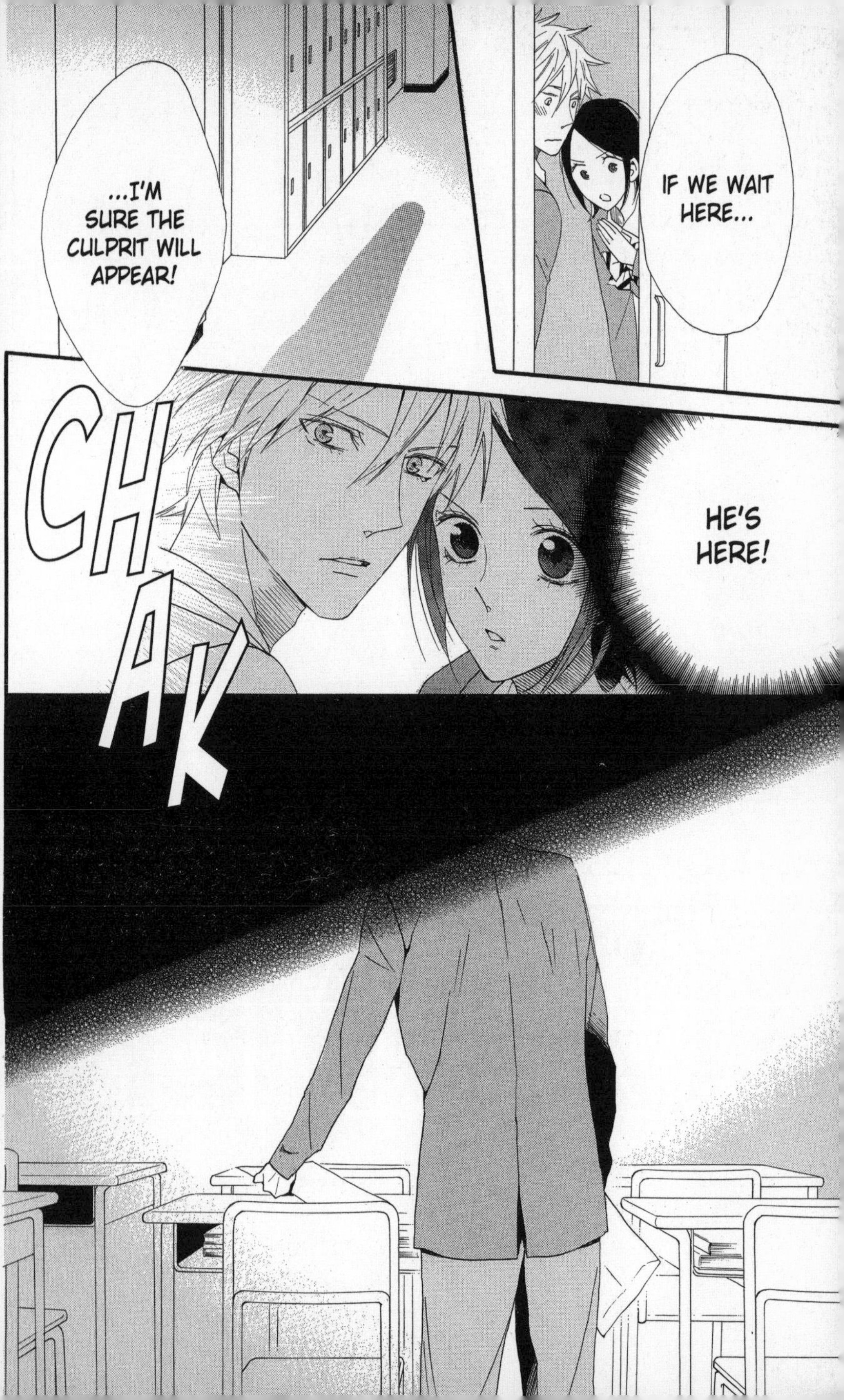
IF WE WAIT HERE...
...I'M SURE THE CULPRIT WILL APPEAR!
HE'S HERE!
CHAK

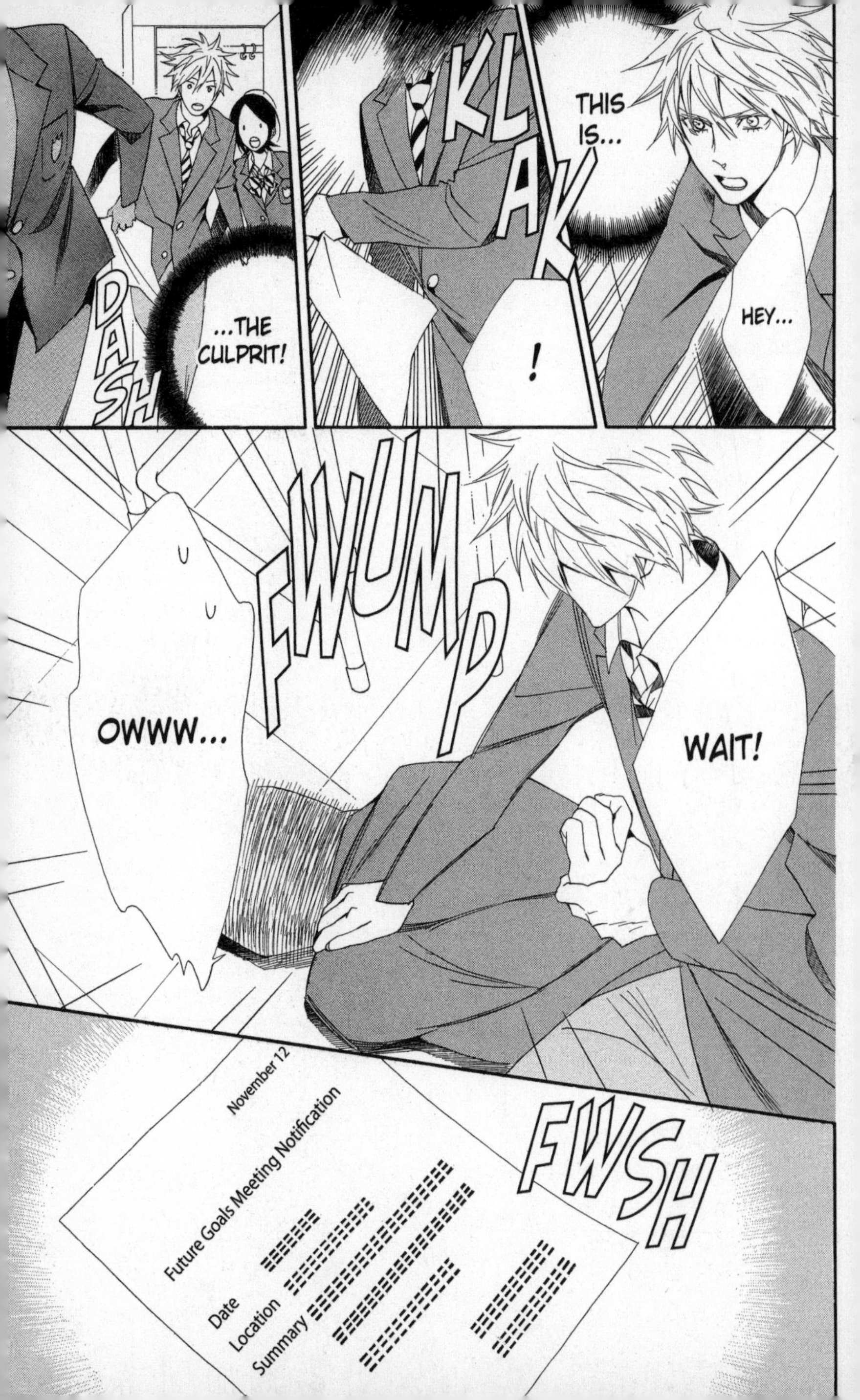
THIS IS...
HEY...
KLAK
!
...THE CULPRIT!
DASH
WAIT!
FWUMP
OWWW...
FWSH
November 12
Future Goals Meeting Notification
Date
Location
Summary

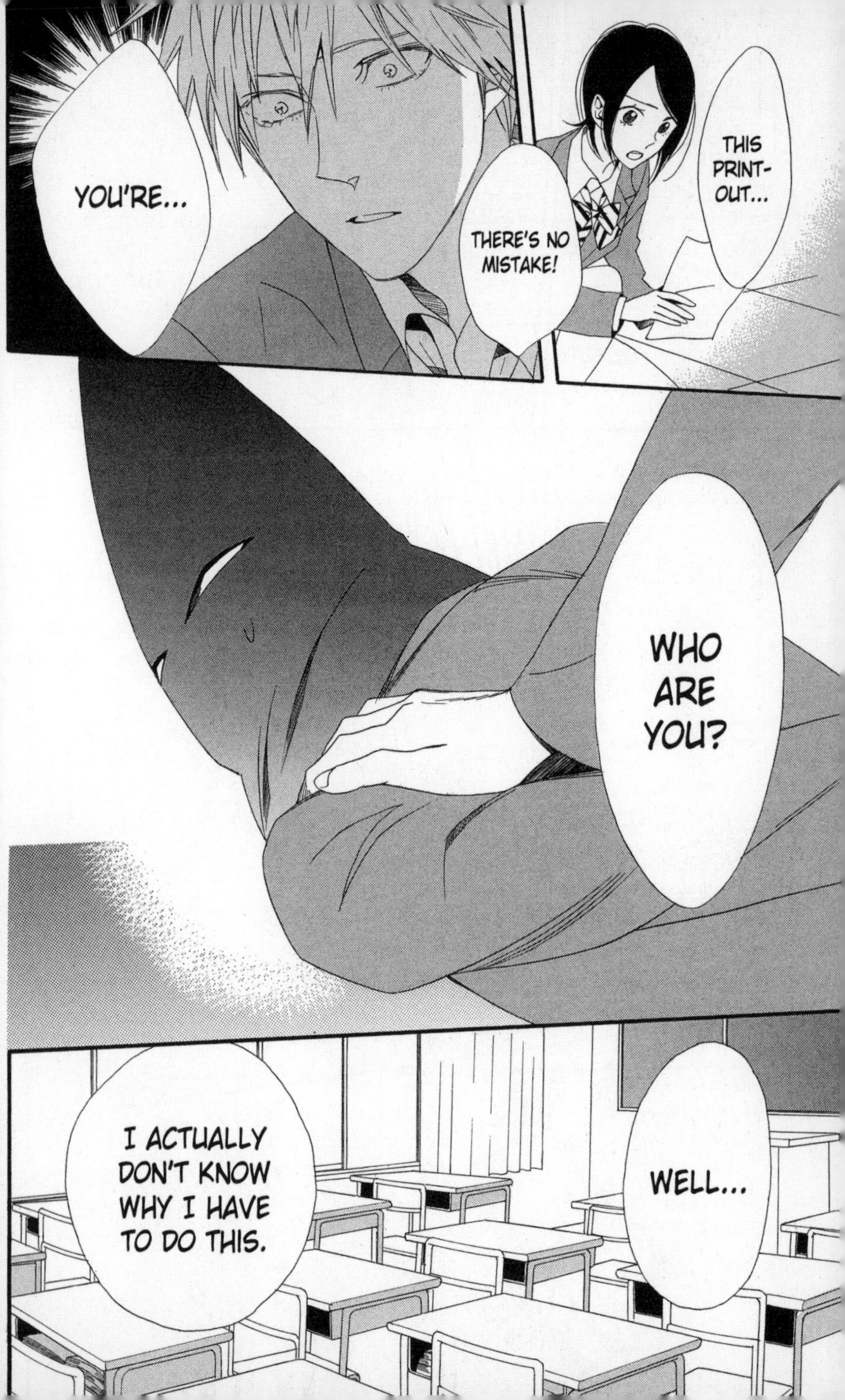
THIS PRINT-OUT...
THERE'S NO MISTAKE!
YOU'RE...
WHO ARE YOU?
WELL...
I ACTUALLY DON'T KNOW WHY I HAVE TO DO THIS.

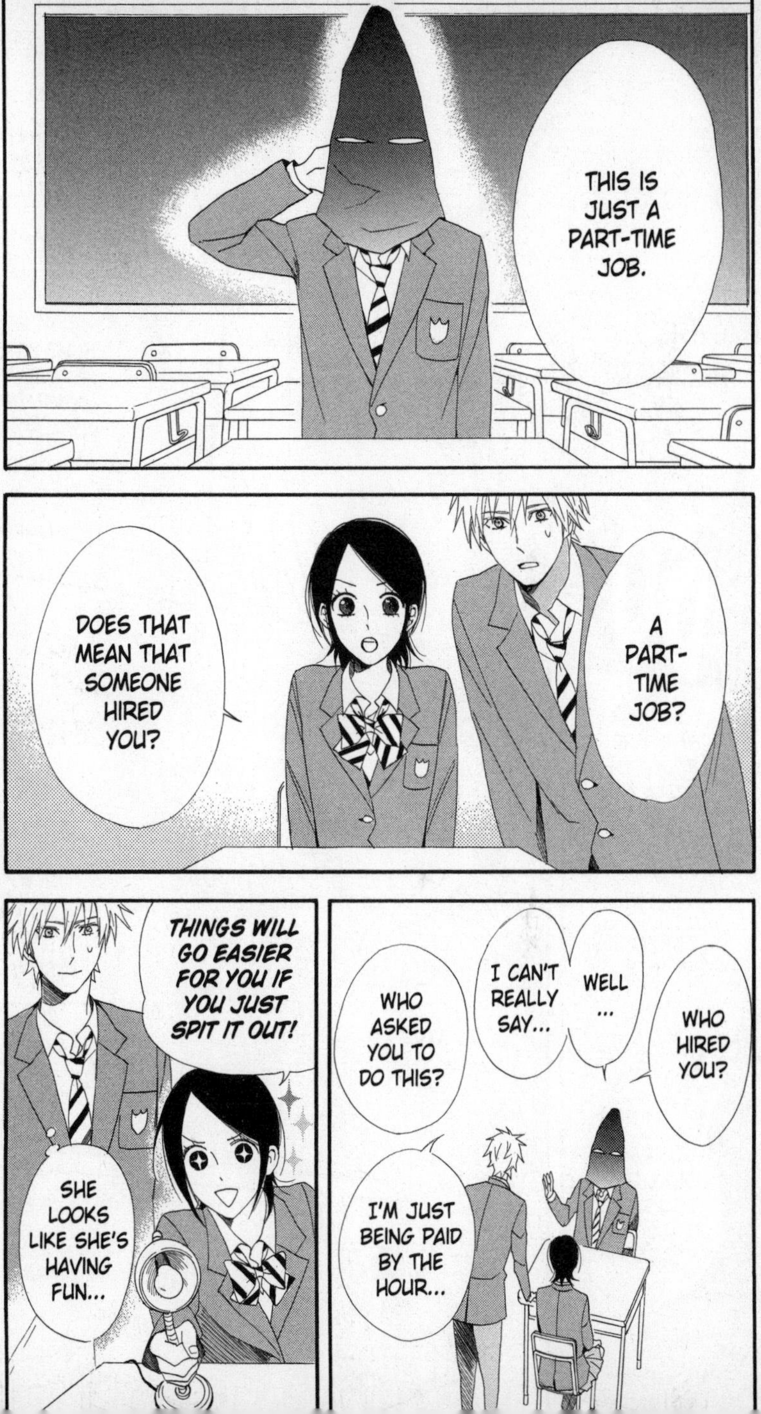
THIS IS JUST A PART-TIME JOB.
A PART-TIME JOB?
DOES THAT MEAN THAT SOMEONE HIRED YOU?
WHO HIRED YOU?
WELL ...
I CAN'T REALLY SAY...
WHO ASKED YOU TO DO THIS?
I'M JUST BEING PAID BY THE HOUR...
THINGS WILL GO EASIER FOR YOU IF YOU JUST SPIT IT OUT!
SHE LOOKS LIKE SHE'S HAVING FUN...

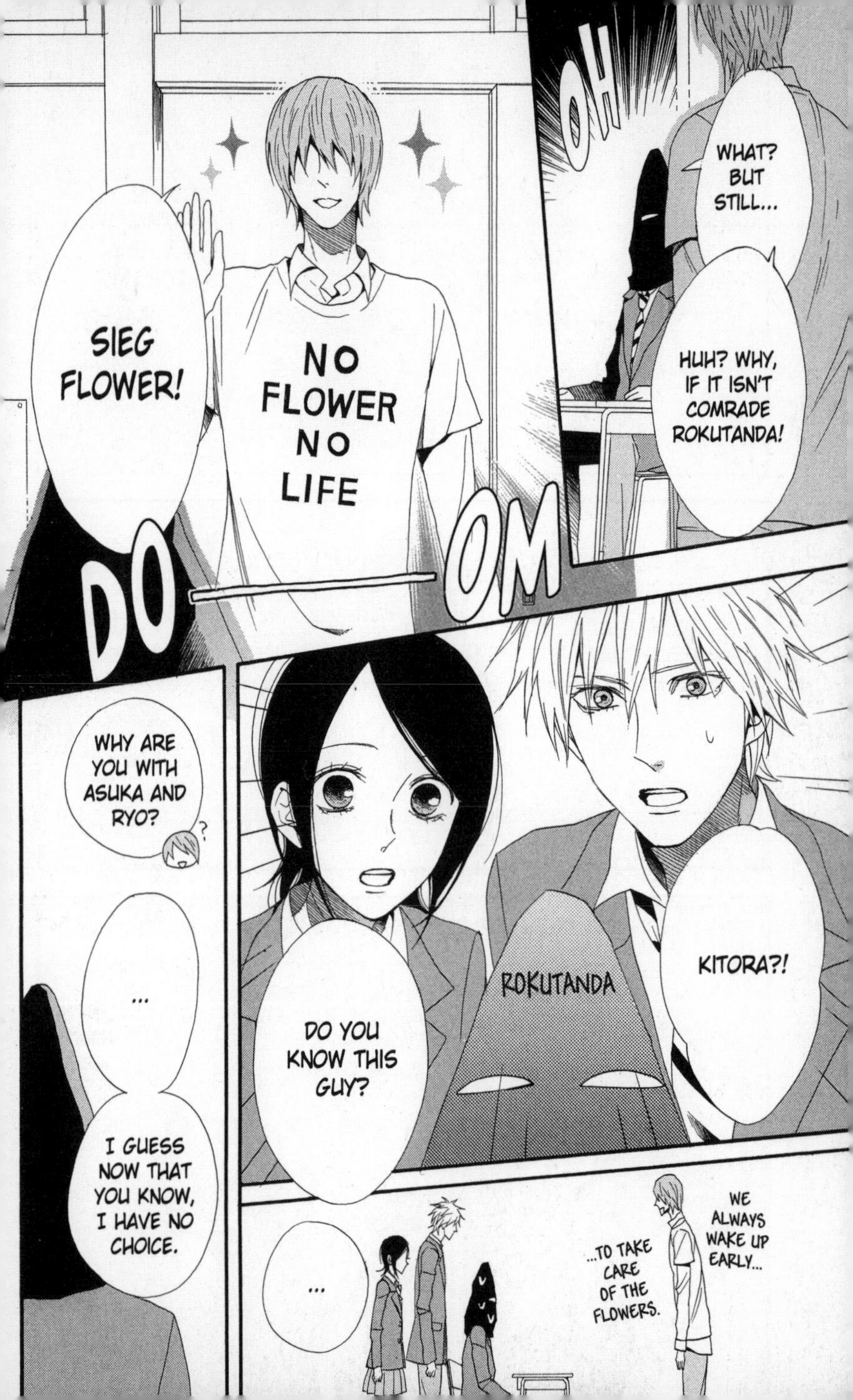
OH
WHAT? BUT STILL...
HUH? WHY, IF IT ISN'T COMRADE ROKUTANDA!
SIEG FLOWER!
NO FLOWER NO LIFE
DO—OM
KITORA?!
ROKUTANDA
DO YOU KNOW THIS GUY?
WE ALWAYS WAKE UP EARLY...
...TO TAKE CARE OF THE FLOWERS.
...
WHY ARE YOU WITH ASUKA AND RYO?
?
...
I GUESS NOW THAT YOU KNOW, I HAVE NO CHOICE.

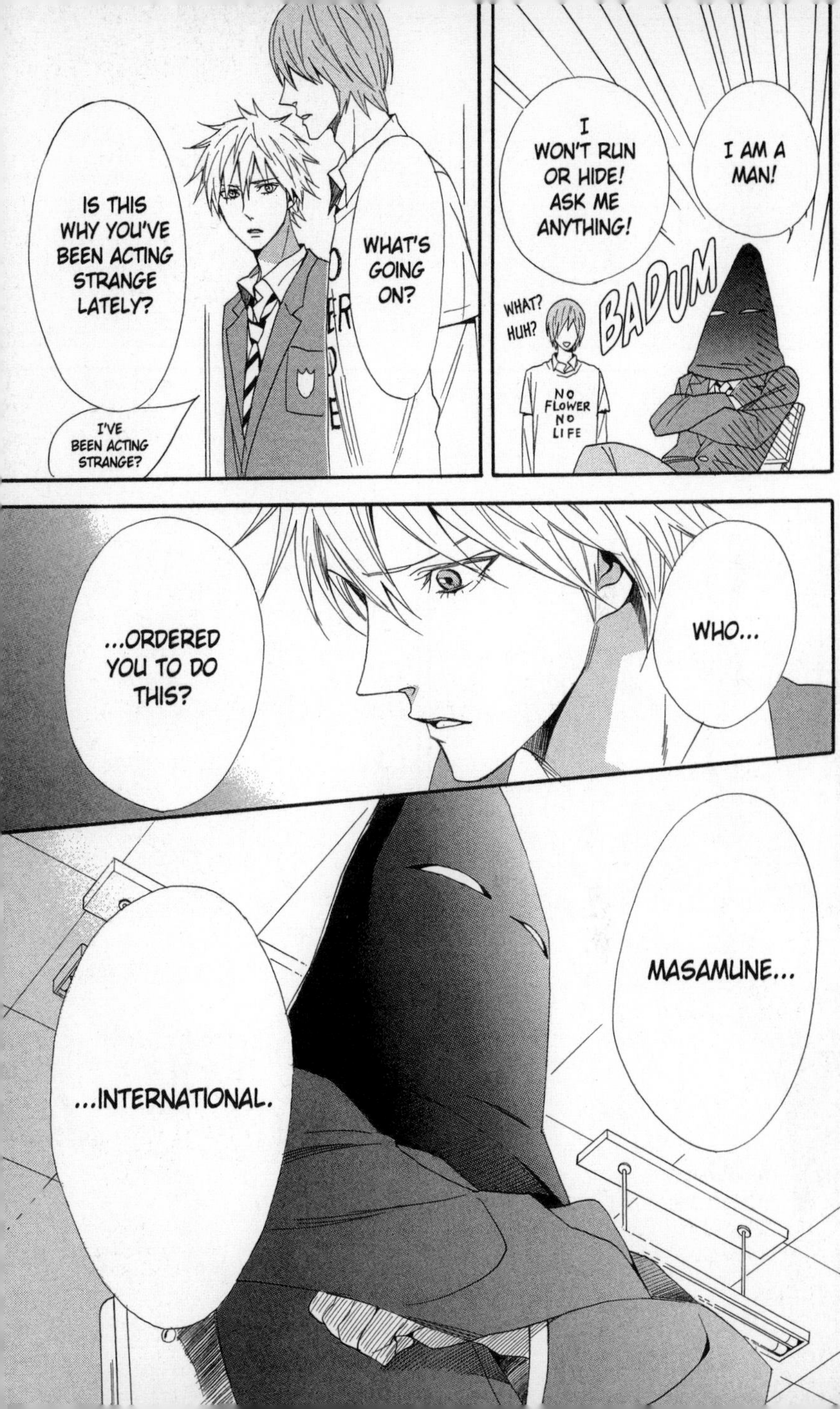
I AM A MAN!
I WON'T RUN OR HIDE! ASK ME ANYTHING!
BADUM
WHAT? HUH?
NO FLOWER NO LIFE
WHAT'S GOING ON?
IS THIS WHY YOU'VE BEEN ACTING STRANGE LATELY?
I'VE BEEN ACTING STRANGE?
WHO...
...ORDERED YOU TO DO THIS?
MASAMUNE...
...INTERNATIONAL.

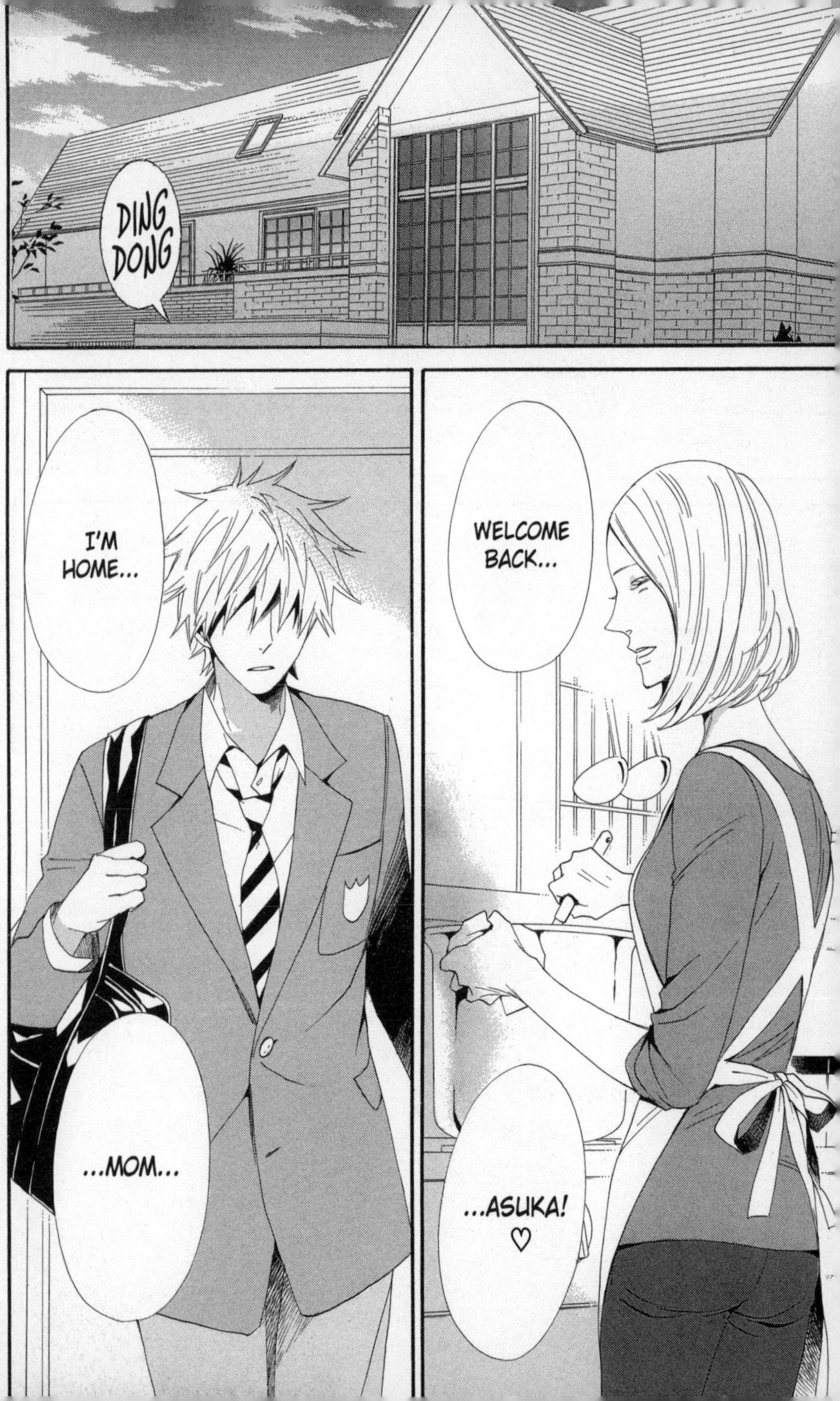
DING DONG
WELCOME BACK...
...ASUKA! ♡
I'M HOME...
...MOM...

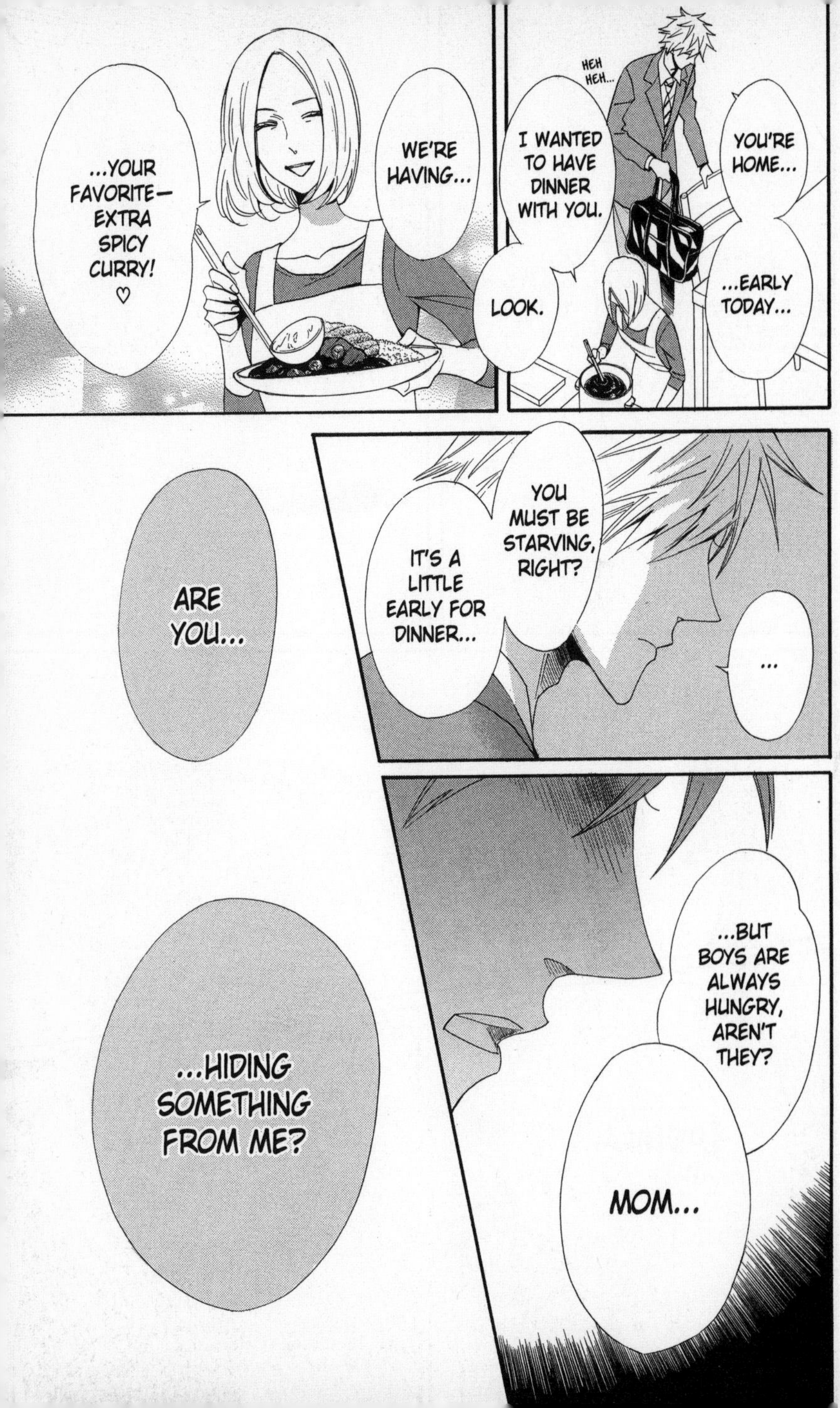
YOU'RE HOME...
...EARLY TODAY...
HEH HEH...
I WANTED TO HAVE DINNER WITH YOU.
LOOK.
WE'RE HAVING...
...YOUR FAVORITE—EXTRA SPICY CURRY! ♡
...
YOU MUST BE STARVING, RIGHT?
IT'S A LITTLE EARLY FOR DINNER...
...BUT BOYS ARE ALWAYS HUNGRY, AREN'T THEY?
MOM...
ARE YOU...
...HIDING SOMETHING FROM ME?

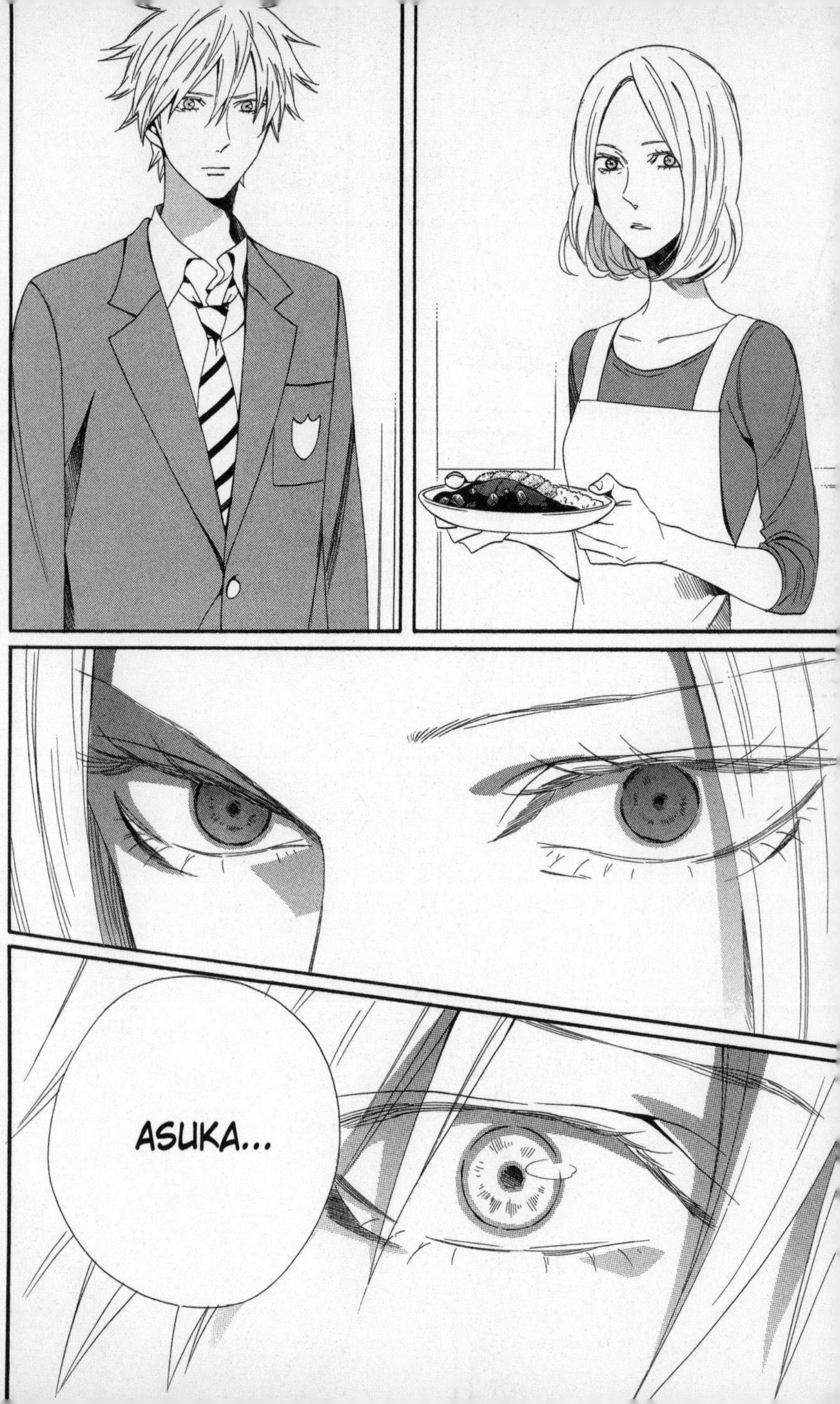
ASUKA...

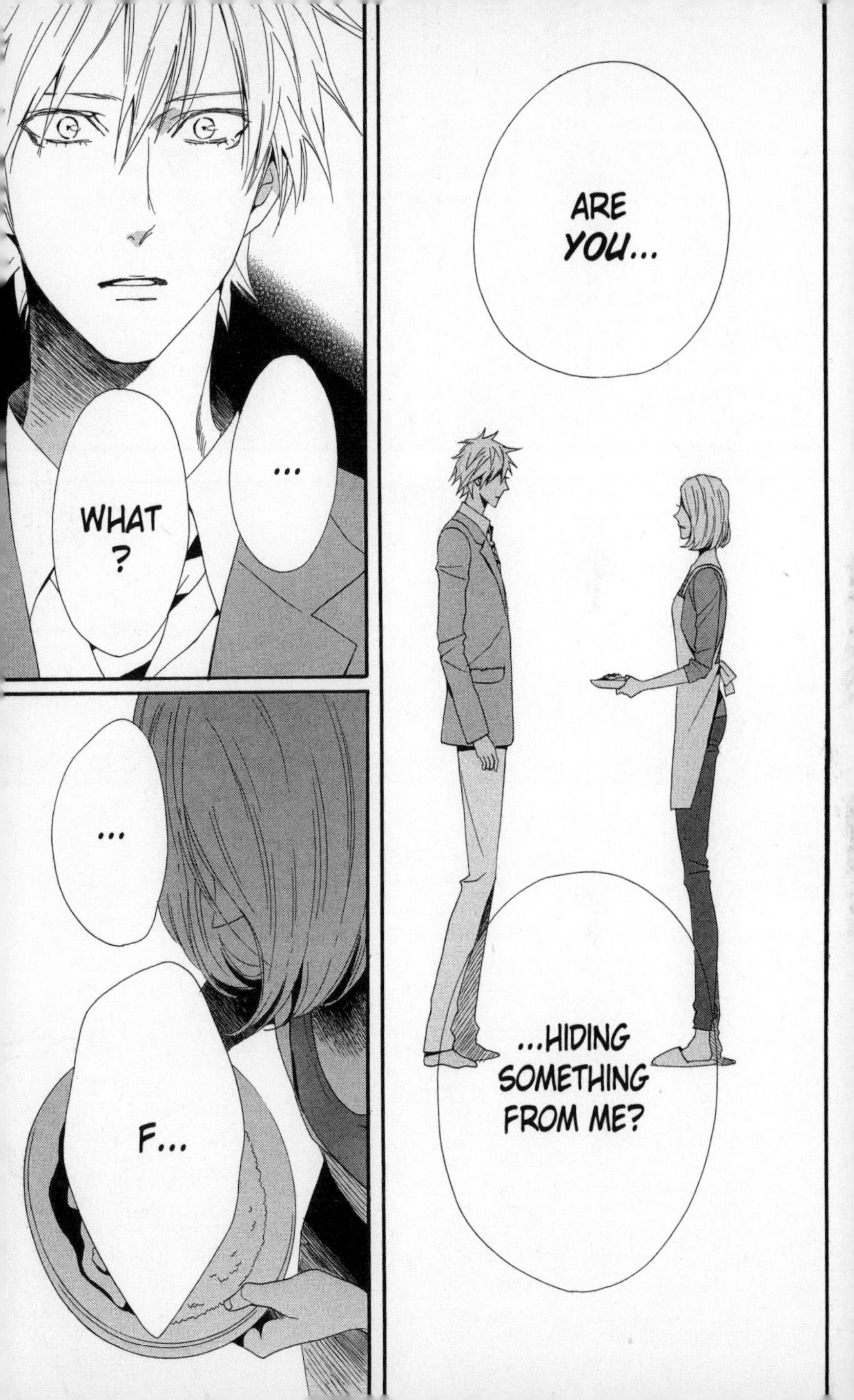
ARE YOU...
...HIDING SOMETHING FROM ME?
...
WHAT ?
...
F...

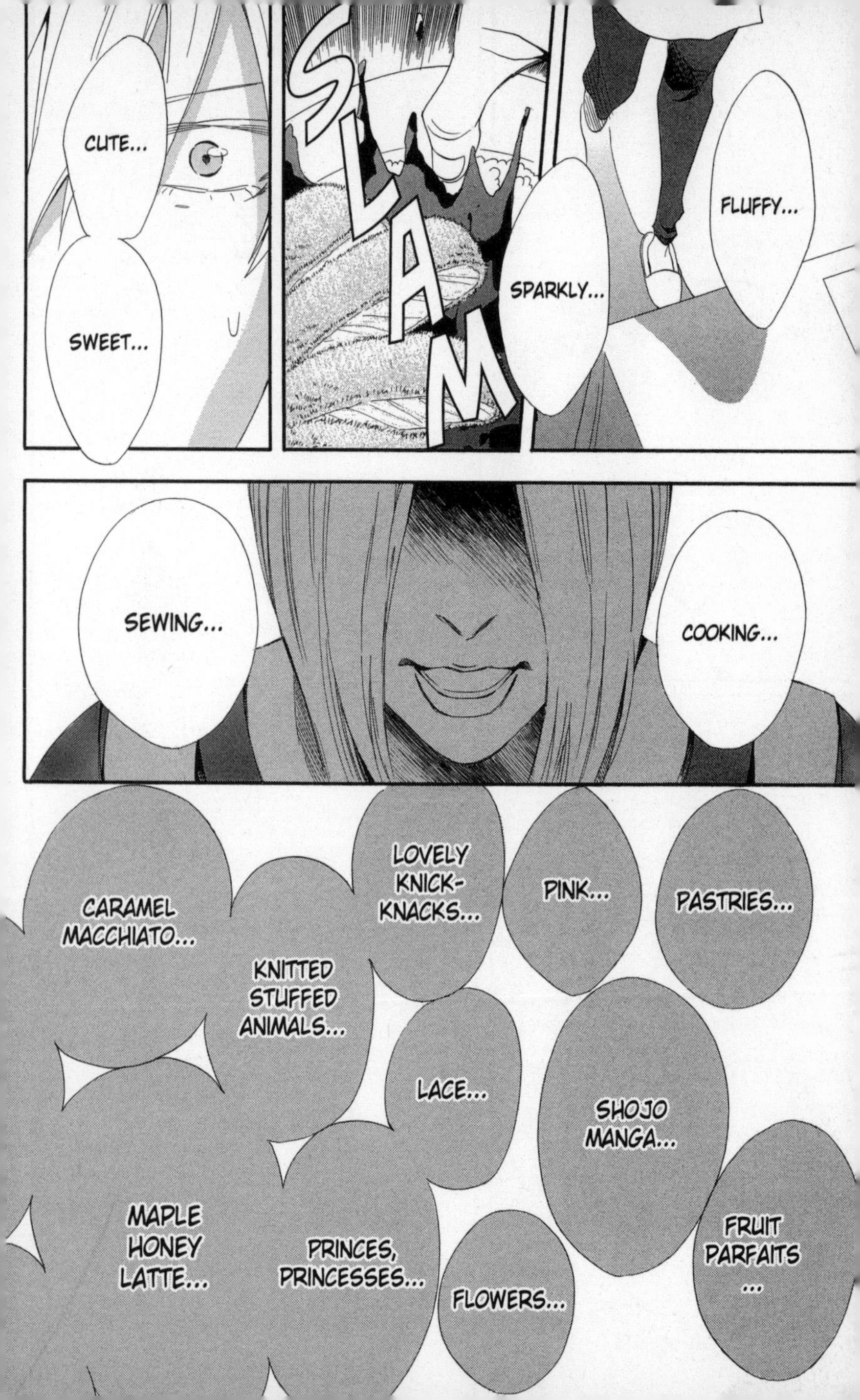
FLUFFY...
SPARKLY...
SLAM
CUTE...
SWEET...
COOKING...
SEWING...
PASTRIES...
PINK...
LOVELY KNICK-KNACKS...
CARAMEL MACCHIATO...
SHOJO MANGA...
LACE...
KNITTED STUFFED ANIMALS...
FRUIT PARFAITS ...
FLOWERS...
PRINCES, PRINCESSES...
MAPLE HONEY LATTE...

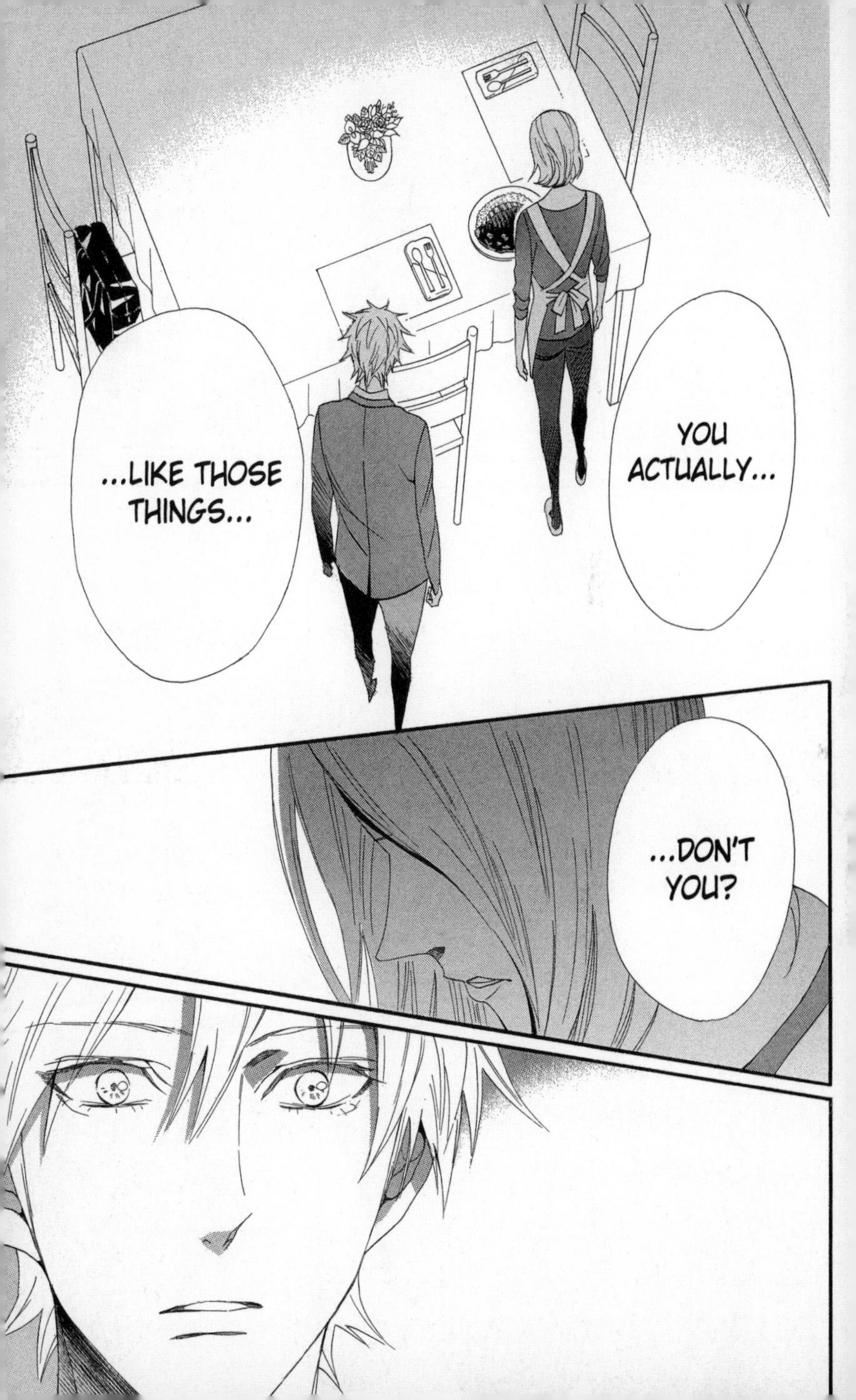
YOU ACTUALLY...
...LIKE THOSE THINGS...
...DON'T YOU?

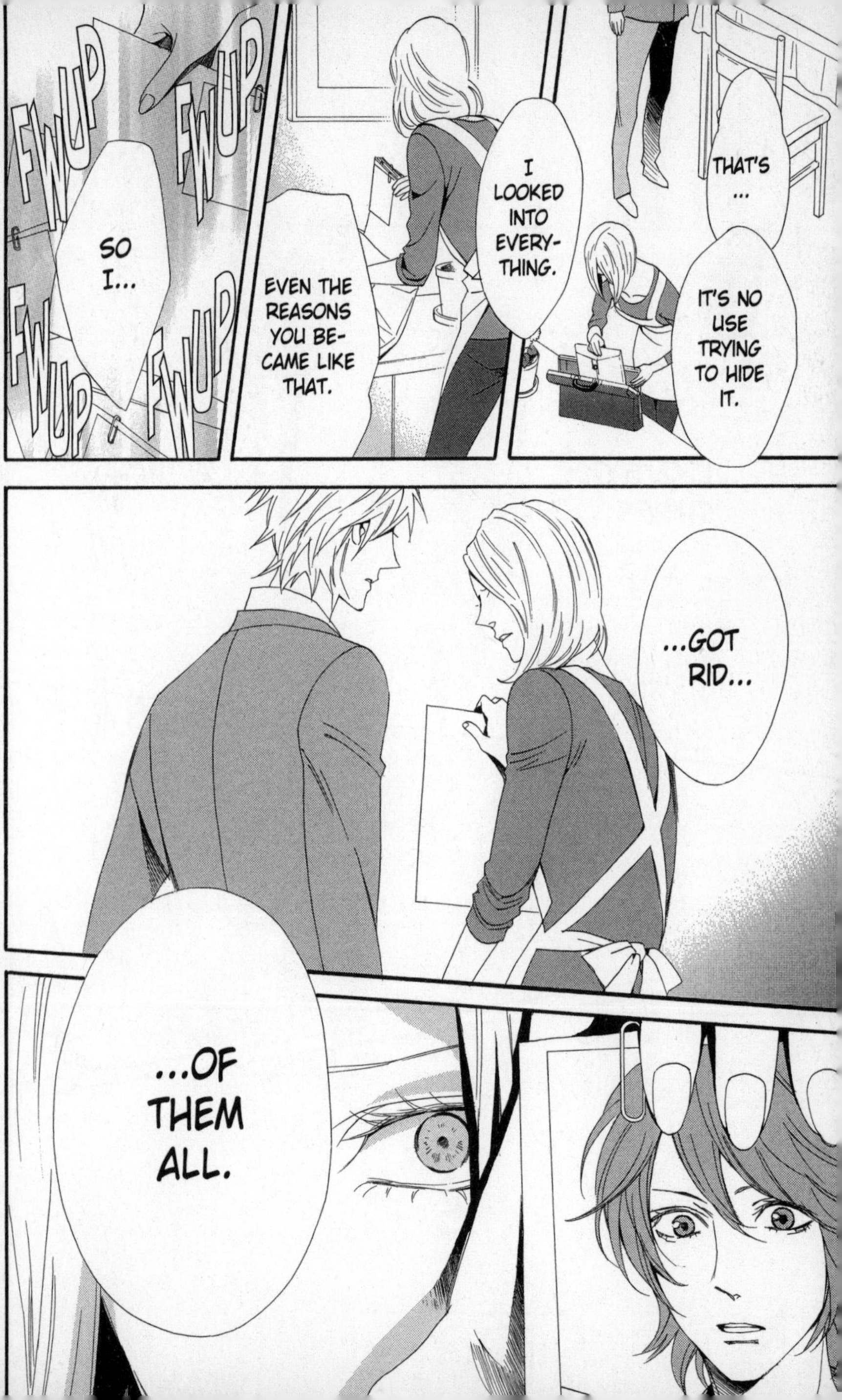
THAT'S ...
IT'S NO USE TRYING TO HIDE IT.
I LOOKED INTO EVERY-THING.
EVEN THE REASONS YOU BE-CAME LIKE THAT.
FWUP
FWUP
SO I...
FWUP
FWUP
...GOT RID...
...OF THEM ALL.

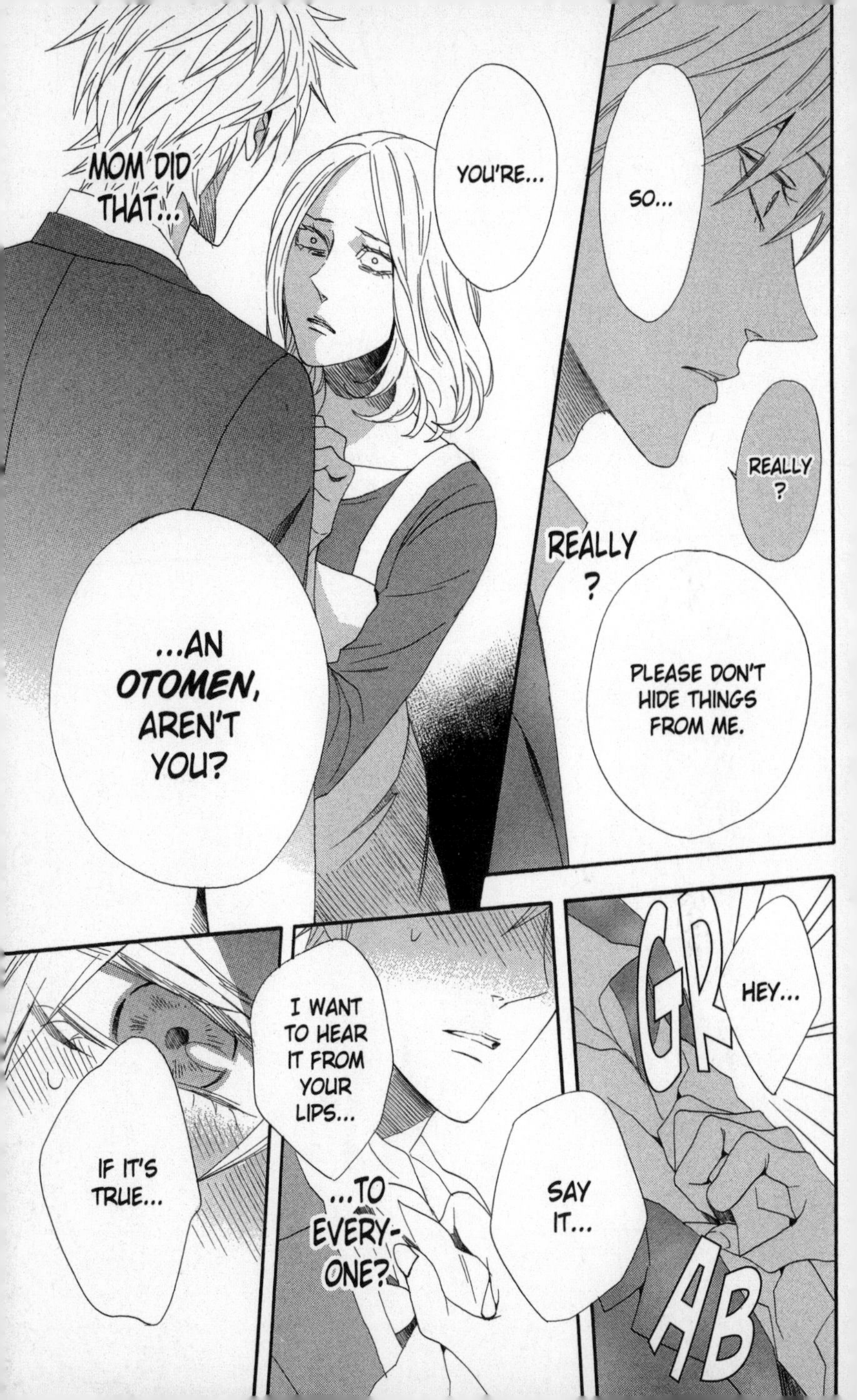
SO...
REALLY ?
REALLY ?
PLEASE DON'T HIDE THINGS FROM ME.
YOU'RE...
MOM DID THAT...
...AN *OTOMEN*, AREN'T YOU?
GRAB
HEY...
I WANT TO HEAR IT FROM YOUR LIPS...
SAY IT...
...TO EVERY-ONE?
IF IT'S TRUE...

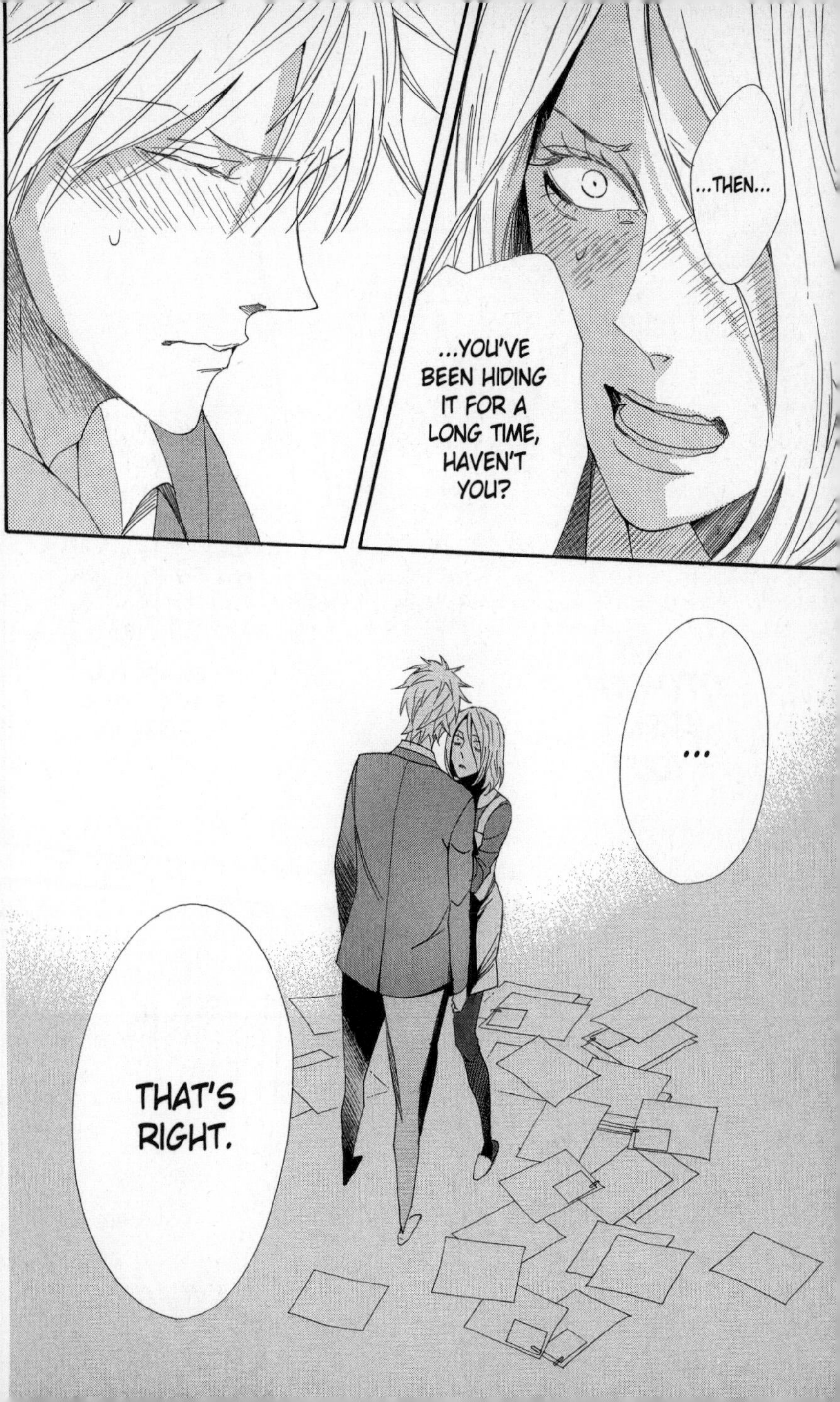
...THEN...
...YOU'VE BEEN HIDING IT FOR A LONG TIME, HAVEN'T YOU?
...
THAT'S RIGHT.

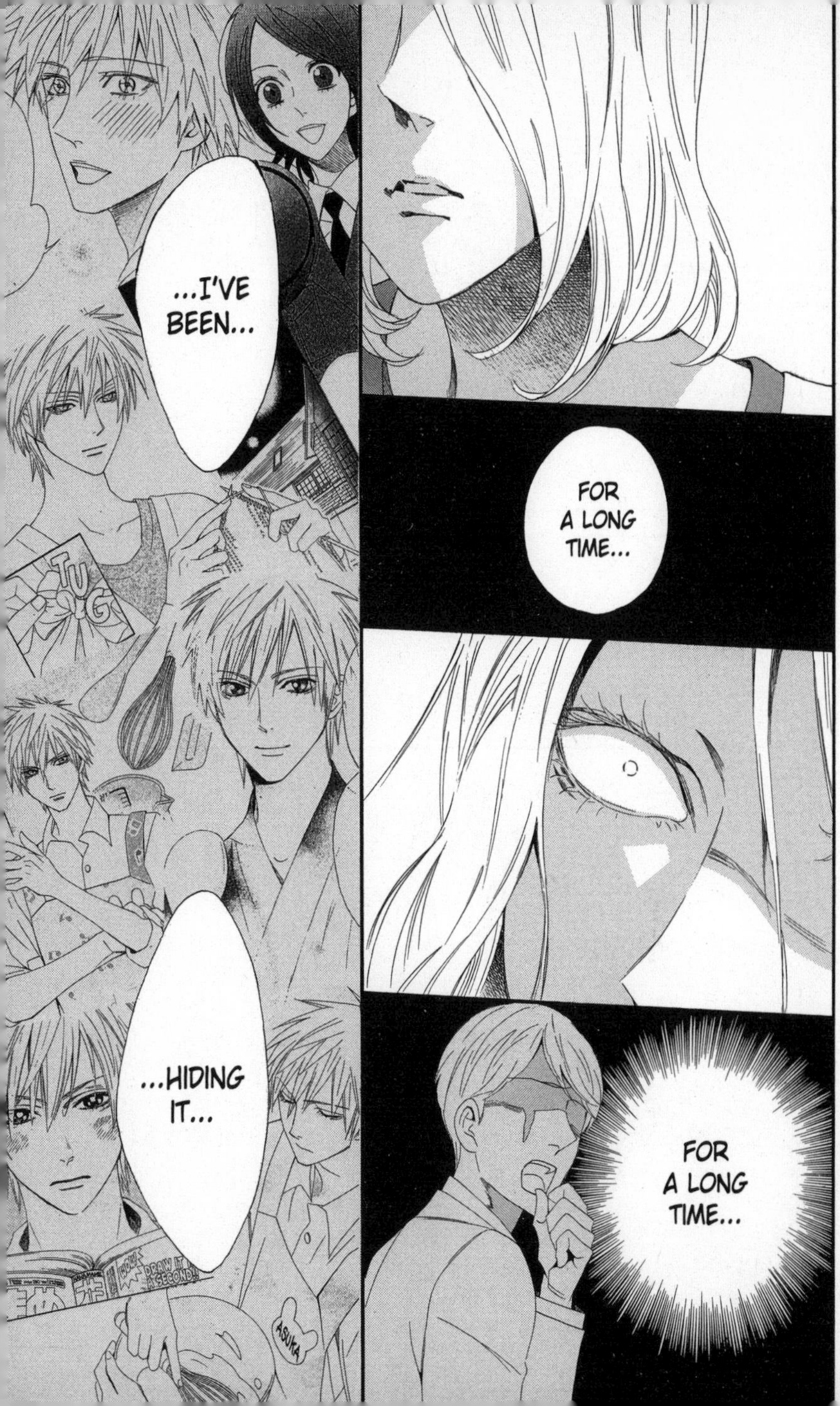
FOR A LONG TIME...
FOR A LONG TIME...
...I'VE BEEN...
...HIDING IT...
DRAW IT A SECOND!
ASUKA

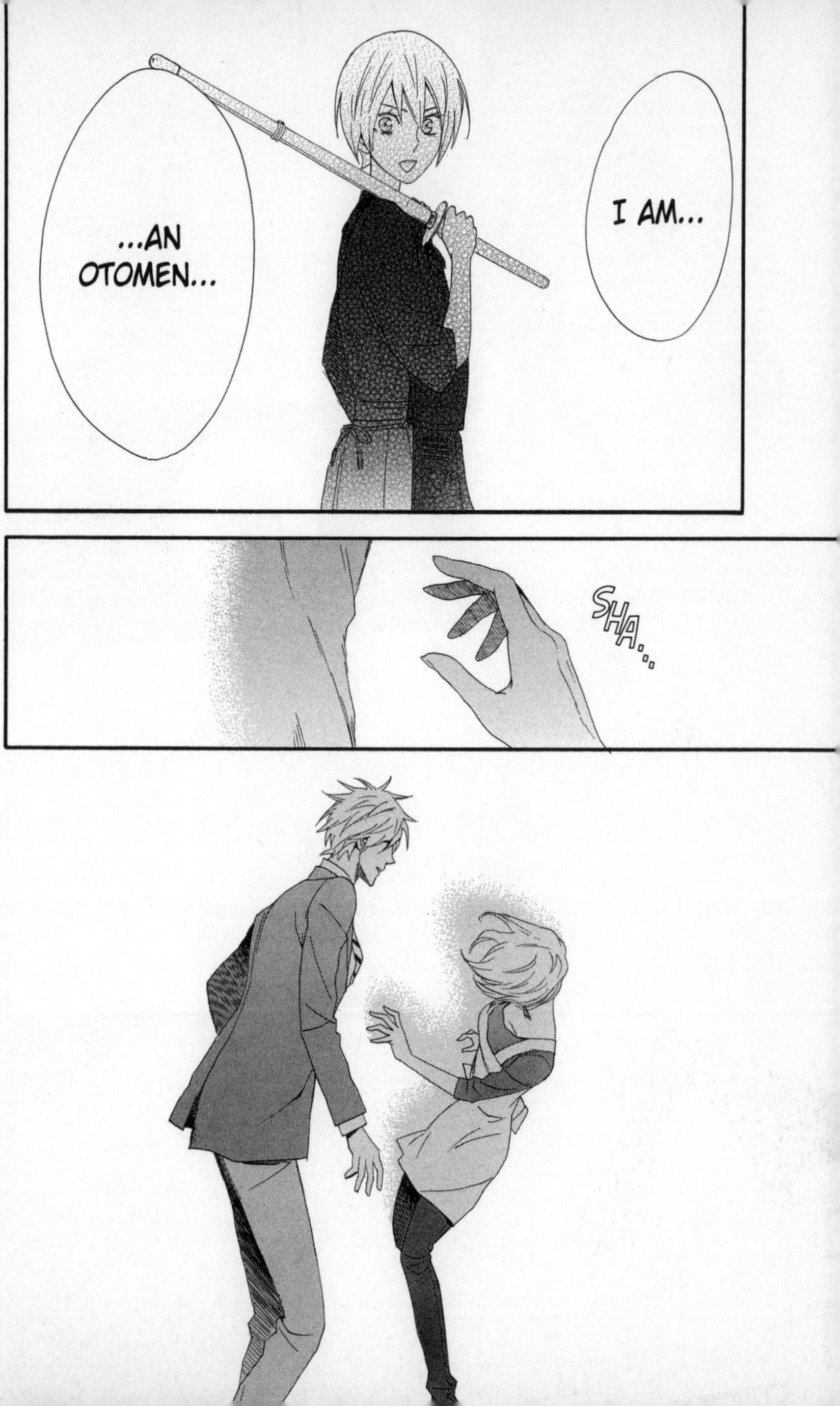
I AM...
...AN OTOMEN...
SHA...

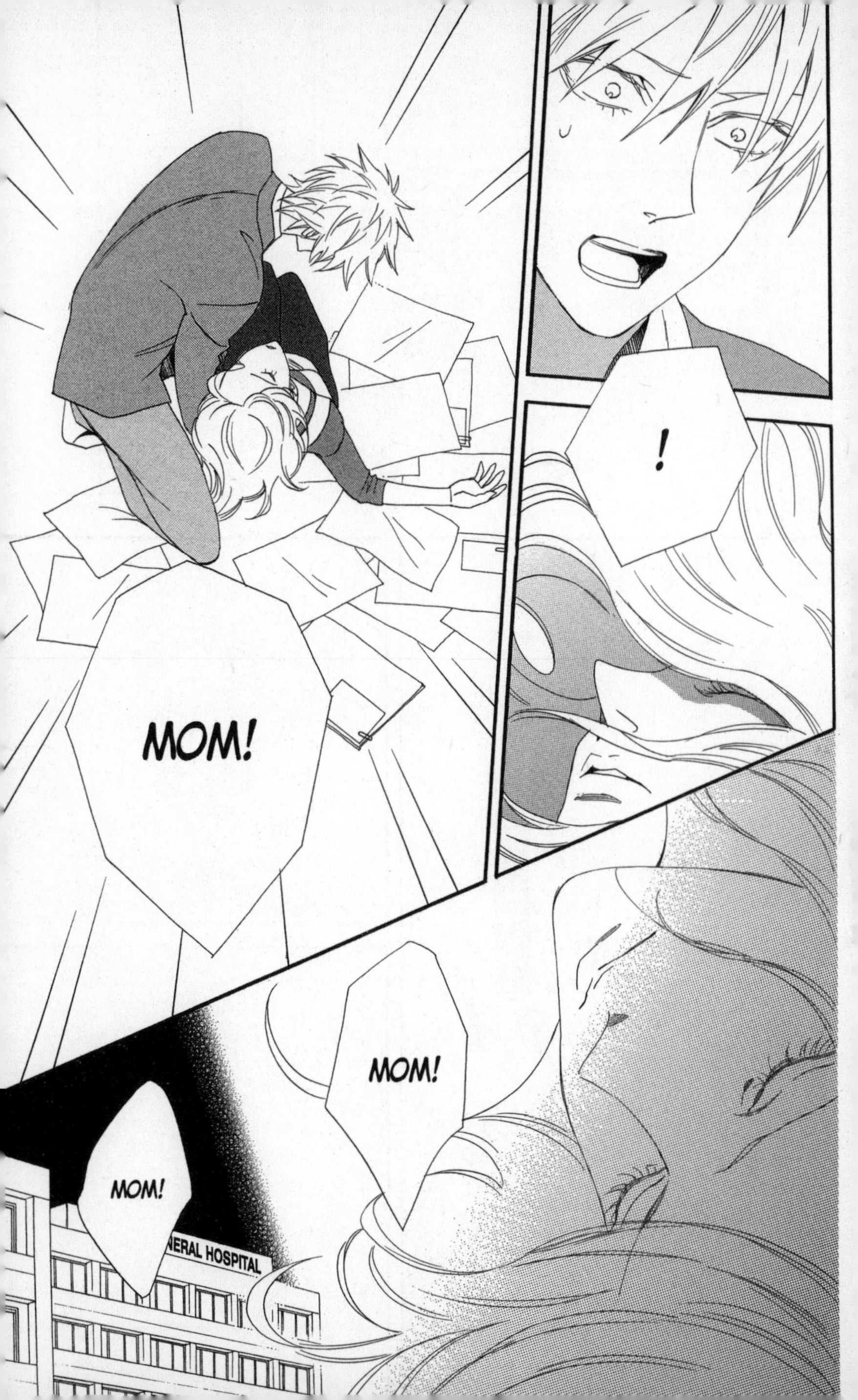
!
MOM!
MOM!
MOM!
NERAL HOSPITAL

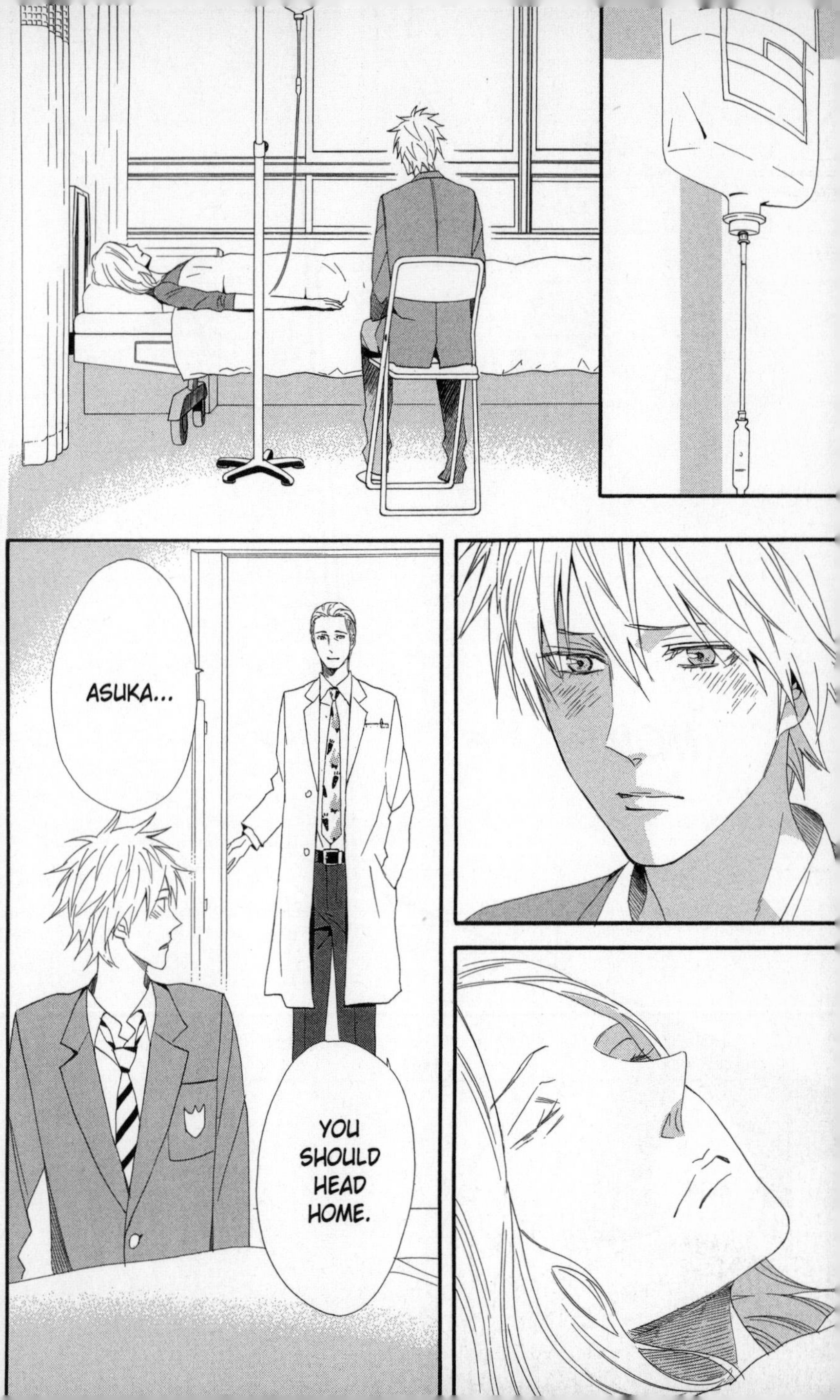
ASUKA...
YOU SHOULD HEAD HOME.

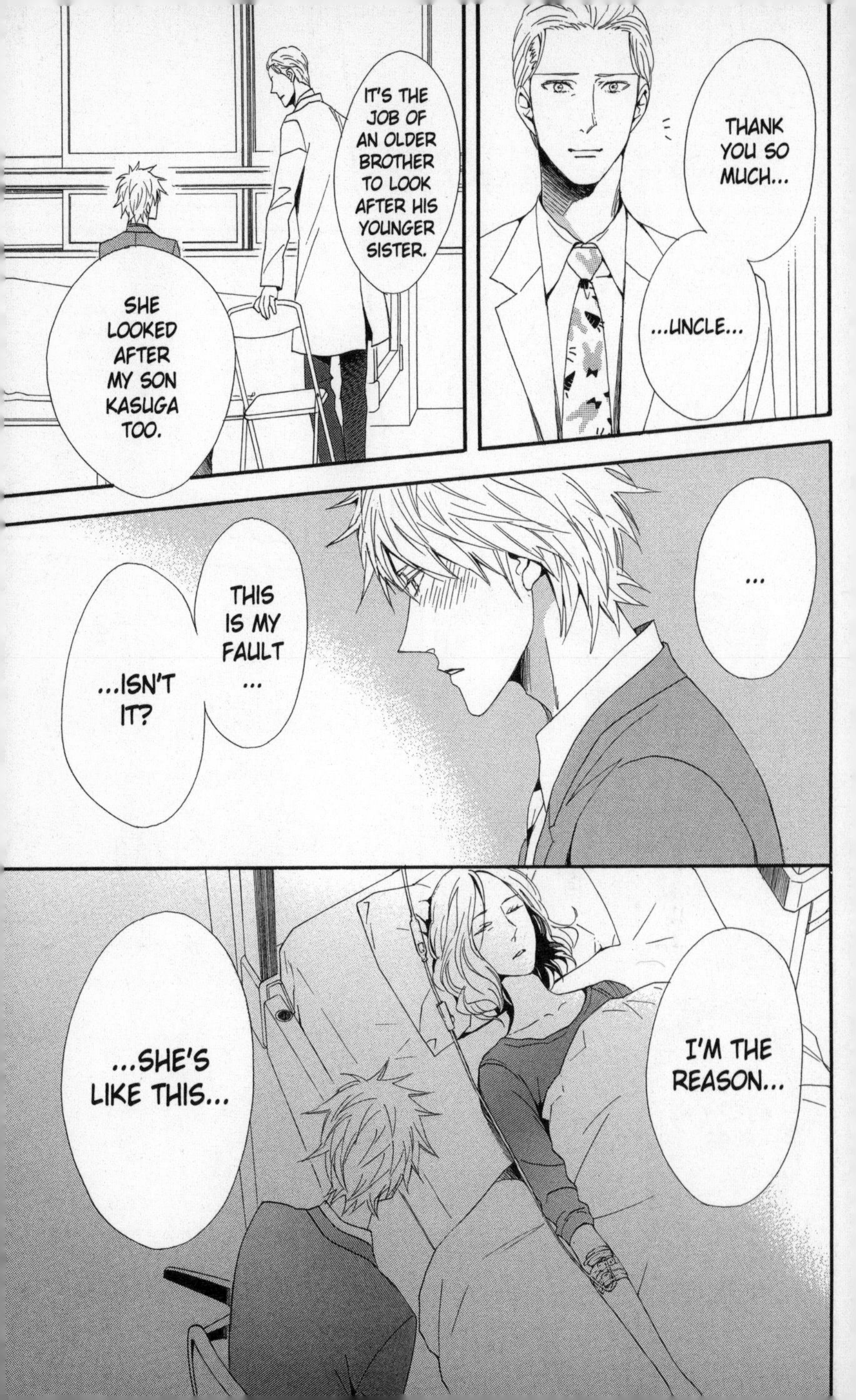
THANK YOU SO MUCH...
...UNCLE...
IT'S THE JOB OF AN OLDER BROTHER TO LOOK AFTER HIS YOUNGER SISTER.
SHE LOOKED AFTER MY SON KASUGA TOO.
...
THIS IS MY FAULT...
...ISN'T IT?
I'M THE REASON...
...SHE'S LIKE THIS...

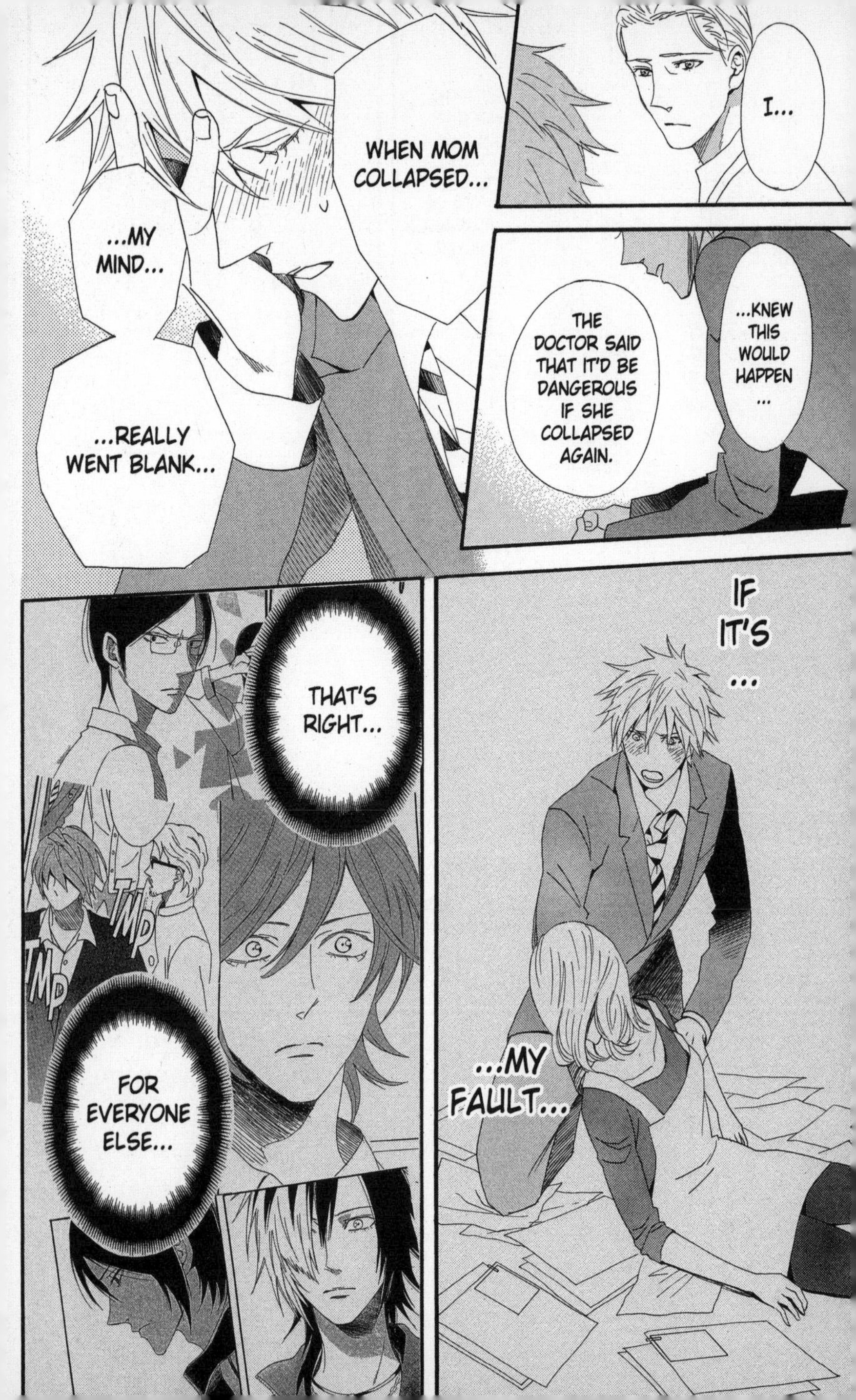
I...
...KNEW THIS WOULD HAPPEN...
THE DOCTOR SAID THAT IT'D BE DANGEROUS IF SHE COLLAPSED AGAIN.
WHEN MOM COLLAPSED...
...MY MIND...
...REALLY WENT BLANK...
IF IT'S...
...MY FAULT...
THAT'S RIGHT...
TMP
TMP
FOR EVERYONE ELSE...

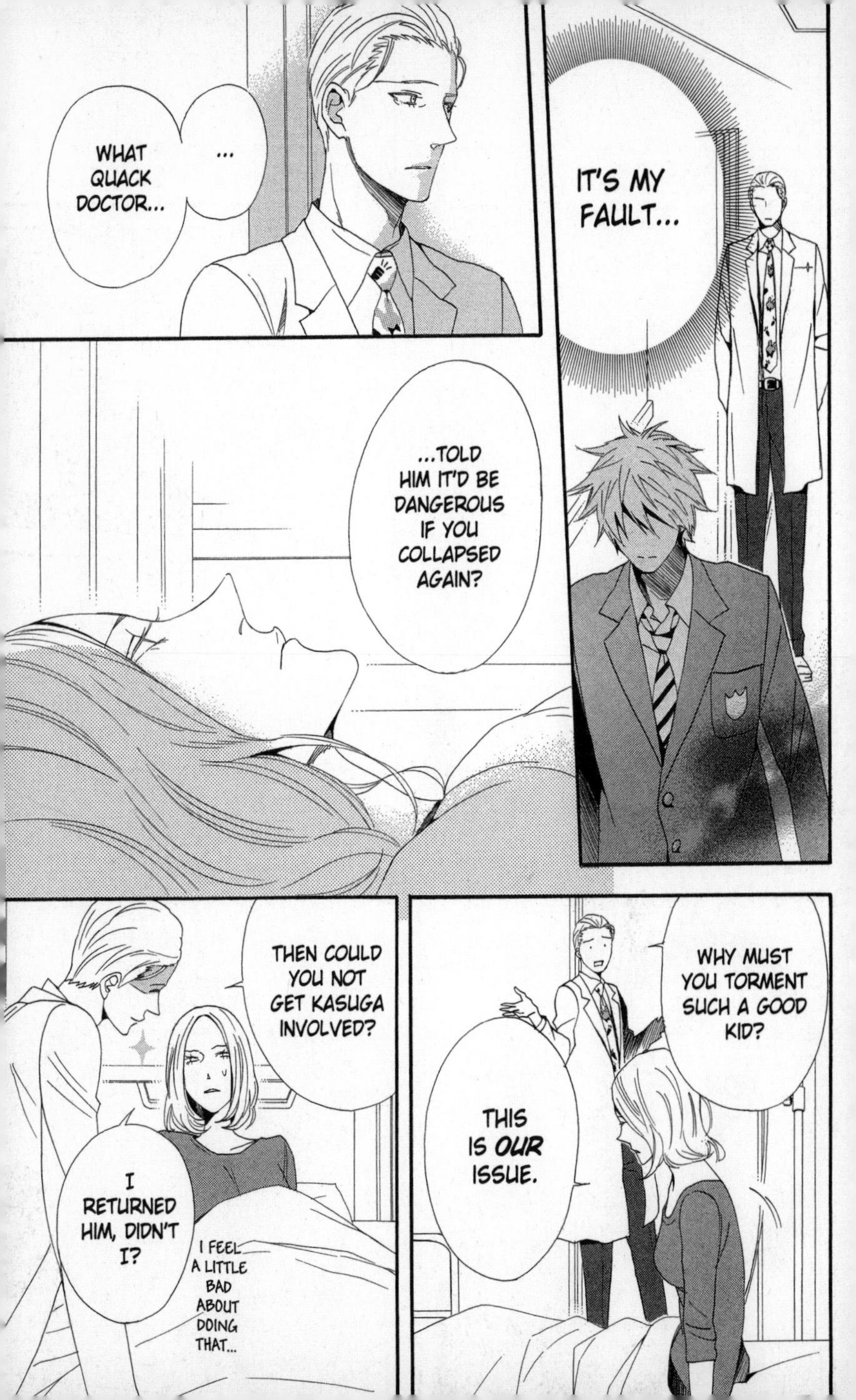
IT'S MY FAULT...
...
WHAT QUACK DOCTOR...
...TOLD HIM IT'D BE DANGEROUS IF YOU COLLAPSED AGAIN?
WHY MUST YOU TORMENT SUCH A GOOD KID?
THIS IS *OUR* ISSUE.
THEN COULD YOU NOT GET KASUGA INVOLVED?
I RETURNED HIM, DIDN'T I?
I FEEL A LITTLE BAD ABOUT DOING THAT...

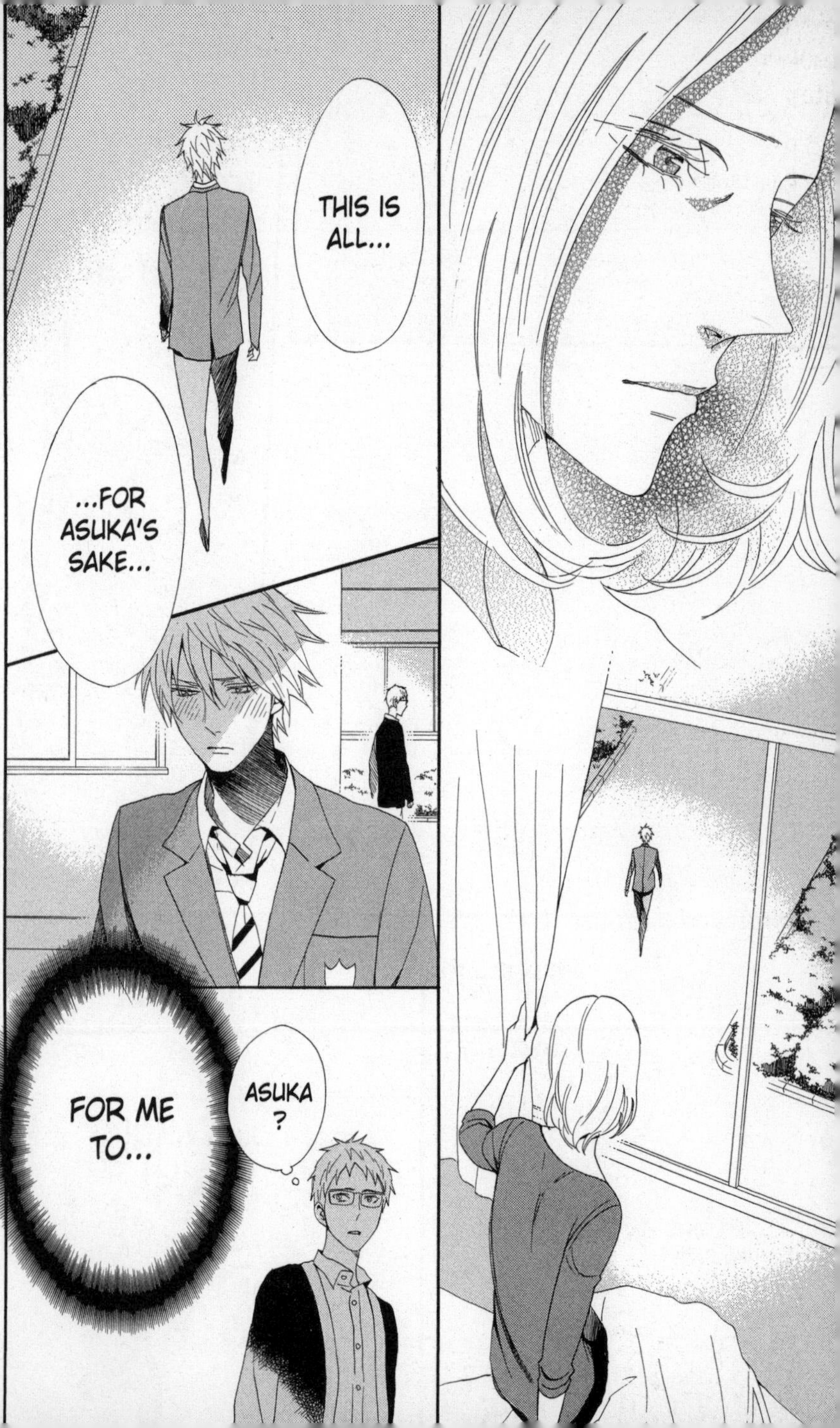
THIS IS ALL...
...FOR ASUKA'S SAKE...
ASUKA?
FOR ME TO...

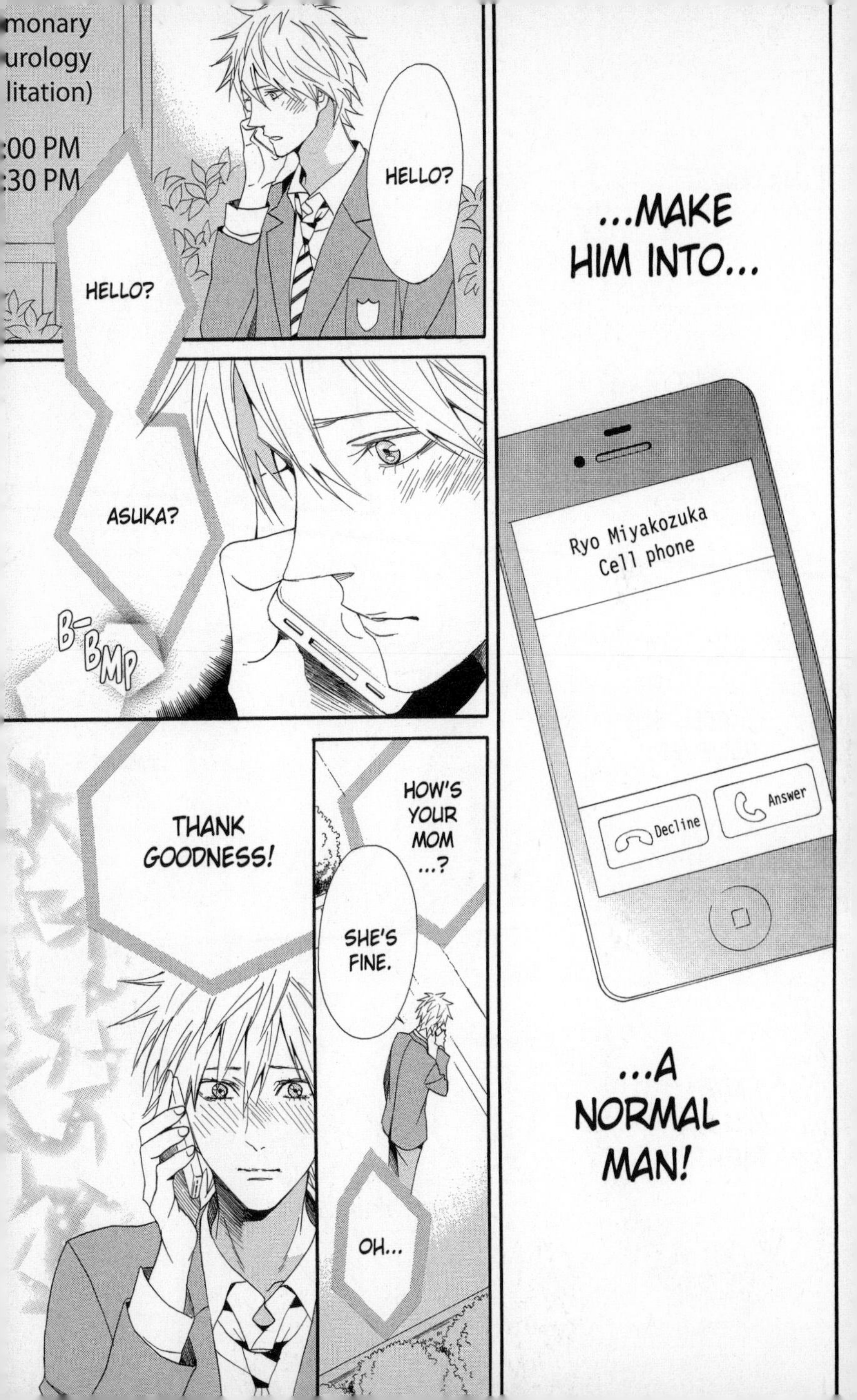
...MAKE HIM INTO...
Ryo Miyakozuka
Cell phone
Decline
Answer
...A NORMAL MAN!
monary
urology
litation)
:00 PM
:30 PM
HELLO?
HELLO?
ASUKA?
B-BMP
HOW'S YOUR MOM ...?
SHE'S FINE.
OH...
THANK GOODNESS!

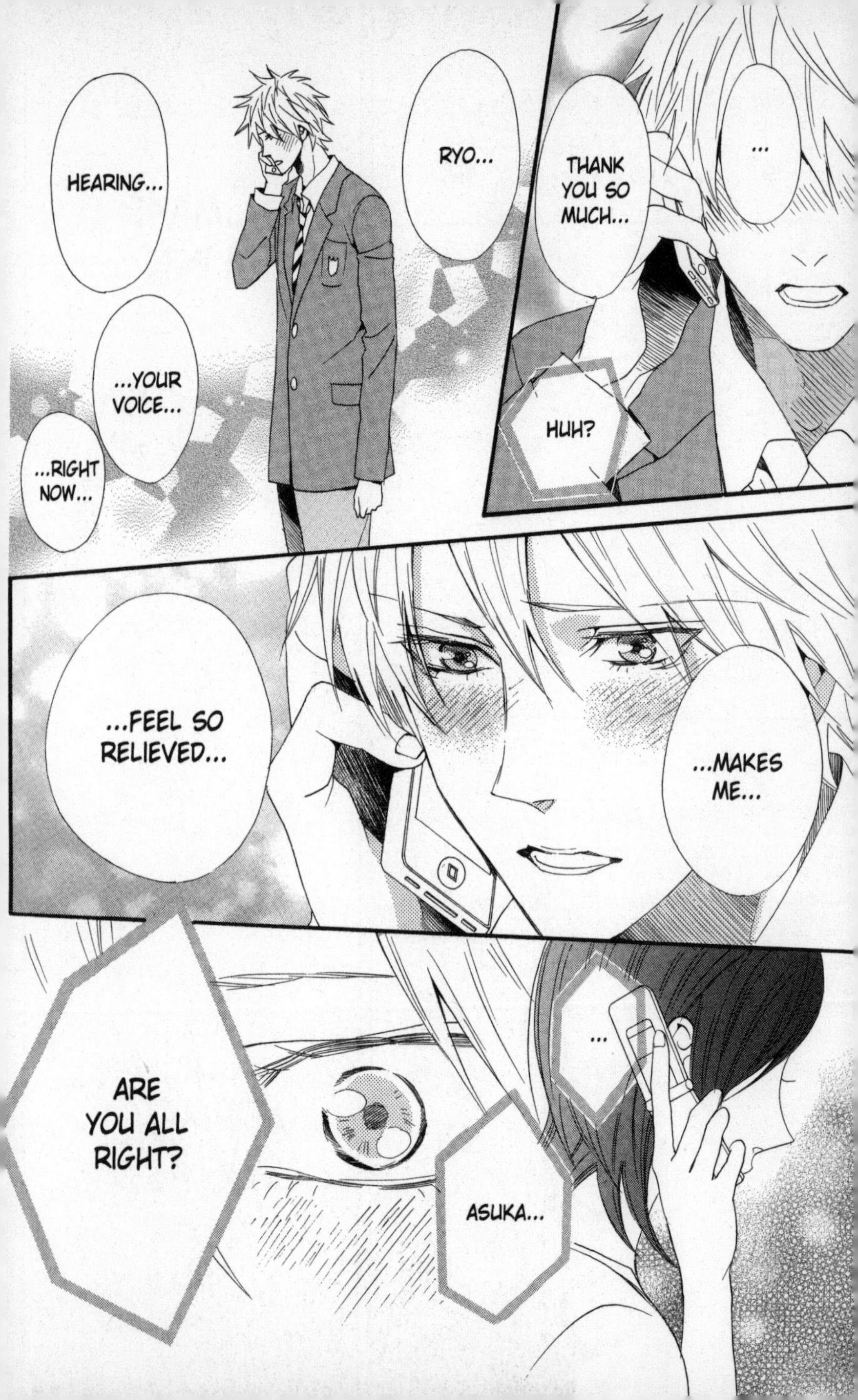
...
THANK YOU SO MUCH...
HUH?
RYO...
HEARING...
...YOUR VOICE...
...RIGHT NOW...
...MAKES ME...
...FEEL SO RELIEVED...
...
ASUKA...
ARE YOU ALL RIGHT?

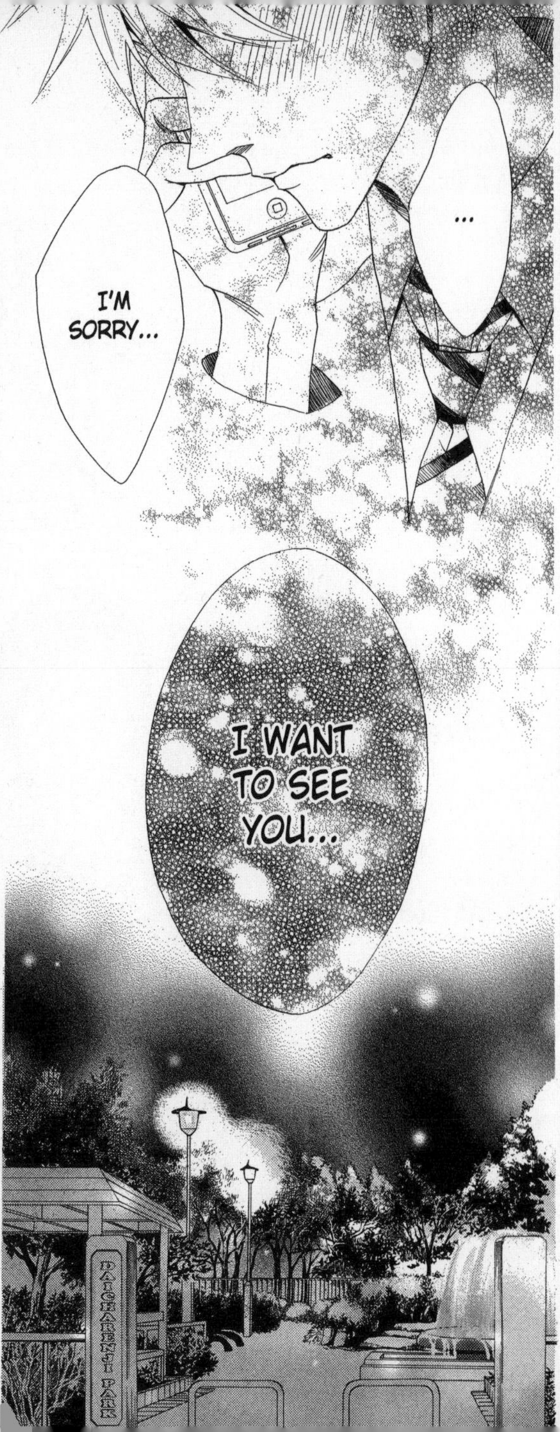
...
I'M SORRY...
I WANT TO SEE YOU...
DAICHARENJI PARK

He used to have black hair.

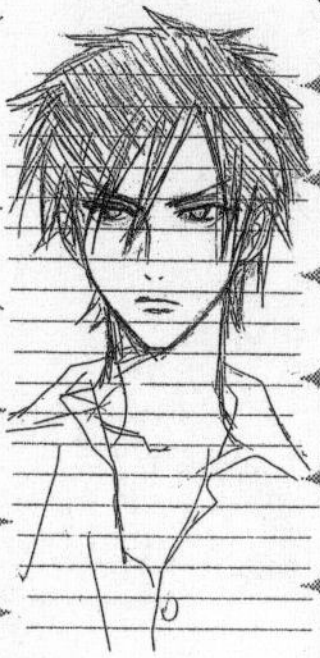

This is the very first picture I drew of Asuka. It was a sketch for a notebook included with a *Hana to Yume* comic. At the time, his name wasn't "Asuka Masamune," but "Masamune Fudo." The reason why I changed it to "Asuka" was because I was completely hooked on the anime *Karate Baka Ichidai* at the time. In the anime version of *Karate Baka*, the main character's name is "Ken Asuka" and his disciple's name is "Shogo Ariake."

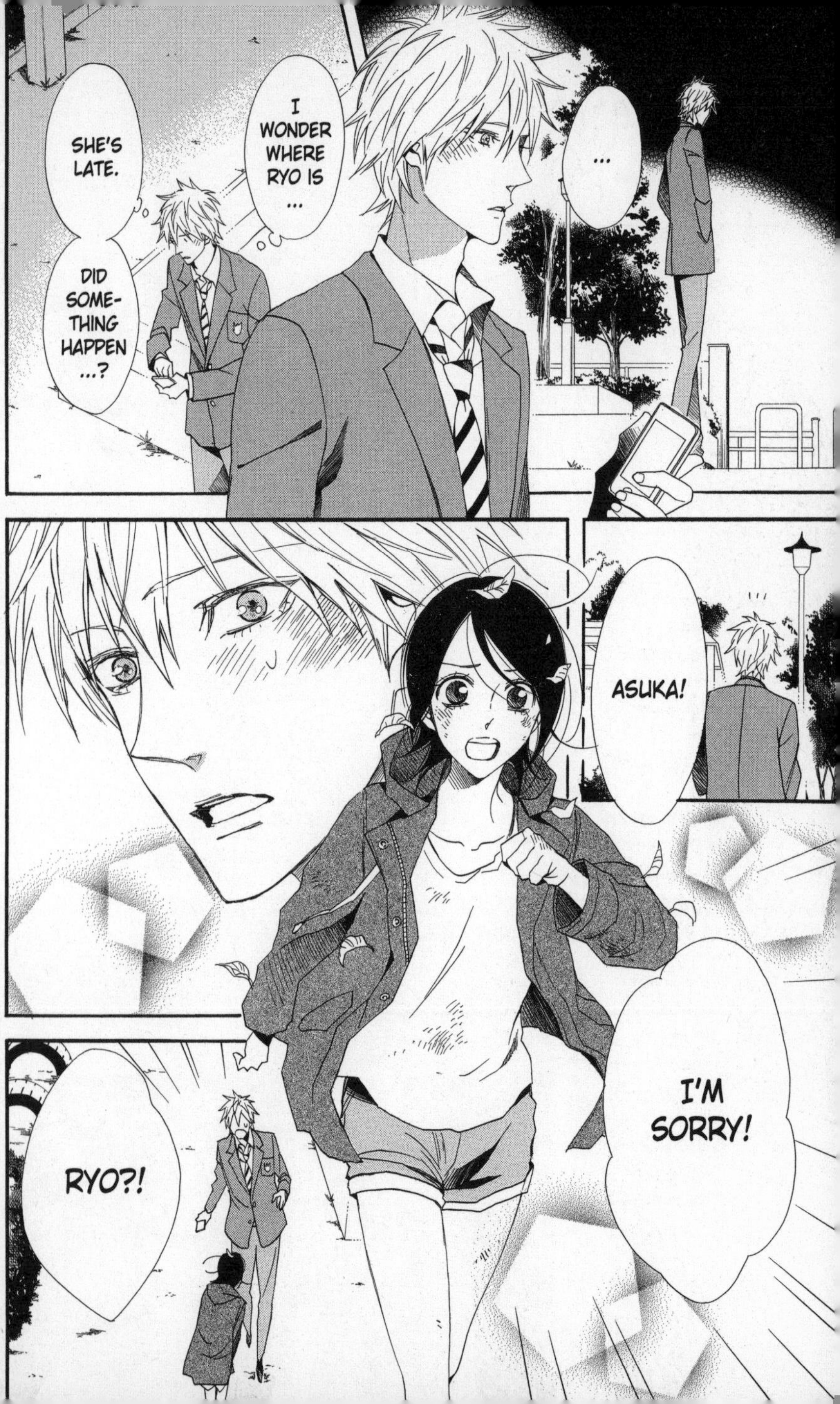
...
I WONDER WHERE RYO IS ...
SHE'S LATE.
DID SOME-THING HAPPEN ...?
ASUKA!
I'M SORRY!
RYO?!

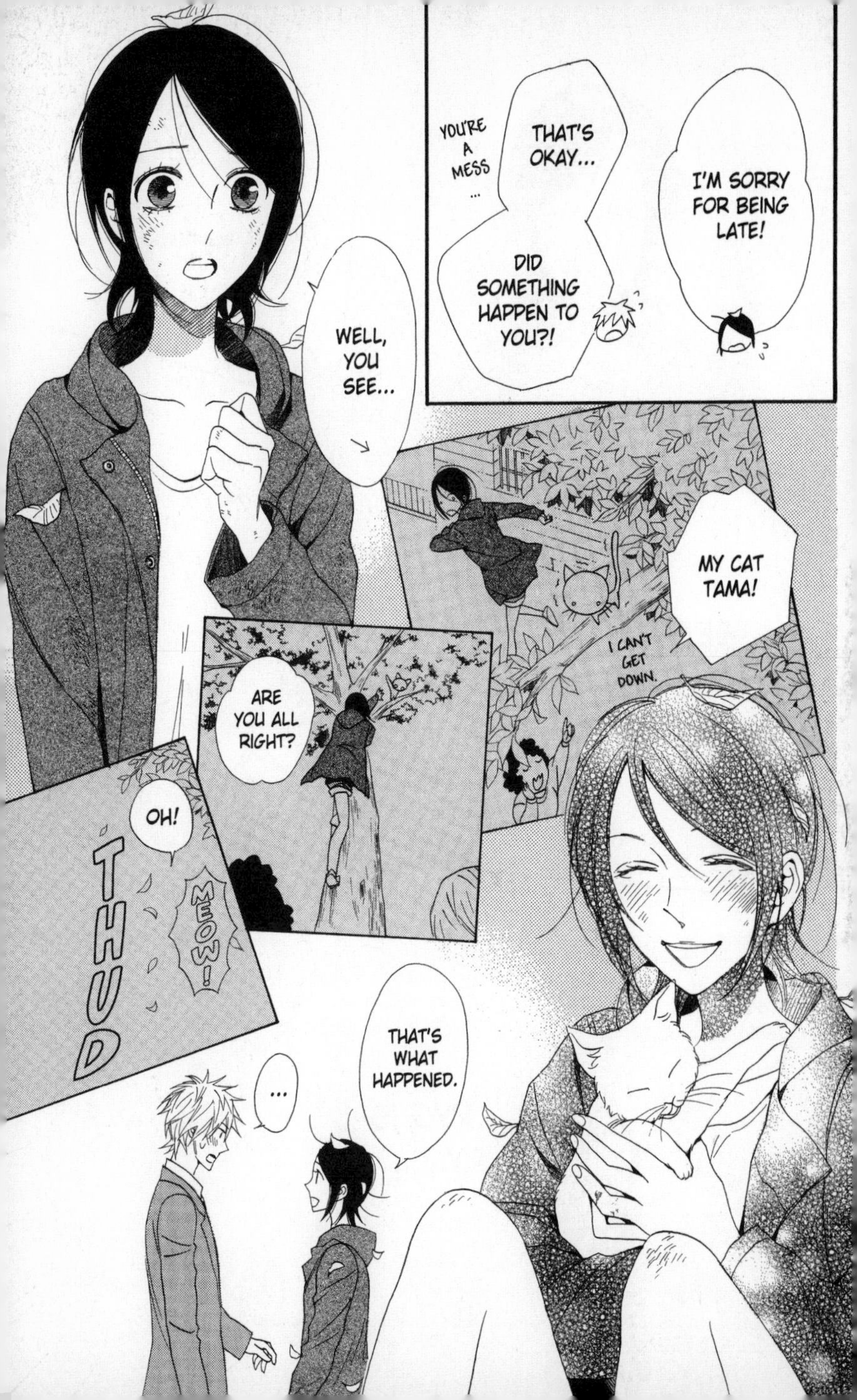
I'M SORRY FOR BEING LATE!
THAT'S OKAY...
YOU'RE A MESS ...
DID SOMETHING HAPPEN TO YOU?!
WELL, YOU SEE...
MY CAT TAMA!
I CAN'T GET DOWN.
ARE YOU ALL RIGHT?
OH!
MEOW!
THUD
THAT'S WHAT HAPPENED.
...

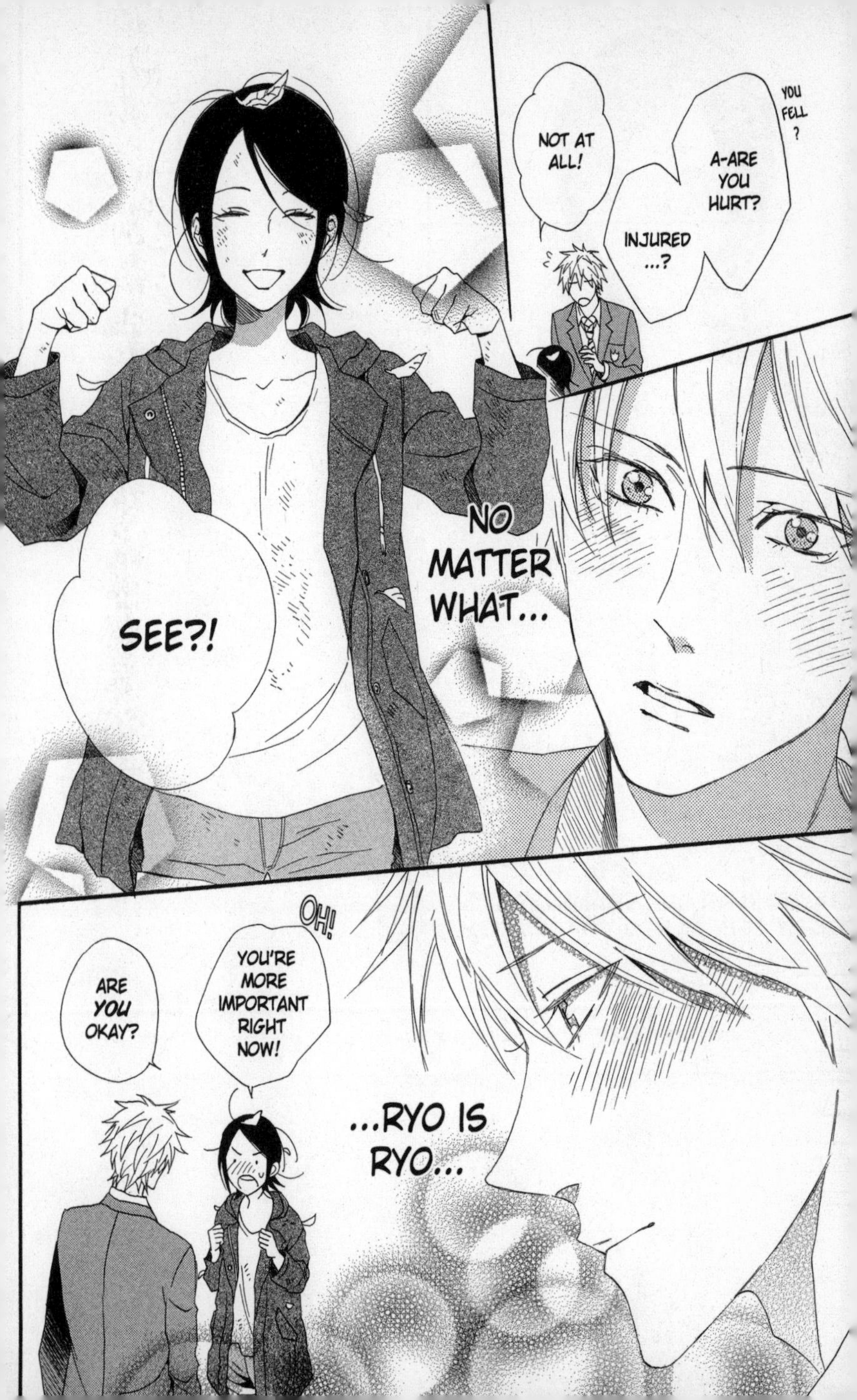

YOU FELL?
A-ARE YOU HURT?
INJURED...?
NOT AT ALL!
NO MATTER WHAT...
SEE?!
...RYO IS RYO...
OH!
YOU'RE MORE IMPORTANT RIGHT NOW!
ARE YOU OKAY?

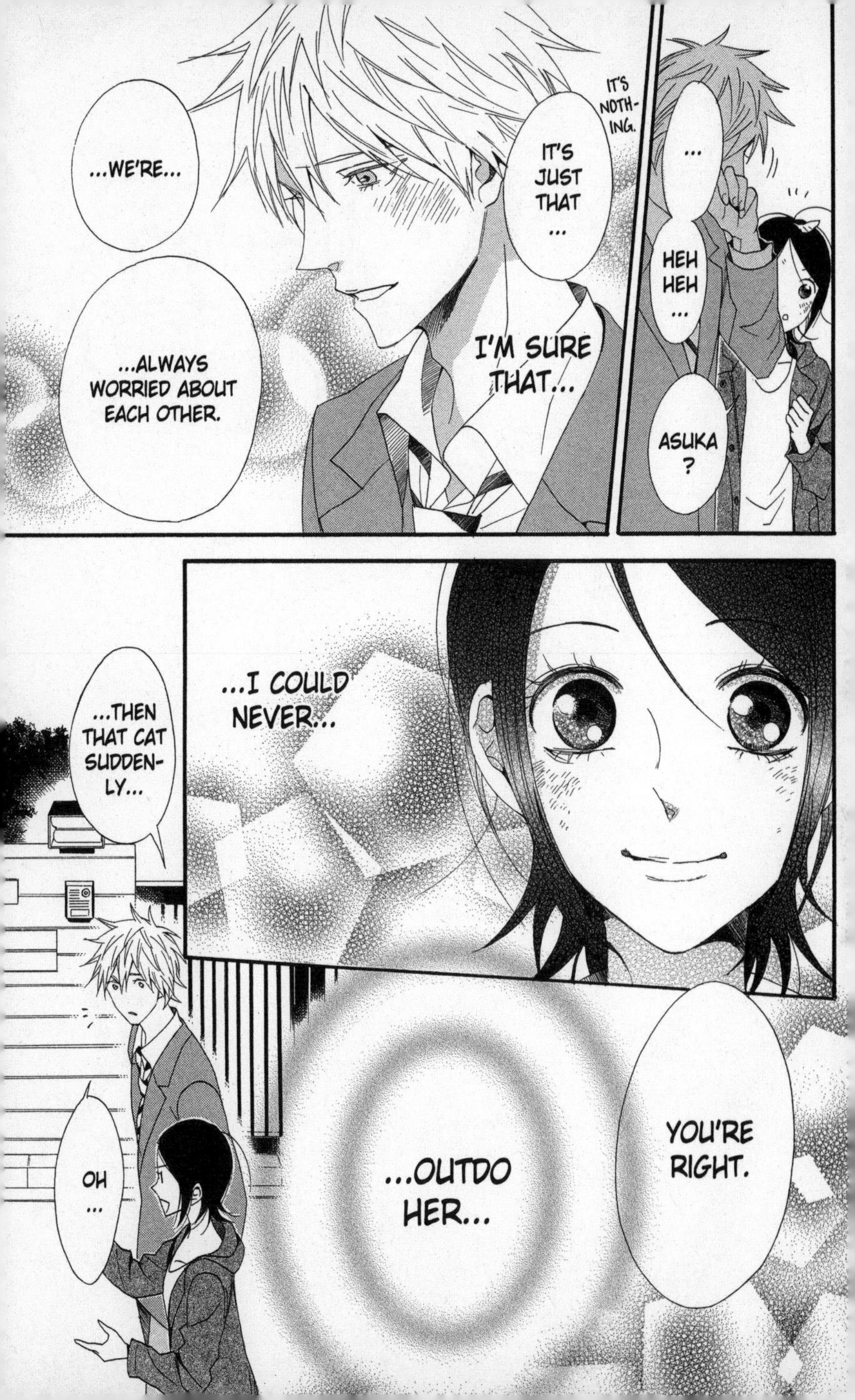
...
HEH HEH ...
ASUKA ?
IT'S NOTHING.
IT'S JUST THAT ...
I'M SURE THAT...
...WE'RE...
...ALWAYS WORRIED ABOUT EACH OTHER.
...I COULD NEVER...
YOU'RE RIGHT.
...OUTDO HER...
...THEN THAT CAT SUDDENLY...
OH ...

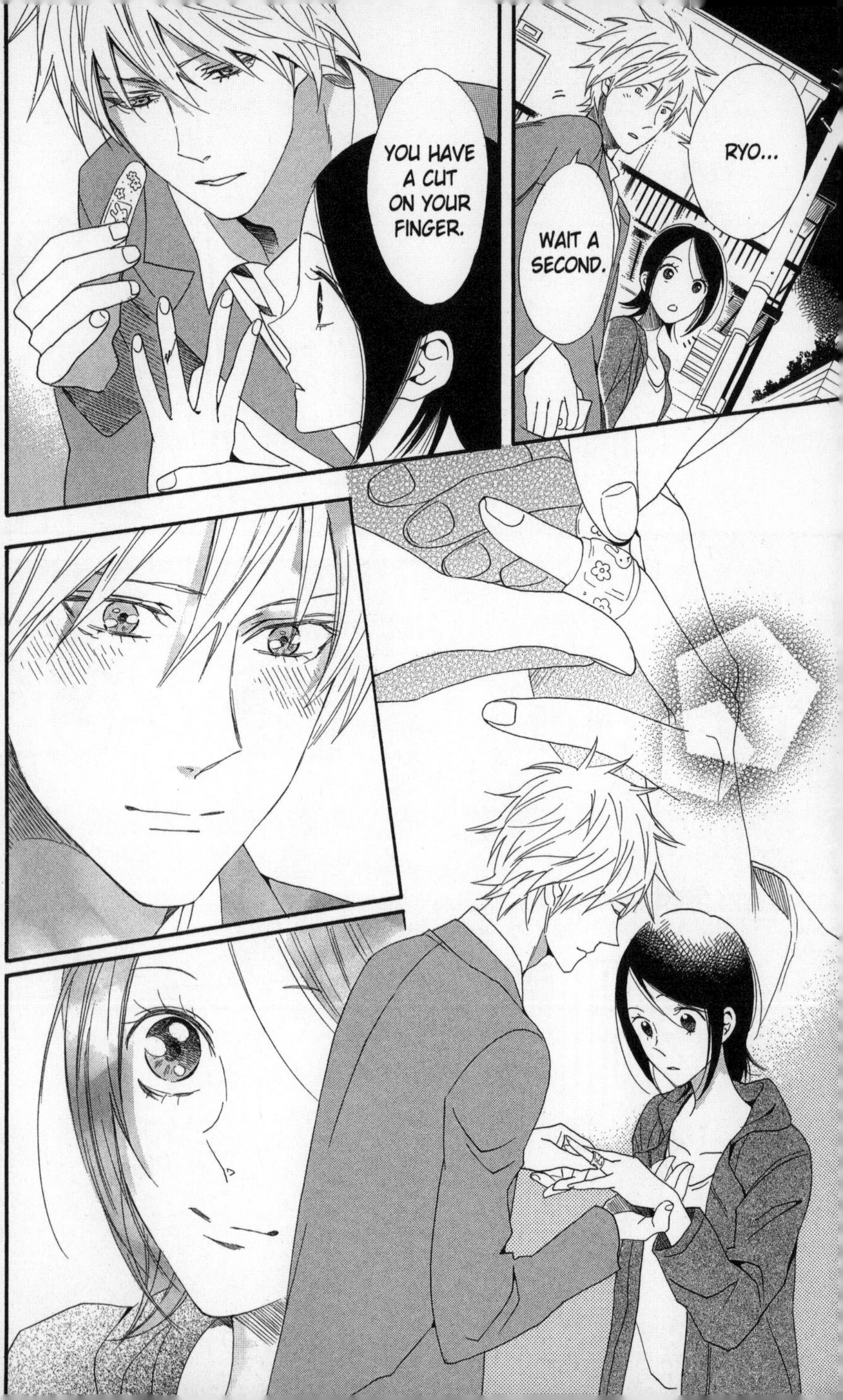
RYO...
WAIT A SECOND.
YOU HAVE A CUT ON YOUR FINGER.

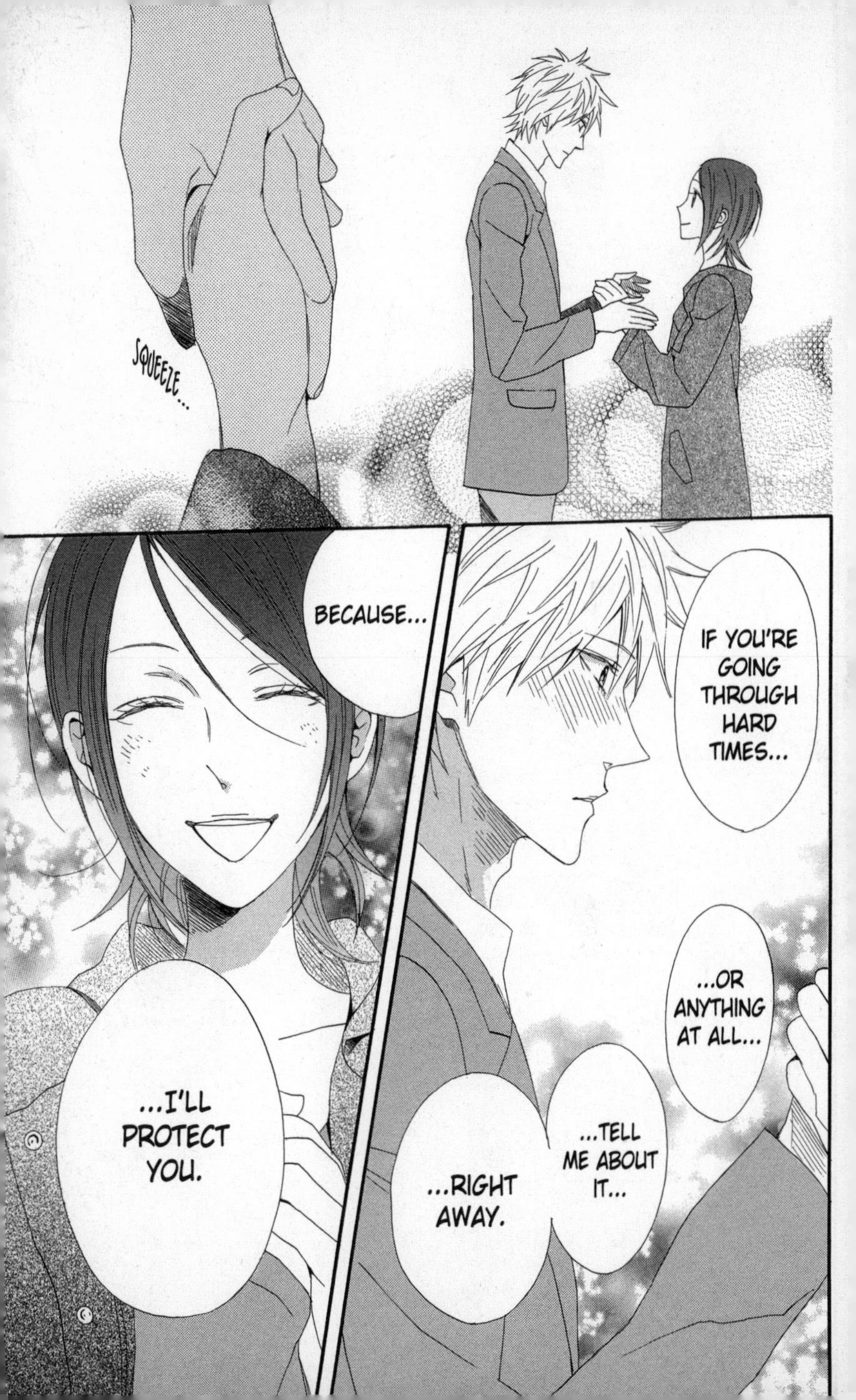
SQUEEZE...
IF YOU'RE GOING THROUGH HARD TIMES...
...OR ANYTHING AT ALL...
...TELL ME ABOUT IT...
...RIGHT AWAY.
BECAUSE...
...I'LL PROTECT YOU.

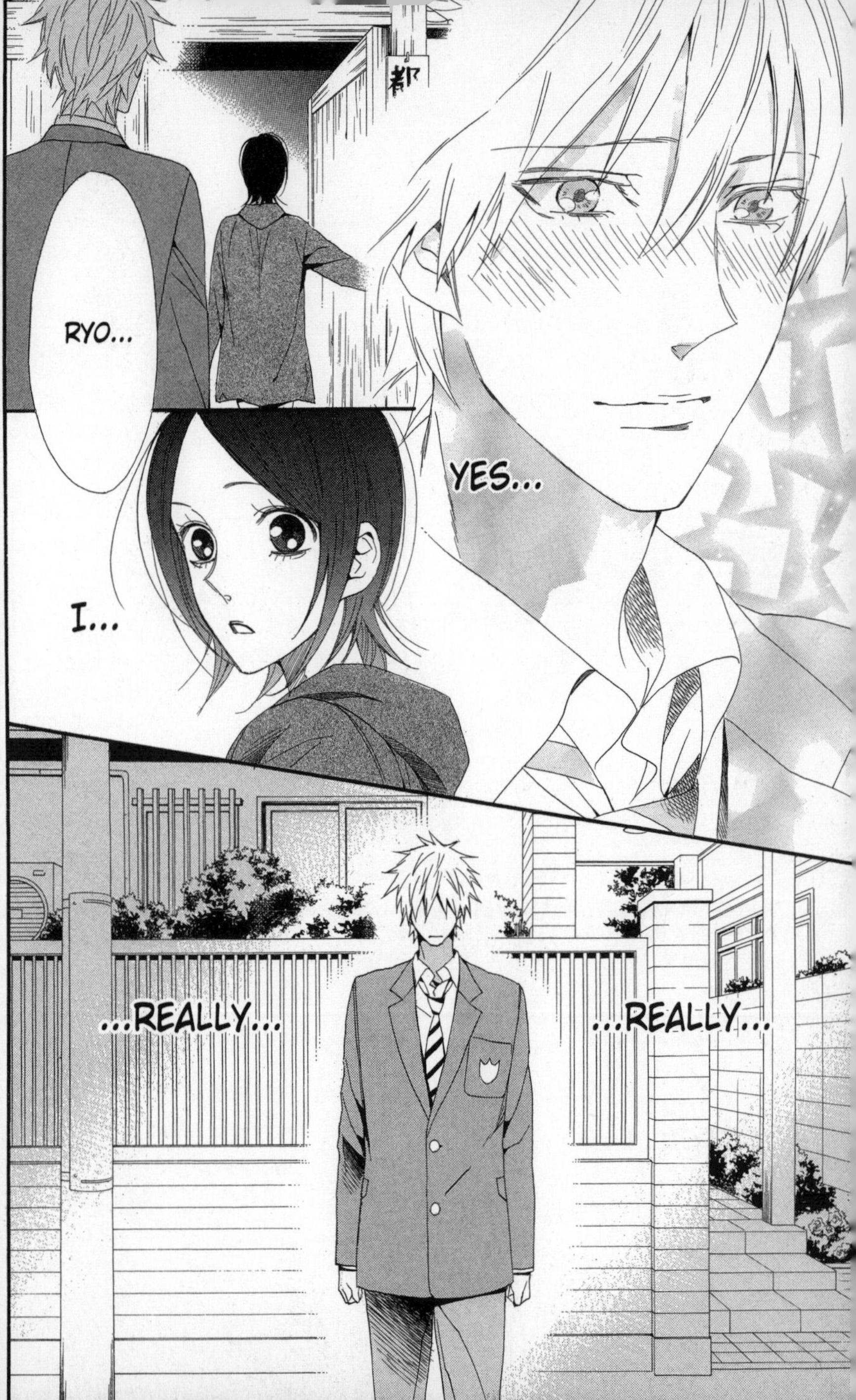
YES...
都
RYO...
I...
...REALLY...
...REALLY...

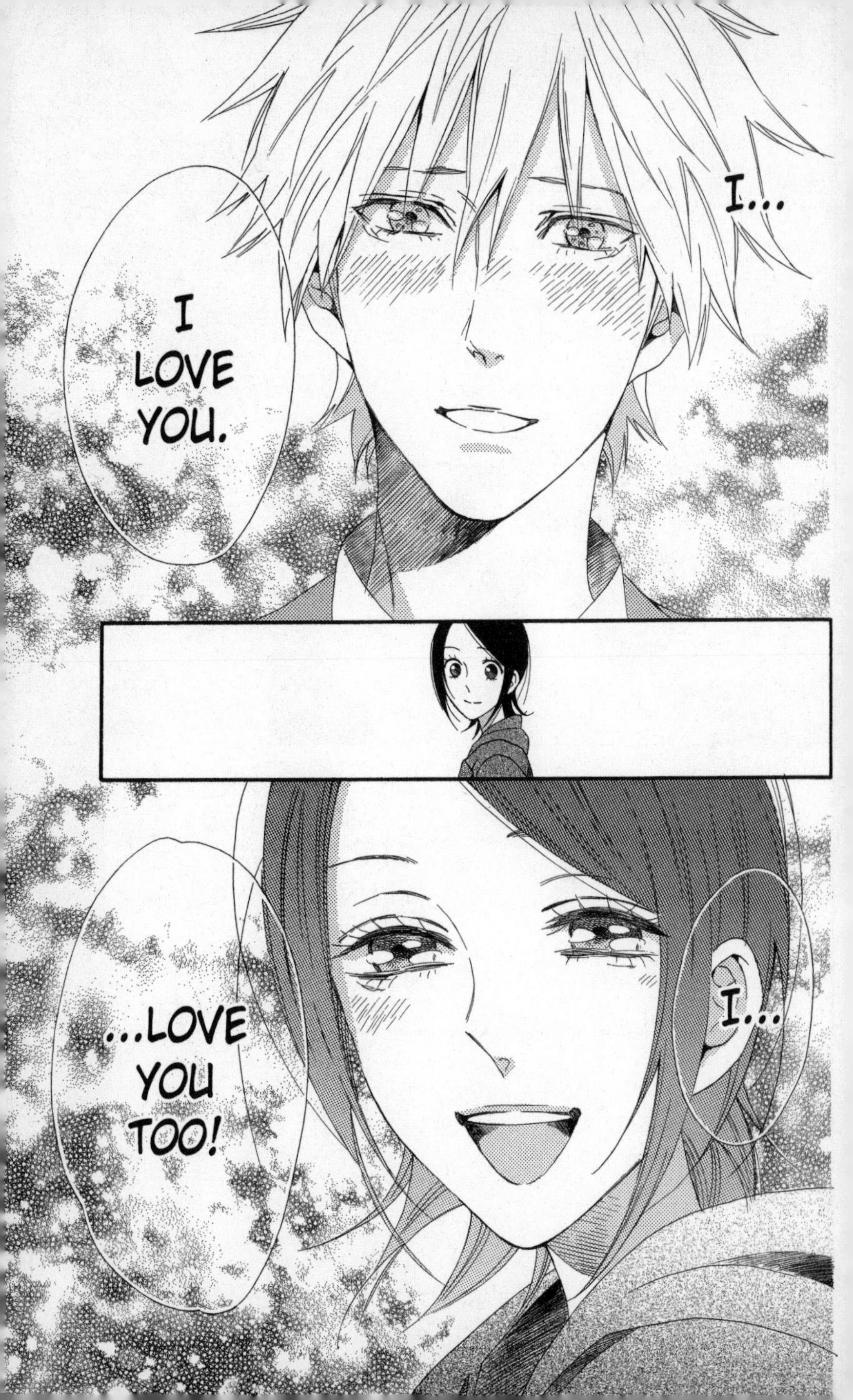
I...
I LOVE YOU.
I...
...LOVE YOU TOO!

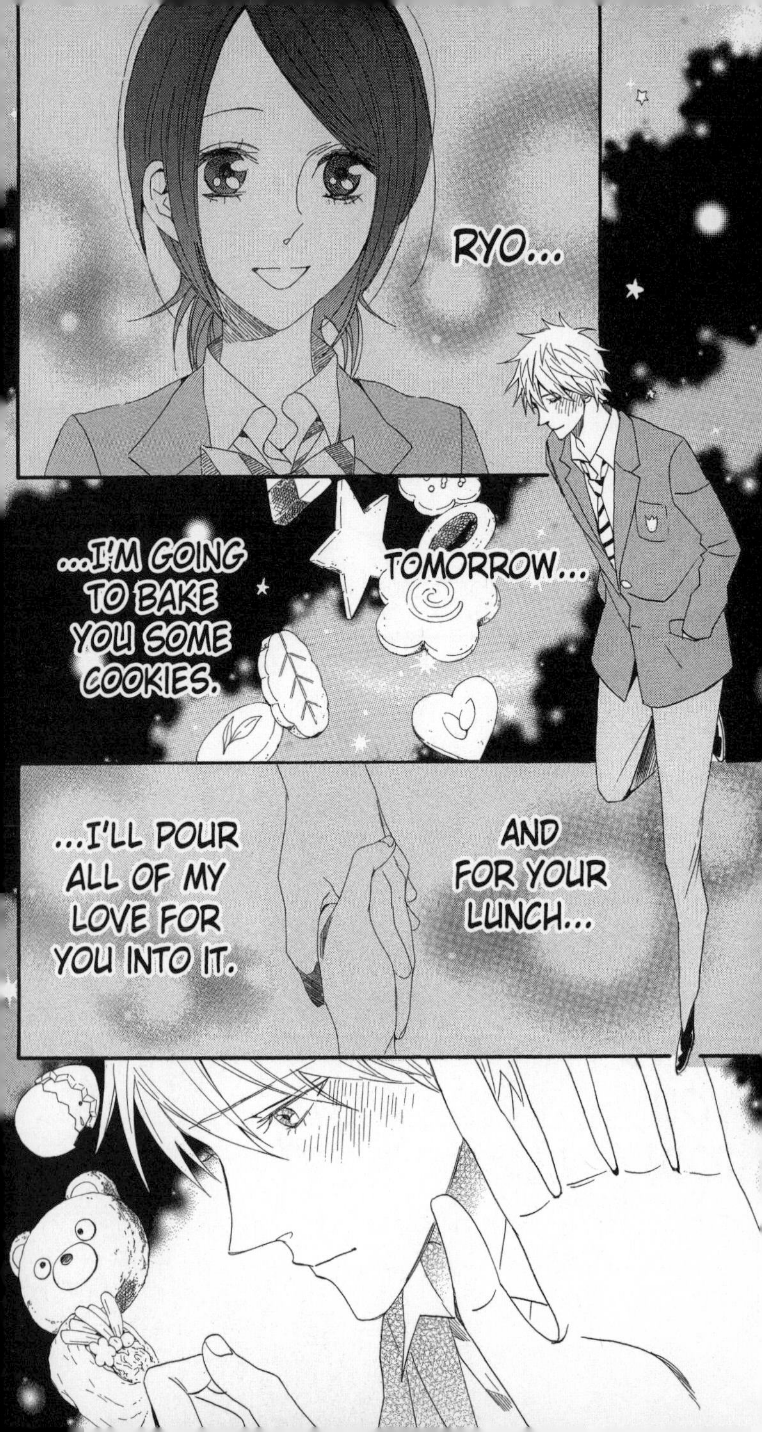
RYO...
TOMORROW...
...I'M GOING TO BAKE YOU SOME COOKIES.
AND FOR YOUR LUNCH...
...I'LL POUR ALL OF MY LOVE FOR YOU INTO IT.

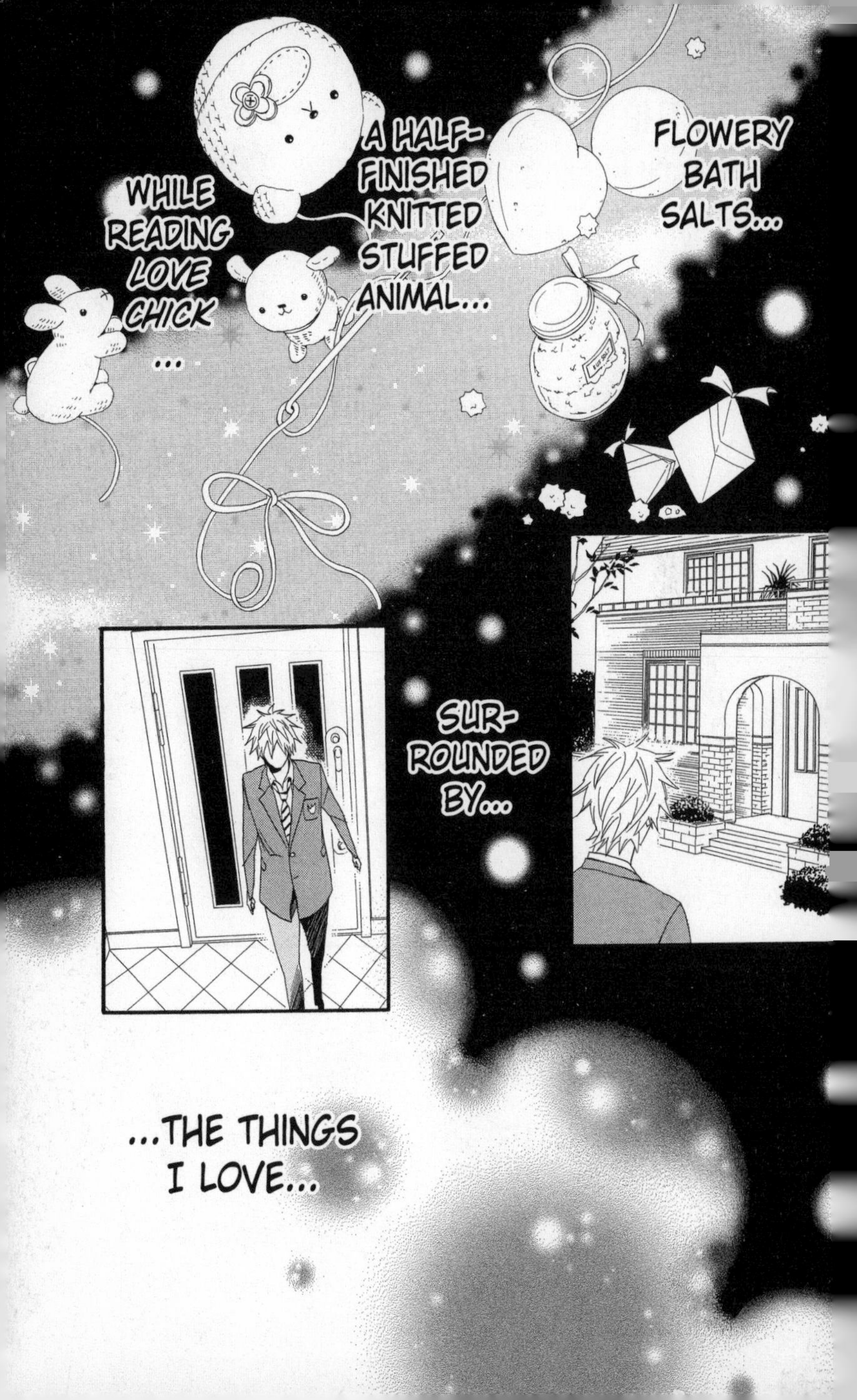
FLOWERY BATH SALTS...
A HALF-FINISHED KNITTED STUFFED ANIMAL...
WHILE READING LOVE CHICK ...
SUR-ROUNDED BY...
...THE THINGS I LOVE...

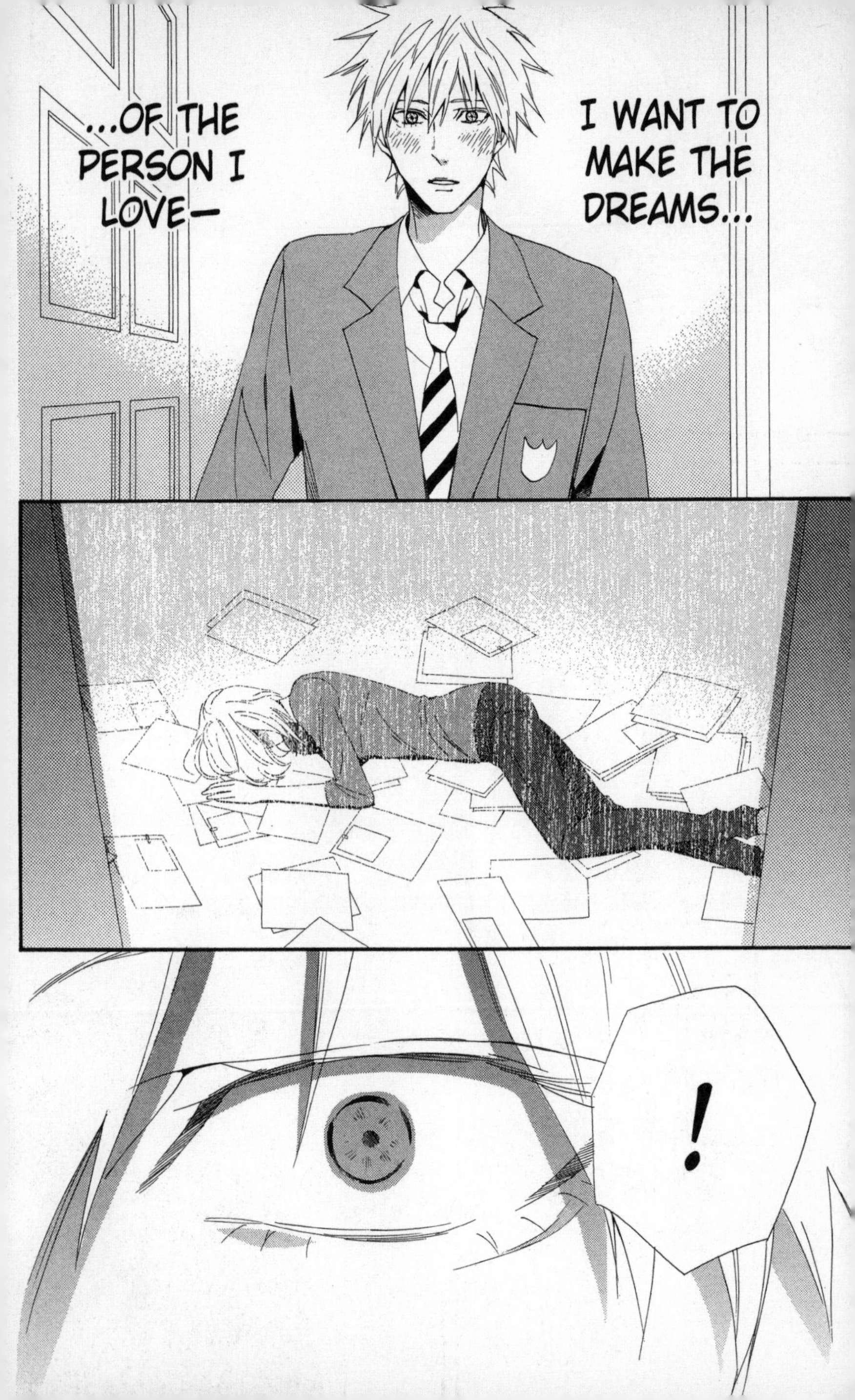
I WANT TO MAKE THE DREAMS...
...OF THE PERSON I LOVE—
!

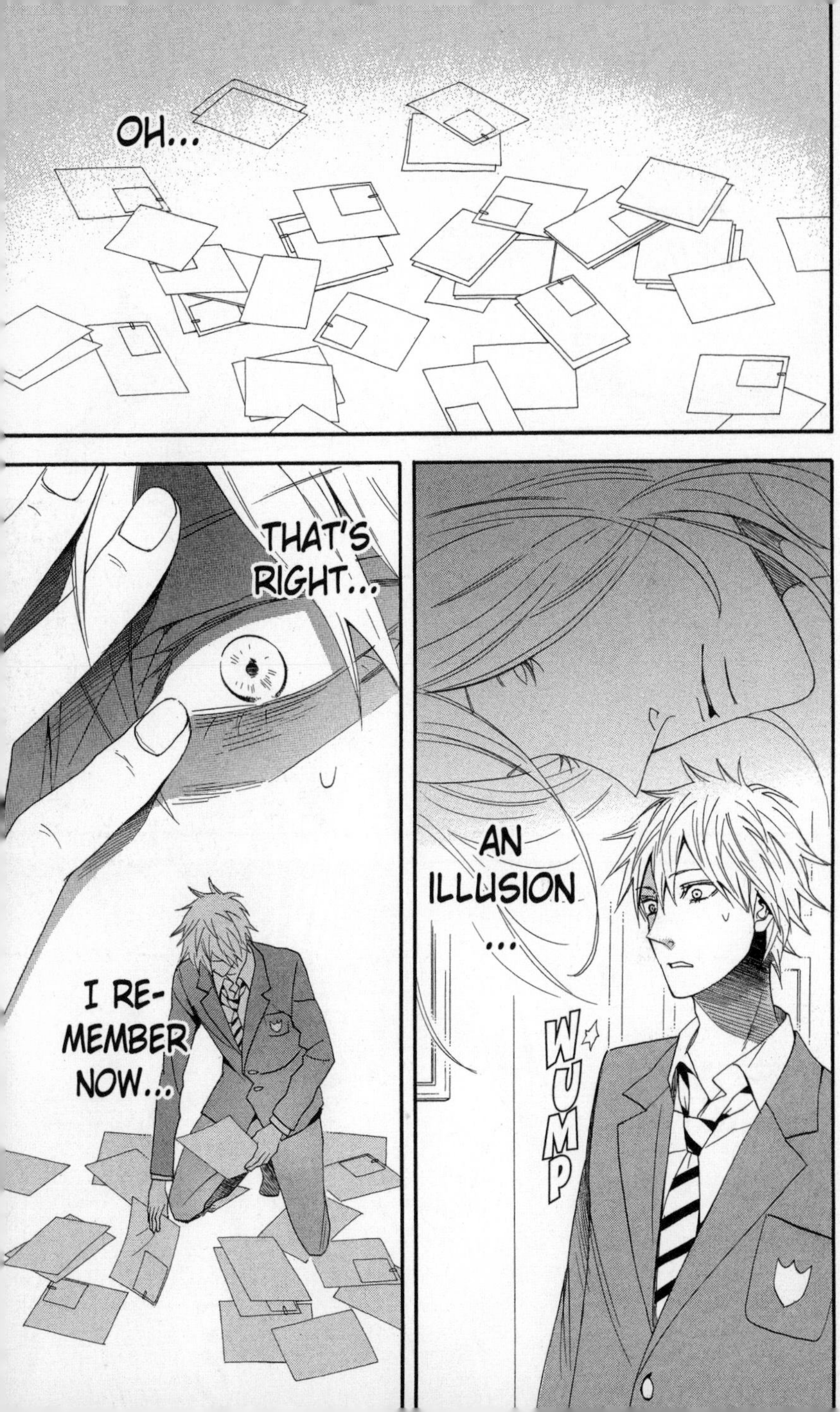
OH...
AN ILLUSION ...
WUMP
THAT'S RIGHT...
I RE-MEMBER NOW...

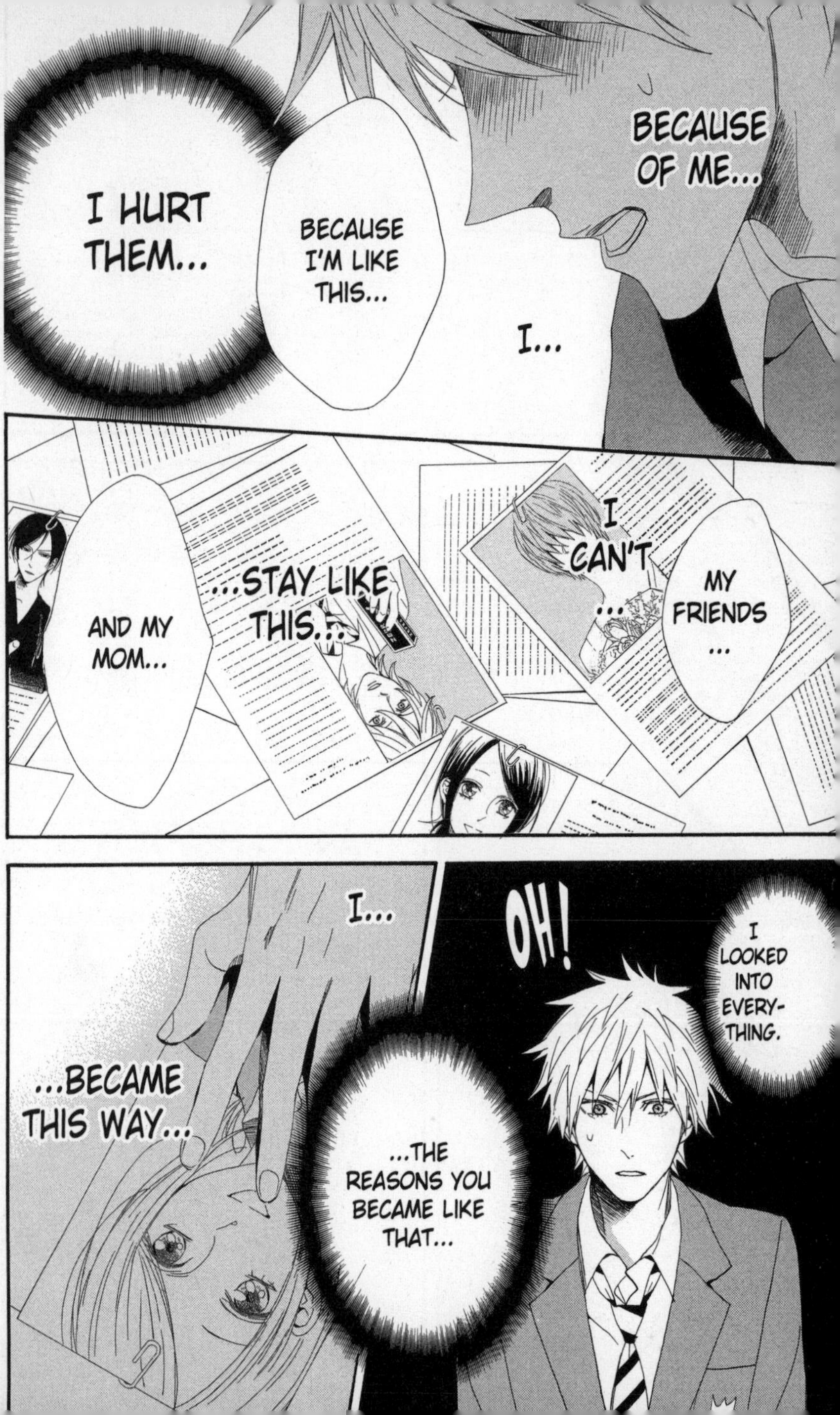
BECAUSE OF ME...
I...
BECAUSE I'M LIKE THIS...
I HURT THEM...
MY FRIENDS ...
I CAN'T ...
...STAY LIKE THIS...
AND MY MOM...
I LOOKED INTO EVERY-THING.
OH!
...THE REASONS YOU BECAME LIKE THAT...
I...
...BECAME THIS WAY...

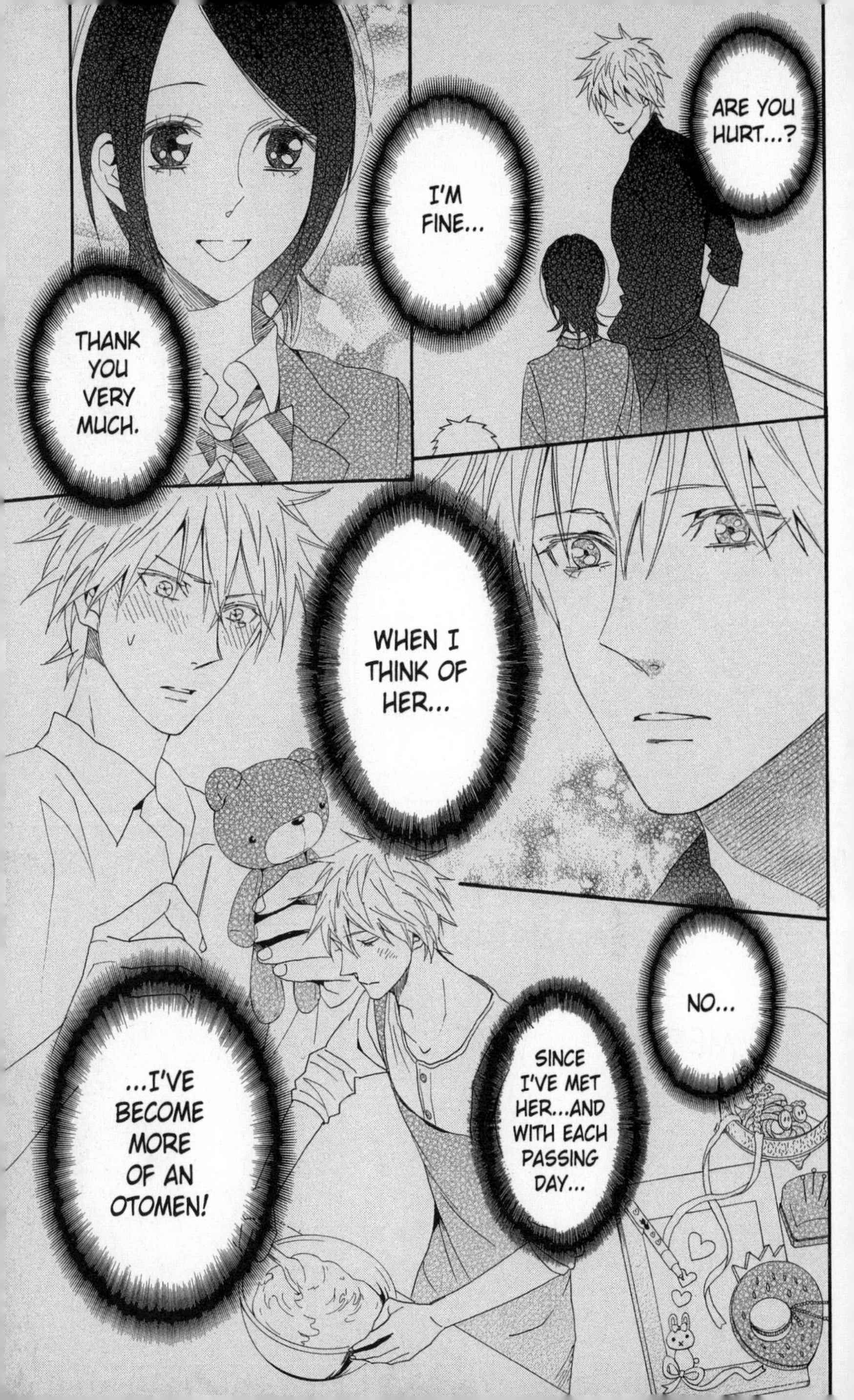
ARE YOU HURT...?
I'M FINE...
THANK YOU VERY MUCH.
WHEN I THINK OF HER...
NO...
SINCE I'VE MET HER...AND WITH EACH PASSING DAY...
...I'VE BECOME MORE OF AN OTOMEN!

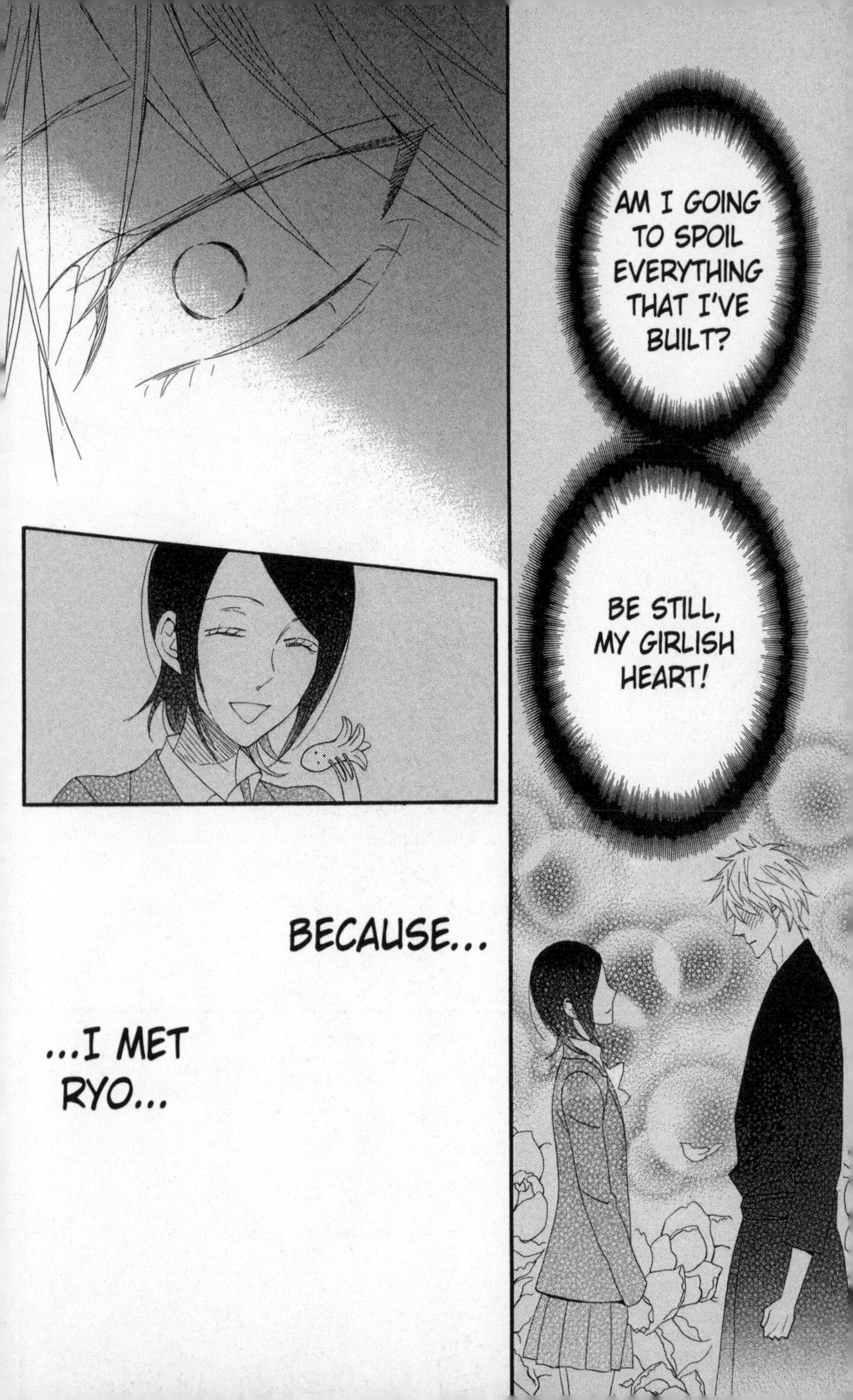
AM I GOING TO SPOIL EVERYTHING THAT I'VE BUILT?
BE STILL, MY GIRLISH HEART!
BECAUSE...
...I MET RYO...

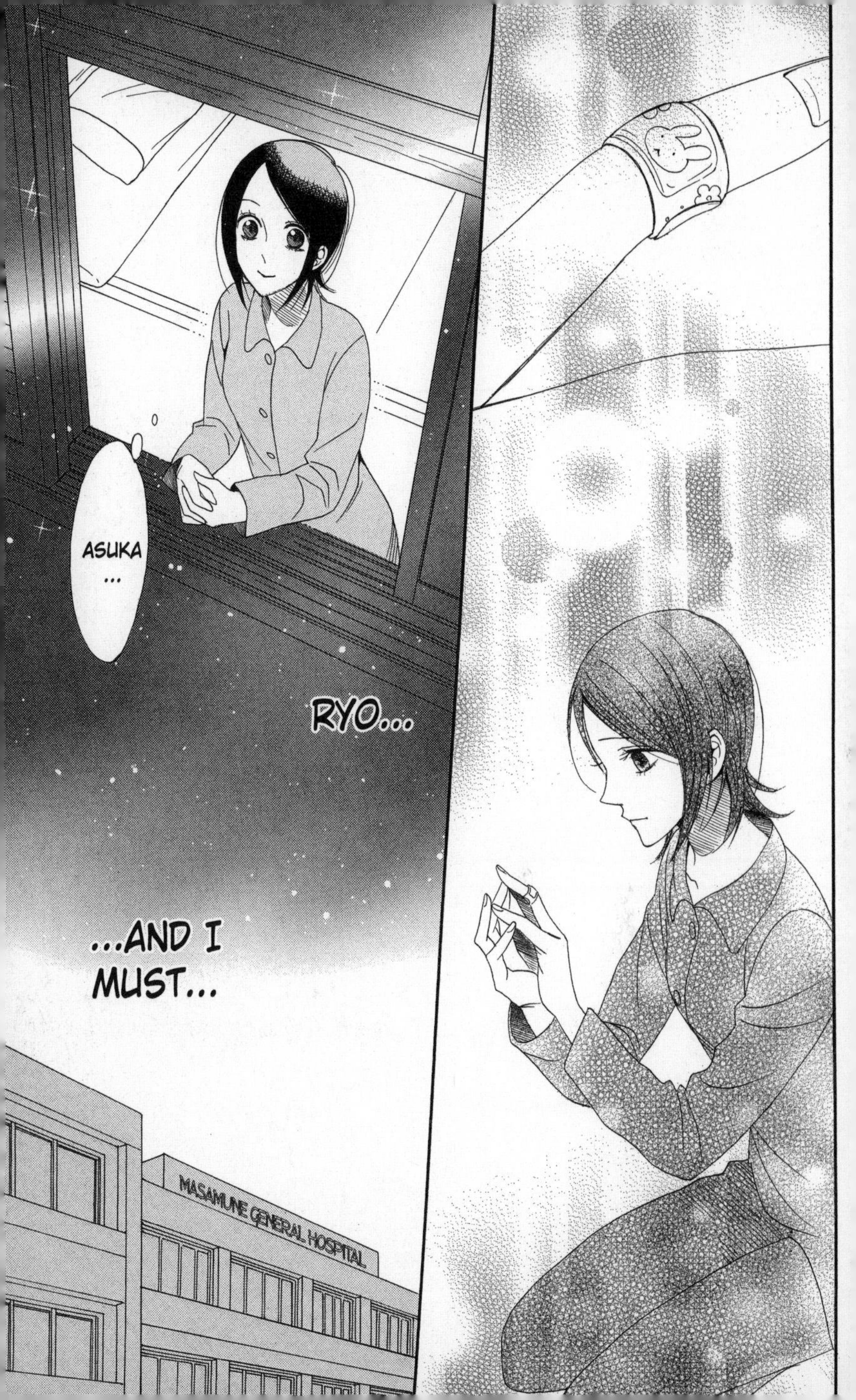
ASUKA ...
RYO...
...AND I MUST...
MASAMUNE GENERAL HOSPITAL

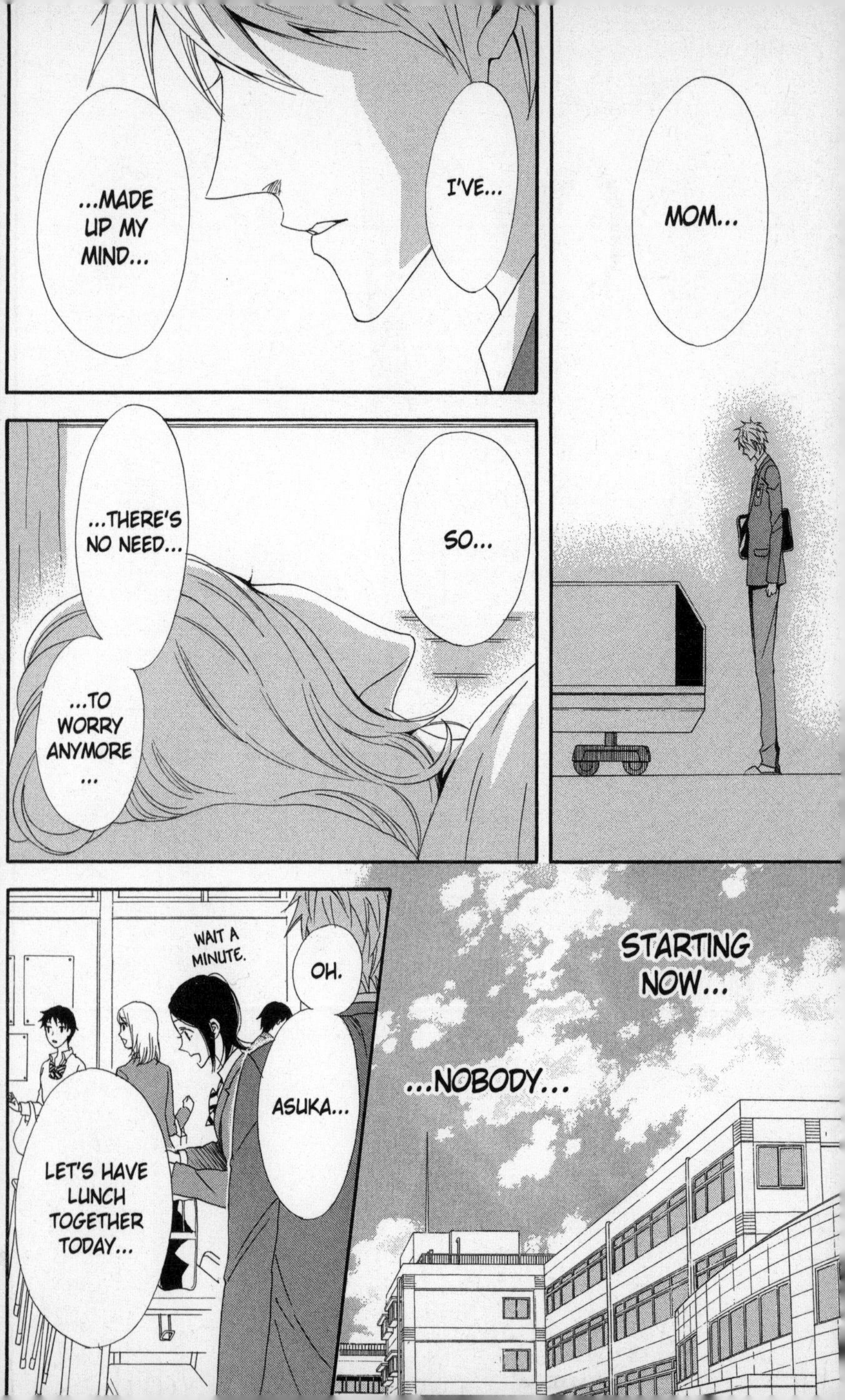
MOM...
I'VE...
...MADE UP MY MIND...
SO...
...THERE'S NO NEED...
...TO WORRY ANYMORE...
STARTING NOW...
...NOBODY...
OH.
WAIT A MINUTE.
ASUKA...
LET'S HAVE LUNCH TOGETHER TODAY...

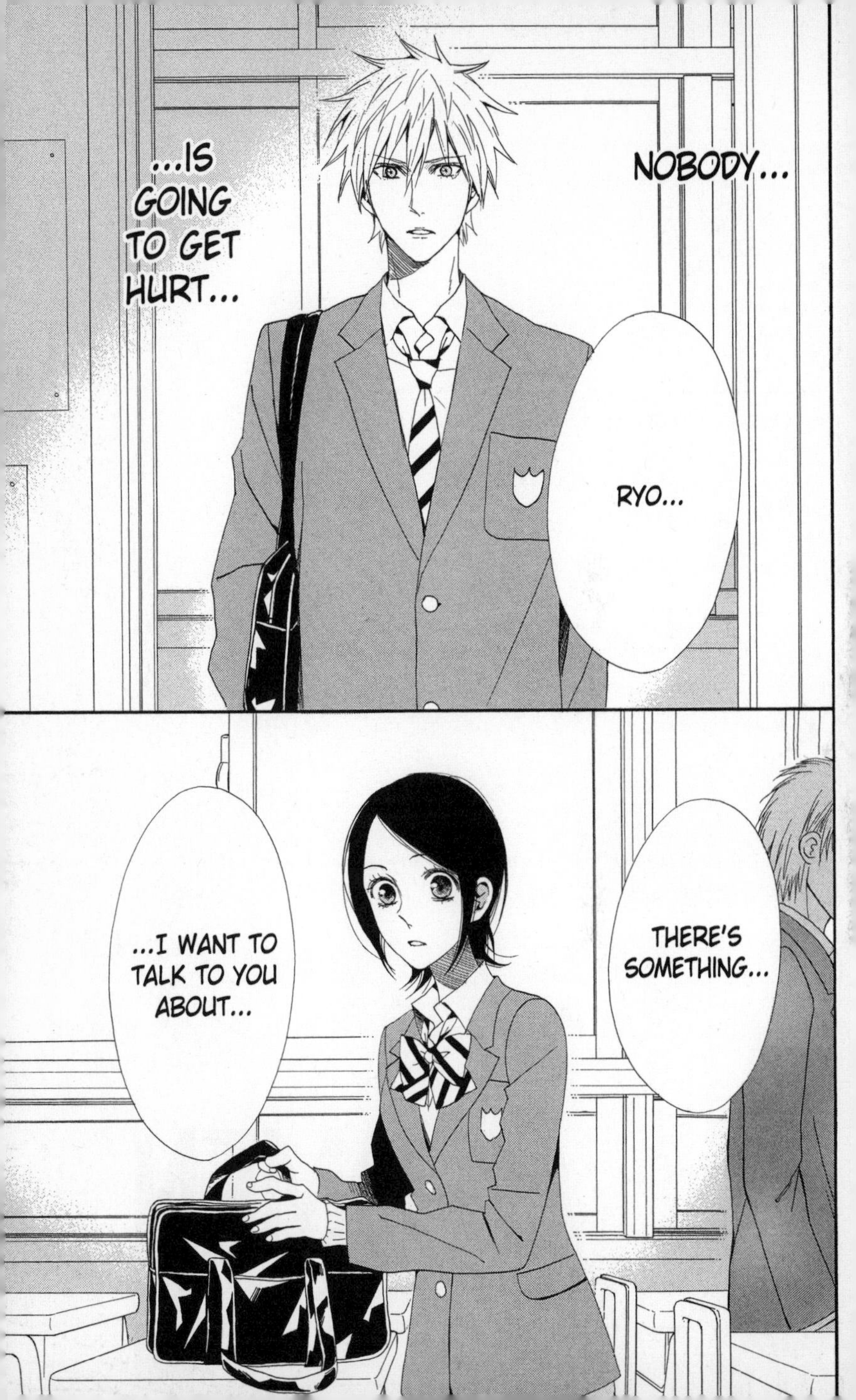
NOBODY...
RYO...
...IS GOING TO GET HURT...
THERE'S SOMETHING...
...I WANT TO TALK TO YOU ABOUT...

OTOMEN

IT'S BEEN SO LONG SINCE WE'VE...
...EATEN LUNCH HERE ON THE ROOF!
OTOMEN

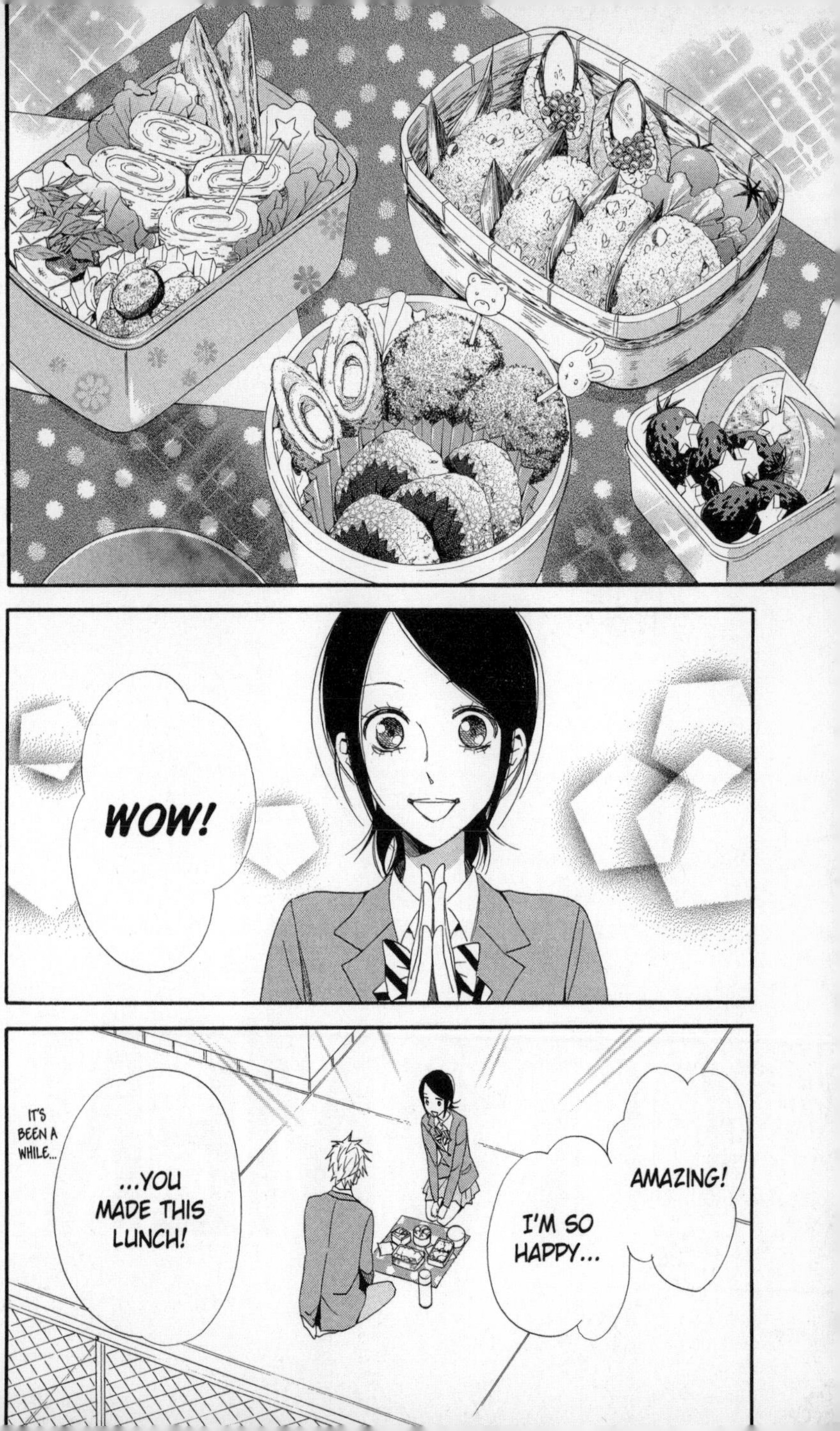
WOW!
AMAZING!
I'M SO HAPPY...
IT'S BEEN A WHILE...
...YOU MADE THIS LUNCH!

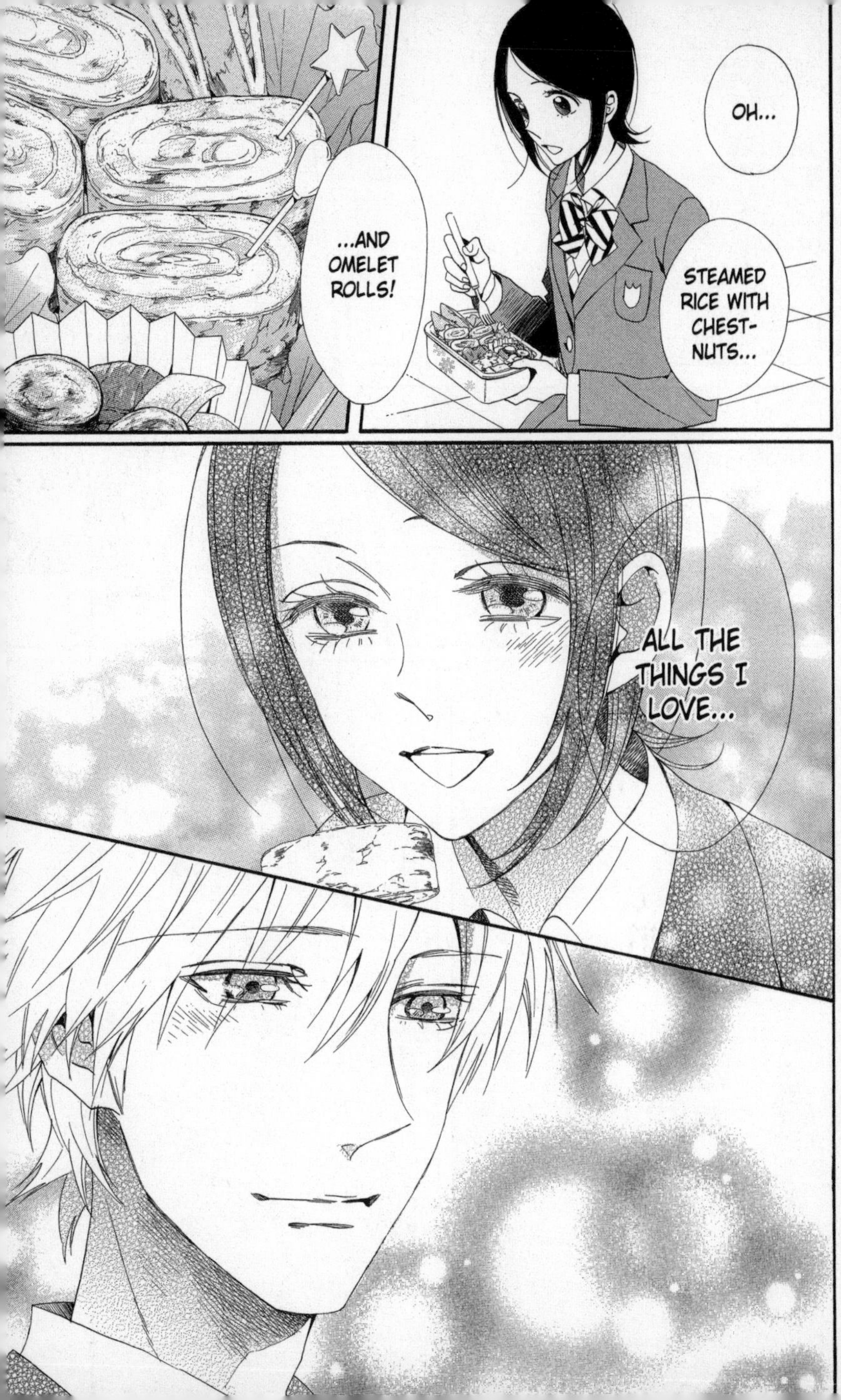
OH...
STEAMED RICE WITH CHEST-NUTS...
...AND OMELET ROLLS!
ALL THE THINGS I LOVE...

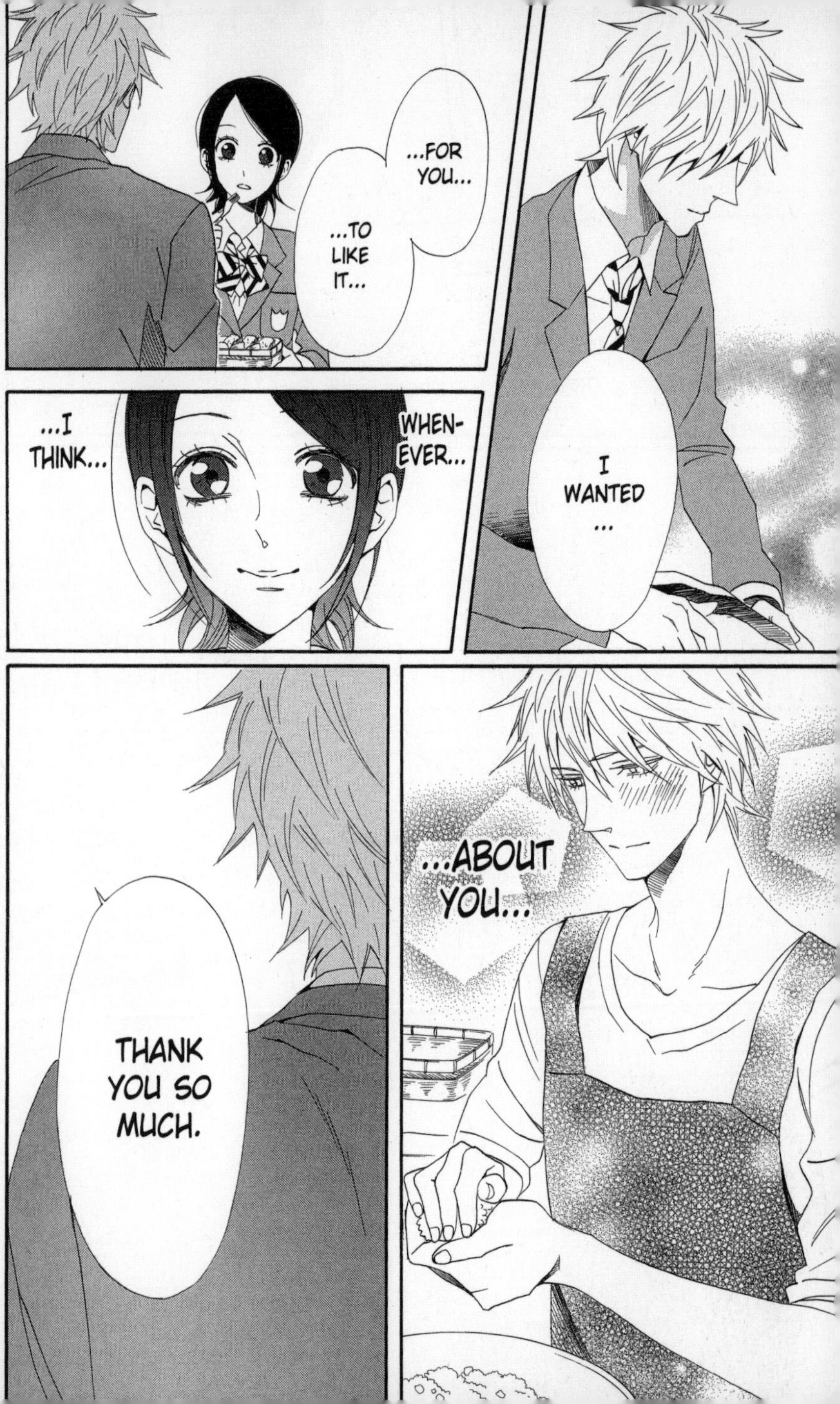
I WANTED ...
...FOR YOU...
...TO LIKE IT...
WHEN-EVER...
...I THINK...
...ABOUT YOU...
THANK YOU SO MUCH.

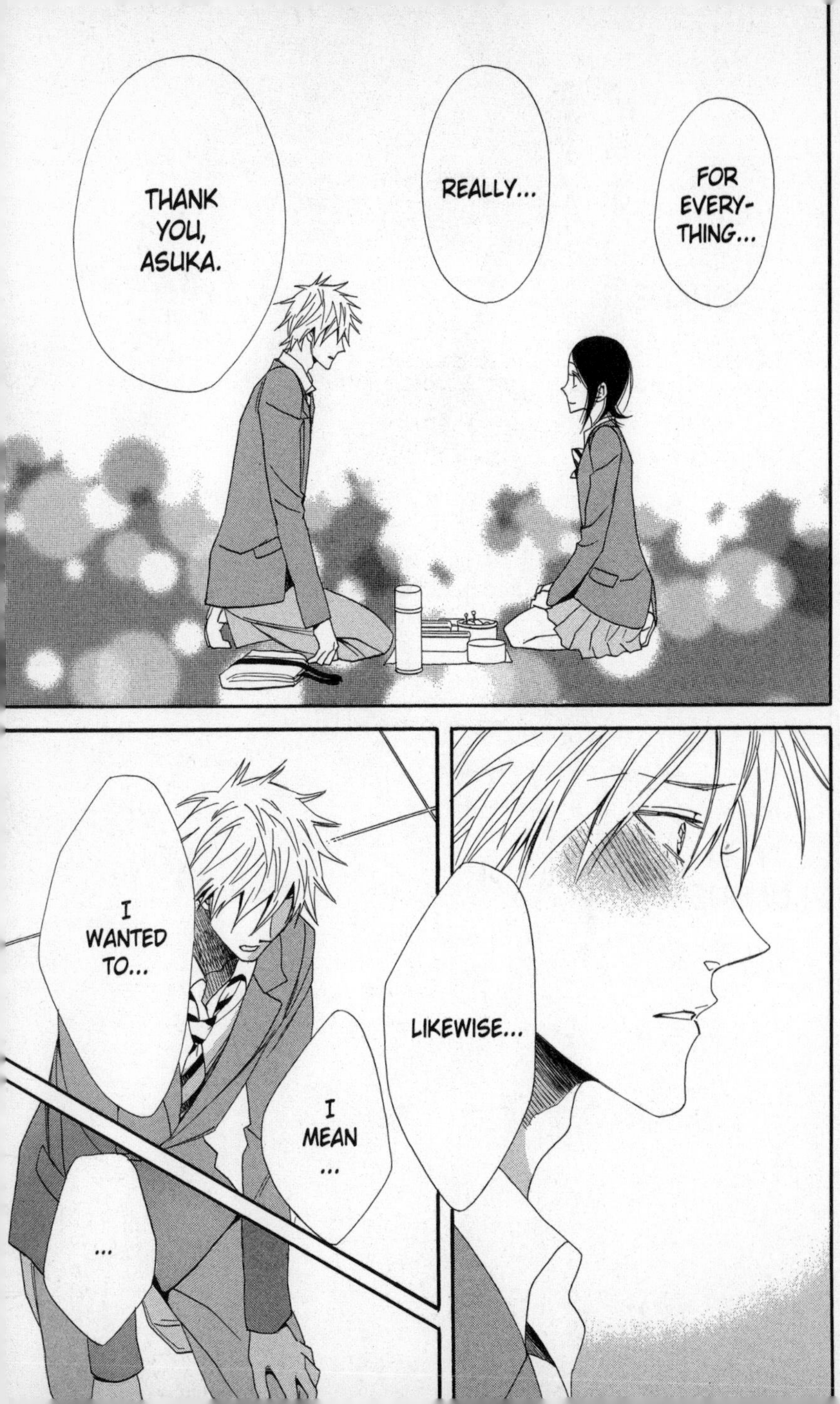
FOR EVERY-THING...
REALLY...
THANK YOU, ASUKA.
LIKEWISE...
I WANTED TO...
I MEAN ...
...

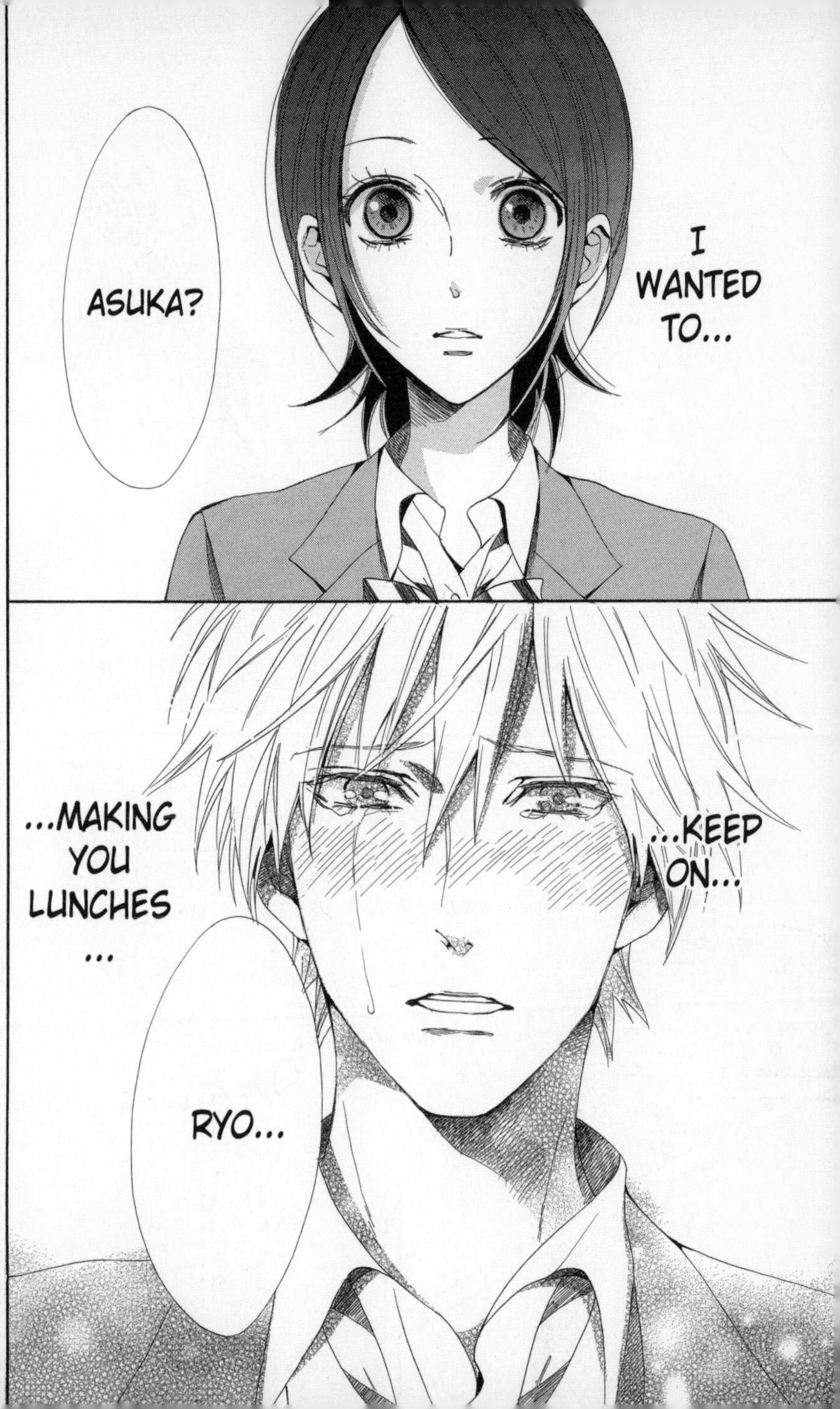
I WANTED TO...
ASUKA?
...KEEP ON...
...MAKING YOU LUNCHES ...
RYO...

...LIKE
THIS...

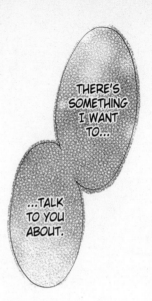

THERE'S
SOMETHING
I WANT
TO...

...TALK
TO YOU
ABOUT.

CON-
VENIENCE
STORE
FOOD...

...TASTES
BLAND.

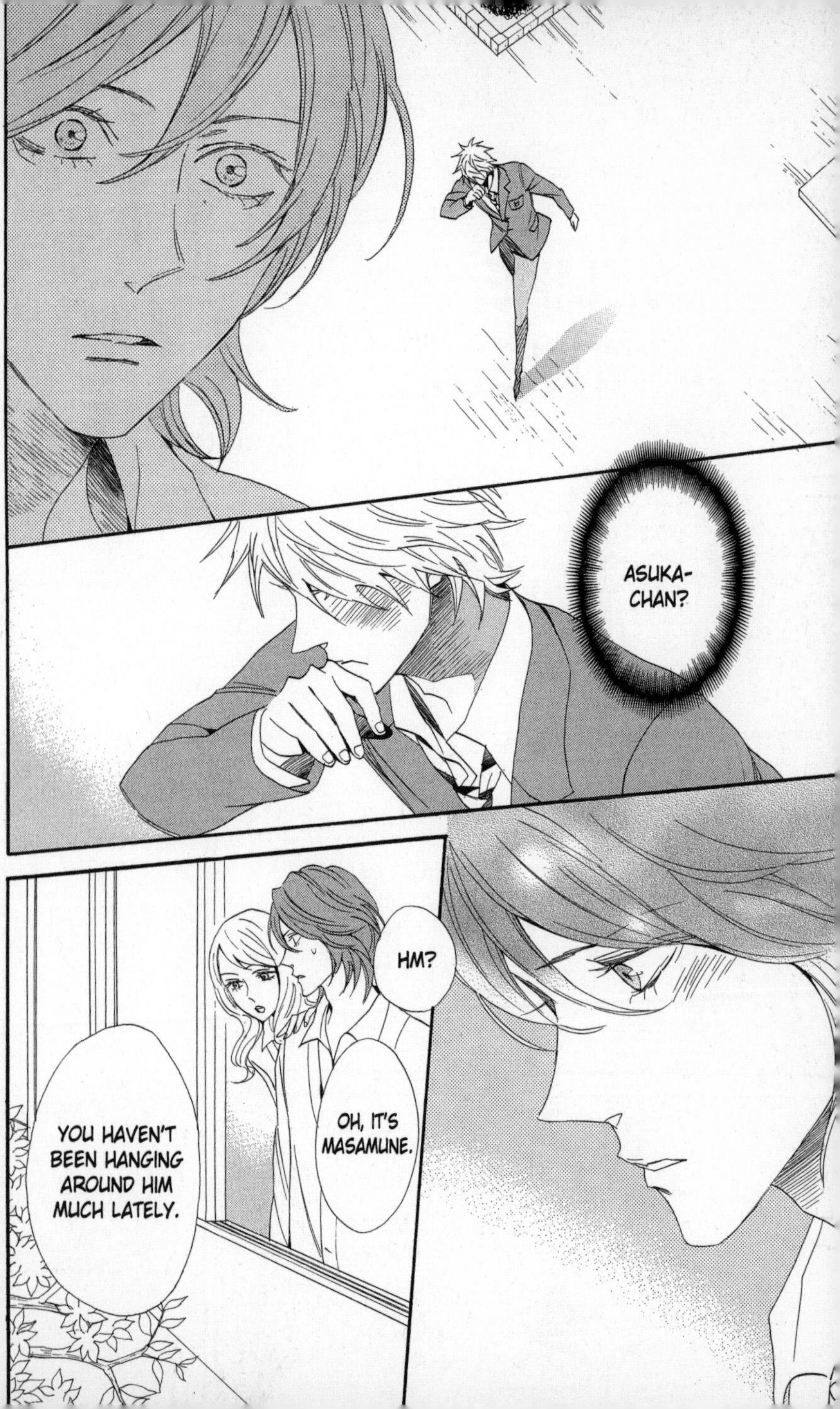
ASUKA-CHAN?
HM?
OH, IT'S MASAMUNE.
YOU HAVEN'T BEEN HANGING AROUND HIM MUCH LATELY.

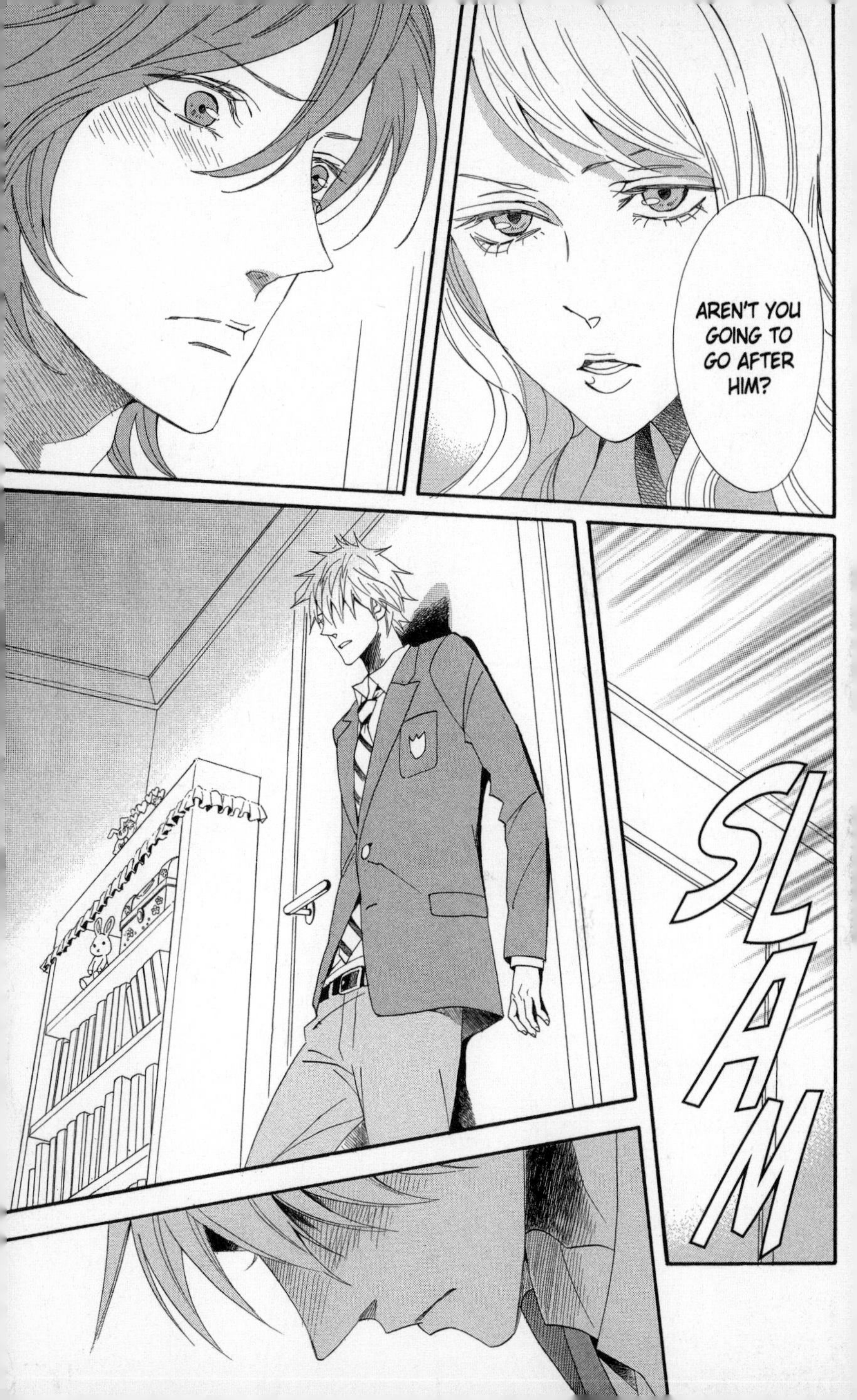
AREN'T YOU GOING TO GO AFTER HIM?
SLAM

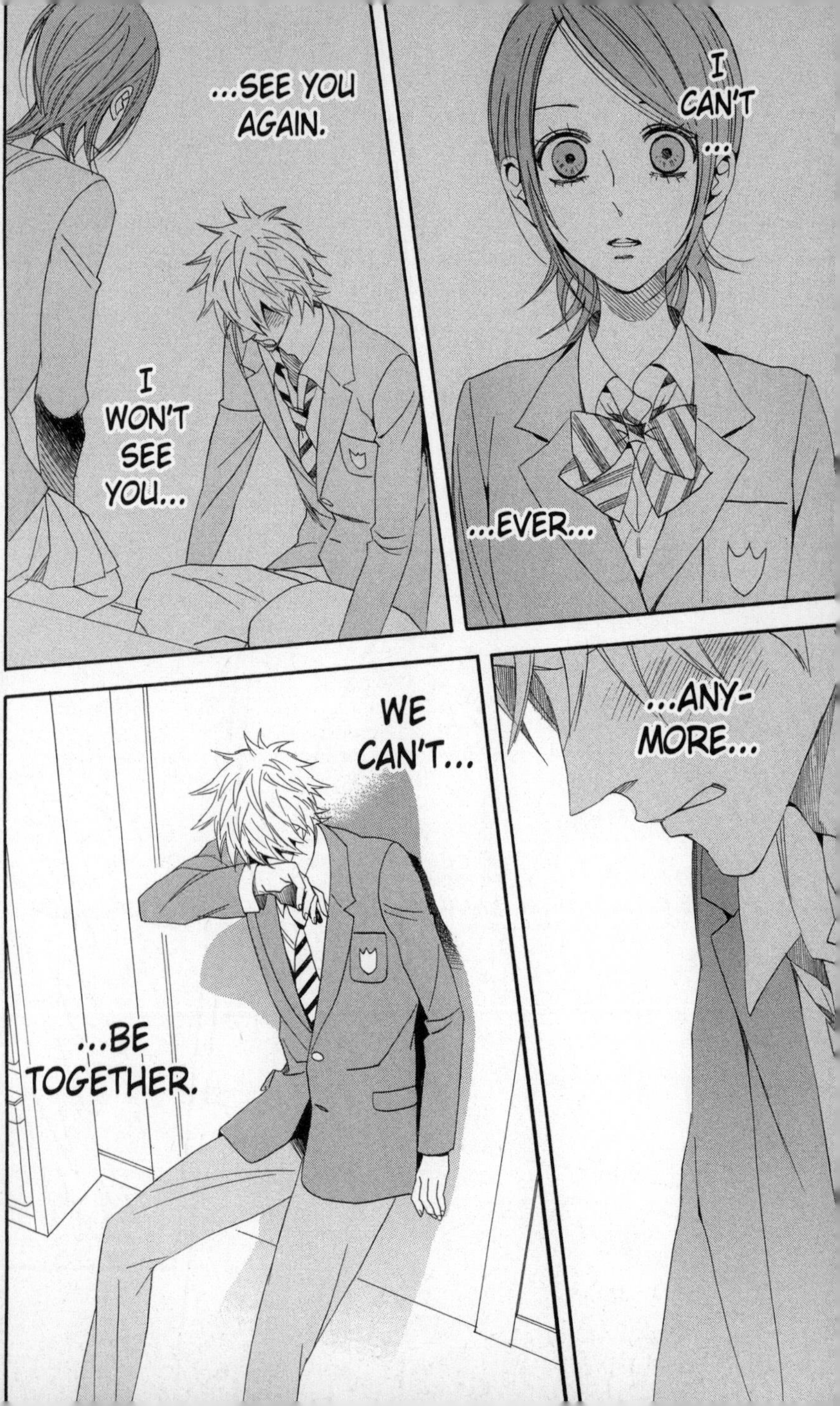
I CAN'T ...
...EVER...
...SEE YOU AGAIN.
I WON'T SEE YOU...
...ANY-MORE...
WE CAN'T...
...BE TOGETHER.

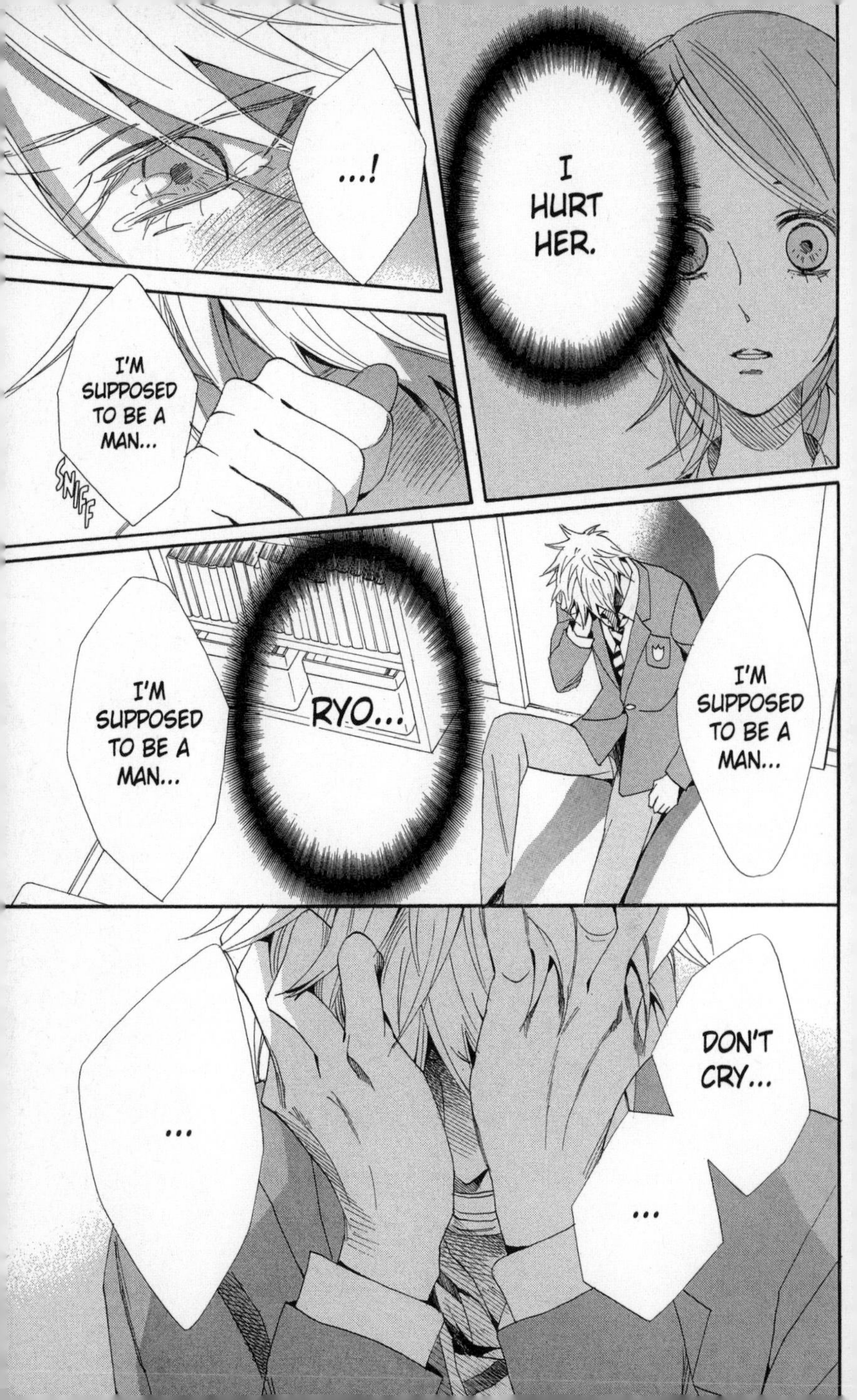
I HURT HER.
...!
I'M SUPPOSED TO BE A MAN...
SNIFF
I'M SUPPOSED TO BE A MAN...
RYO...
I'M SUPPOSED TO BE A MAN...
DON'T CRY...
...
...

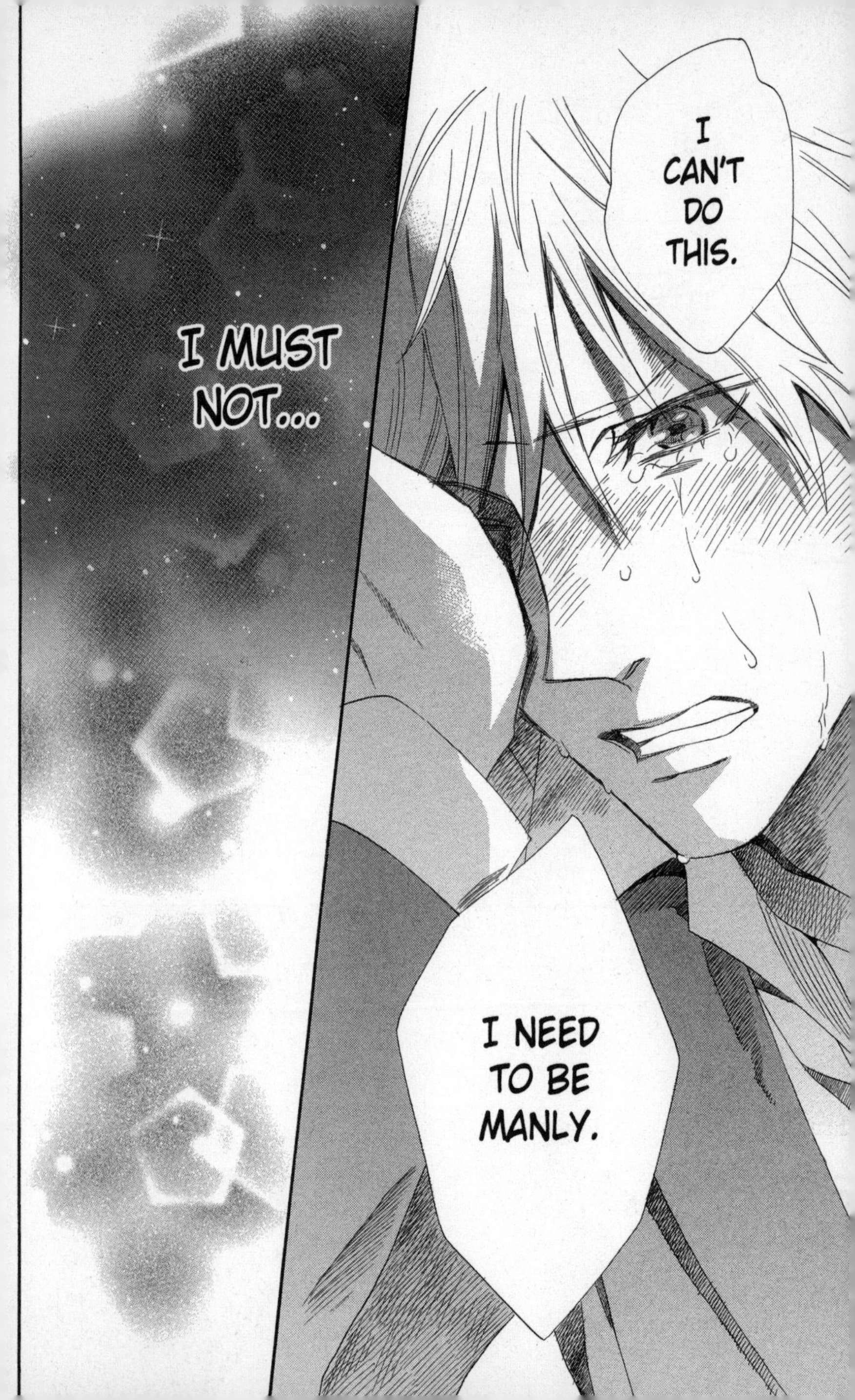
I CAN'T DO THIS.
I NEED TO BE MANLY.
I MUST NOT...

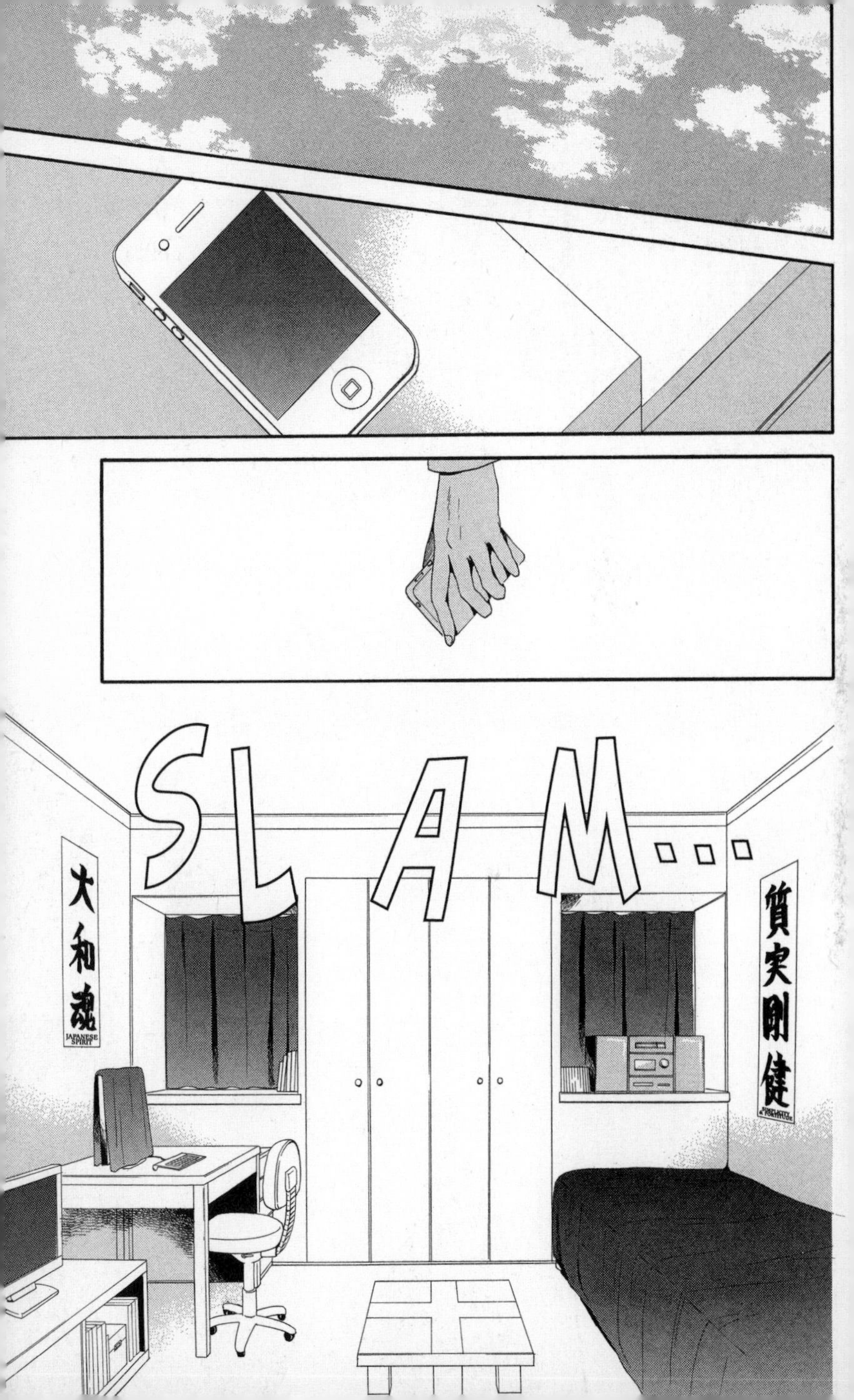
SLAM...
質実剛健
SIMPLICITY & FORTITUDE
大和魂
JAPANESE SPIRIT

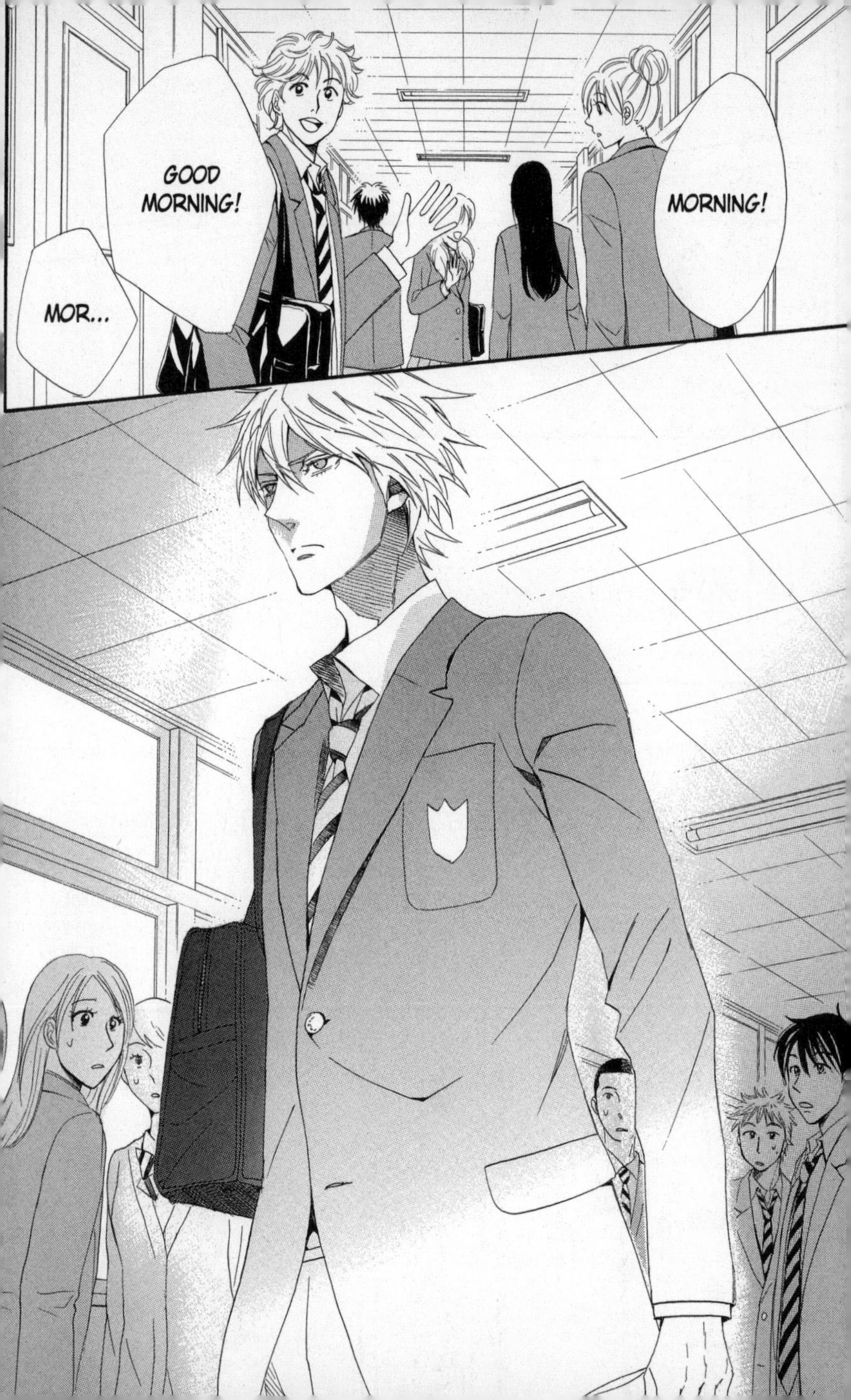
MORNING!
GOOD MORNING!
MOR...

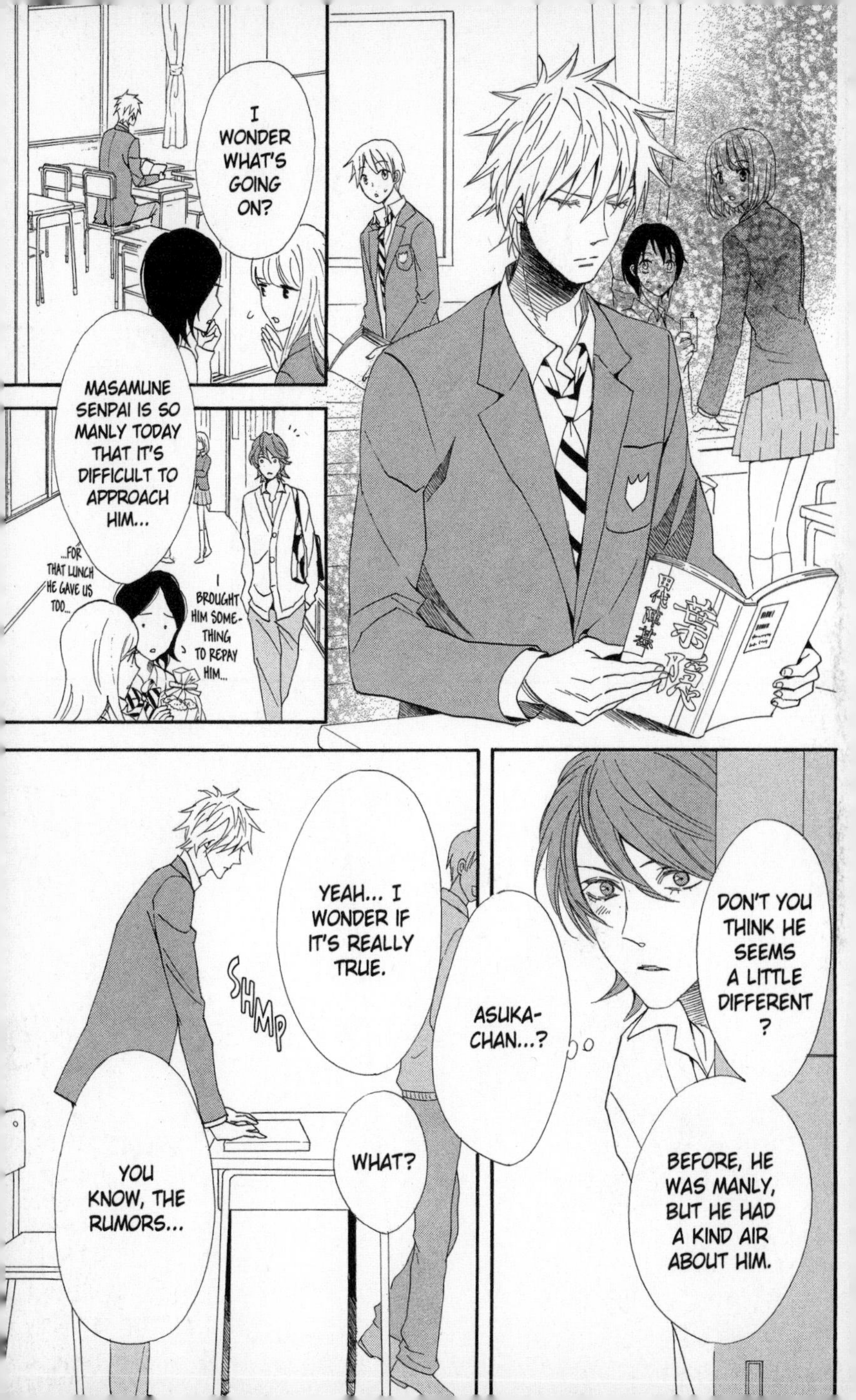
I WONDER WHAT'S GOING ON?
MASAMUNE SENPAI IS SO MANLY TODAY THAT IT'S DIFFICULT TO APPROACH HIM...
I BROUGHT HIM SOME-THING TO REPAY HIM...
...FOR THAT LUNCH HE GAVE US TOO...
DON'T YOU THINK HE SEEMS A LITTLE DIFFERENT?
ASUKA-CHAN...?
BEFORE, HE WAS MANLY, BUT HE HAD A KIND AIR ABOUT HIM.
WHAT?
YEAH... I WONDER IF IT'S REALLY TRUE.
SHMP
YOU KNOW, THE RUMORS...

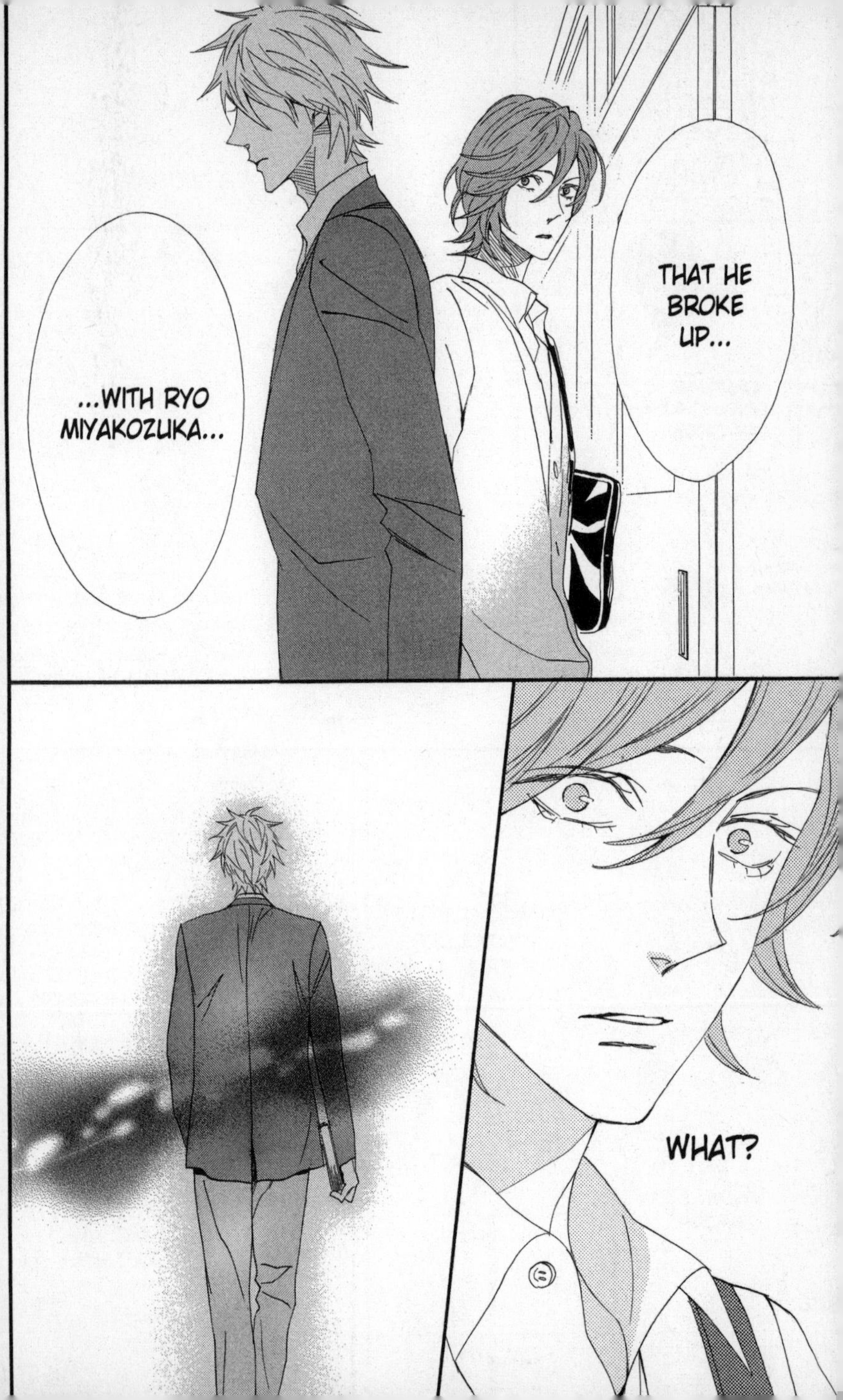
THAT HE BROKE UP...
...WITH RYO MIYAKOZUKA...
WHAT?

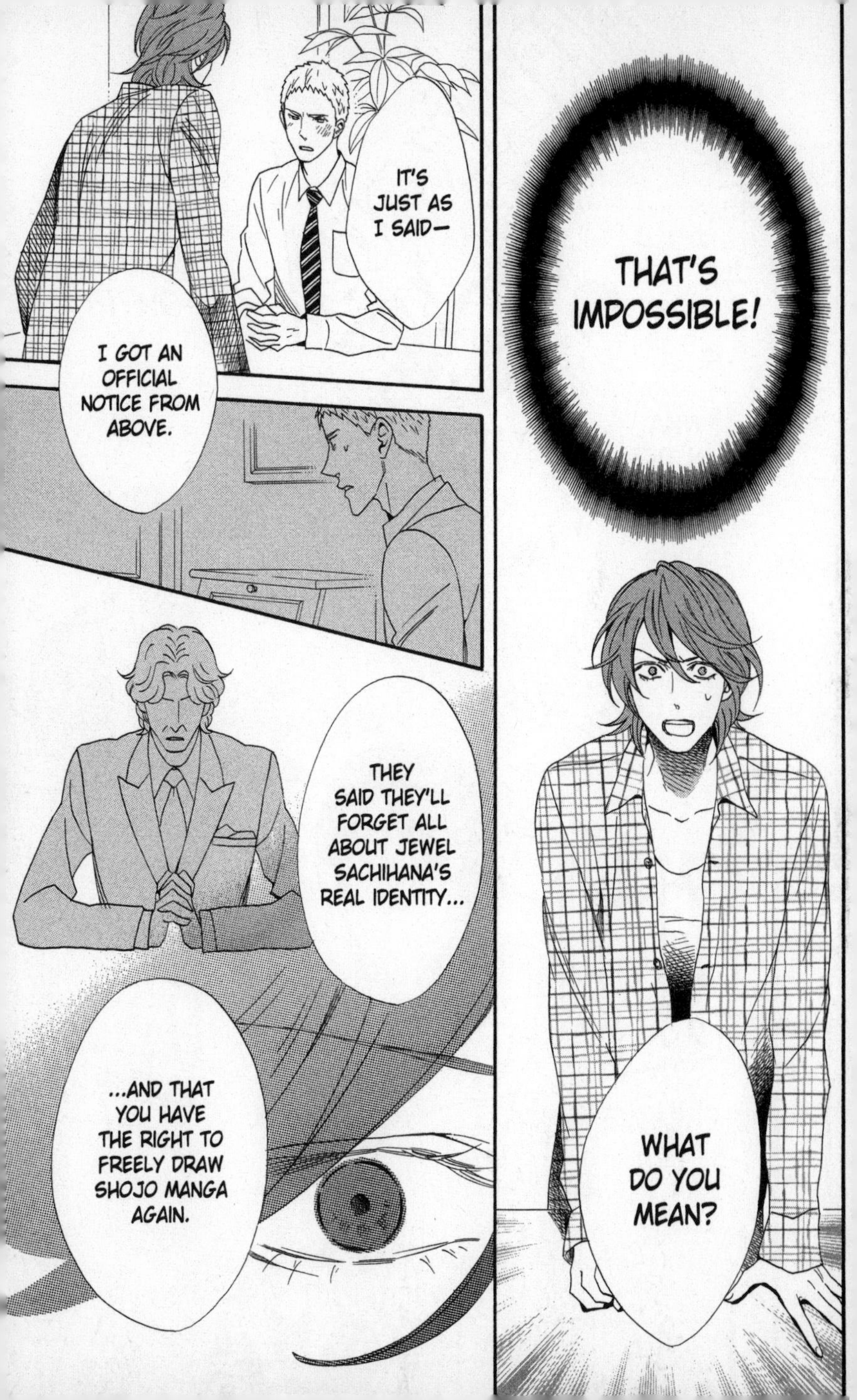
THAT'S IMPOSSIBLE!
WHAT DO YOU MEAN?
IT'S JUST AS I SAID—
I GOT AN OFFICIAL NOTICE FROM ABOVE.
THEY SAID THEY'LL FORGET ALL ABOUT JEWEL SACHIHANA'S REAL IDENTITY...
...AND THAT YOU HAVE THE RIGHT TO FREELY DRAW SHOJO MANGA AGAIN.

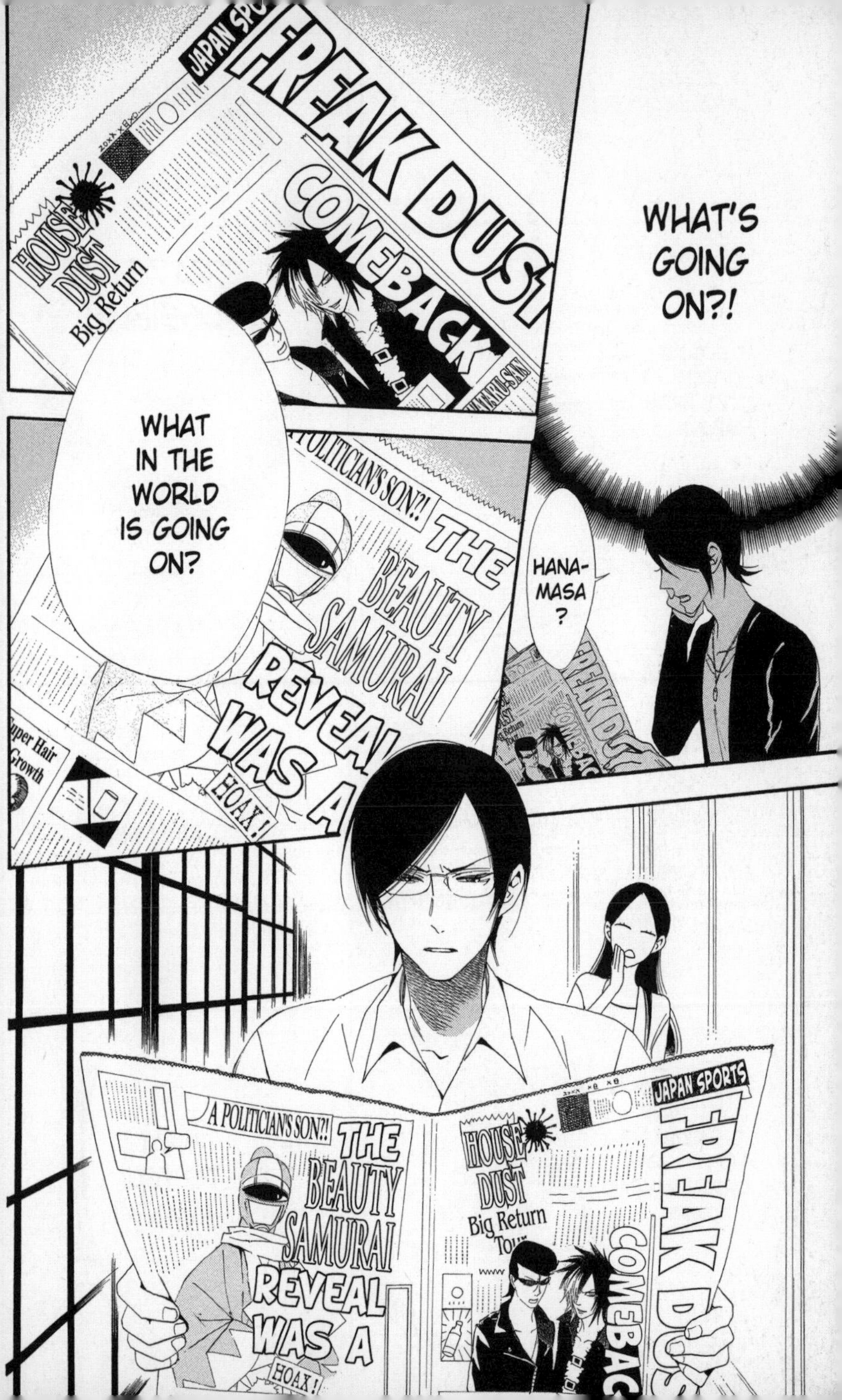
WHAT'S GOING ON?!
JAPAN SPO
FREAK DUST
COMEBACK
HOUSE DUST
Big Return
HANA-MASA?
A POLITICIAN'S SON?!
THE BEAUTY SAMURAI REVEAL WAS A HOAX!
WHAT IN THE WORLD IS GOING ON?
JAPAN SPORTS
FREAK DUS
COMEBAC
HOUSE DUST
Big Return Tour
A POLITICIAN'S SON?!
THE BEAUTY SAMURAI REVEAL WAS A HOAX!

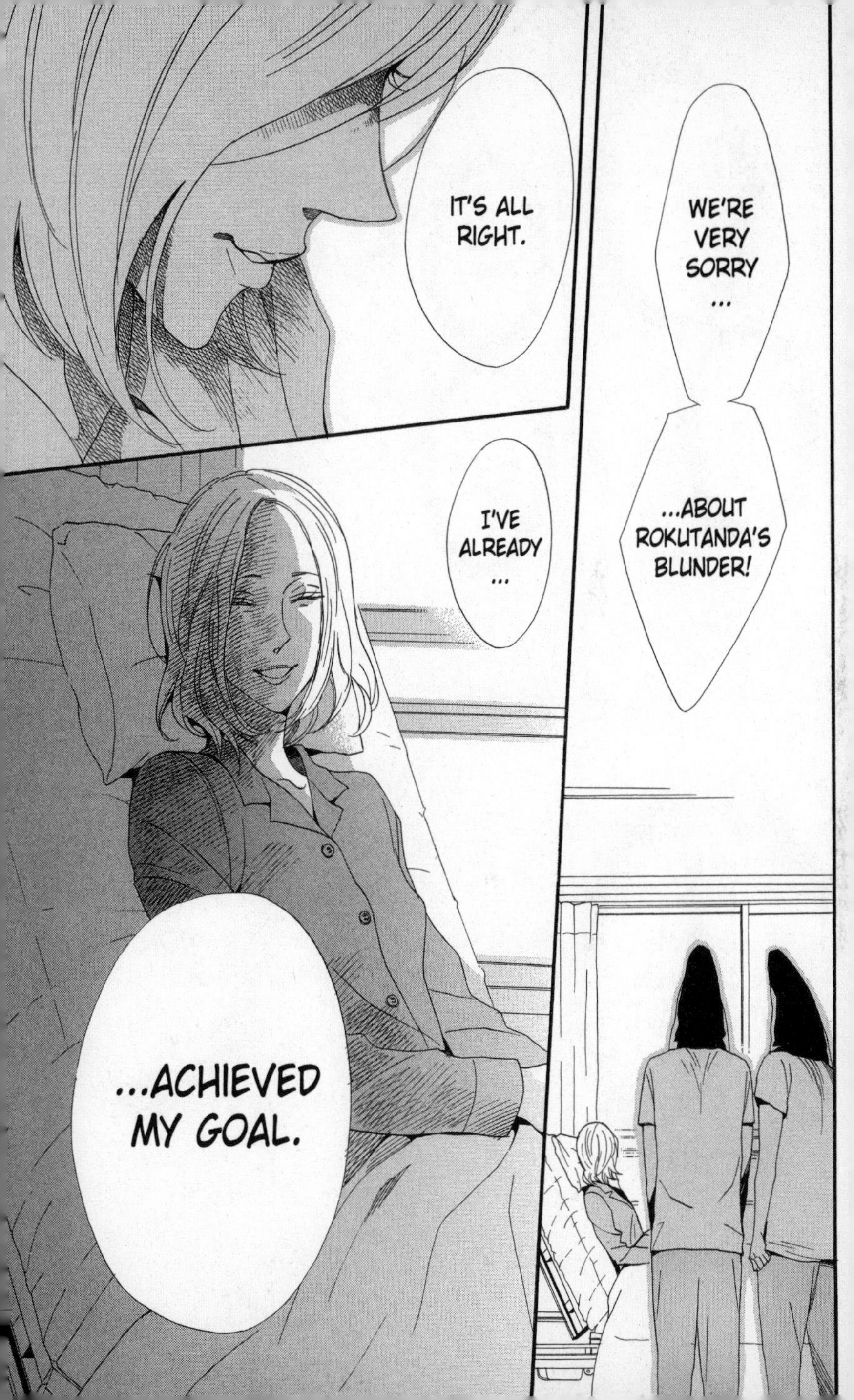
WE'RE VERY SORRY ...
...ABOUT ROKUTANDA'S BLUNDER!
IT'S ALL RIGHT.
I'VE ALREADY ...
...ACHIEVED MY GOAL.

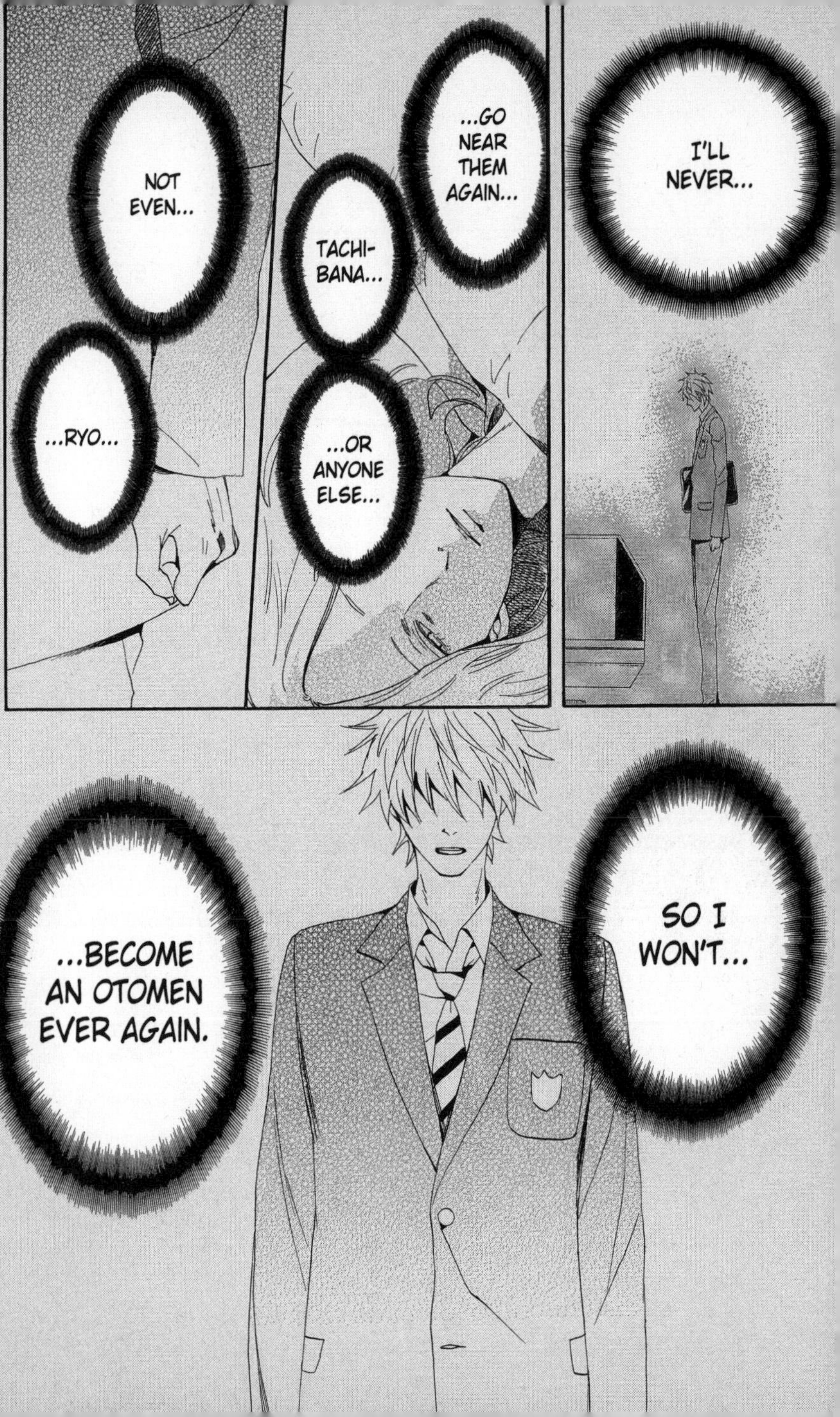

I'LL NEVER...
...GO NEAR THEM AGAIN...
TACHI-BANA...
...OR ANYONE ELSE...
NOT EVEN...
...RYO...
SO I WON'T...
...BECOME AN OTOMEN EVER AGAIN.

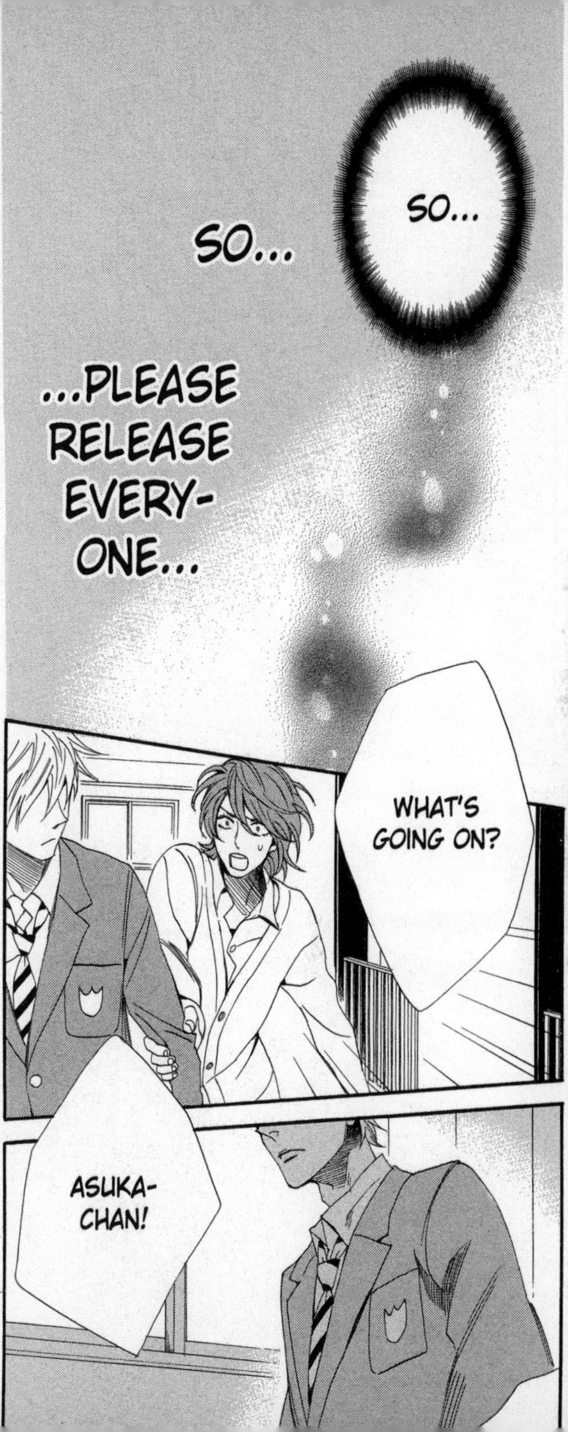
SO...
SO...
...PLEASE RELEASE EVERY-ONE...
WHAT'S GOING ON?
ASUKA-CHAN!

She used to have white hair.

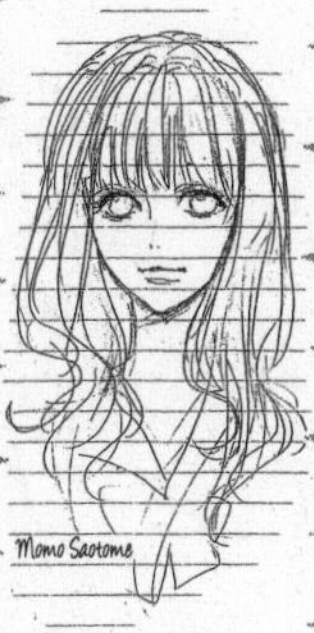
Momo Saotome

This is a very different Ryo from the one now. You can see it scribbled there that her name used to be "Momo Saotome." Since Asuka is a feminine sounding name, I figured that the heroine should have a manly sounding name, so I changed it to "Ryo Miyakozuka." I wanted the heroine to look feminine, and I wasn't sure whether to make her a Western- or Japanese-style beauty. In the end, I decided on a traditional Japanese woman. Since I turned Ryo's hair black, I made Asuka's hair white.

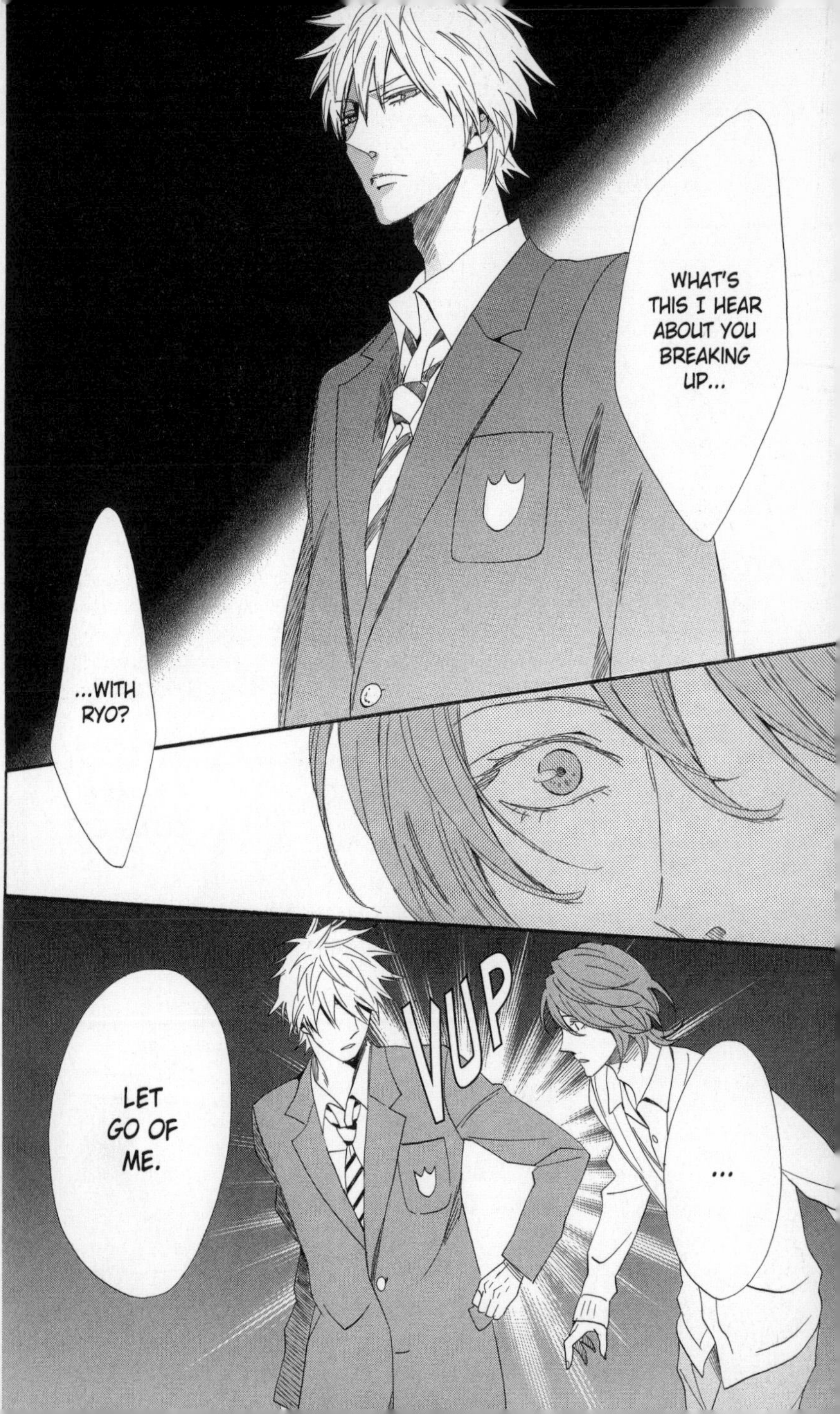
WHAT'S THIS I HEAR ABOUT YOU BREAKING UP...
...WITH RYO?
...
VUP
LET GO OF ME.

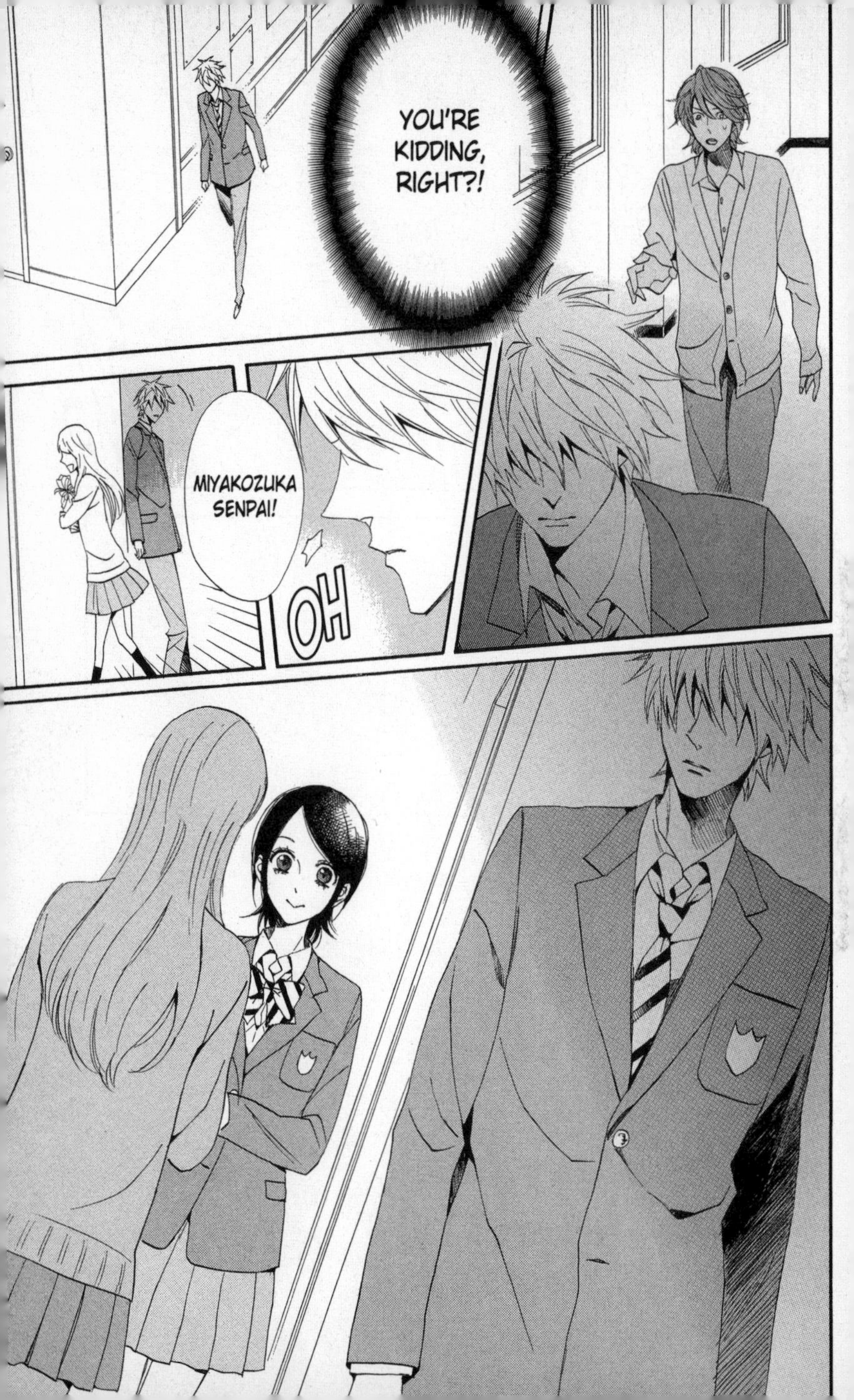
YOU'RE KIDDING, RIGHT?!
OH
MIYAKOZUKA SENPAI!

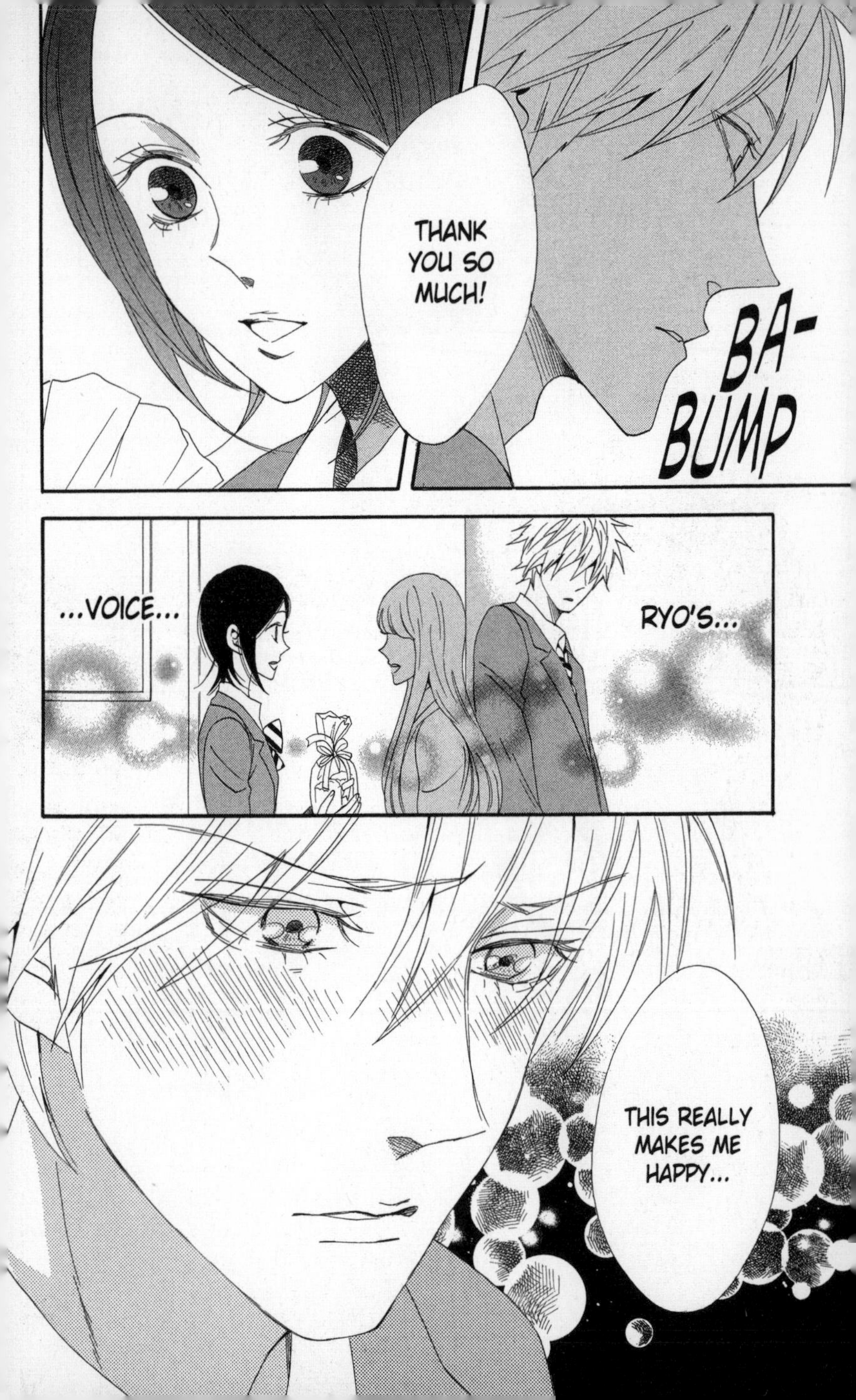
THANK YOU SO MUCH!
BA-BUMP
RYO'S...
...VOICE...
THIS REALLY MAKES ME HAPPY...

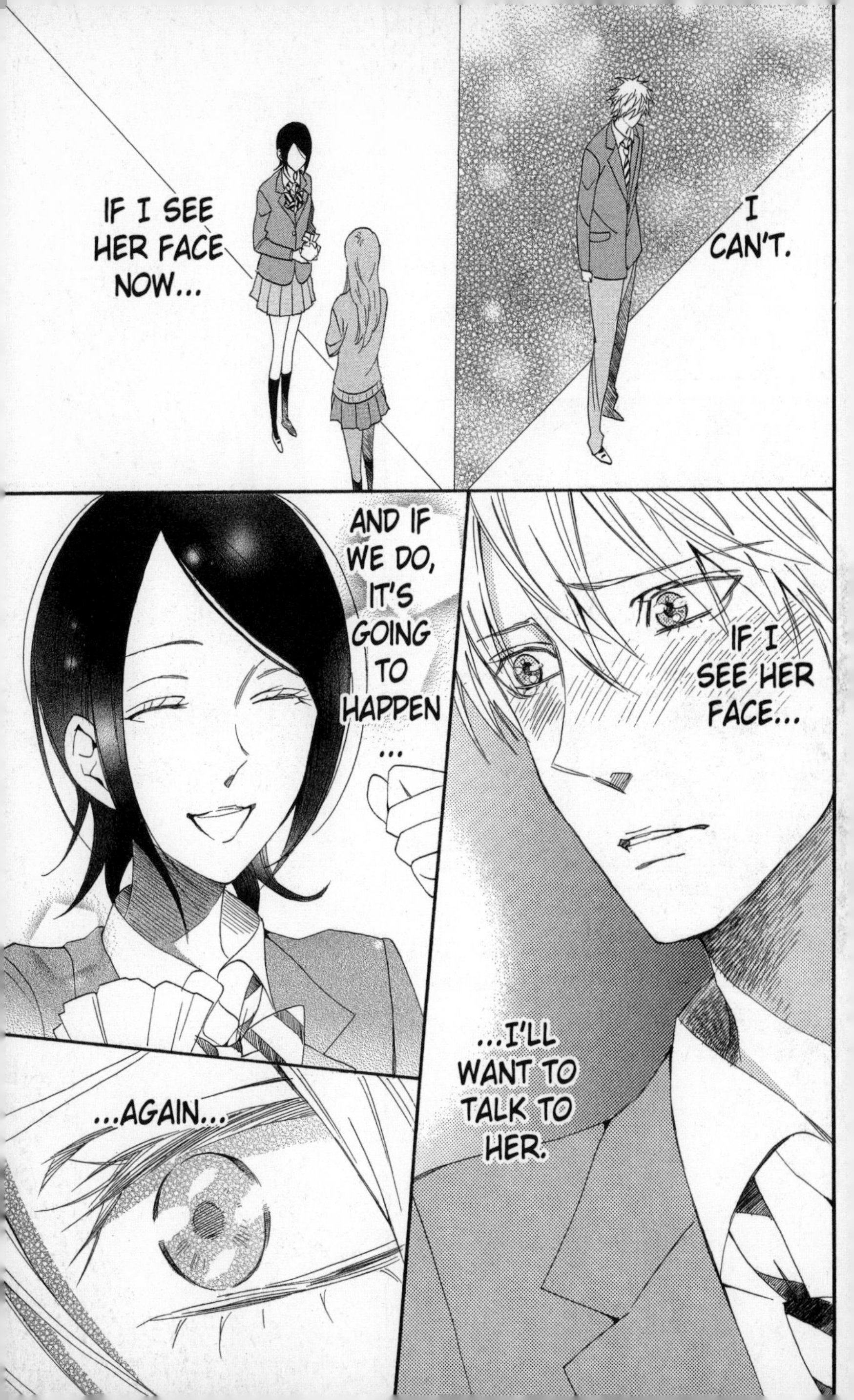
I CAN'T.
IF I SEE HER FACE NOW...
IF I SEE HER FACE...
...I'LL WANT TO TALK TO HER.
AND IF WE DO, IT'S GOING TO HAPPEN...
...AGAIN...

THANK GOOD-NESS.

RYO...

...IS STILL HER-SELF...

...NO MATTER WHAT.

I'M JUST GLAD THAT SHE'S...

...THE SAME...

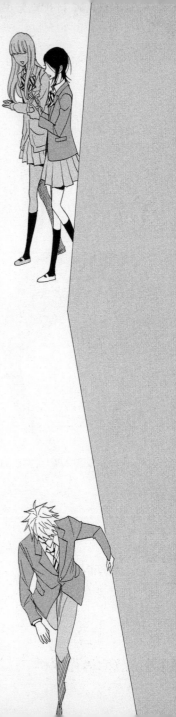

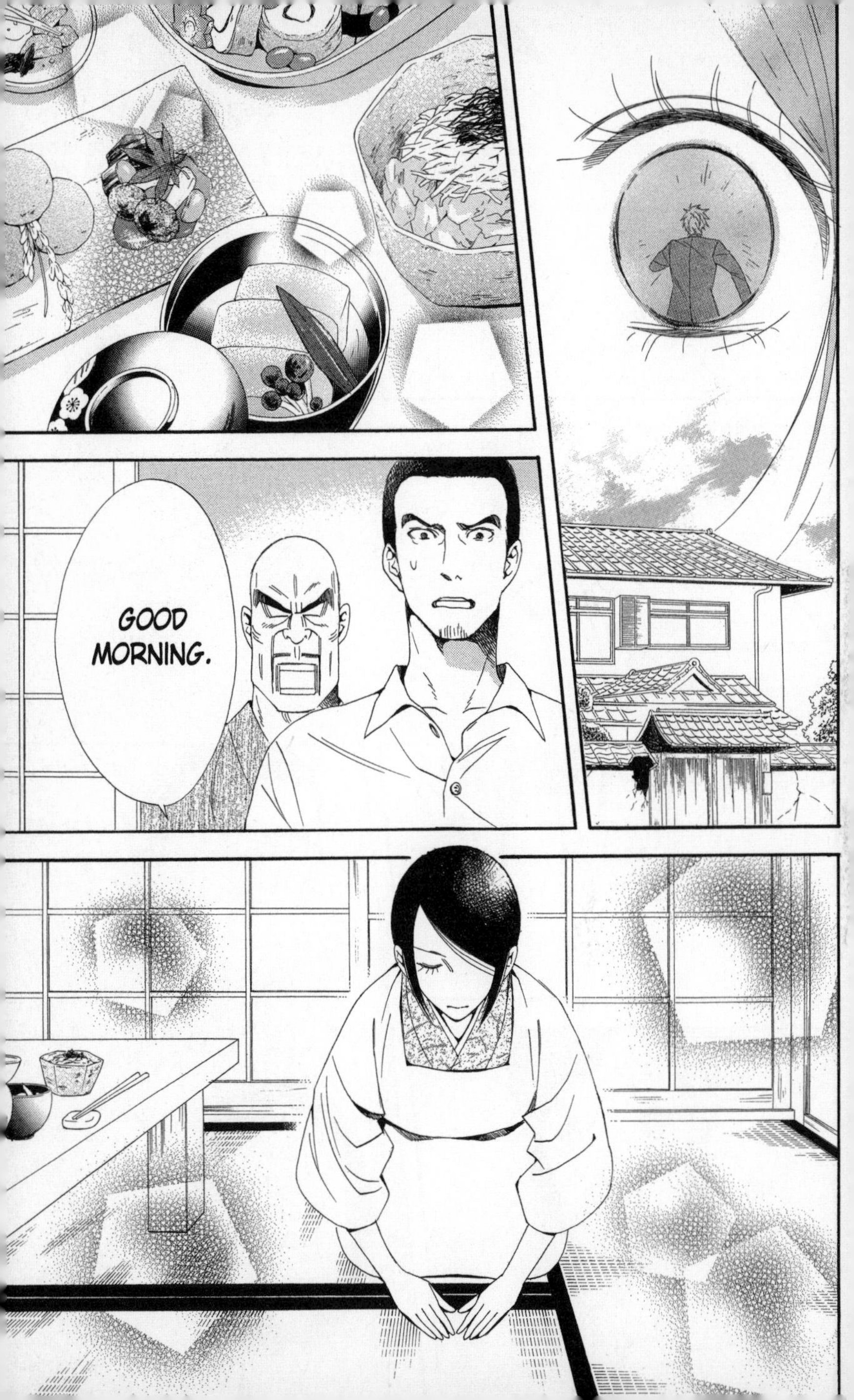
GOOD MORNING.

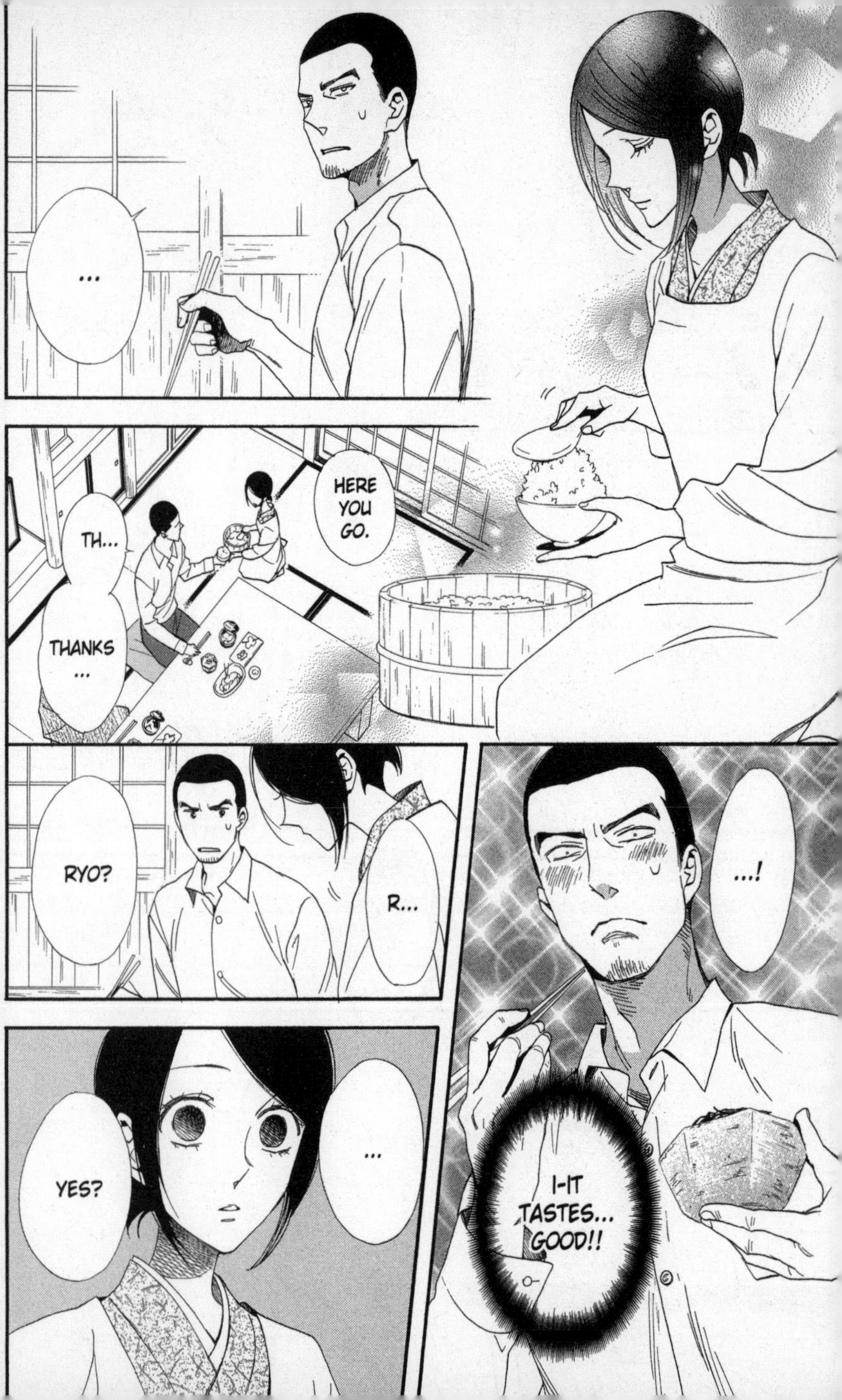
...
HERE YOU GO.
TH...
THANKS...
...!
I-IT TASTES... GOOD!!
R...
RYO?
...
YES?

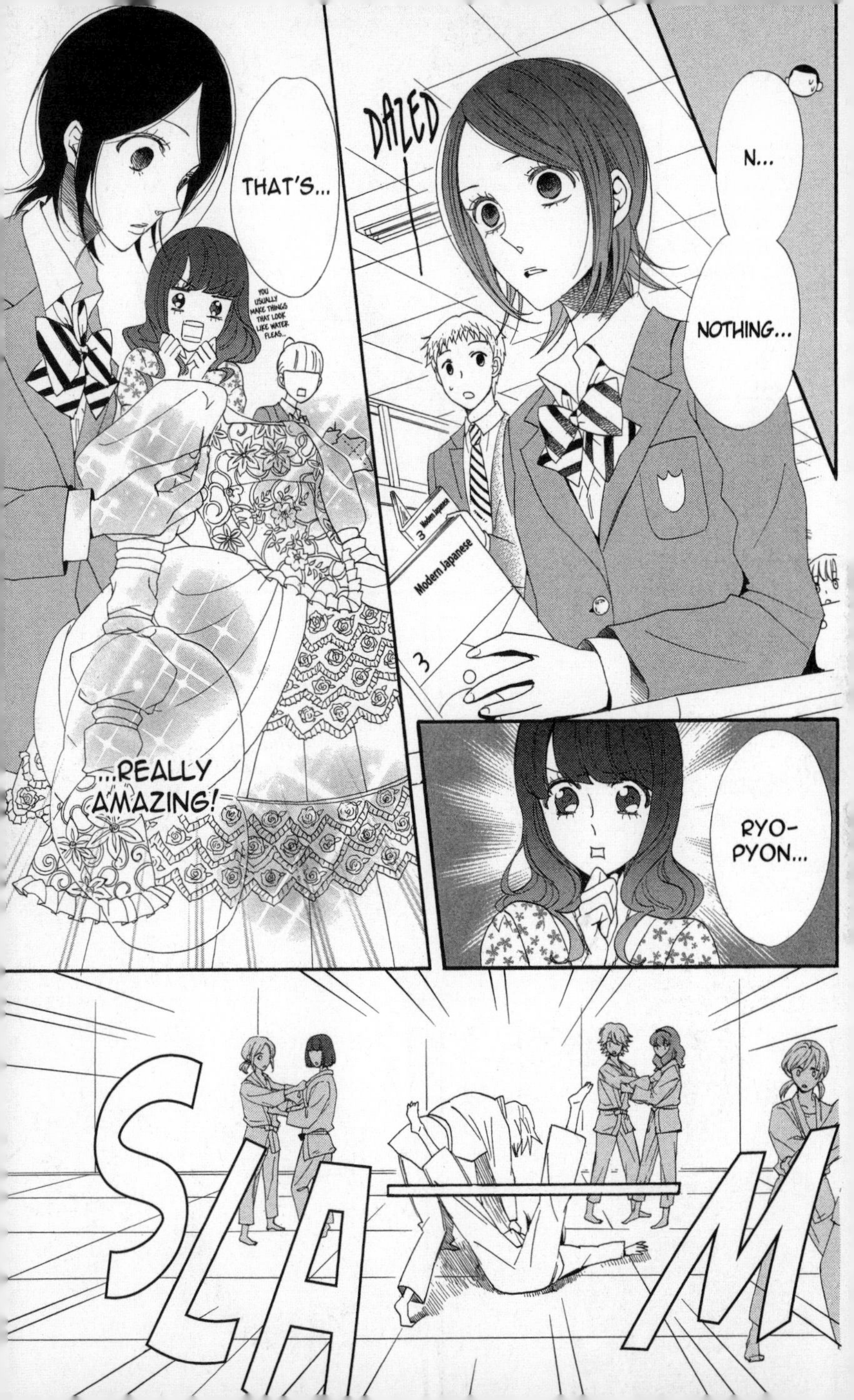
N... NOTHING...
DAZED
Modern Japanese
3
RYO-PYON...
THAT'S...
YOU USUALLY MAKE THINGS THAT LOOK LIKE WATER FLEAS...
...REALLY AMAZING!
SLAM

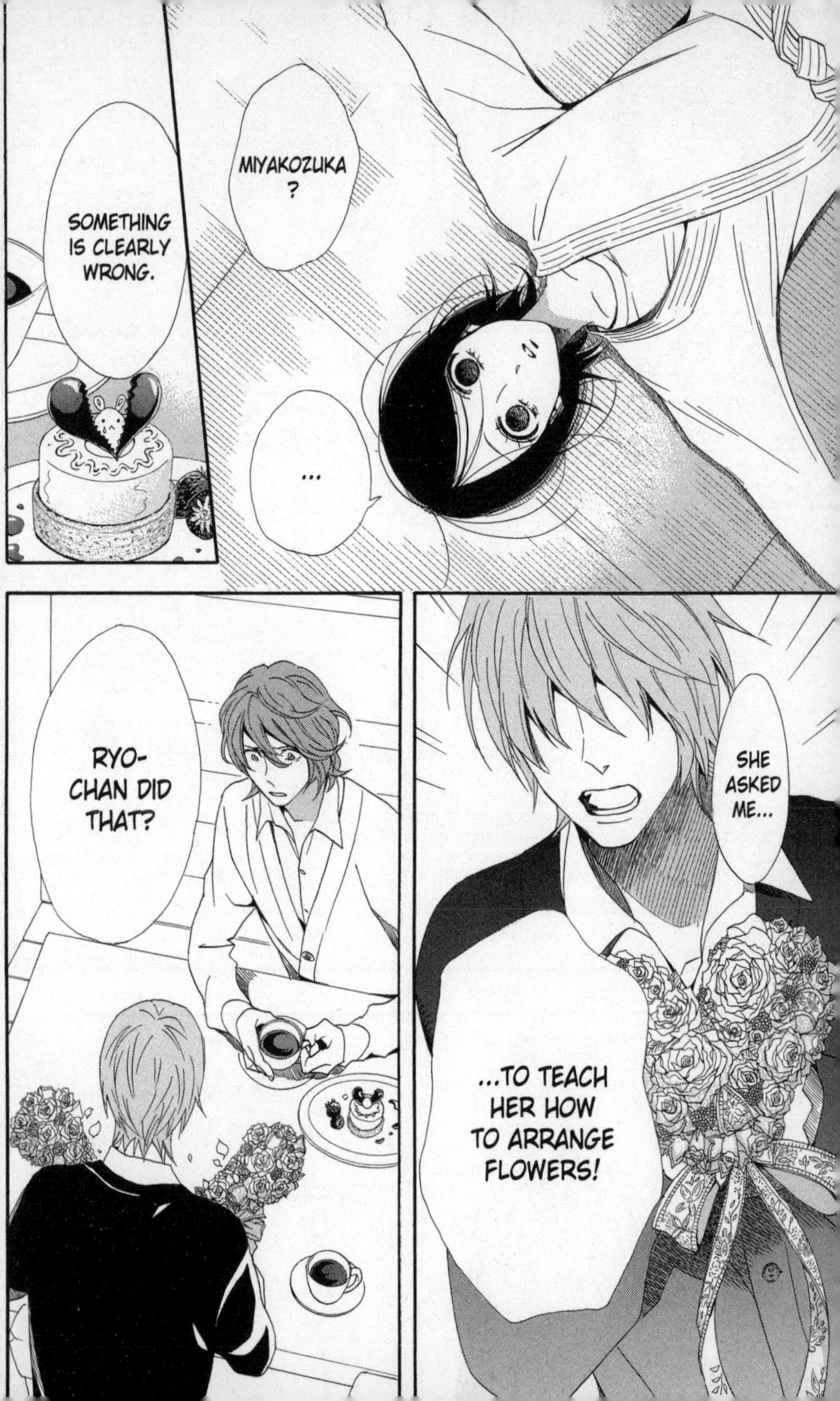
MIYAKOZUKA ?
...
SOMETHING IS CLEARLY WRONG.
SHE ASKED ME...
...TO TEACH HER HOW TO ARRANGE FLOWERS!
RYO-CHAN DID THAT?

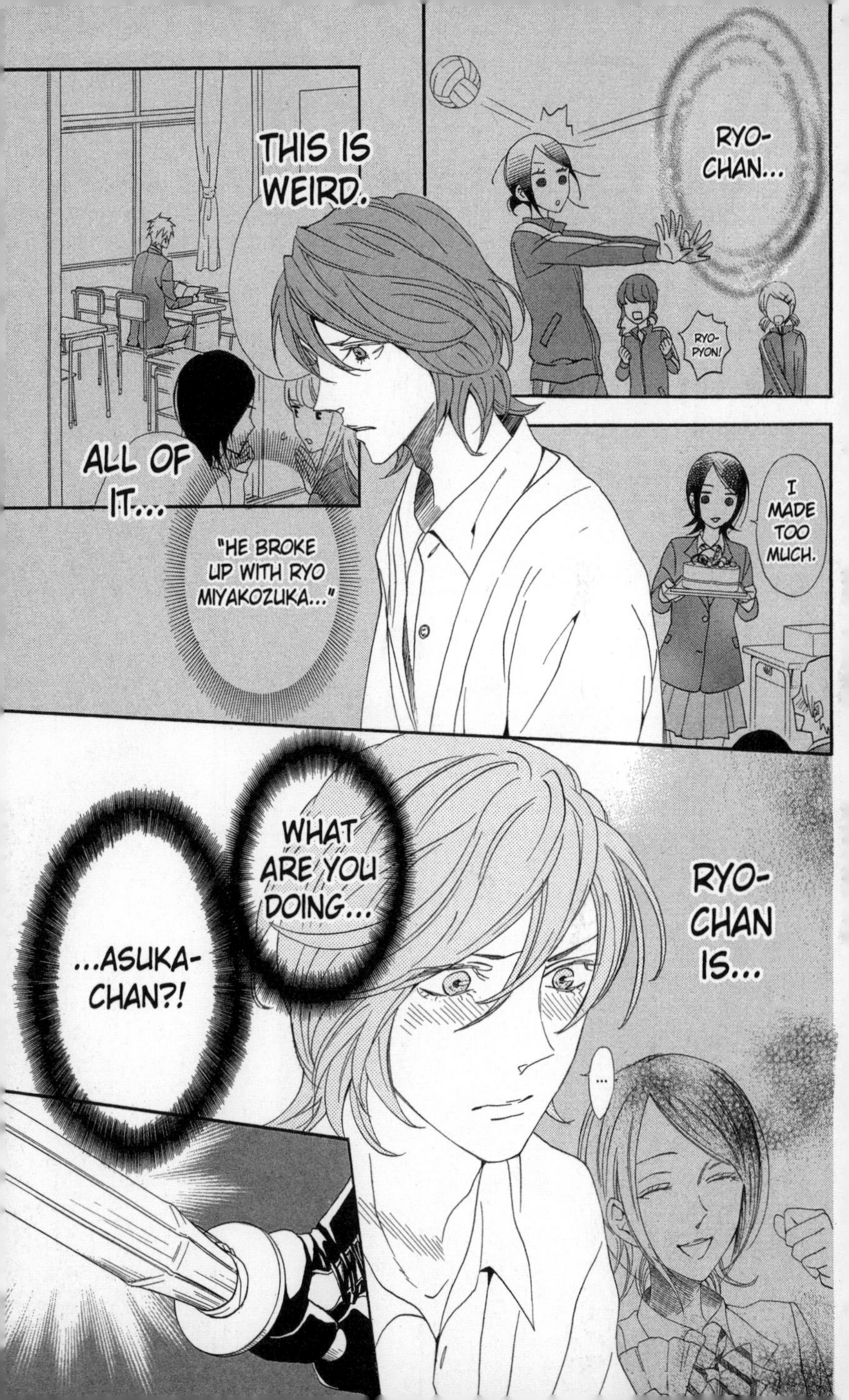
RYO-CHAN...
RYO-PYON!
THIS IS WEIRD.
ALL OF IT...
I MADE TOO MUCH.
"HE BROKE UP WITH RYO MIYAKOZUKA..."
RYO-CHAN IS...
...
WHAT ARE YOU DOING...
...ASUKA-CHAN?!

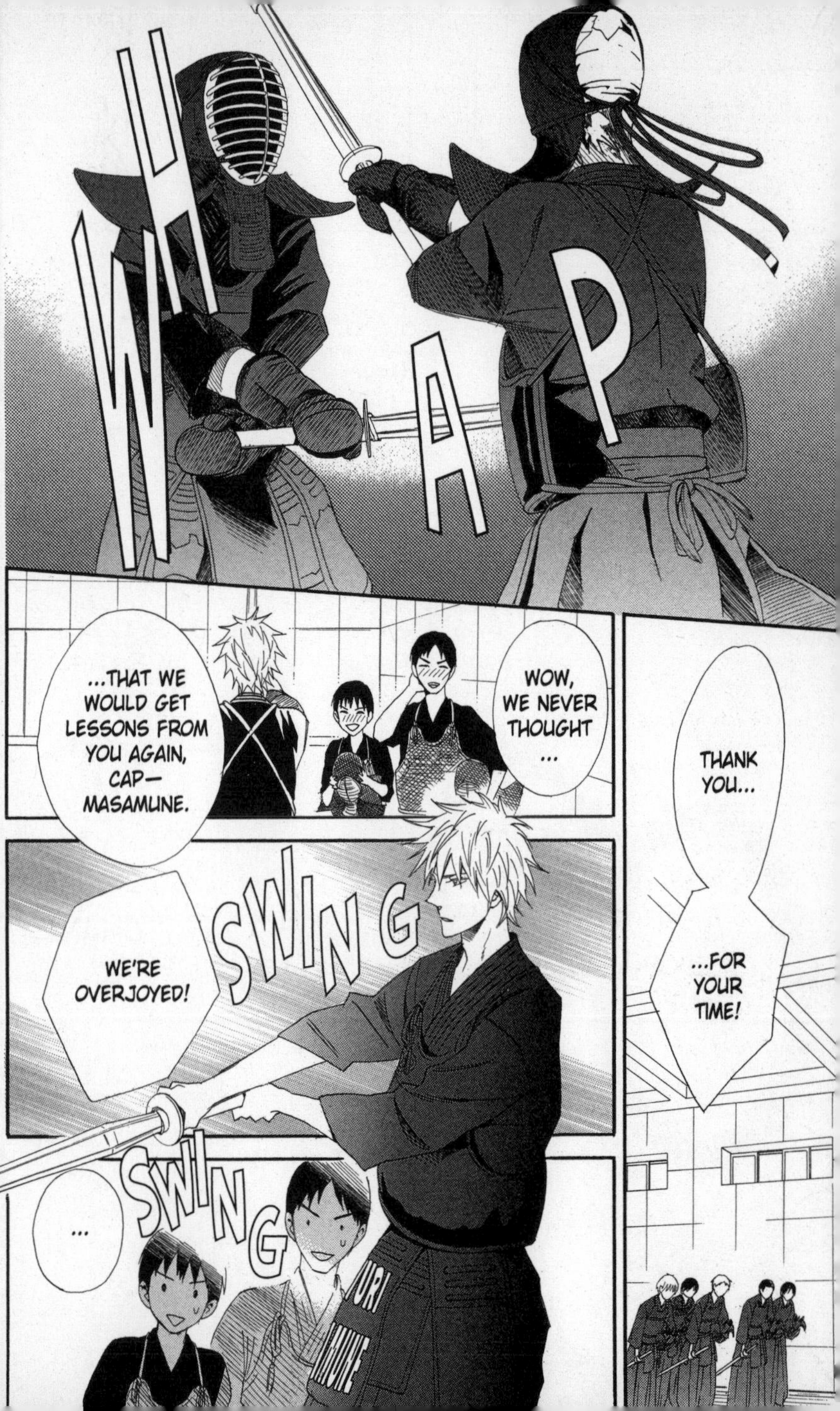
WHAP
THANK YOU...
...FOR YOUR TIME!
WOW, WE NEVER THOUGHT...
...THAT WE WOULD GET LESSONS FROM YOU AGAIN, CAP—MASAMUNE.
WE'RE OVERJOYED!
SWING
SWING
...

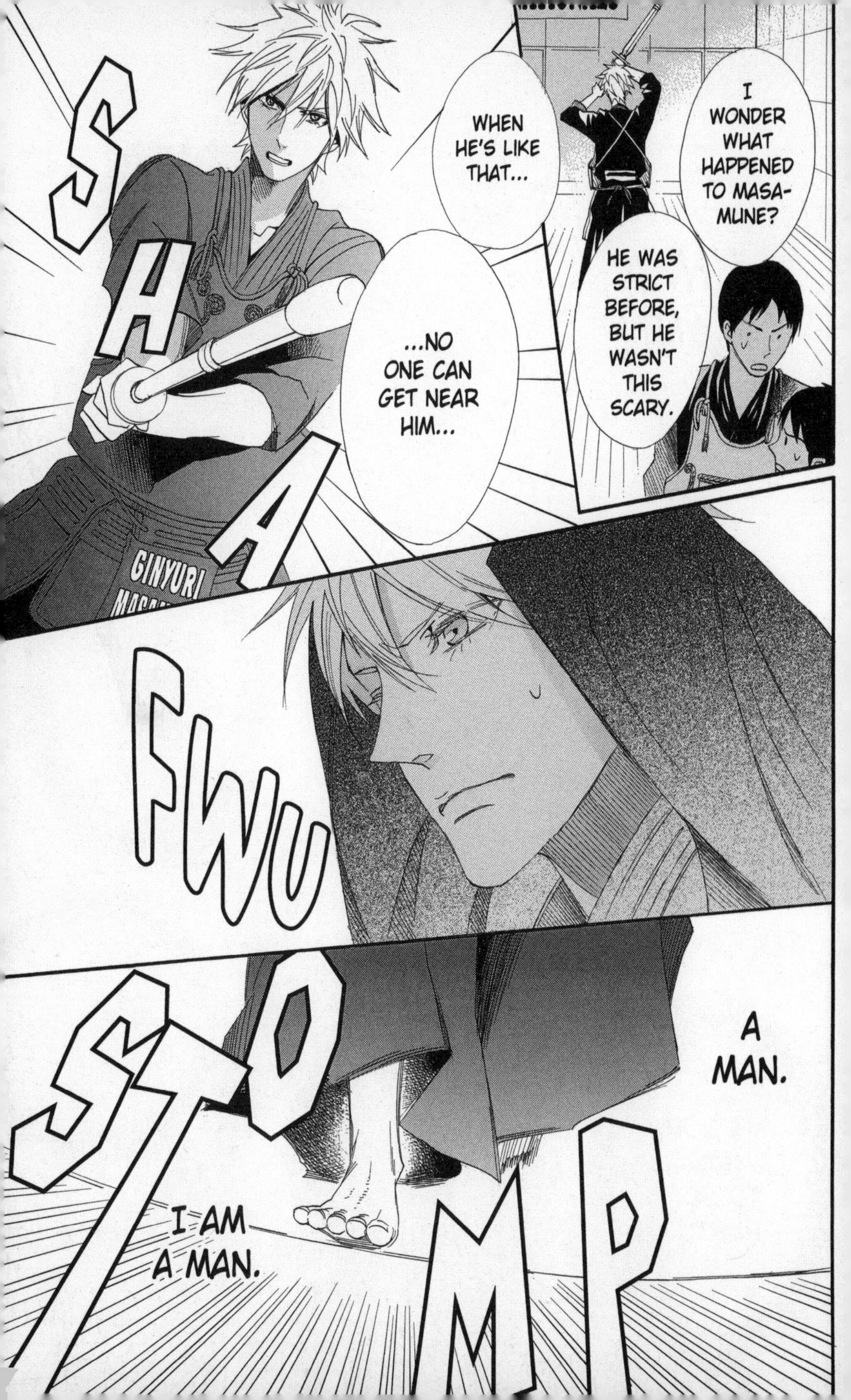
I WONDER WHAT HAPPENED TO MASAMUNE?
HE WAS STRICT BEFORE, BUT HE WASN'T THIS SCARY.
WHEN HE'S LIKE THAT...
...NO ONE CAN GET NEAR HIM...
SHAA
GINYURI
FWU
A MAN.
I AM A MAN.
STOMP

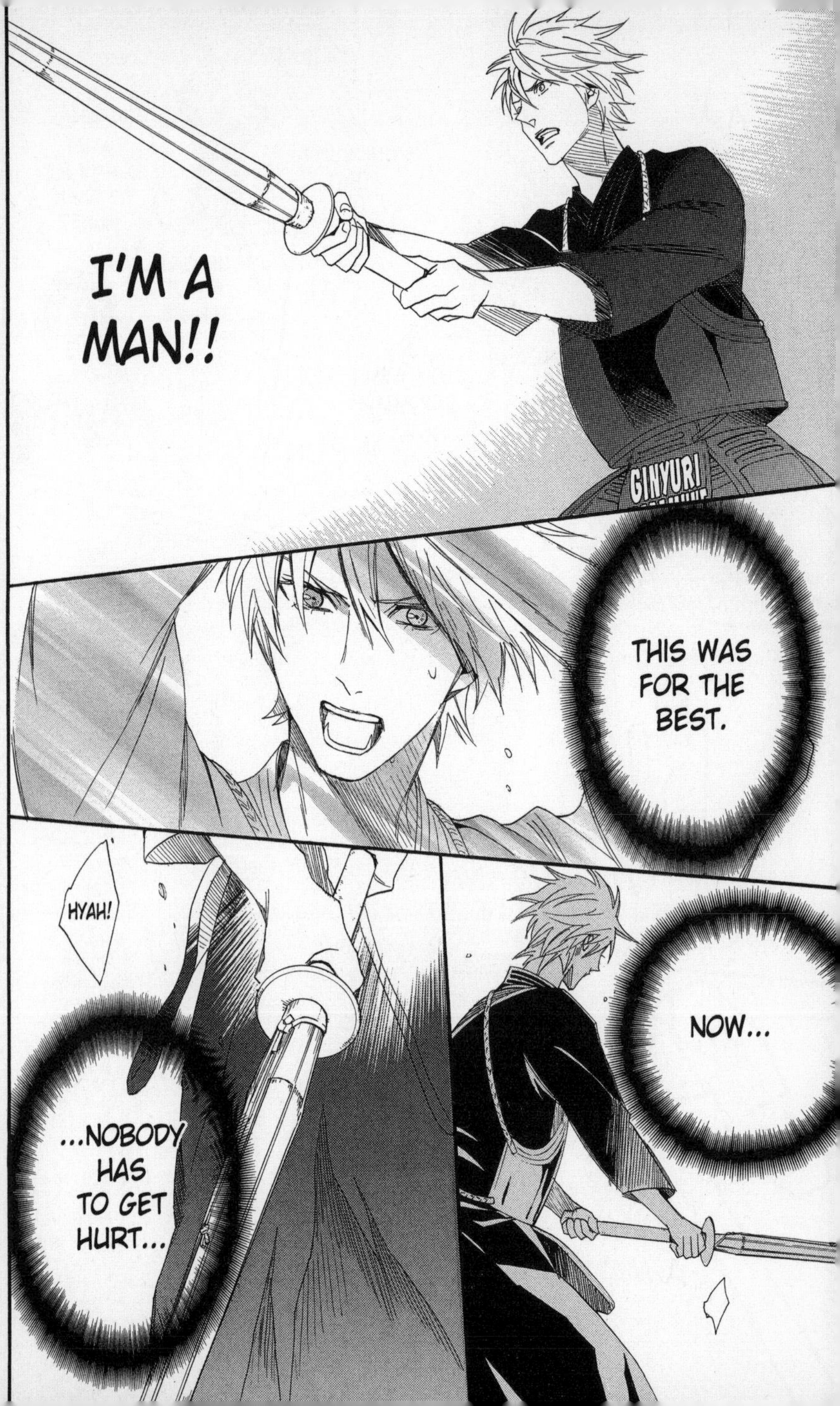
I'M A MAN!!
GINYURI
THIS WAS FOR THE BEST.
NOW...
HYAH!
...NOBODY HAS TO GET HURT...

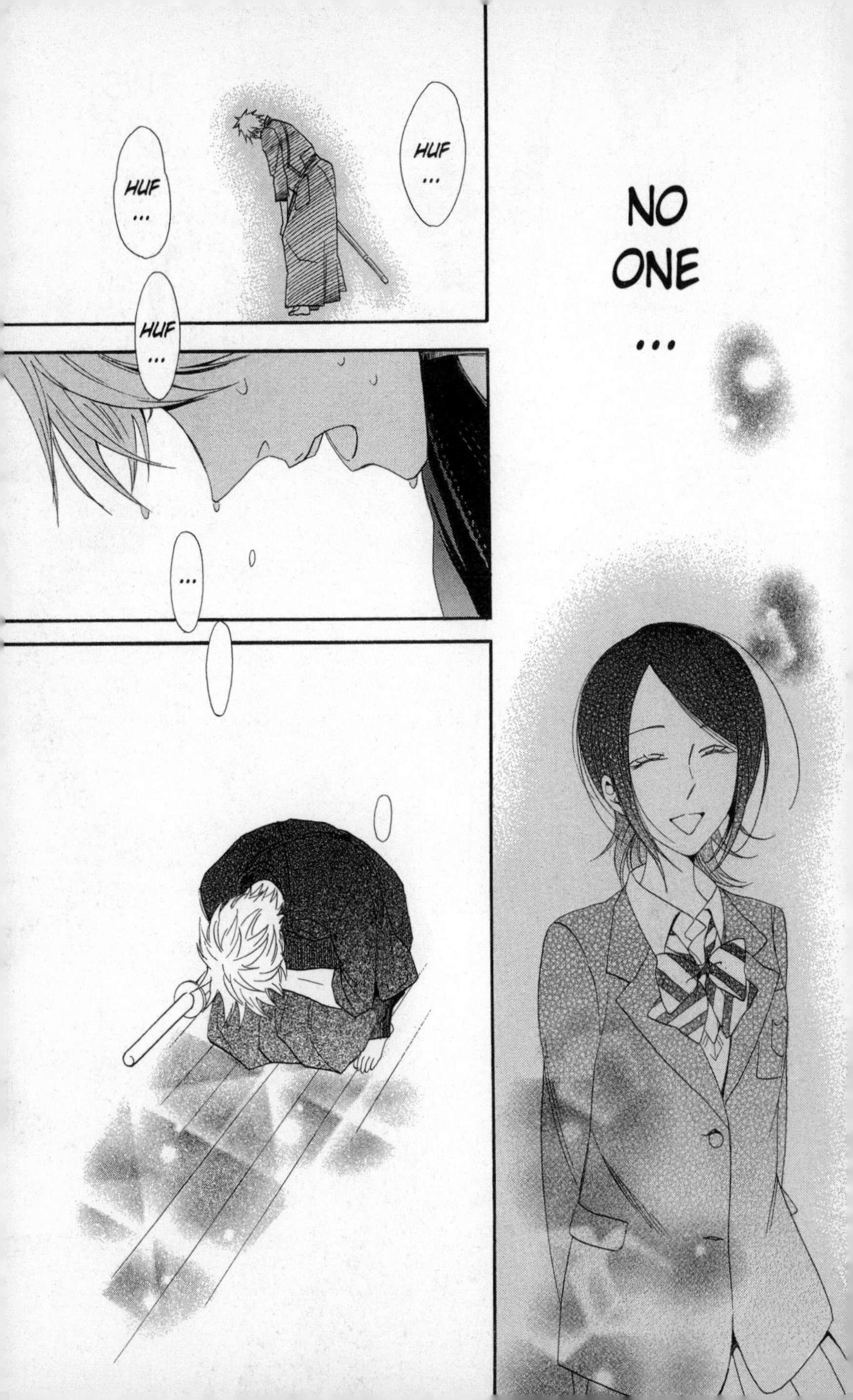
NO ONE ...
HUF ...
HUF ...
HUF ...
...

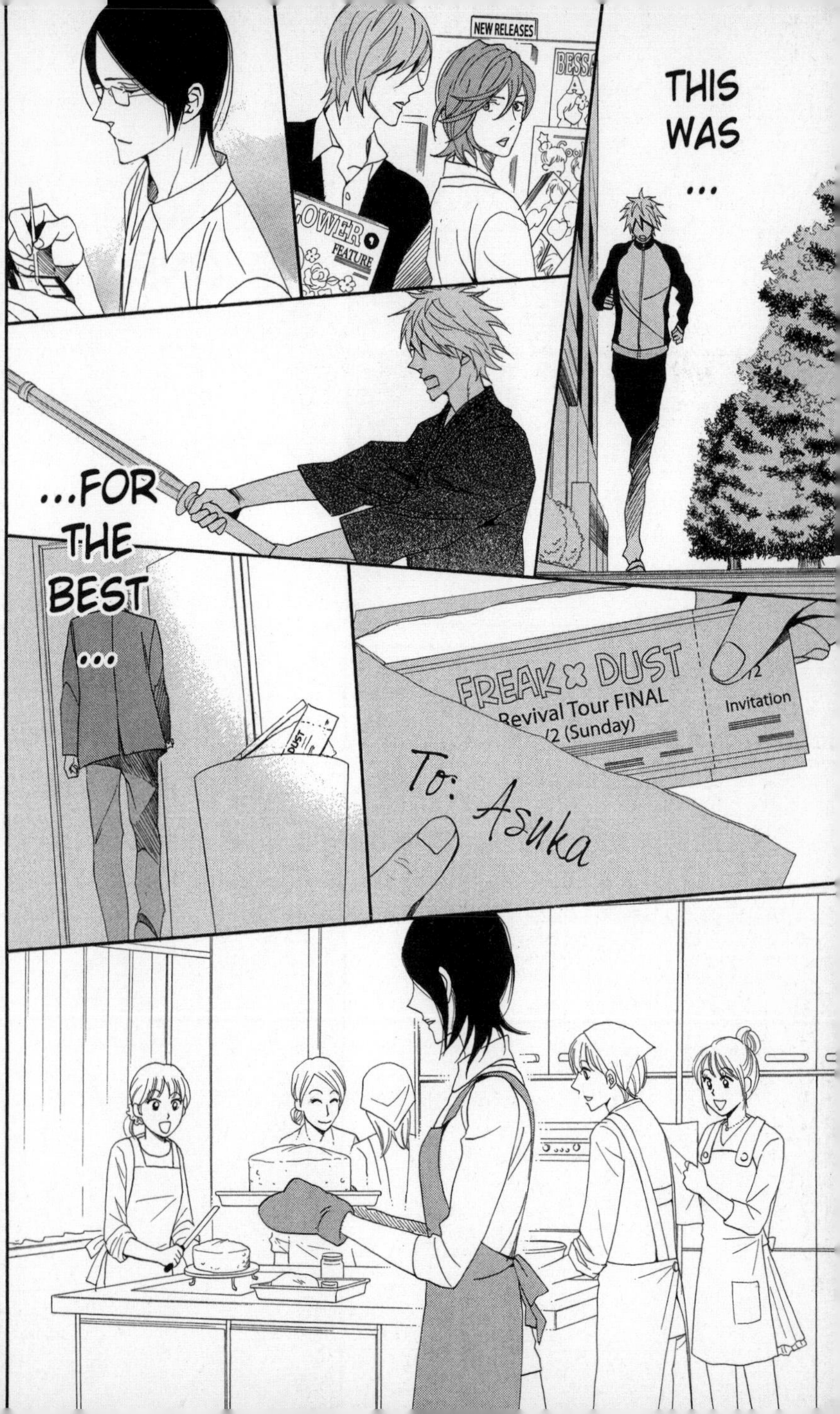
THIS WAS ...
NEW RELEASES
LOWER
FEATURE
...FOR THE BEST ...
FREAK DUST
Revival Tour FINAL
/2 (Sunday)
/2
Invitation
To: Asuka

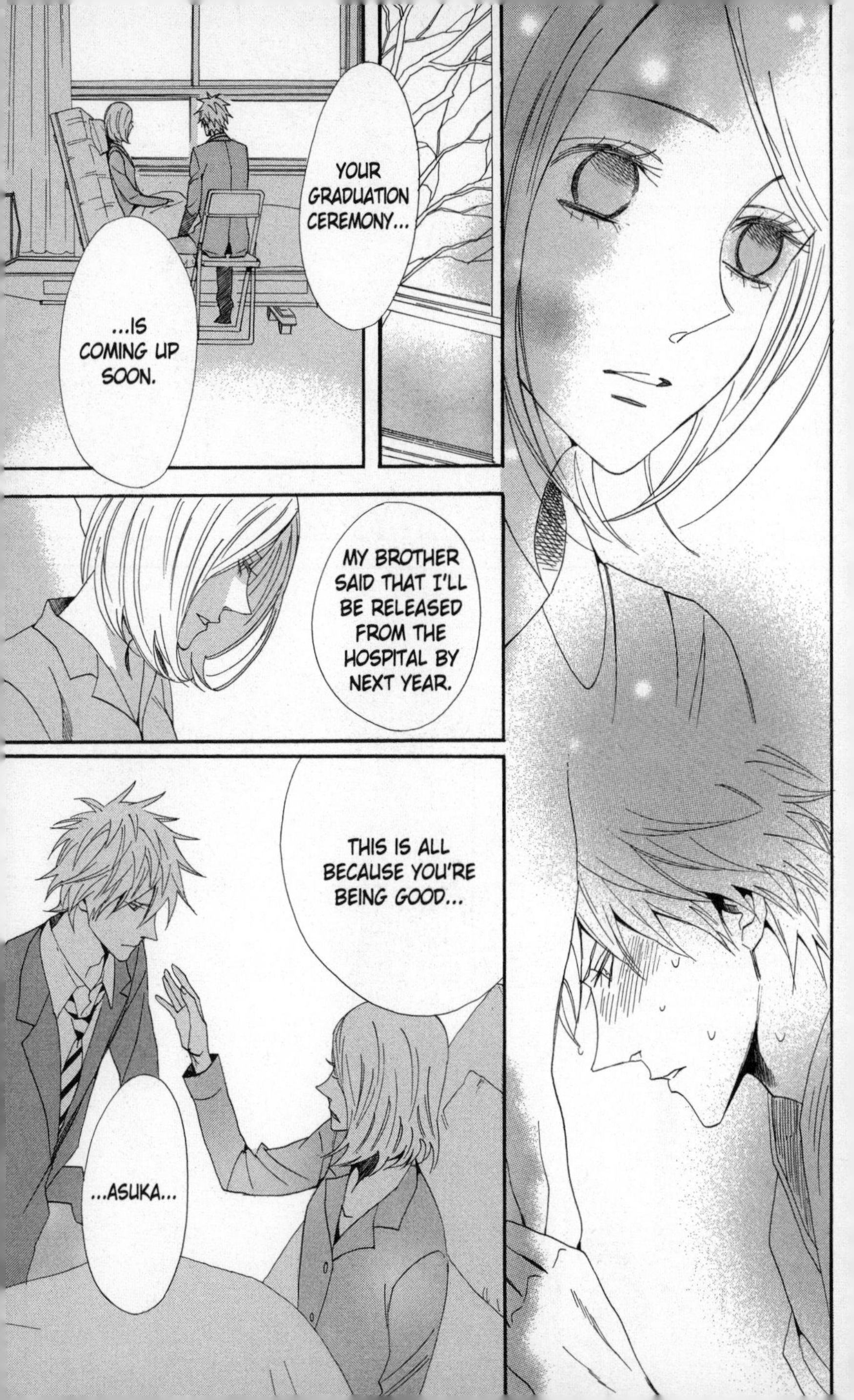
YOUR GRADUATION CEREMONY...
...IS COMING UP SOON.
MY BROTHER SAID THAT I'LL BE RELEASED FROM THE HOSPITAL BY NEXT YEAR.
THIS IS ALL BECAUSE YOU'RE BEING GOOD...
...ASUKA...

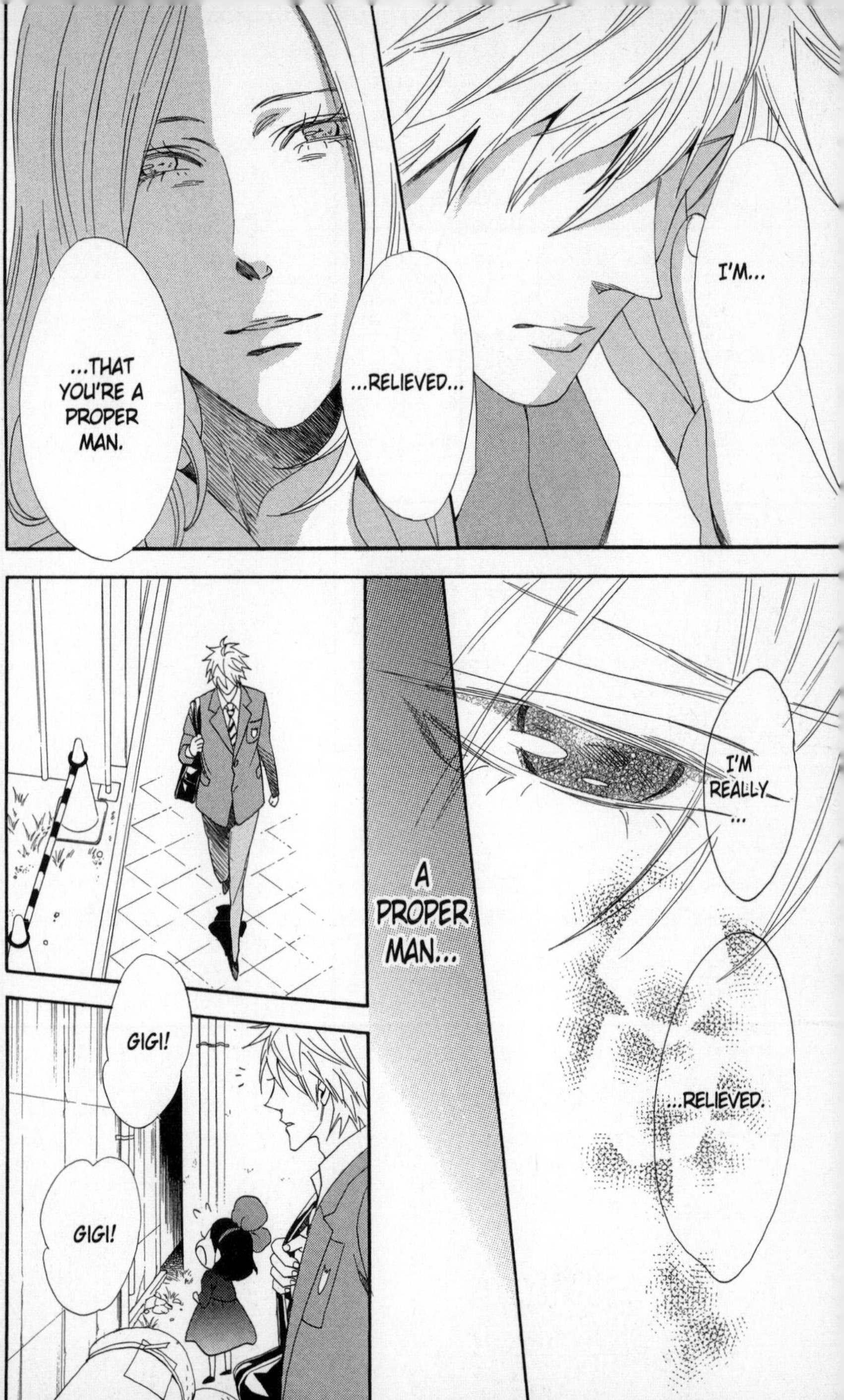
I'M...
...RELIEVED...
...THAT YOU'RE A PROPER MAN.
I'M REALLY...
...RELIEVED.
A PROPER MAN...
GIGI!
GIGI!

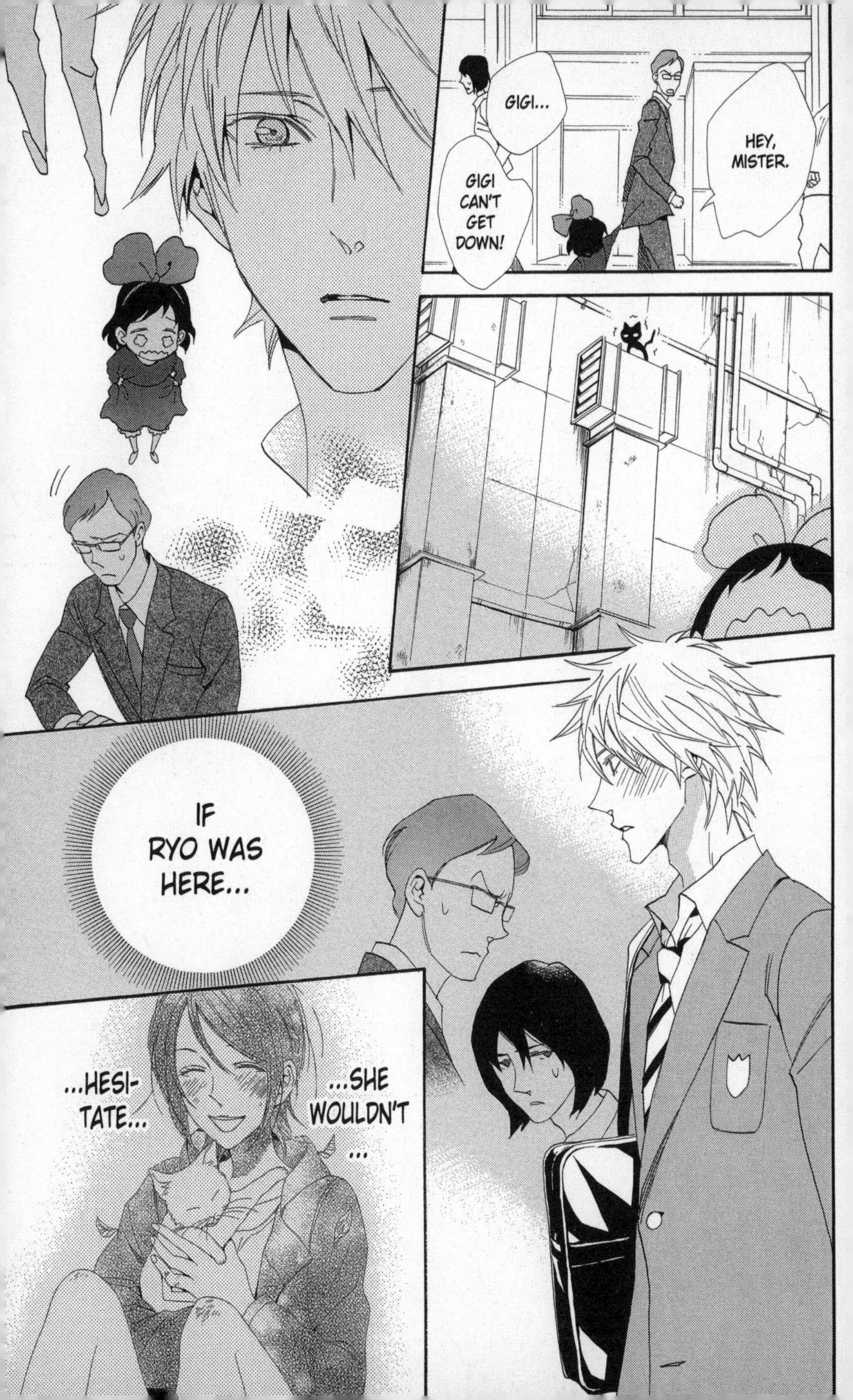
HEY, MISTER.
GIGI...
GIGI CAN'T GET DOWN!
IF RYO WAS HERE...
...SHE WOULDN'T ...
...HESI-TATE...

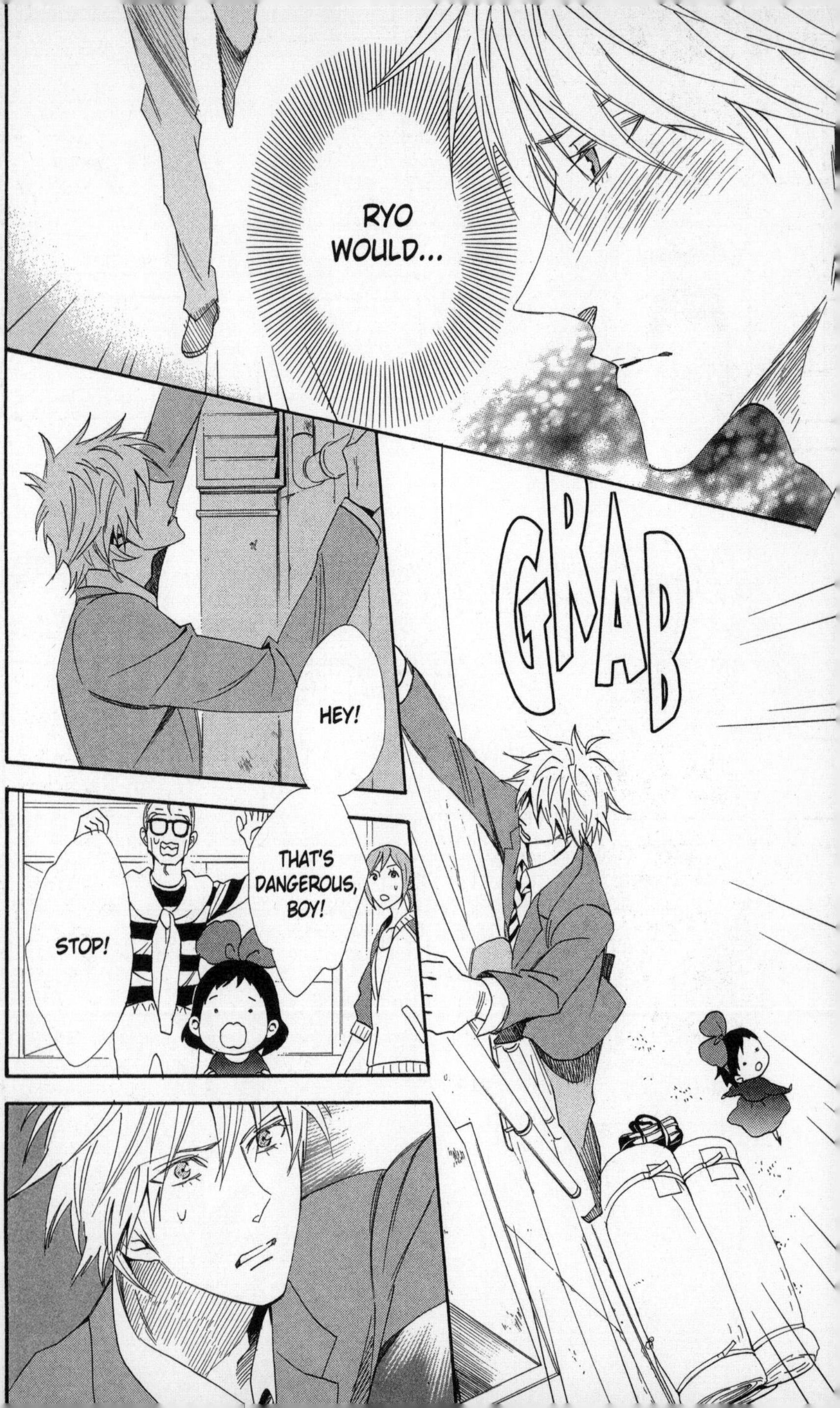
RYO WOULD...
GRAB
HEY!
THAT'S DANGEROUS, BOY!
STOP!

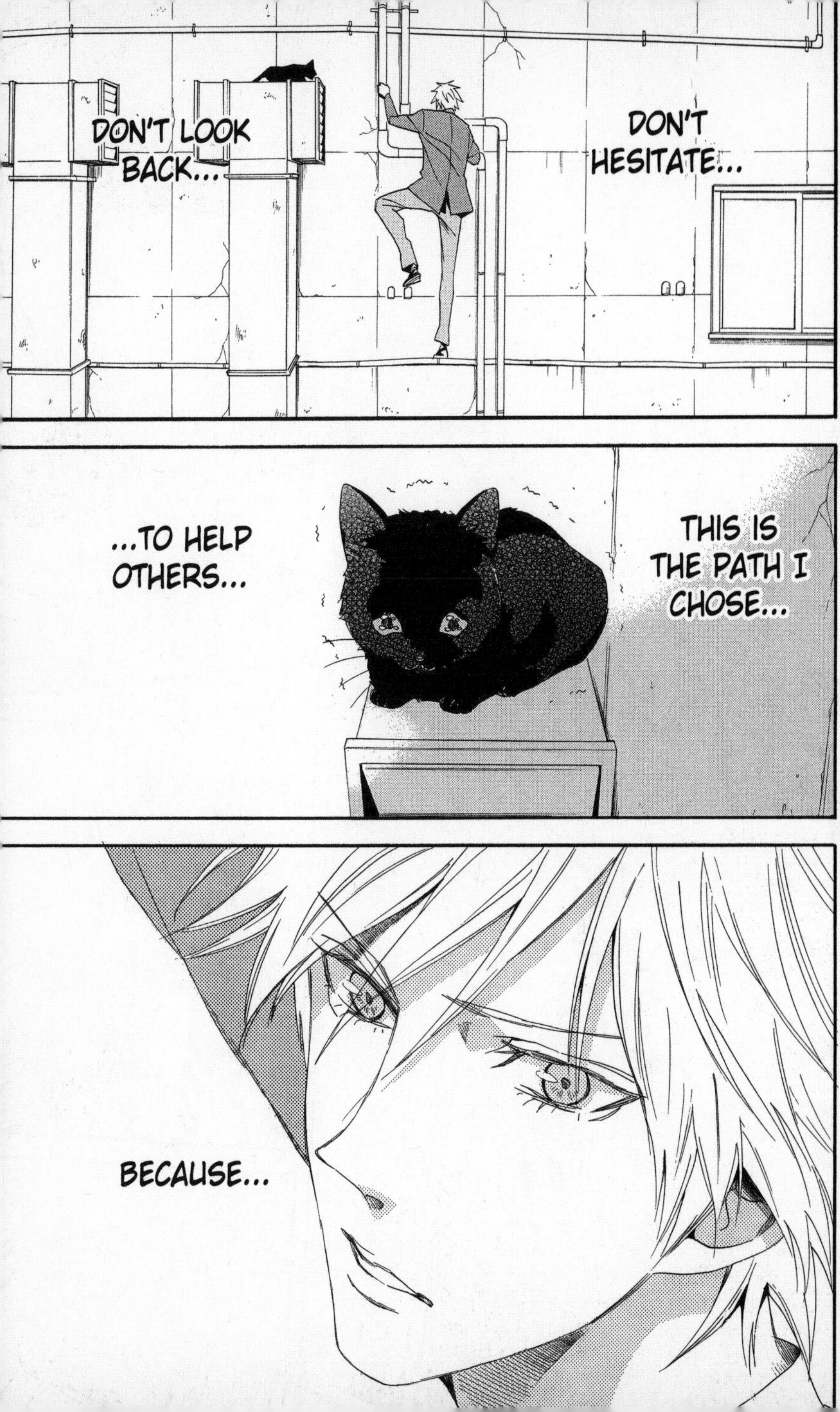
DON'T HESITATE...
DON'T LOOK BACK...
THIS IS THE PATH I CHOSE...
...TO HELP OTHERS...
BECAUSE...

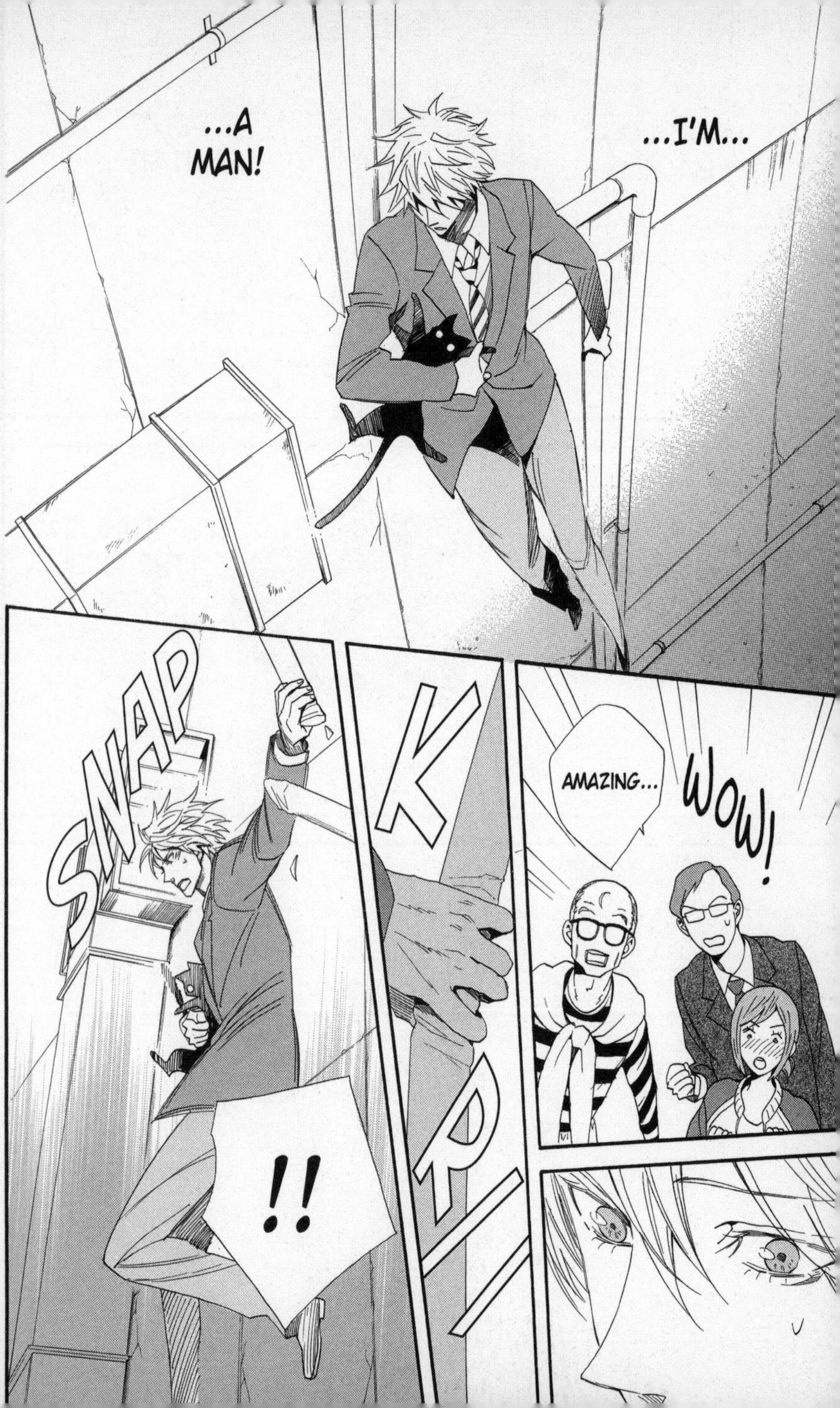
...I'M...
...A MAN!
WOW!
AMAZING...
KR
SNAP
!!

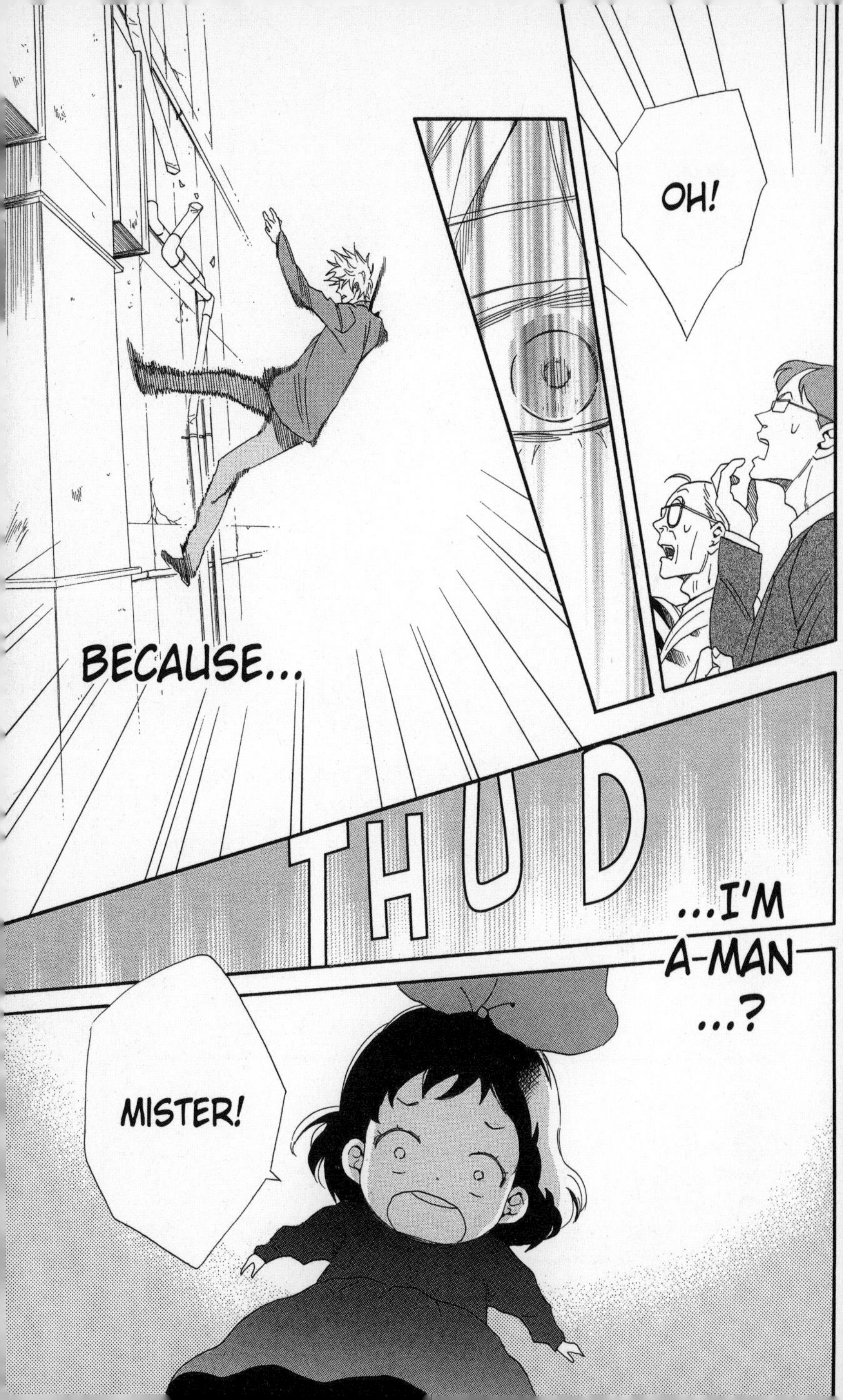
OH!
BECAUSE...
THUD
...I'M A-MAN ...?
MISTER!

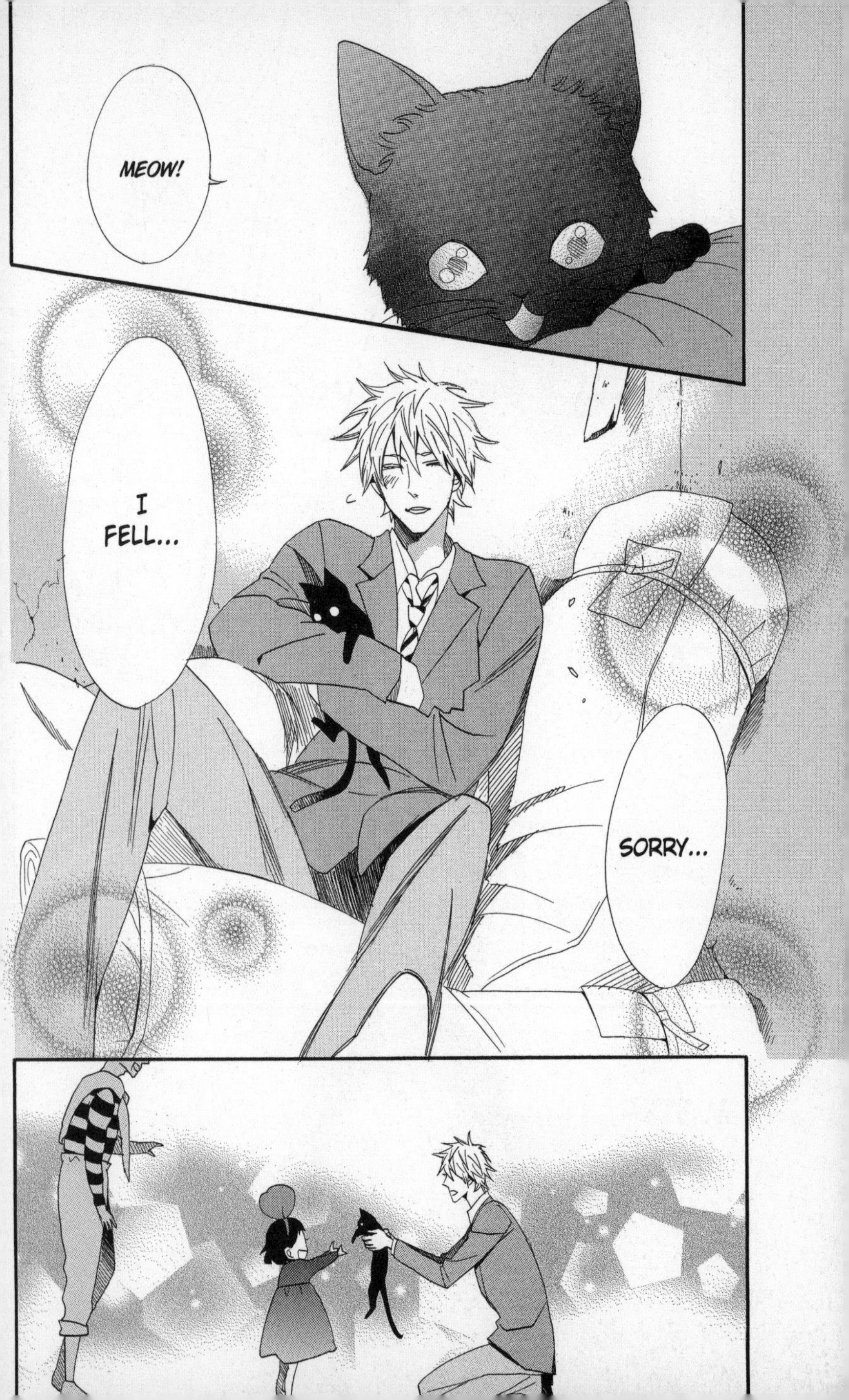
MEOW!
SORRY...
I FELL...

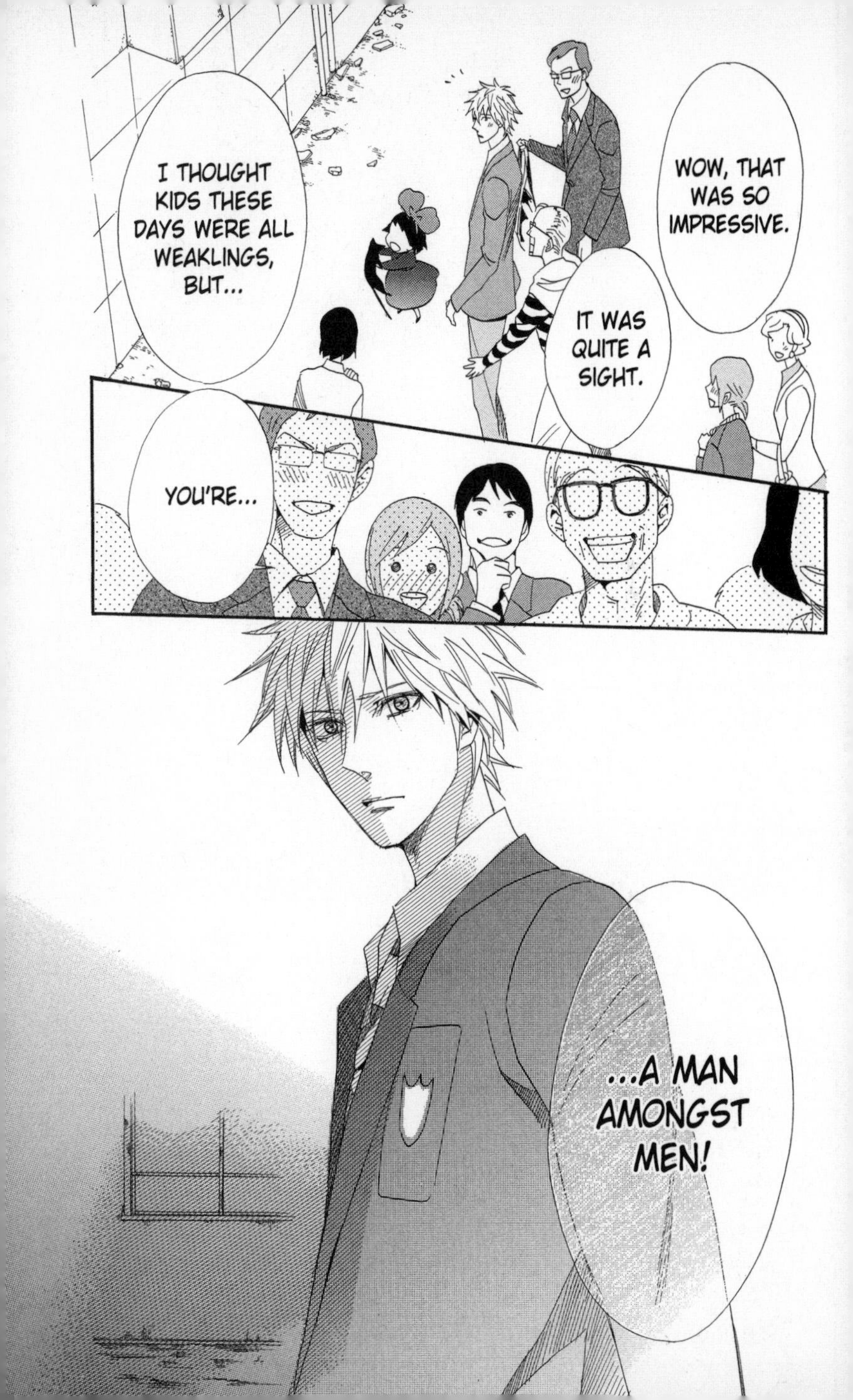
WOW, THAT WAS SO IMPRESSIVE.
IT WAS QUITE A SIGHT.
I THOUGHT KIDS THESE DAYS WERE ALL WEAKLINGS, BUT...
YOU'RE...
...A MAN AMONGST MEN!

OTOMEN

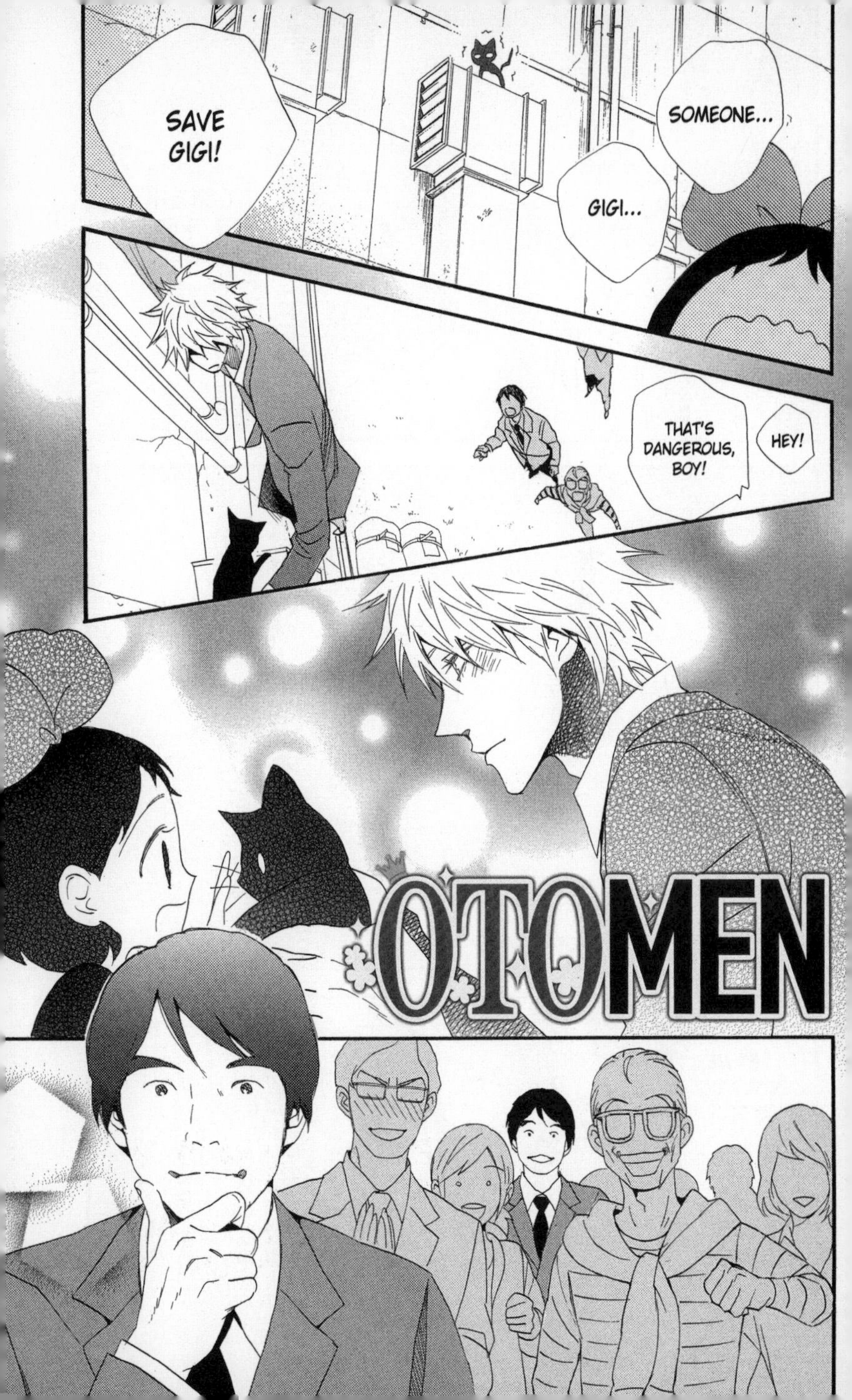
SOMEONE...
GIGI...
SAVE GIGI!
HEY!
THAT'S DANGEROUS, BOY!
OTOMEN

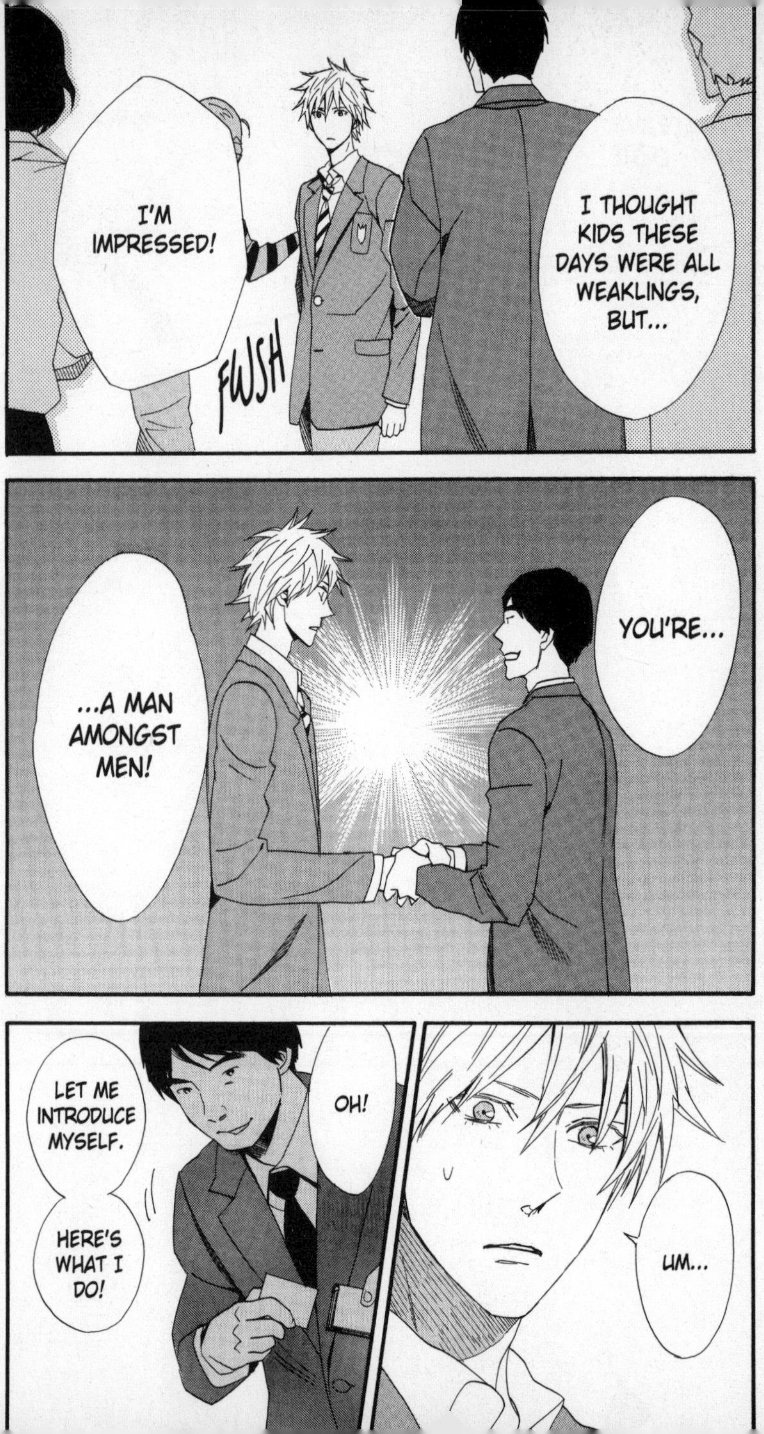
I THOUGHT KIDS THESE DAYS WERE ALL WEAKLINGS, BUT...
I'M IMPRESSED!
FWSH
YOU'RE...
...A MAN AMONGST MEN!
UM...
OH!
LET ME INTRODUCE MYSELF.
HERE'S WHAT I DO!

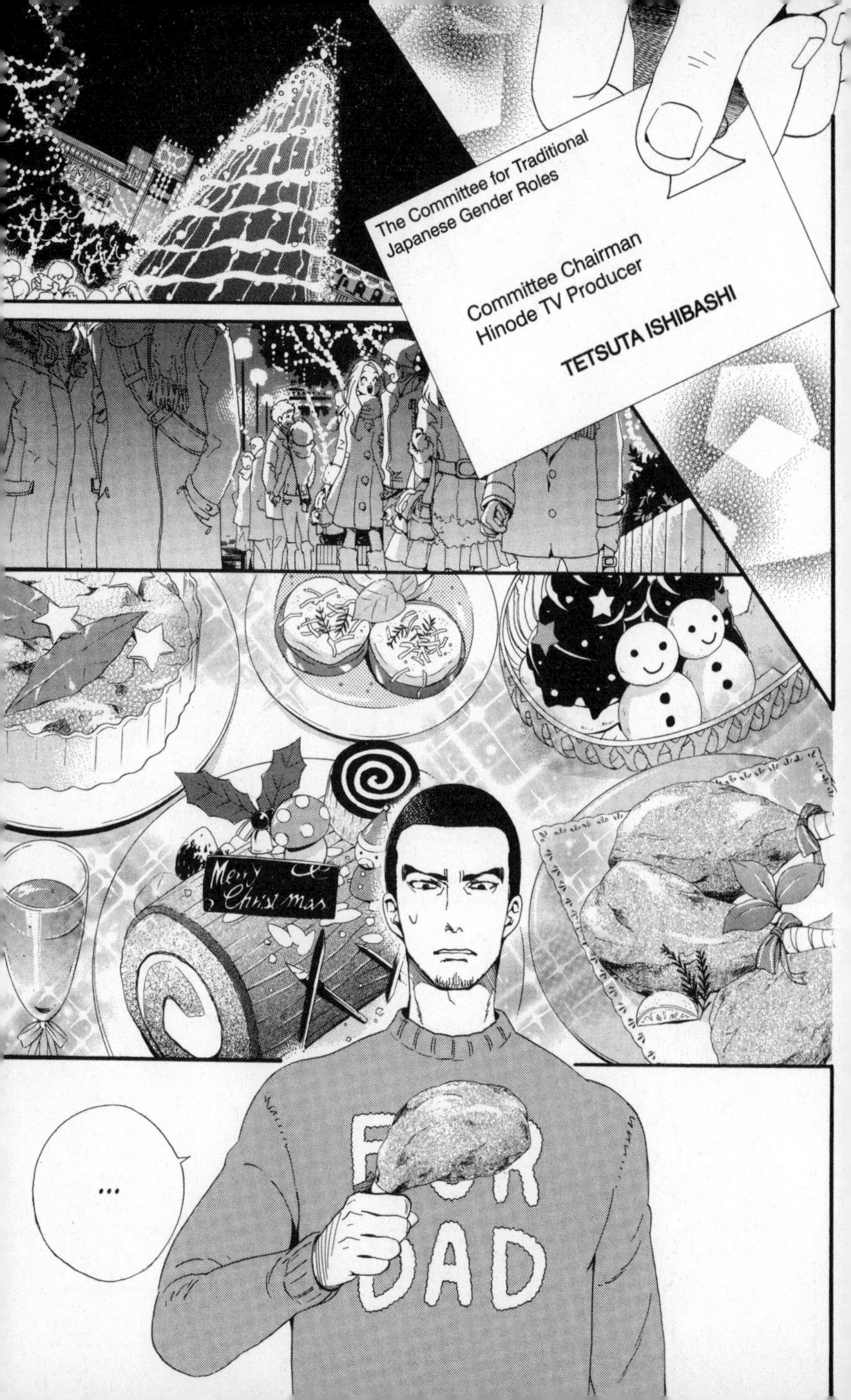
The Committee for Traditional Japanese Gender Roles
Committee Chairman
Hinode TV Producer
TETSUTA ISHIBASHI
Merry Christmas
...
FOR DAD

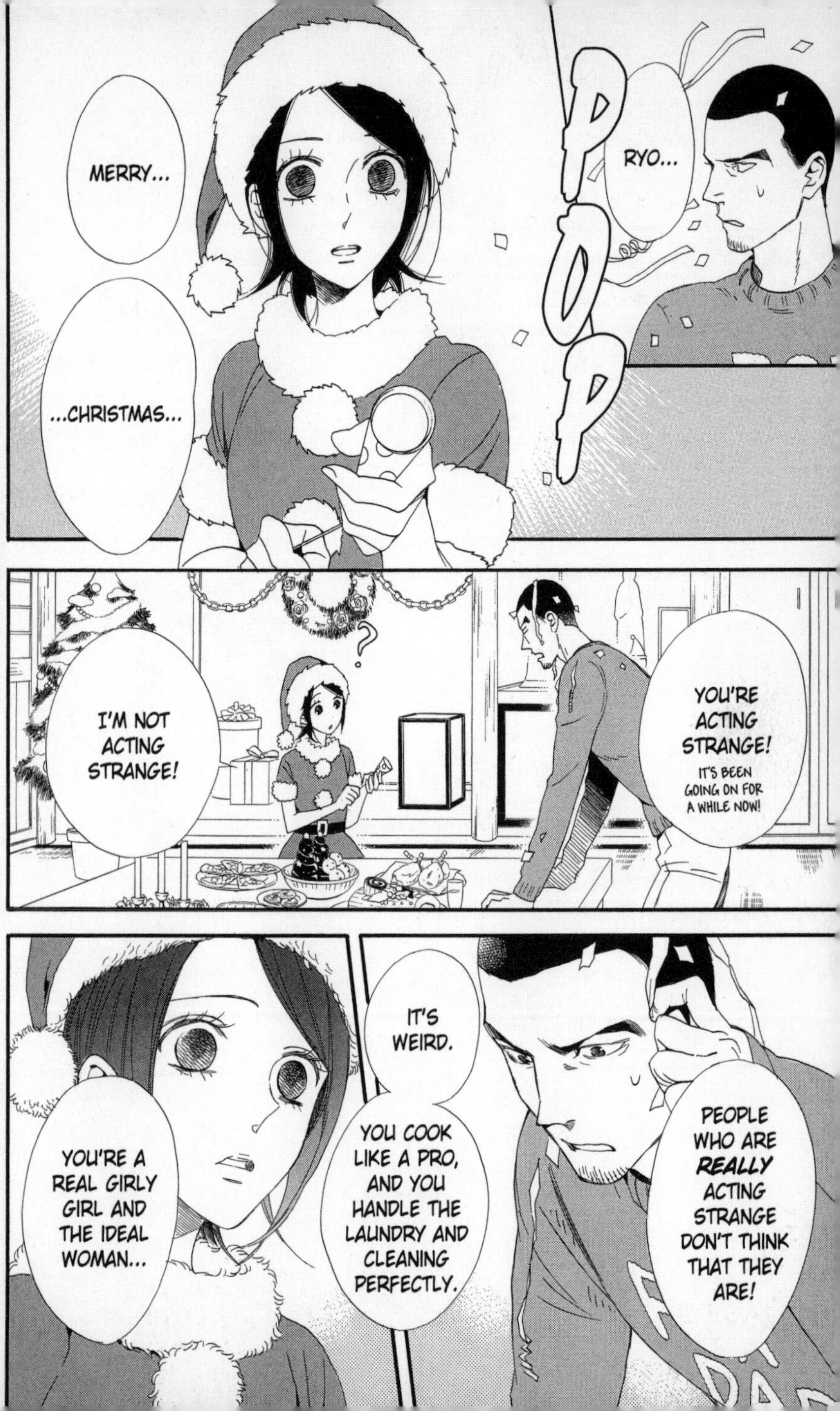
POP
RYO...
MERRY...
...CHRISTMAS...
YOU'RE ACTING STRANGE!
IT'S BEEN GOING ON FOR A WHILE NOW!
I'M NOT ACTING STRANGE!
PEOPLE WHO ARE REALLY ACTING STRANGE DON'T THINK THAT THEY ARE!
IT'S WEIRD.
YOU COOK LIKE A PRO, AND YOU HANDLE THE LAUNDRY AND CLEANING PERFECTLY.
YOU'RE A REAL GIRLY GIRL AND THE IDEAL WOMAN...

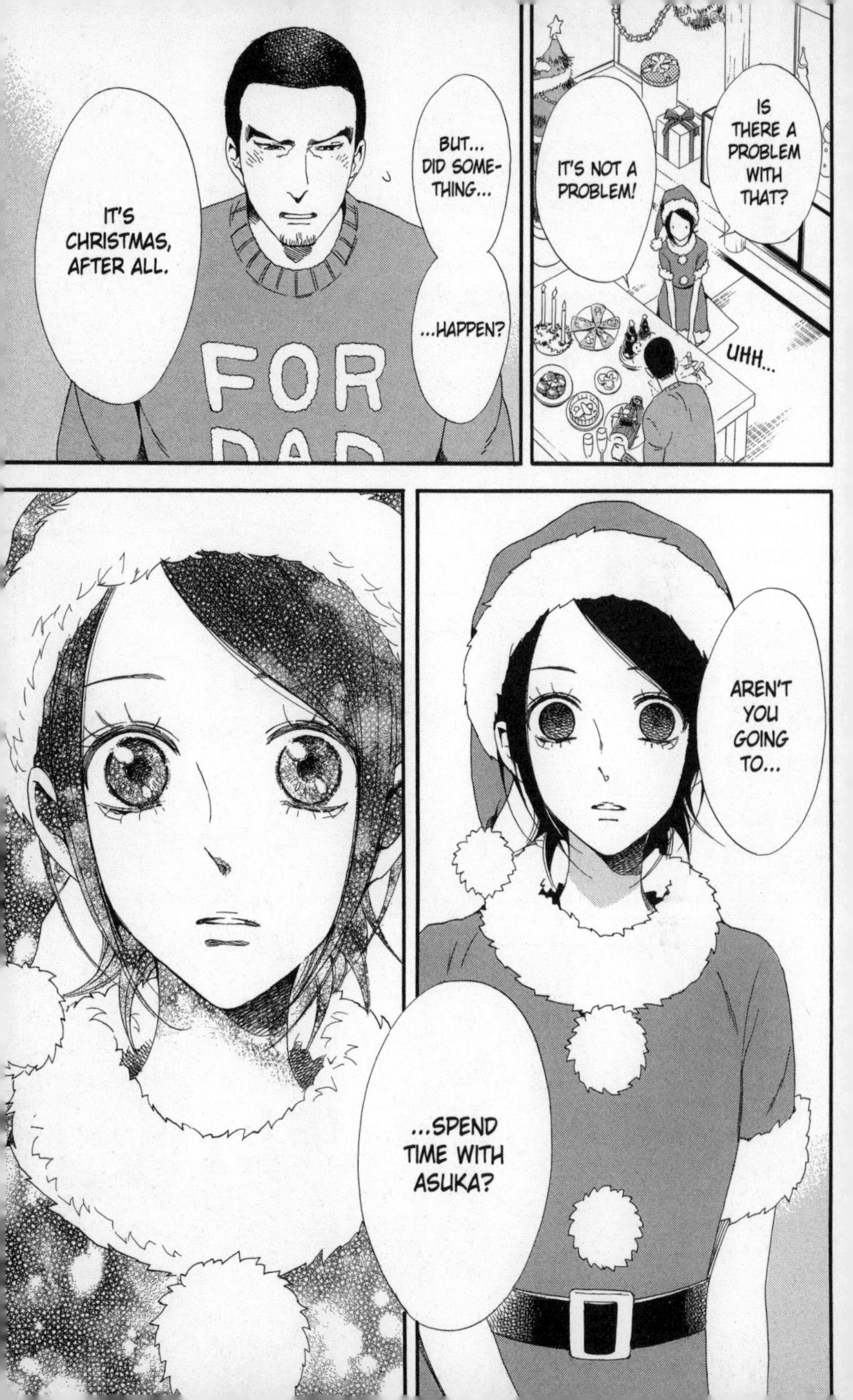
IS THERE A PROBLEM WITH THAT?
IT'S NOT A PROBLEM!
UHH...
BUT... DID SOME-THING...
...HAPPEN?
IT'S CHRISTMAS, AFTER ALL.
FOR
AREN'T YOU GOING TO...
...SPEND TIME WITH ASUKA?

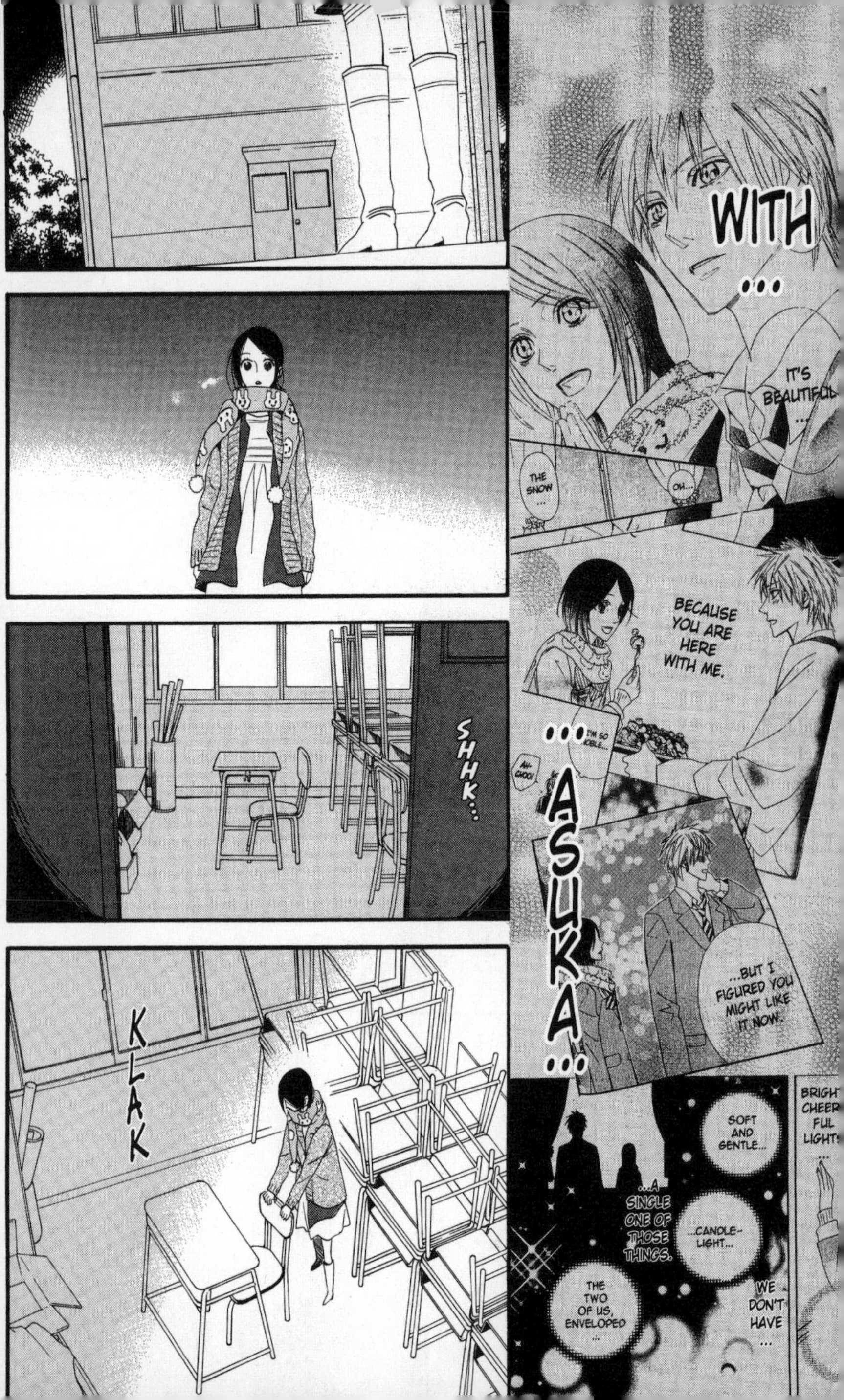
WITH ...
IT'S BEAUTIFUL ...
OH...
THE SNOW ...
BECAUSE YOU ARE HERE WITH ME.
... ASUKA...
AH-CHOO!
...BUT I FIGURED YOU MIGHT LIKE IT NOW.
BRIGHT CHEERFUL LIGHTS ...
SOFT AND GENTLE...
...CANDLE-LIGHT...
THE TWO OF US, ENVELOPED ...
WE DON'T HAVE ...
...A SINGLE ONE OF THOSE THINGS.
SHHK...
KLAK

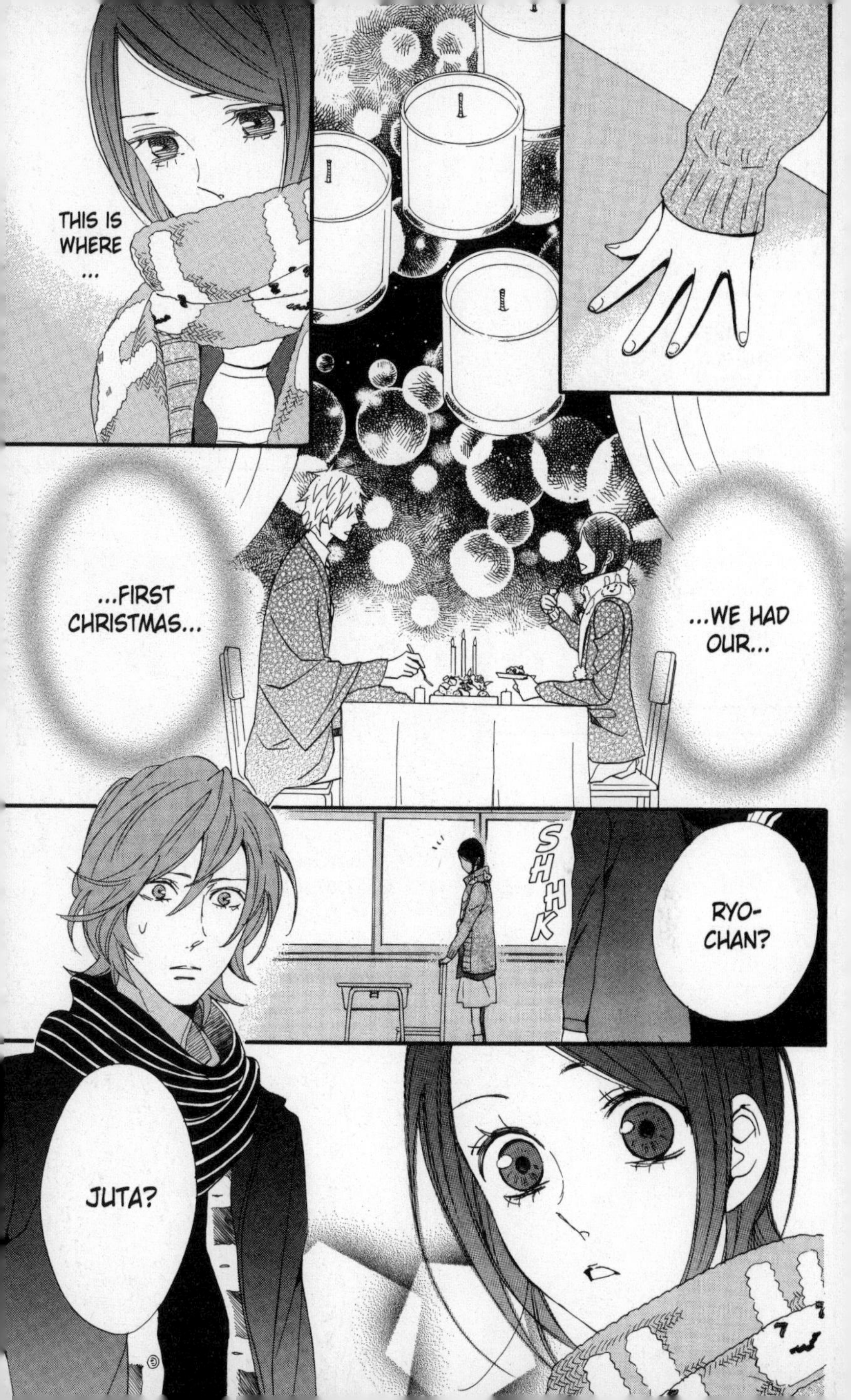
THIS IS WHERE ...
...WE HAD OUR...
...FIRST CHRISTMAS...
RYO-CHAN?
SHHK
JUTA?

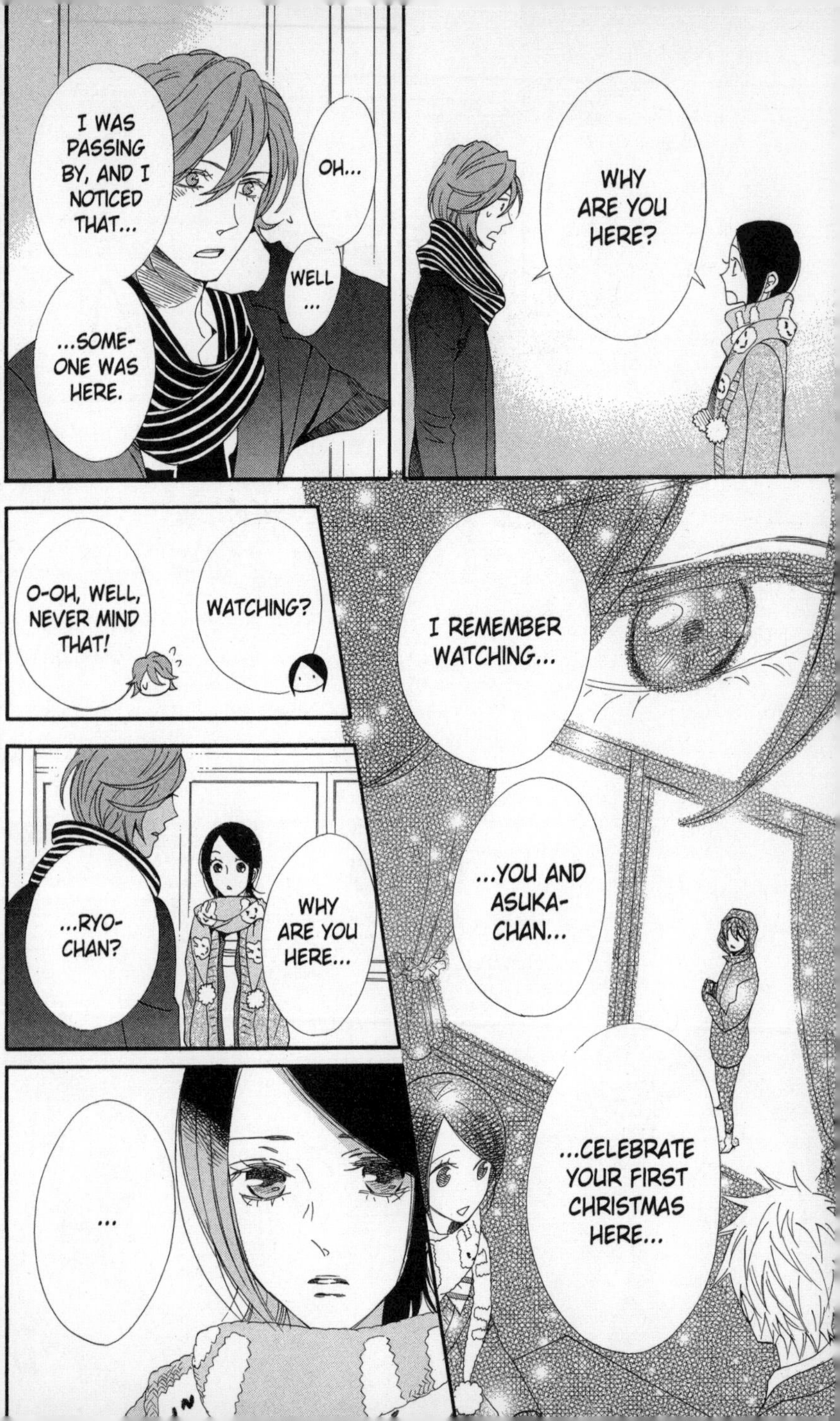
WHY ARE YOU HERE?
OH...
WELL...
I WAS PASSING BY, AND I NOTICED THAT...
...SOME-ONE WAS HERE.
I REMEMBER WATCHING...
...YOU AND ASUKA-CHAN...
...CELEBRATE YOUR FIRST CHRISTMAS HERE...
WATCHING?
O-OH, WELL, NEVER MIND THAT!
WHY ARE YOU HERE...
...RYO-CHAN?
...

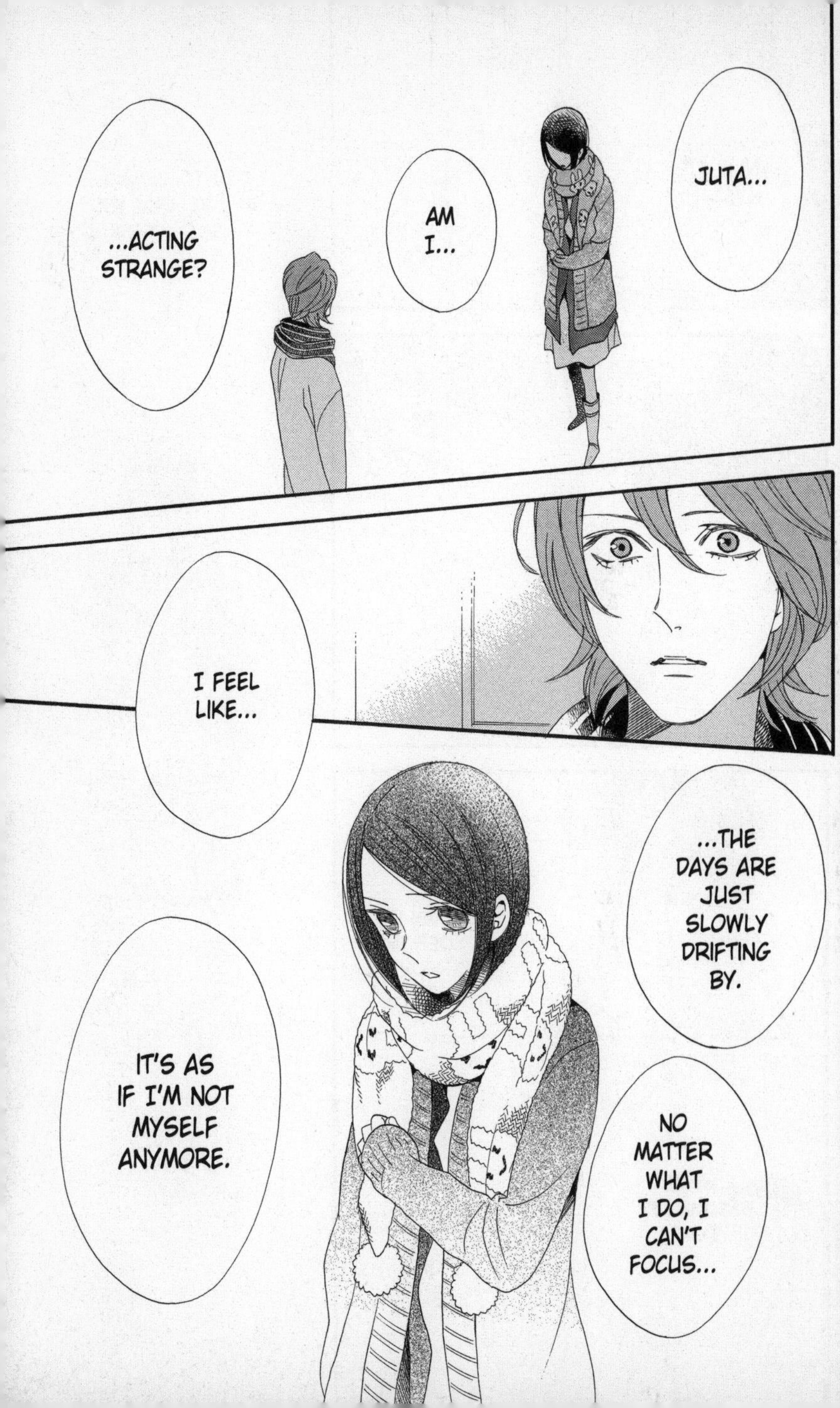
JUTA...
AM I...
...ACTING STRANGE?
I FEEL LIKE...
...THE DAYS ARE JUST SLOWLY DRIFTING BY.
NO MATTER WHAT I DO, I CAN'T FOCUS...
IT'S AS IF I'M NOT MYSELF ANYMORE.

JUTA,
DO YOU
THINK...

NOT AT
ALL.

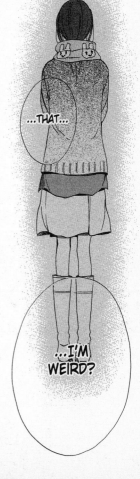

...THAT...

...I'M
WEIRD?

YOU'RE
NOT
WEIRD.

WHEN WE
LOSE THE
PERSON WE
LOVE...

...WE ALL
BECOME LIKE
THAT.

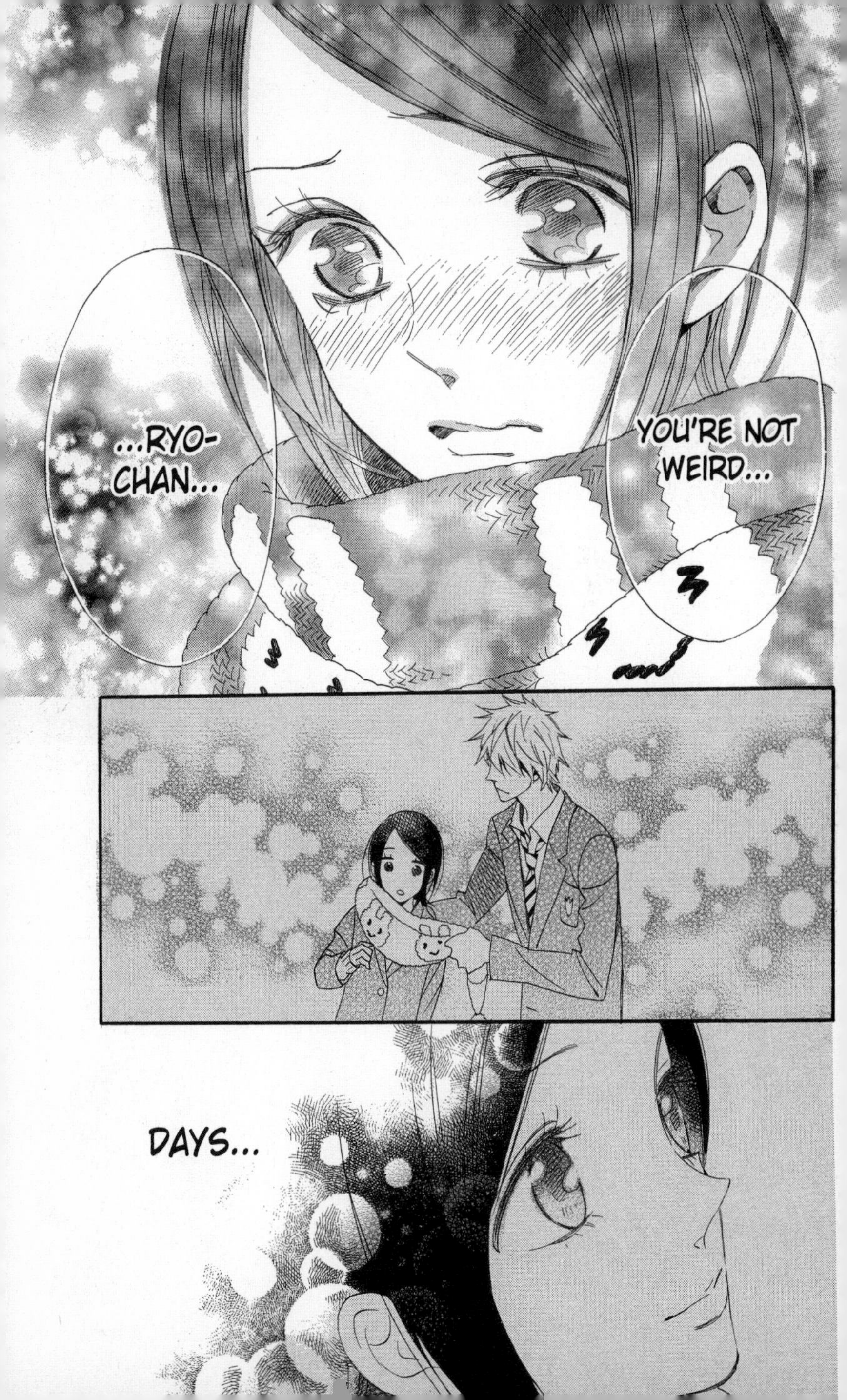
YOU'RE NOT WEIRD...
...RYO-CHAN...
DAYS...

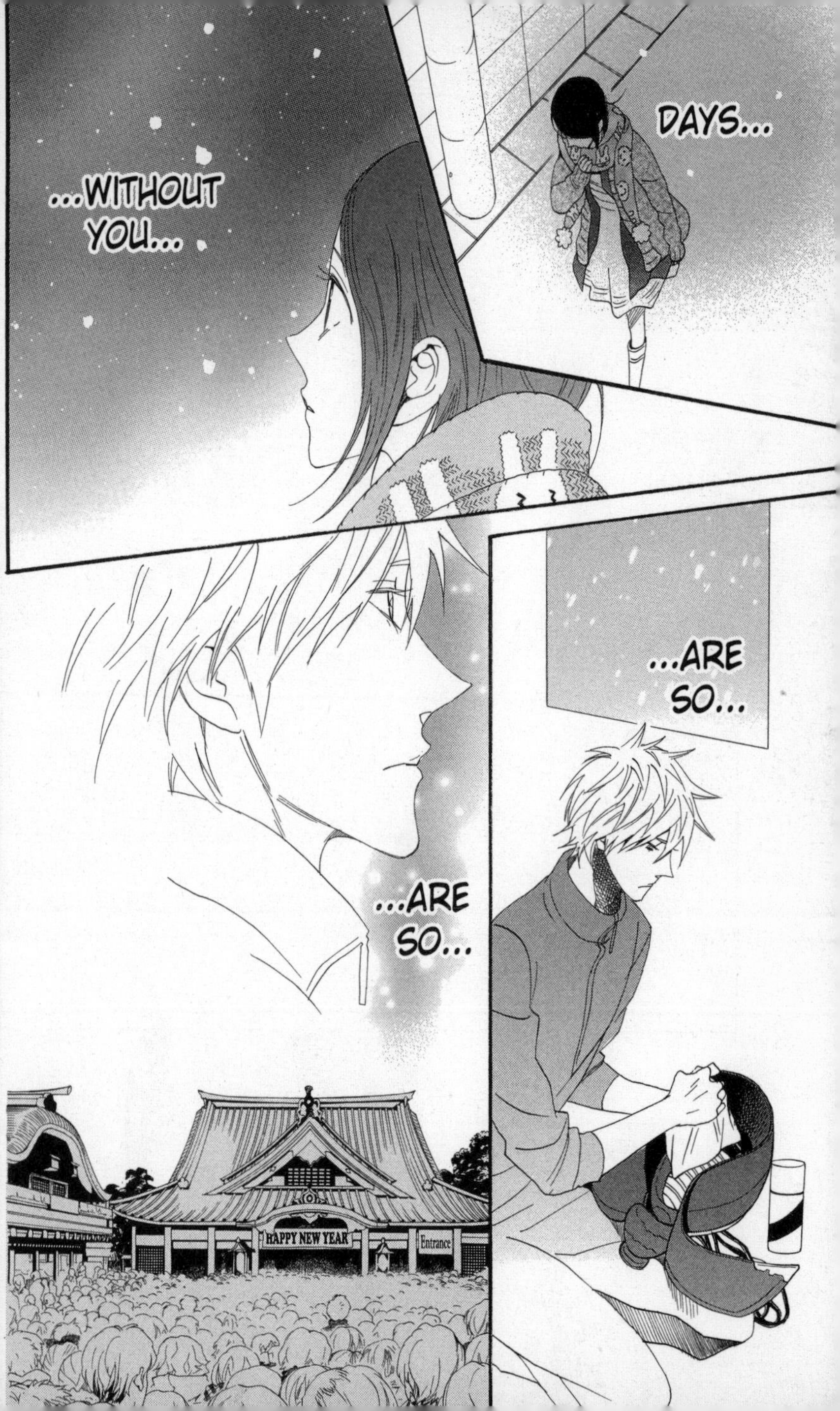
DAYS...
...WITHOUT YOU...
...ARE SO...
...ARE SO...
HAPPY NEW YEAR
Entrance

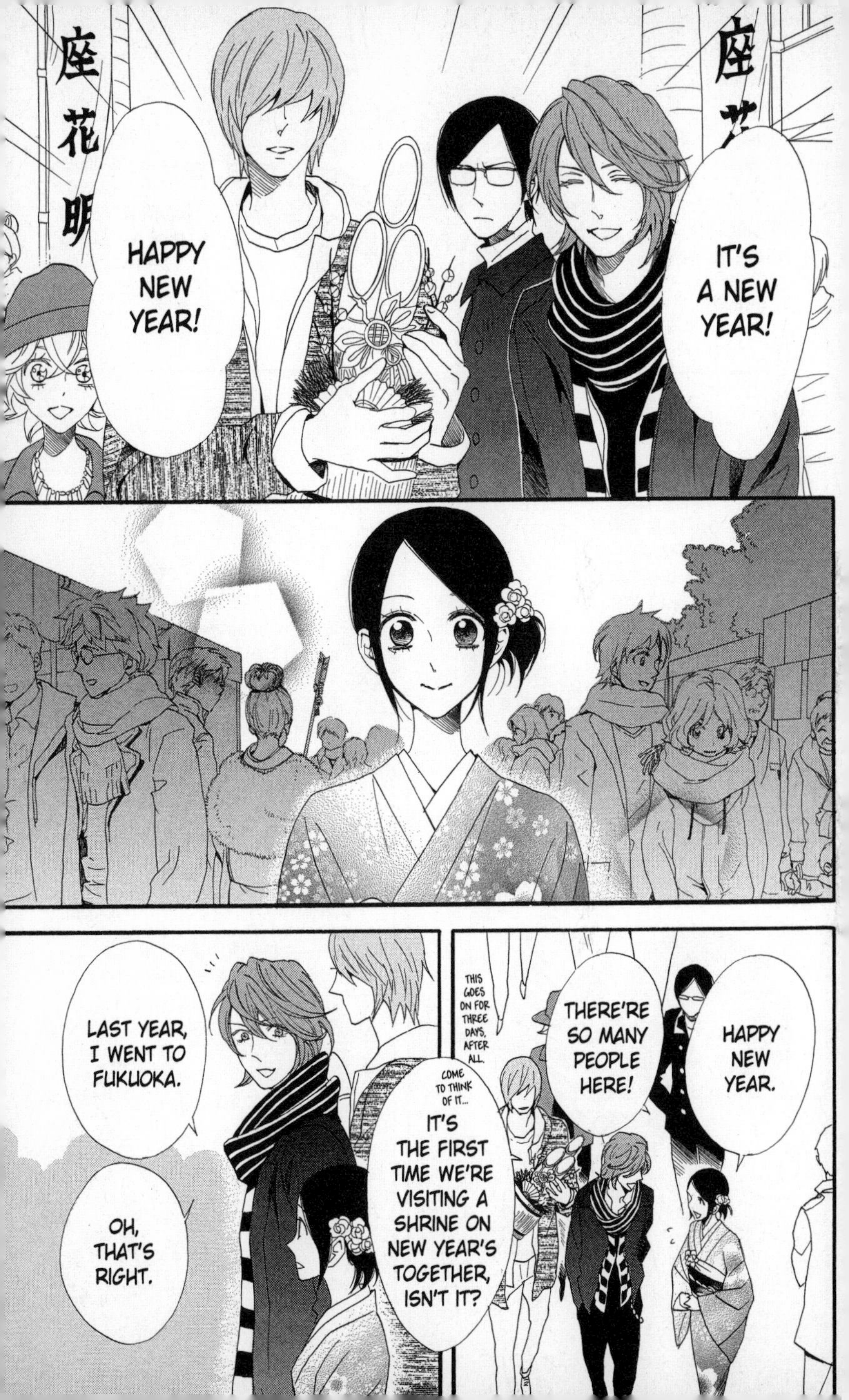
座
IT'S A NEW YEAR!
座花明
HAPPY NEW YEAR!
HAPPY NEW YEAR.
THERE'RE SO MANY PEOPLE HERE!
THIS GOES ON FOR THREE DAYS, AFTER ALL.
COME TO THINK OF IT...
IT'S THE FIRST TIME WE'RE VISITING A SHRINE ON NEW YEAR'S TOGETHER, ISN'T IT?
LAST YEAR, I WENT TO FUKUOKA.
OH, THAT'S RIGHT.

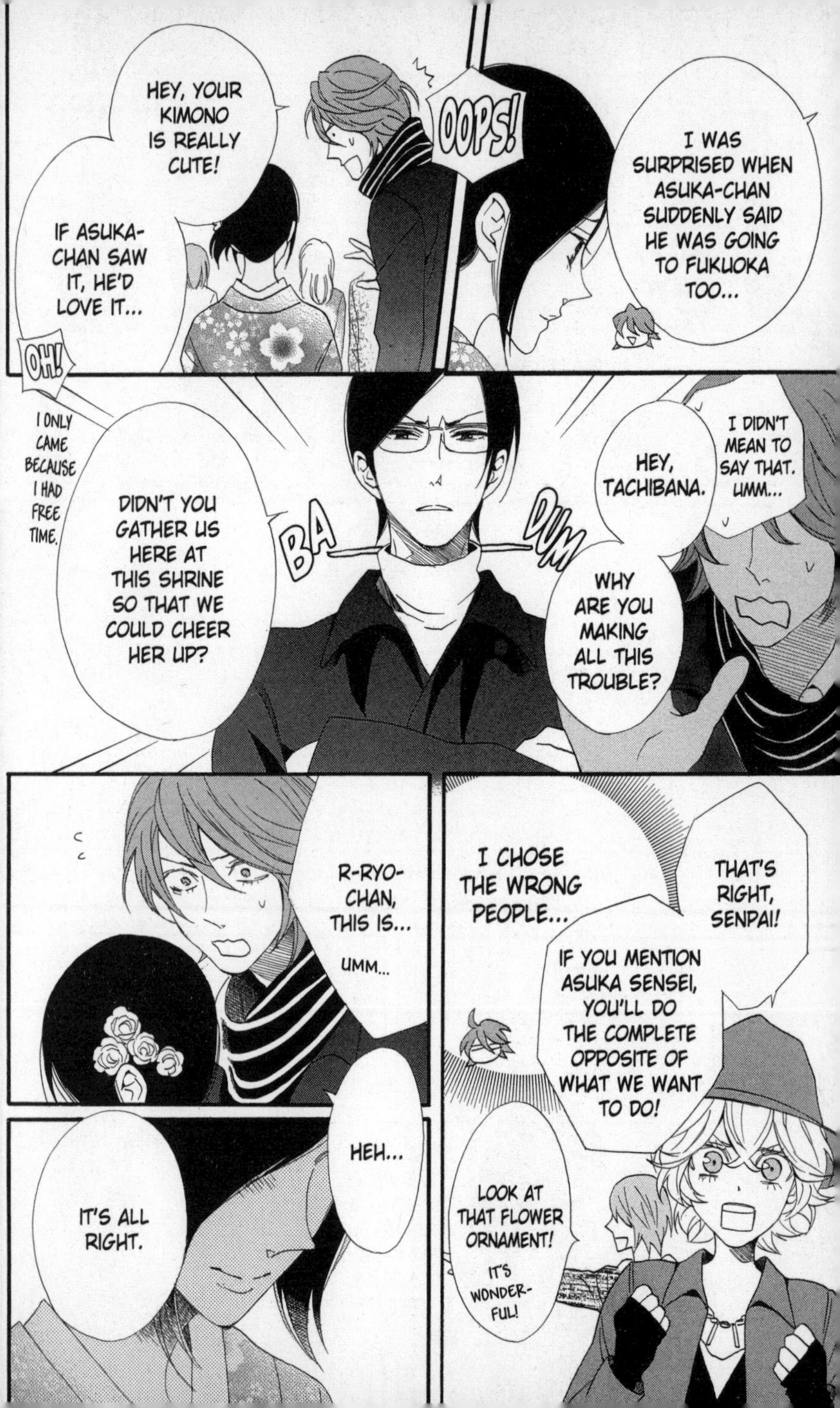
I WAS SURPRISED WHEN ASUKA-CHAN SUDDENLY SAID HE WAS GOING TO FUKUOKA TOO...
OOPS!
HEY, YOUR KIMONO IS REALLY CUTE!
IF ASUKA-CHAN SAW IT, HE'D LOVE IT...
OH!
I DIDN'T MEAN TO SAY THAT. UMM...
HEY, TACHIBANA.
WHY ARE YOU MAKING ALL THIS TROUBLE?
BA DUM
DIDN'T YOU GATHER US HERE AT THIS SHRINE SO THAT WE COULD CHEER HER UP?
I ONLY CAME BECAUSE I HAD FREE TIME.
THAT'S RIGHT, SENPAI!
I CHOSE THE WRONG PEOPLE...
IF YOU MENTION ASUKA SENSEI, YOU'LL DO THE COMPLETE OPPOSITE OF WHAT WE WANT TO DO!
LOOK AT THAT FLOWER ORNAMENT!
IT'S WONDERFUL!
R-RYO-CHAN, THIS IS...
UMM...
HEH...
IT'S ALL RIGHT.

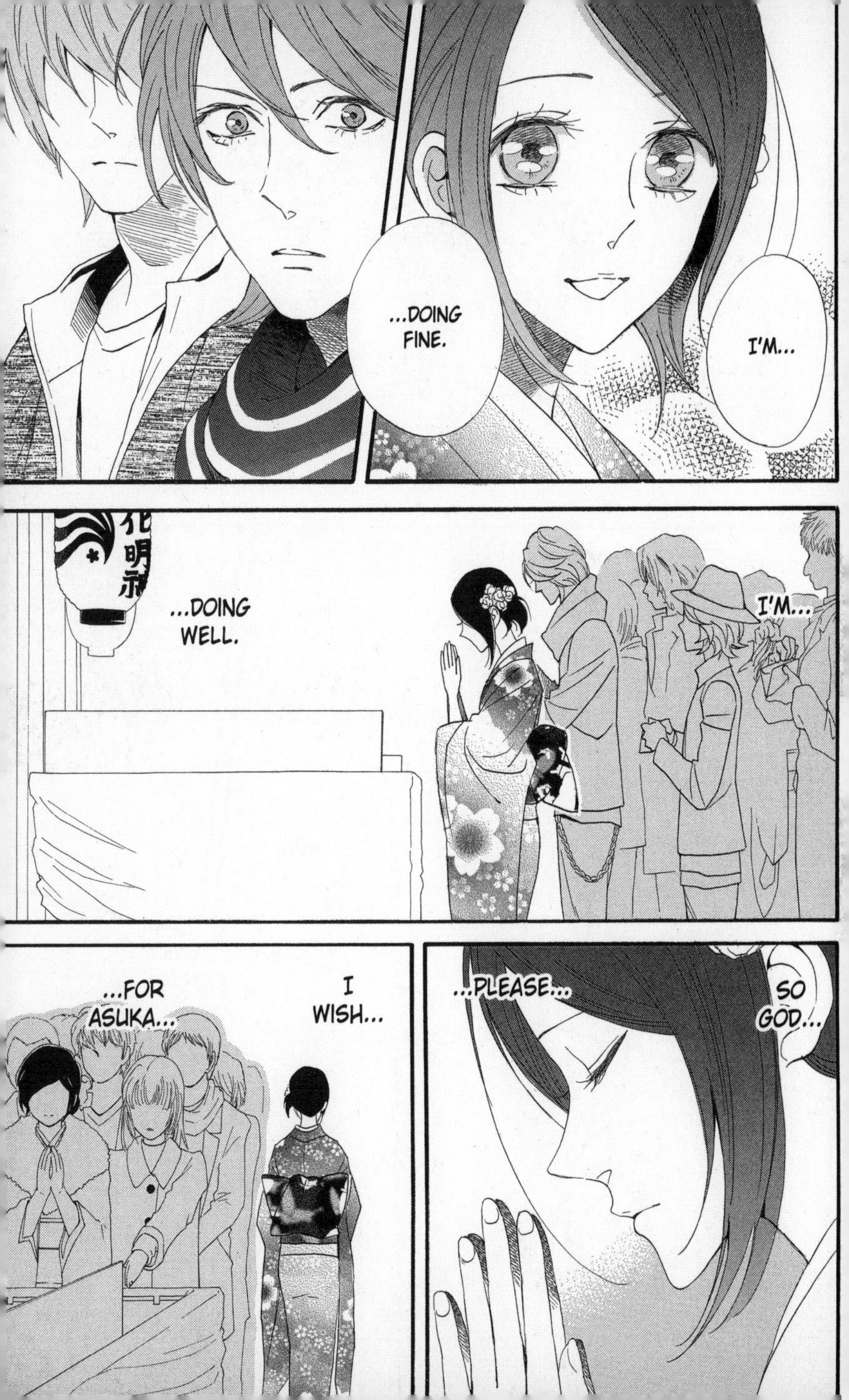
I'M...
...DOING FINE.
I'M...
...DOING WELL.
SO GOD...
...PLEASE...
I WISH...
...FOR ASUKA...

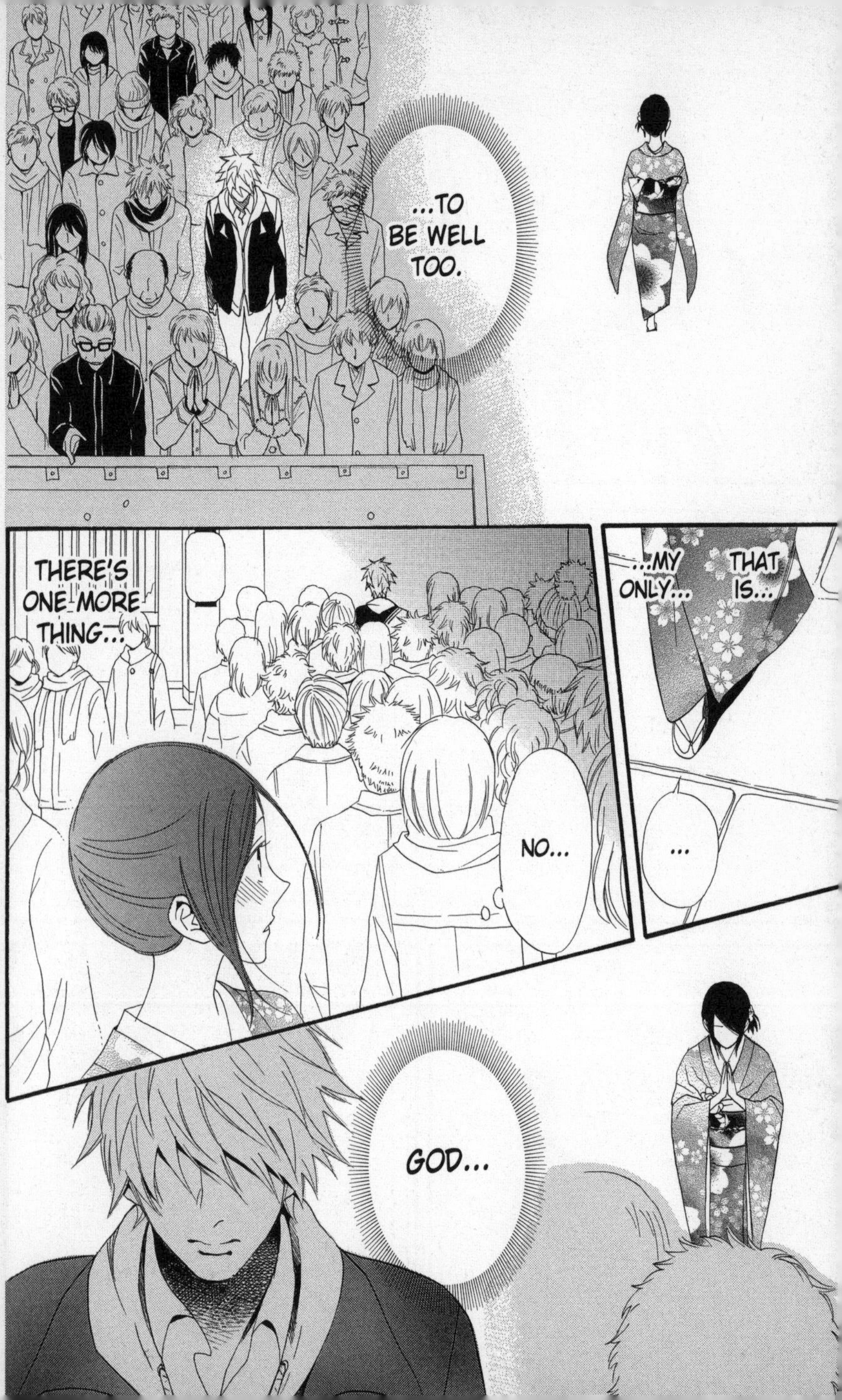
...TO BE WELL TOO.
THAT IS...
...MY ONLY...
...
THERE'S ONE MORE THING...
NO...
GOD...

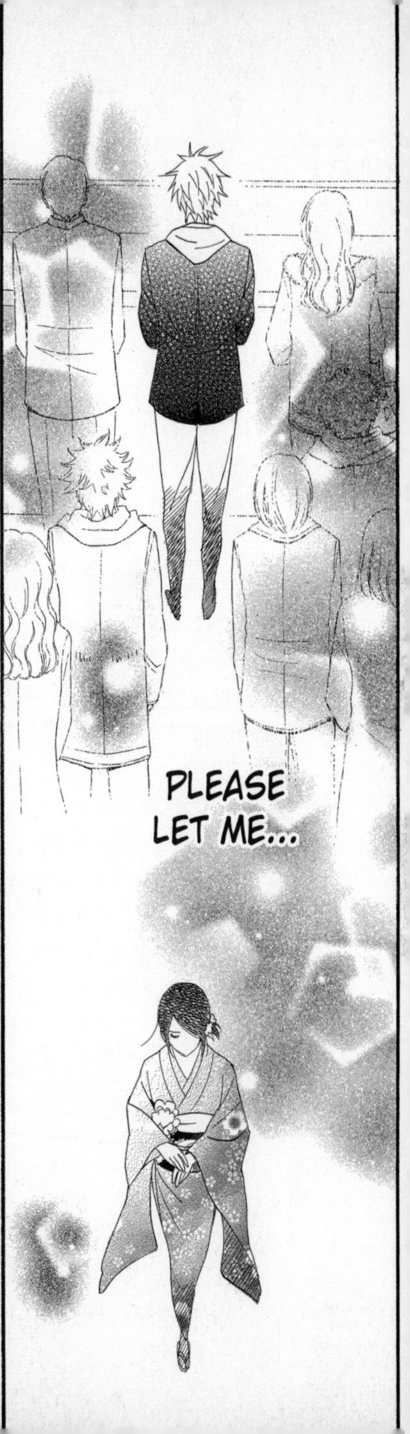
PLEASE LET ME...

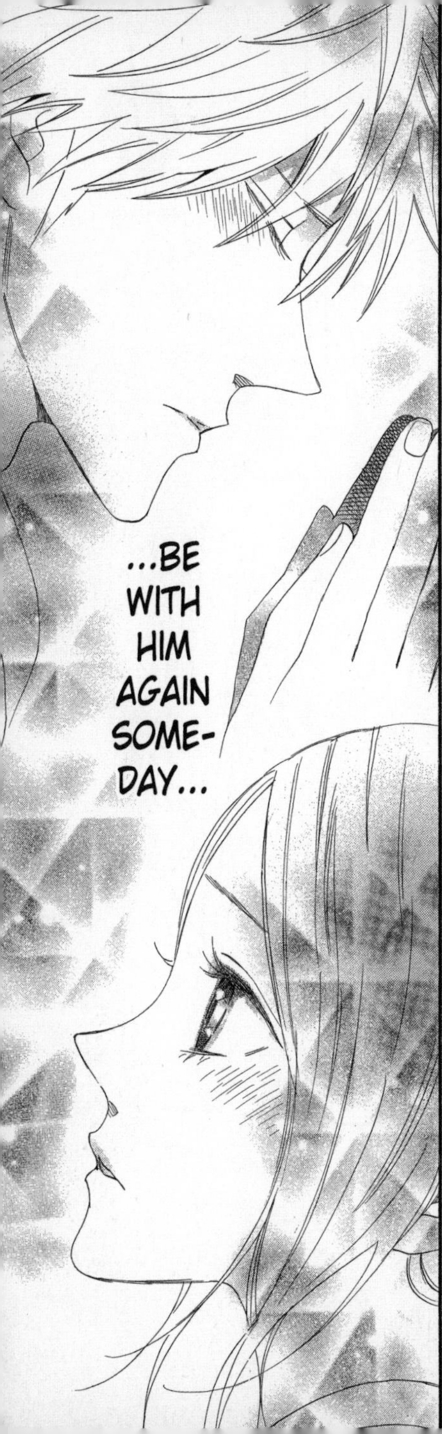
...BE WITH HIM AGAIN SOME-DAY...

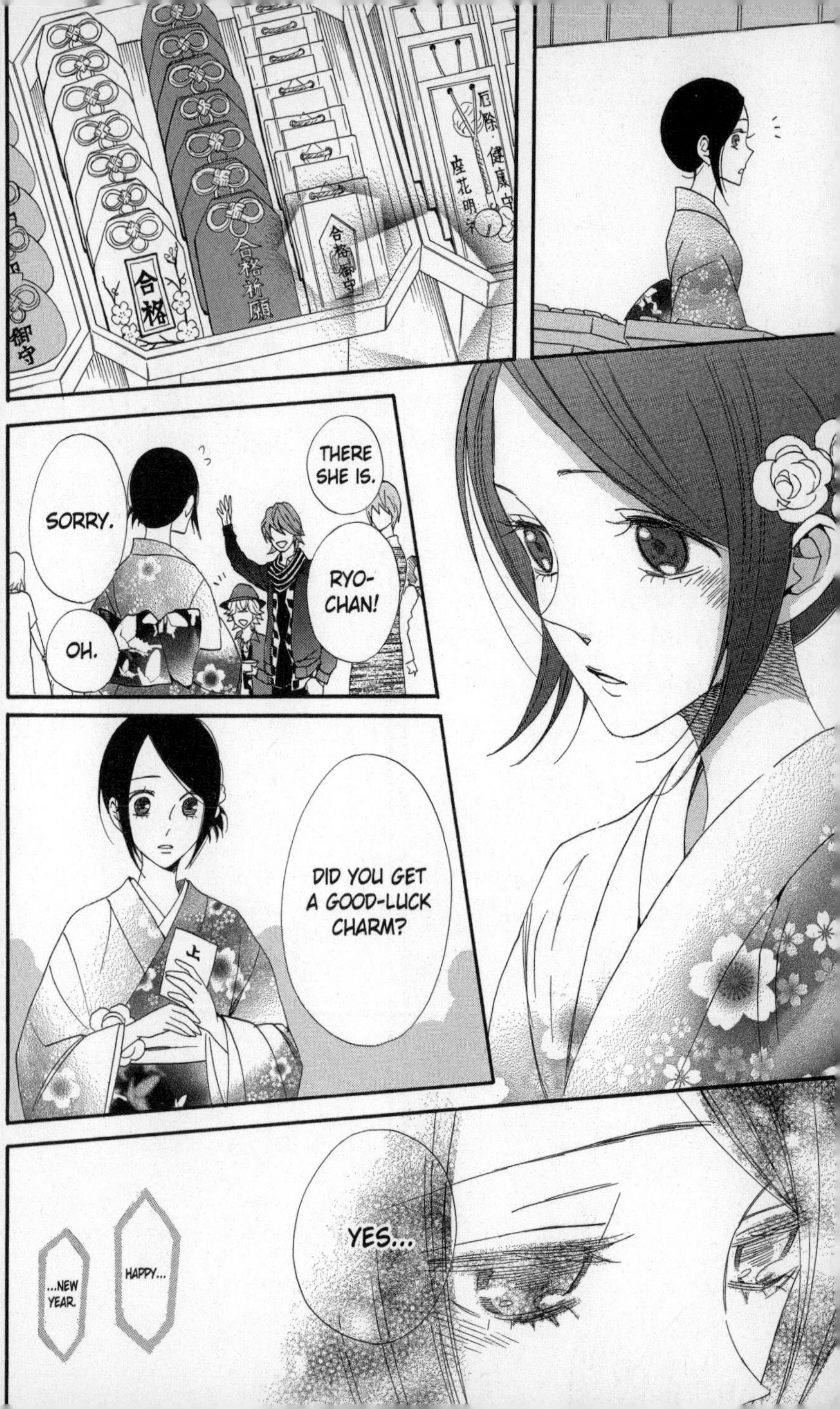
厄除・健康守
合格御守
合格祈願
合格
御守
THERE SHE IS.
RYO-CHAN!
SORRY.
OH.
DID YOU GET A GOOD-LUCK CHARM?
YES...
HAPPY...
...NEW YEAR.

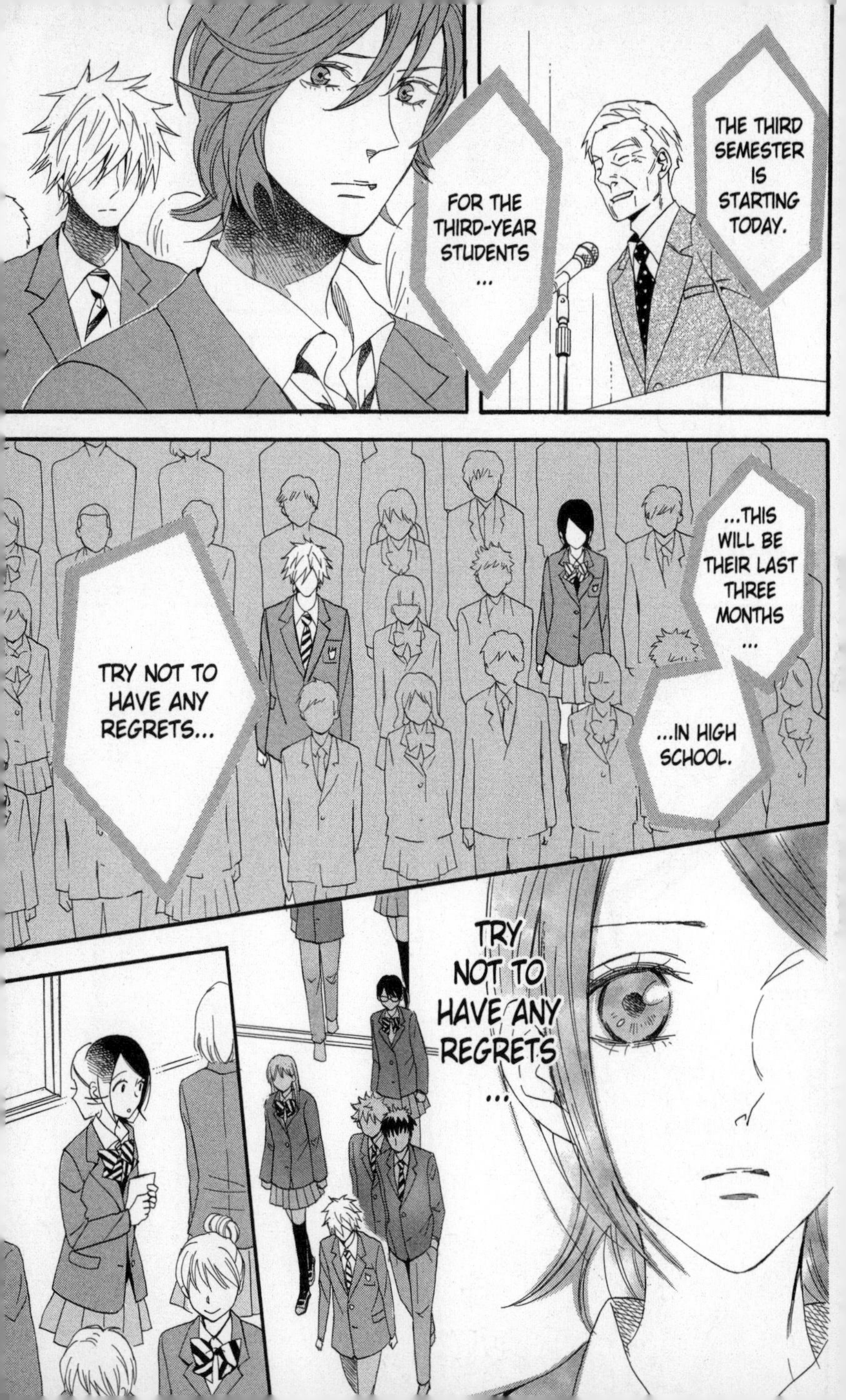
THE THIRD SEMESTER IS STARTING TODAY.
FOR THE THIRD-YEAR STUDENTS ...
...THIS WILL BE THEIR LAST THREE MONTHS ...
...IN HIGH SCHOOL.
TRY NOT TO HAVE ANY REGRETS...
TRY NOT TO HAVE ANY REGRETS ...

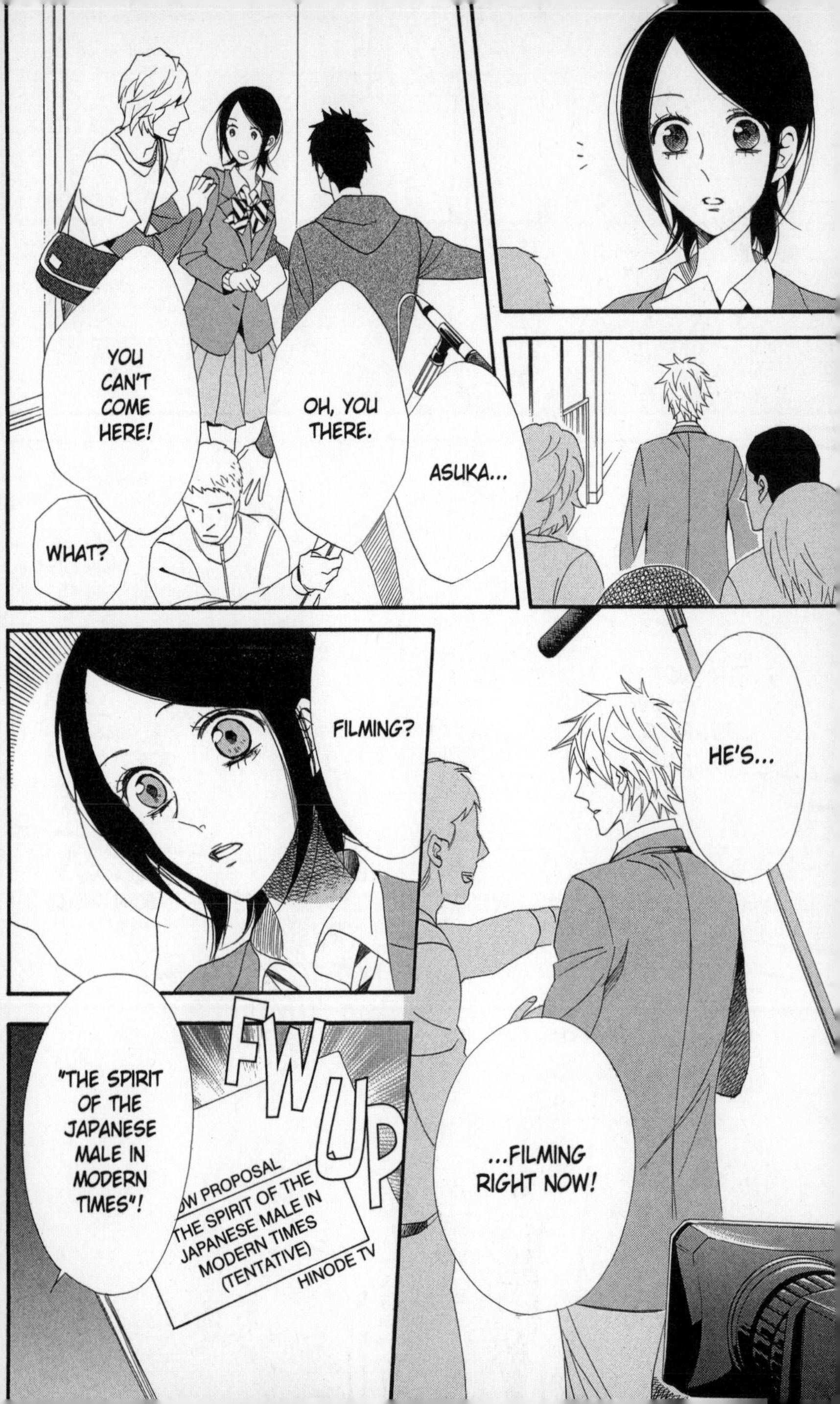
ASUKA...
OH, YOU THERE.
YOU CAN'T COME HERE!
WHAT?
HE'S...
...FILMING RIGHT NOW!
FILMING?
FWUP
"THE SPIRIT OF THE JAPANESE MALE IN MODERN TIMES"!
...OW PROPOSAL
THE SPIRIT OF THE JAPANESE MALE IN MODERN TIMES (TENTATIVE)
HINODE TV

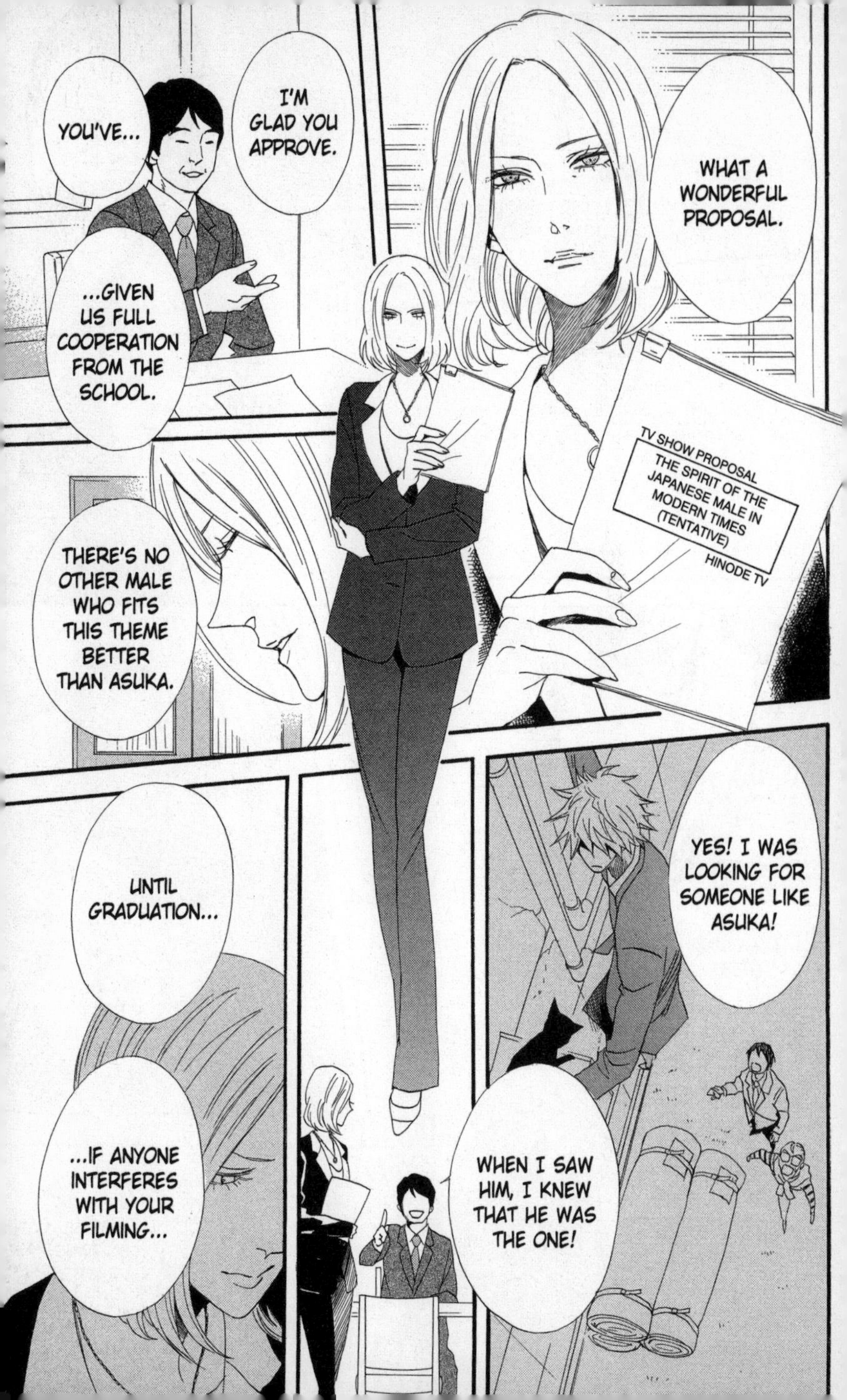
WHAT A WONDERFUL PROPOSAL.
I'M GLAD YOU APPROVE.
YOU'VE...
...GIVEN US FULL COOPERATION FROM THE SCHOOL.
TV SHOW PROPOSAL
THE SPIRIT OF THE JAPANESE MALE IN MODERN TIMES (TENTATIVE)
HINODE TV
THERE'S NO OTHER MALE WHO FITS THIS THEME BETTER THAN ASUKA.
YES! I WAS LOOKING FOR SOMEONE LIKE ASUKA!
WHEN I SAW HIM, I KNEW THAT HE WAS THE ONE!
UNTIL GRADUATION...
...IF ANYONE INTERFERES WITH YOUR FILMING...

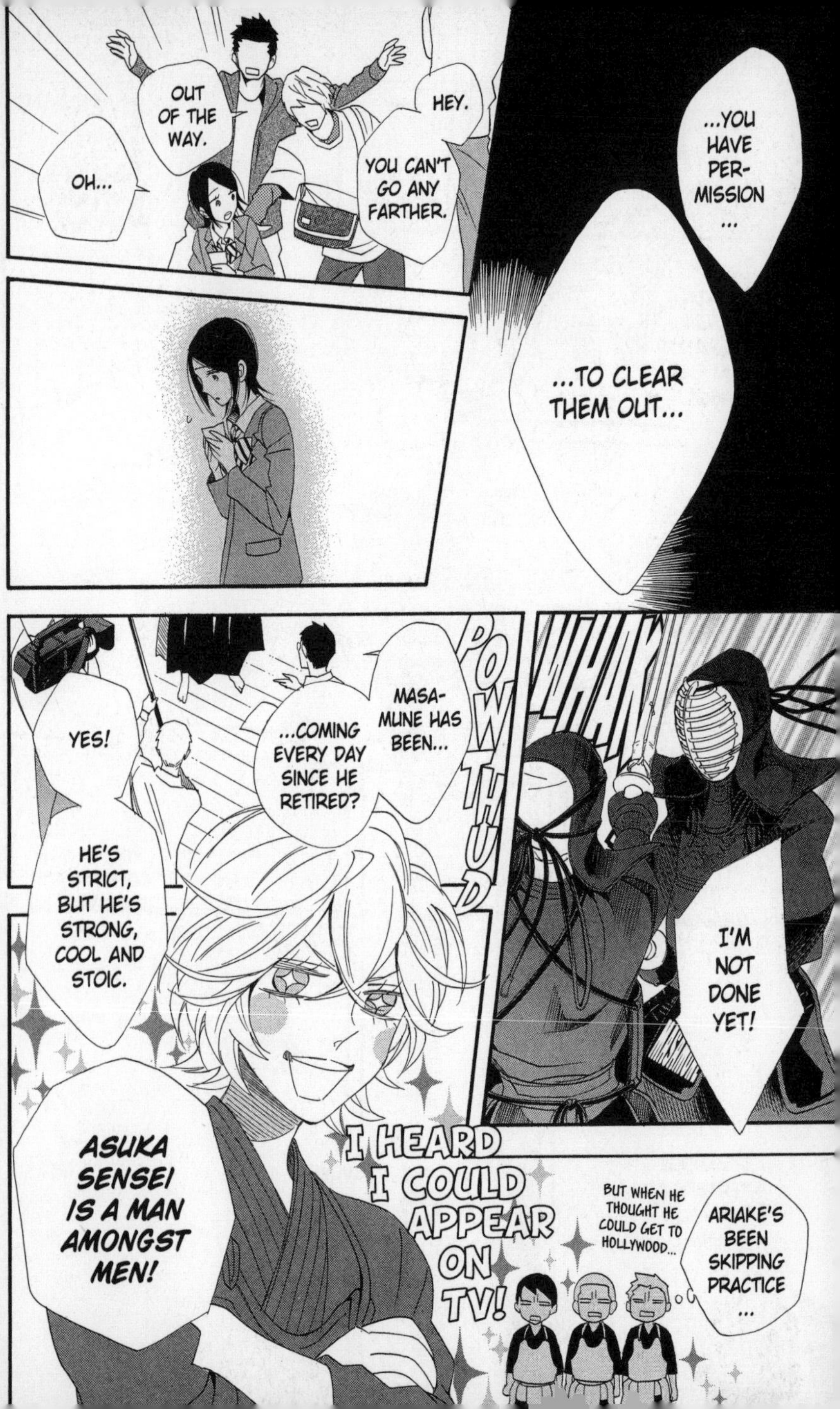
...YOU HAVE PER-MISSION ...
...TO CLEAR THEM OUT...
HEY.
YOU CAN'T GO ANY FARTHER.
OUT OF THE WAY.
OH...
POW
THUD
I'M NOT DONE YET!
MASA-MUNE HAS BEEN...
...COMING EVERY DAY SINCE HE RETIRED?
YES!
HE'S STRICT, BUT HE'S STRONG, COOL AND STOIC.
ARIAKE'S BEEN SKIPPING PRACTICE ...
BUT WHEN HE THOUGHT HE COULD GET TO HOLLYWOOD...
I HEARD I COULD APPEAR ON TV!
ASUKA SENSEI IS A MAN AMONGST MEN!

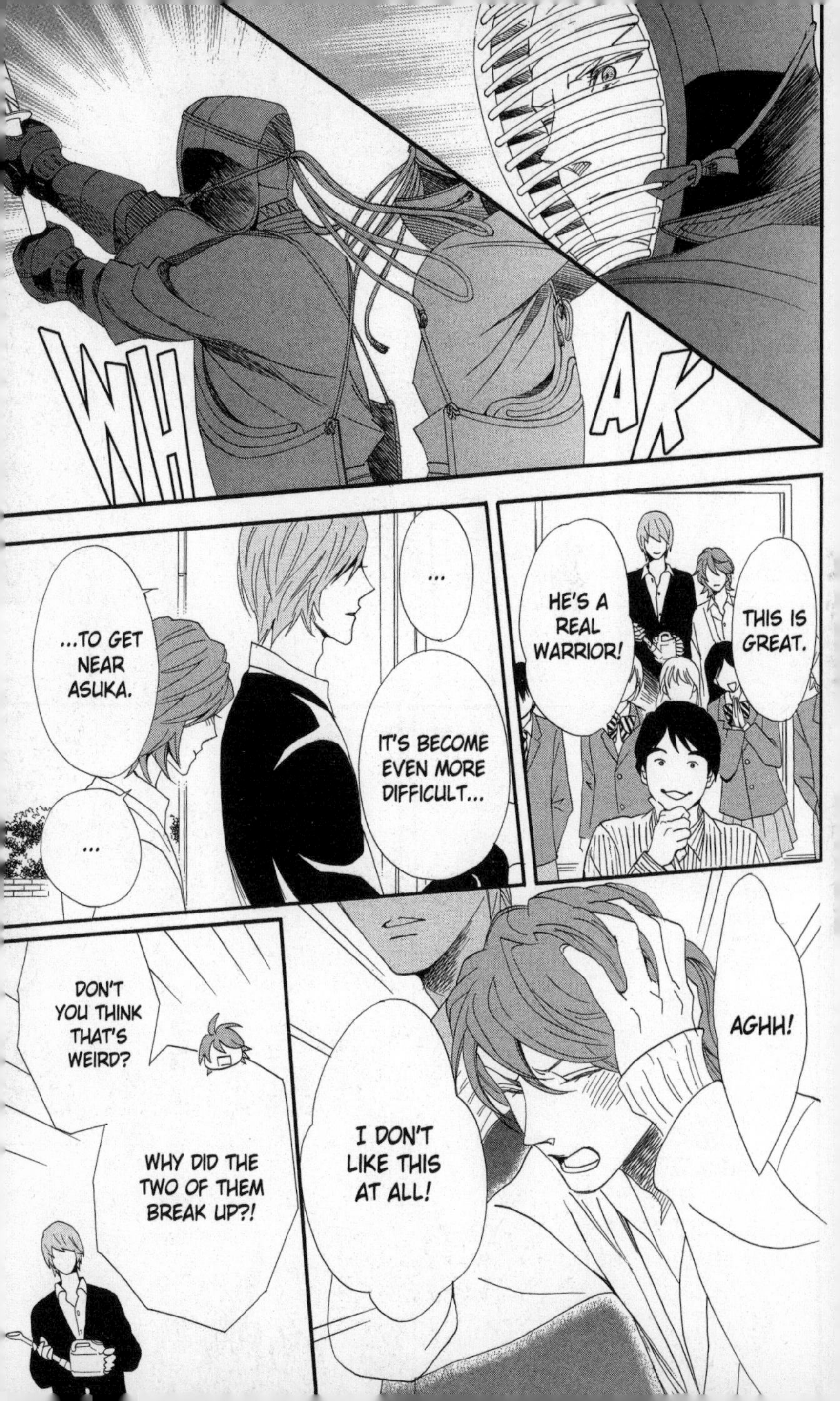
WHAK
THIS IS GREAT.
HE'S A REAL WARRIOR!
...
IT'S BECOME EVEN MORE DIFFICULT...
...TO GET NEAR ASUKA.
...
AGHH!
I DON'T LIKE THIS AT ALL!
DON'T YOU THINK THAT'S WEIRD?
WHY DID THE TWO OF THEM BREAK UP?!

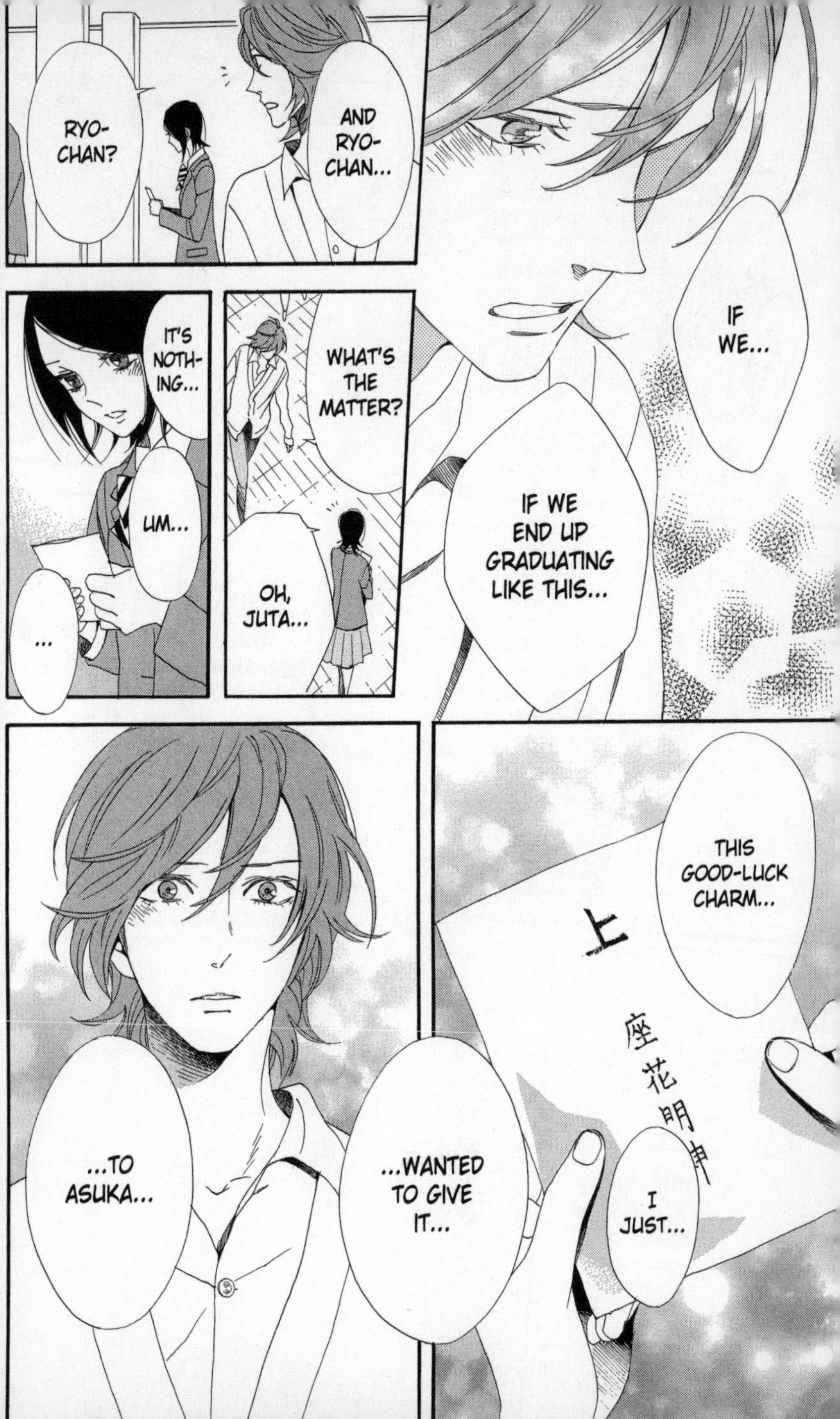
IF WE...
IF WE END UP GRADUATING LIKE THIS...
AND RYO-CHAN...
RYO-CHAN?
WHAT'S THE MATTER?
OH, JUTA...
IT'S NOTHING...
UM...
...
THIS GOOD-LUCK CHARM...
I JUST...
...WANTED TO GIVE IT...
...TO ASUKA...

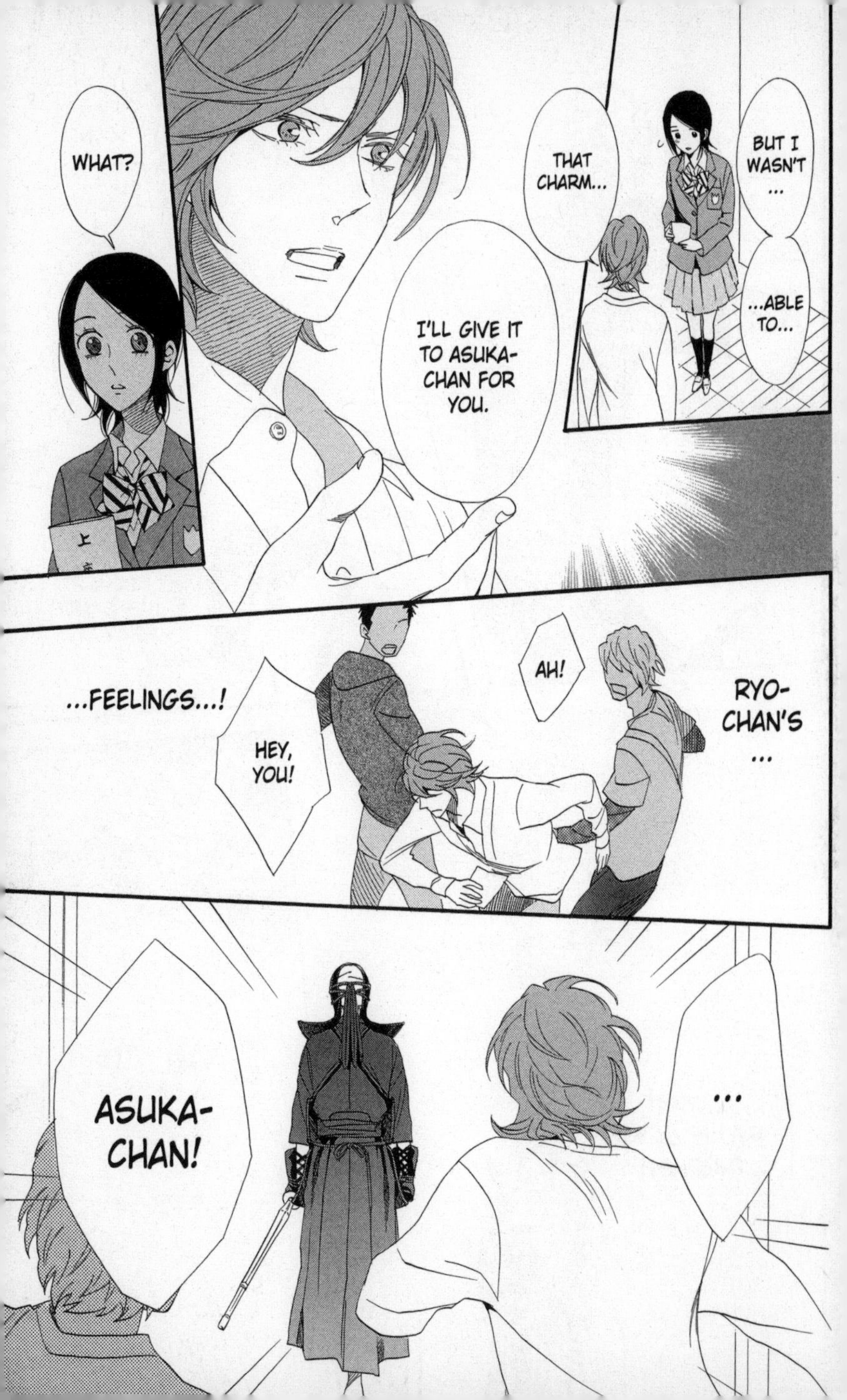

BUT I WASN'T ...
...ABLE TO...
THAT CHARM...
I'LL GIVE IT TO ASUKA-CHAN FOR YOU.
WHAT?
RYO-CHAN'S ...
AH!
HEY, YOU!
...FEELINGS...!
...
ASUKA-CHAN!

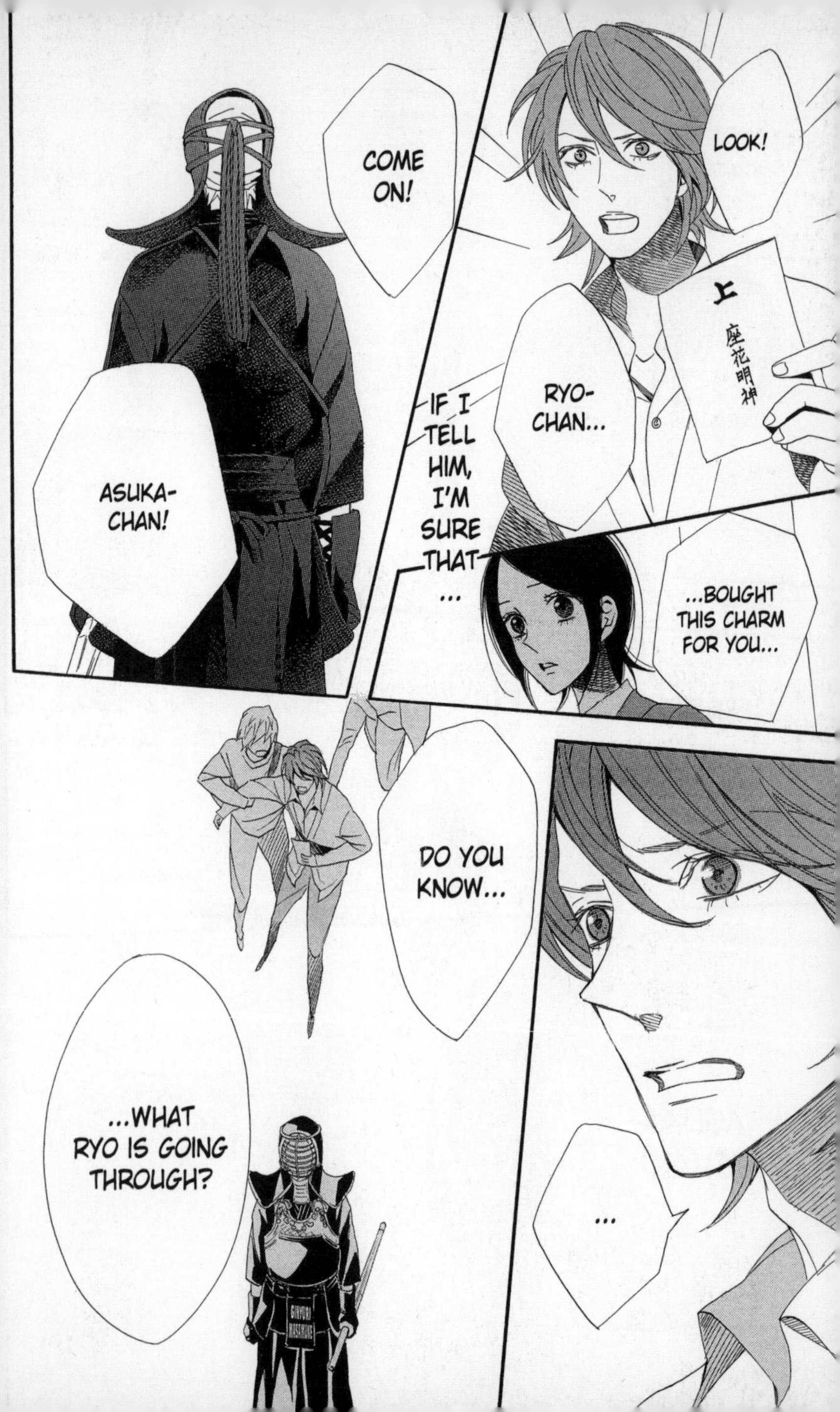
LOOK!
RYO-CHAN...
...BOUGHT THIS CHARM FOR YOU...
IF I TELL HIM, I'M SURE THAT...
COME ON!
ASUKA-CHAN!
...
DO YOU KNOW...
...WHAT RYO IS GOING THROUGH?

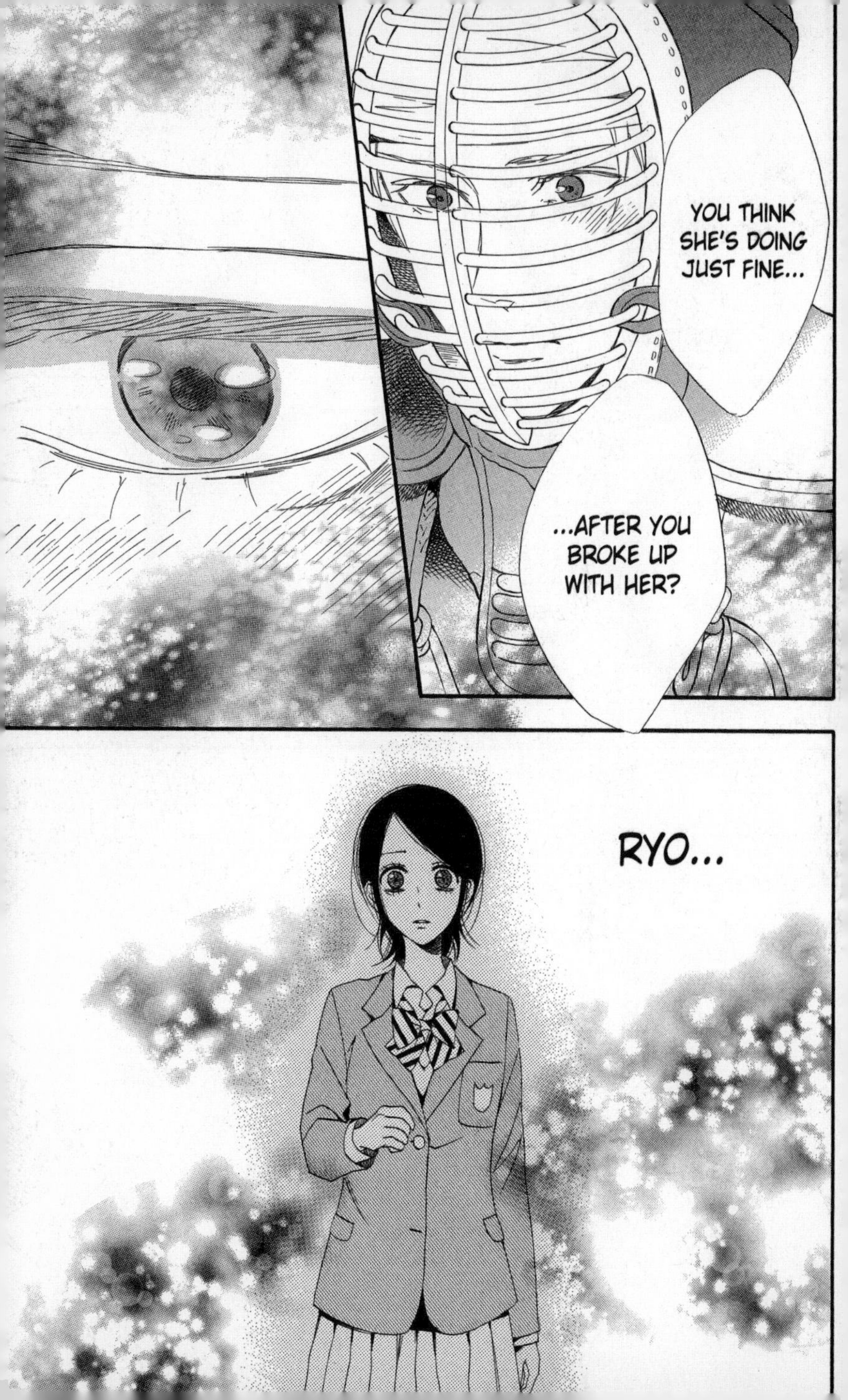
YOU THINK SHE'S DOING JUST FINE...
...AFTER YOU BROKE UP WITH HER?
RYO...

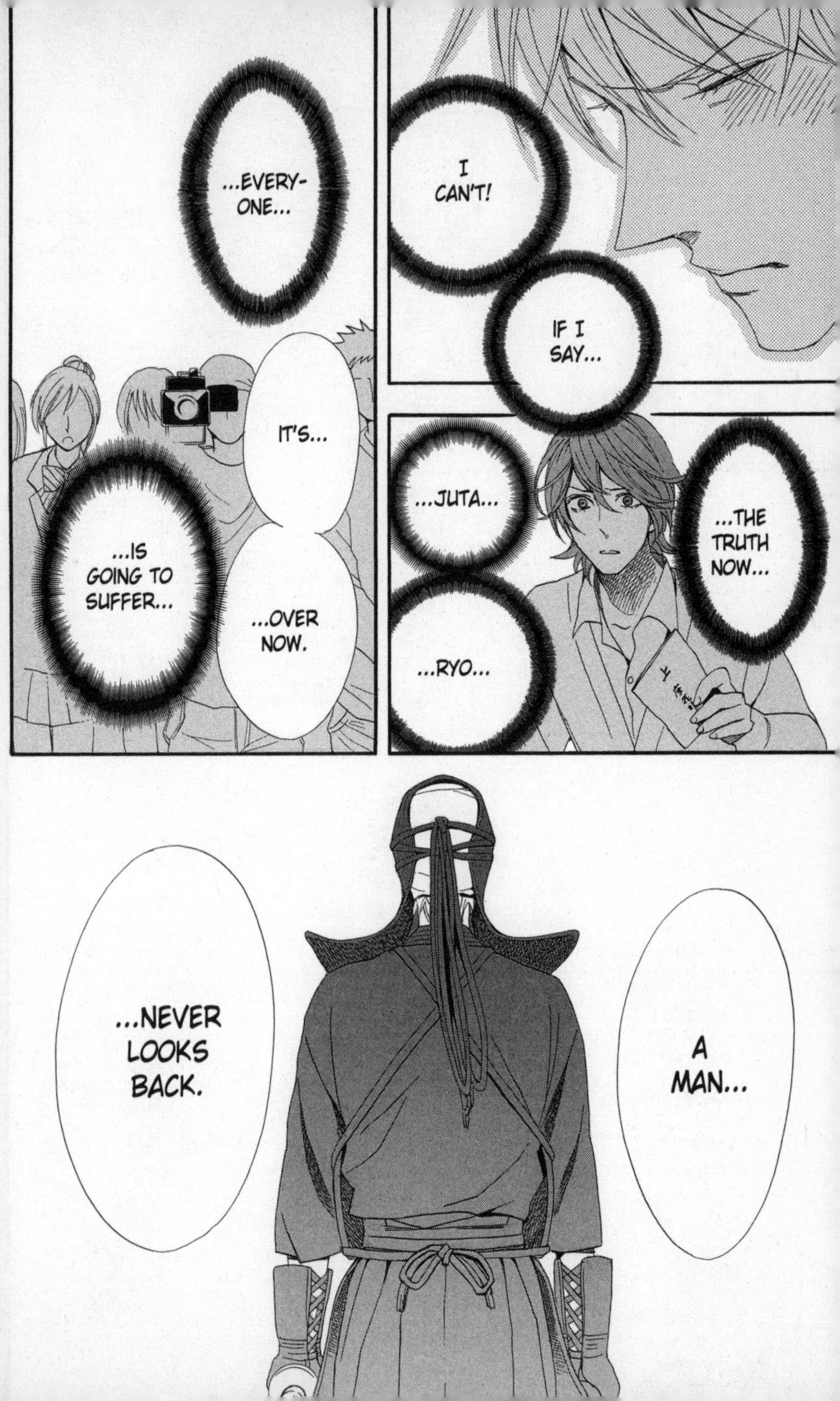
I CAN'T!
IF I SAY...
...THE TRUTH NOW...
...JUTA...
...RYO...
...EVERY-ONE...
...IS GOING TO SUFFER...
IT'S...
...OVER NOW.
A MAN...
...NEVER LOOKS BACK.

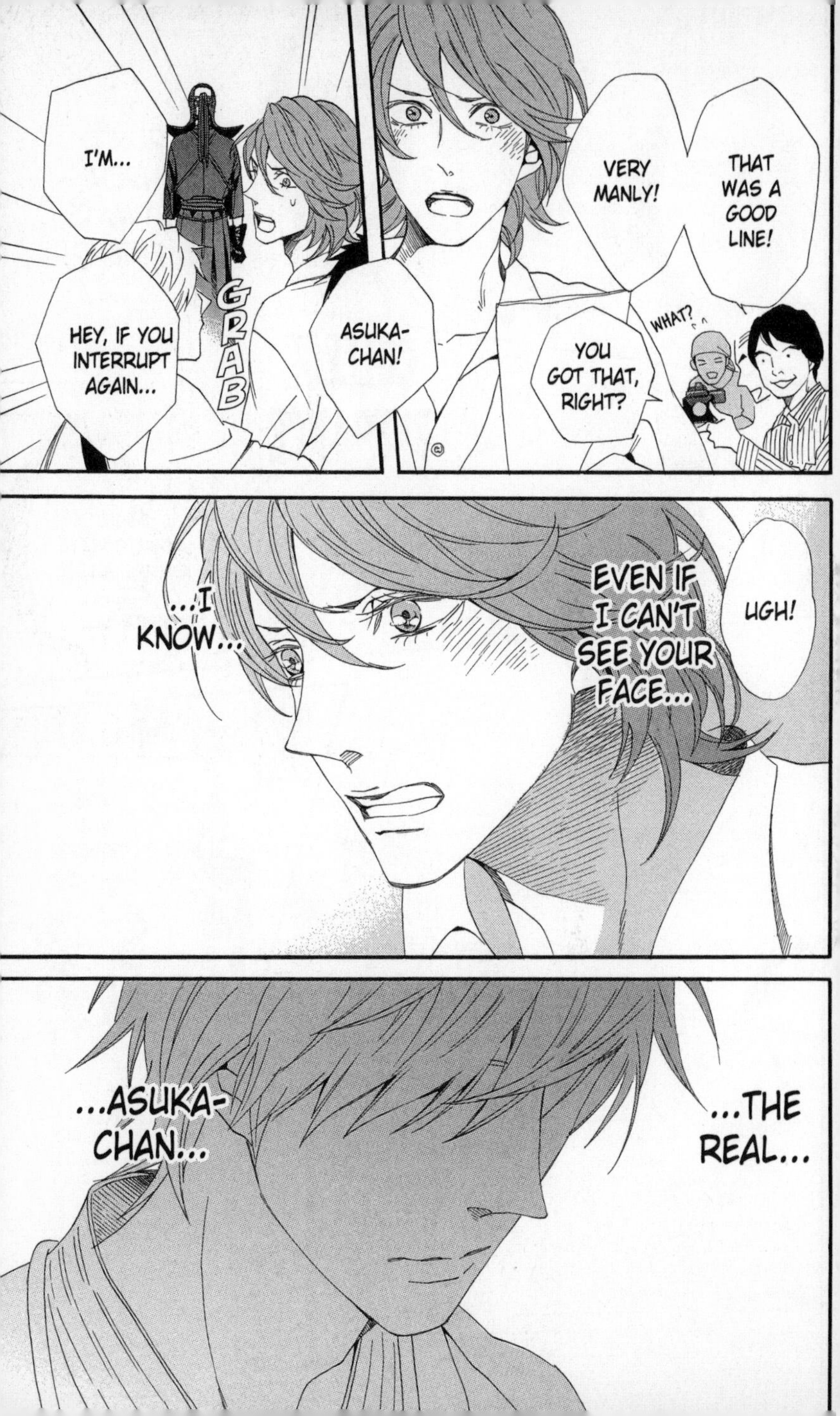
THAT WAS A GOOD LINE!
VERY MANLY!
WHAT?
YOU GOT THAT, RIGHT?
ASUKA-CHAN!
I'M...
GRAB
HEY, IF YOU INTERRUPT AGAIN...
UGH!
EVEN IF I CAN'T SEE YOUR FACE...
...I KNOW...
...THE REAL...
...ASUKA-CHAN...

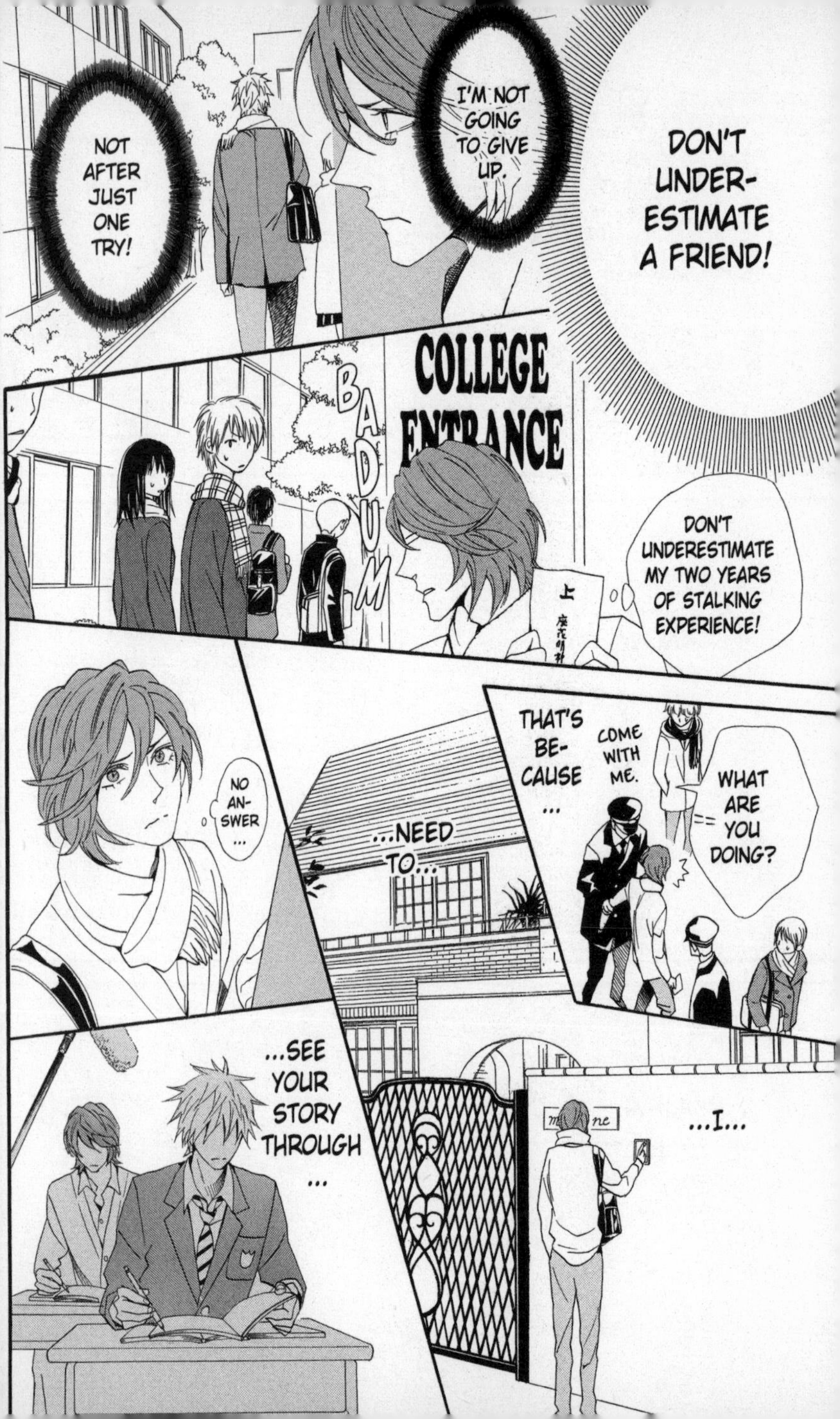
DON'T UNDER-ESTIMATE A FRIEND!
I'M NOT GOING TO GIVE UP.
NOT AFTER JUST ONE TRY!
DON'T UNDERESTIMATE MY TWO YEARS OF STALKING EXPERIENCE!
COLLEGE ENTRANCE
BADUM
WHAT ARE YOU DOING?
COME WITH ME.
THAT'S BE-CAUSE ...
...NEED TO...
NO AN-SWER ...
...I...
...SEE YOUR STORY THROUGH ...

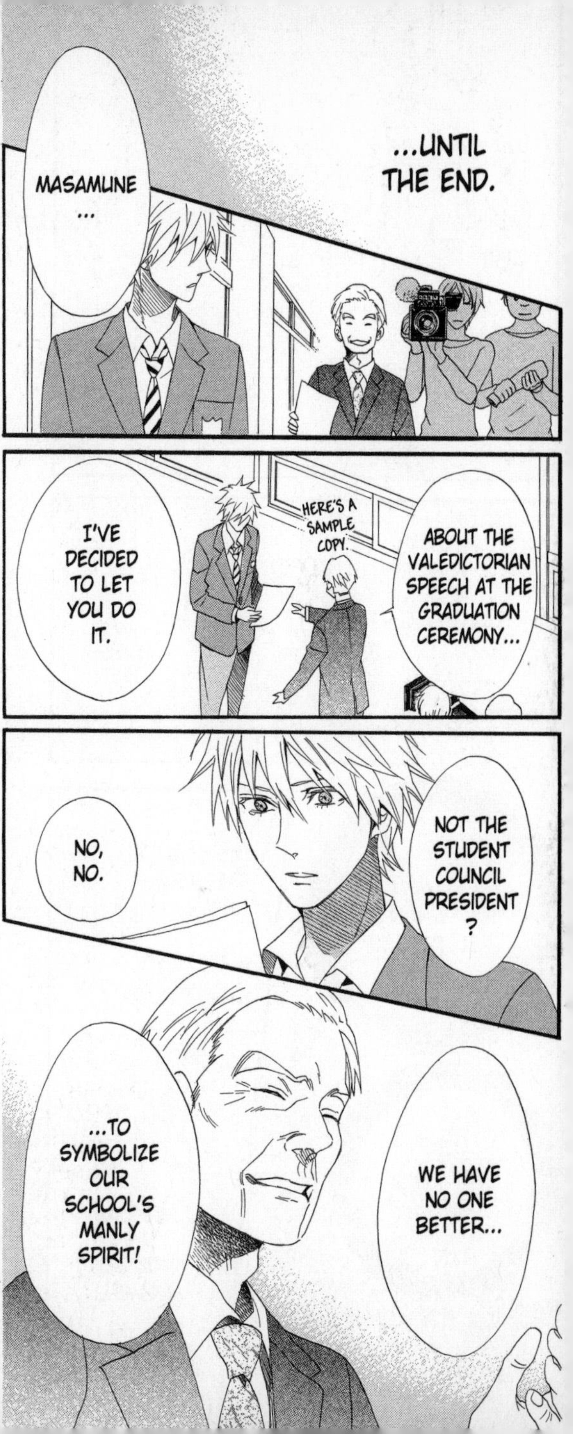
...UNTIL THE END.
MASAMUNE ...
ABOUT THE VALEDICTORIAN SPEECH AT THE GRADUATION CEREMONY...
HERE'S A SAMPLE COPY.
I'VE DECIDED TO LET YOU DO IT.
NOT THE STUDENT COUNCIL PRESIDENT?
NO, NO.
WE HAVE NO ONE BETTER...
...TO SYMBOLIZE OUR SCHOOL'S MANLY SPIRIT!

Yamato Ariake's original form

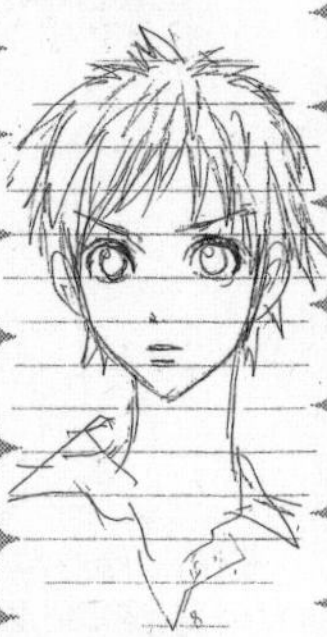

The next character I decided on after Asuka and Ryo was actually Yamato. He used to be named "Kei." When I was still vague on the story, Asuka even had a younger sister by the name of "Kikuka." She became the basis of Kuriko. ↓

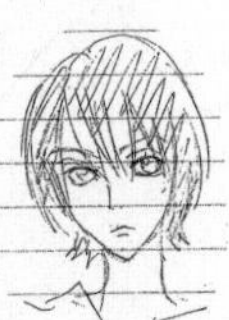

To be continued in volume 18.

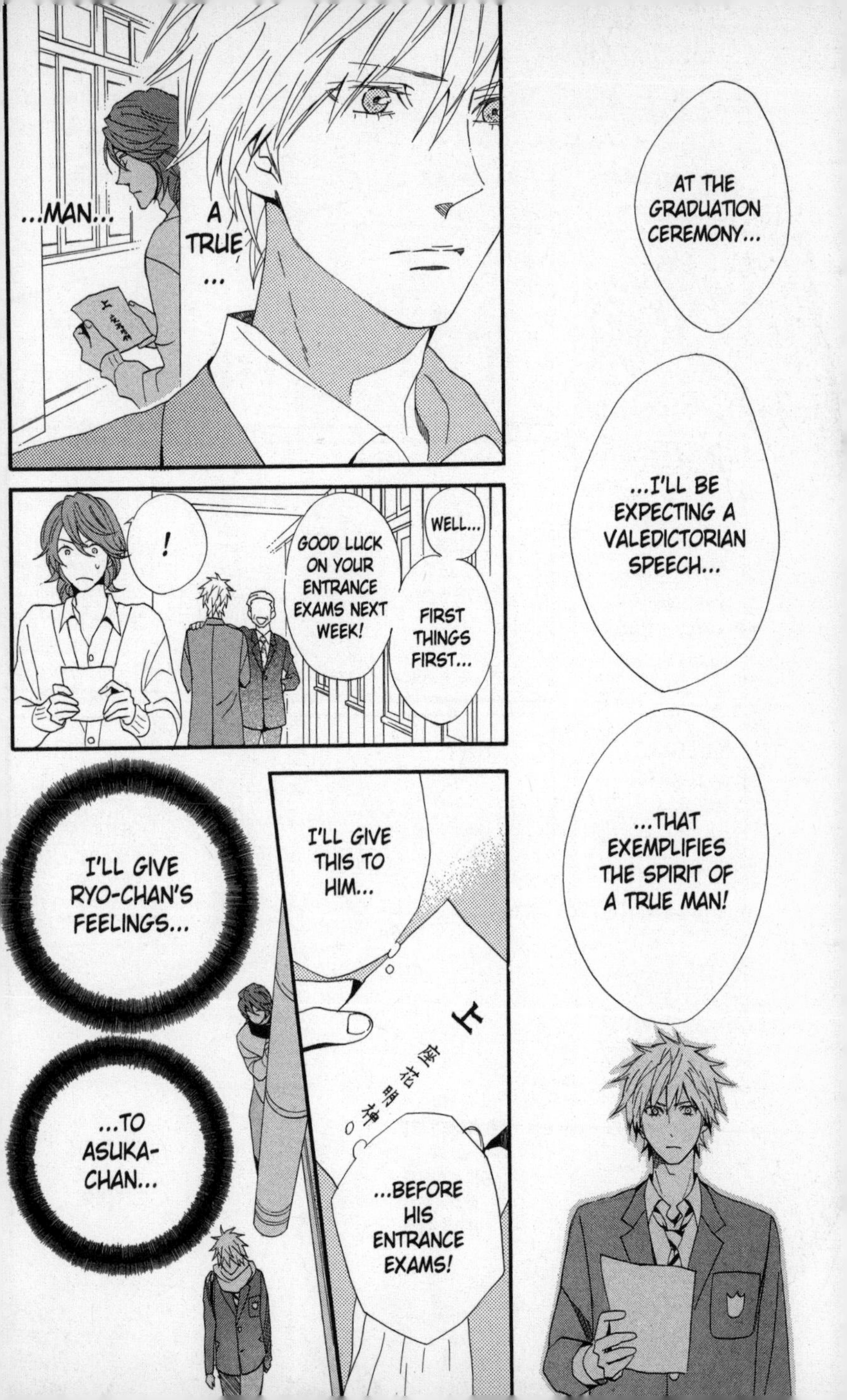
AT THE GRADUATION CEREMONY...
...I'LL BE EXPECTING A VALEDICTORIAN SPEECH...
...THAT EXEMPLIFIES THE SPIRIT OF A TRUE MAN!
A TRUE...
...MAN...
WELL...
FIRST THINGS FIRST...
GOOD LUCK ON YOUR ENTRANCE EXAMS NEXT WEEK!
!
I'LL GIVE THIS TO HIM...
...BEFORE HIS ENTRANCE EXAMS!
I'LL GIVE RYO-CHAN'S FEELINGS...
...TO ASUKA-CHAN...

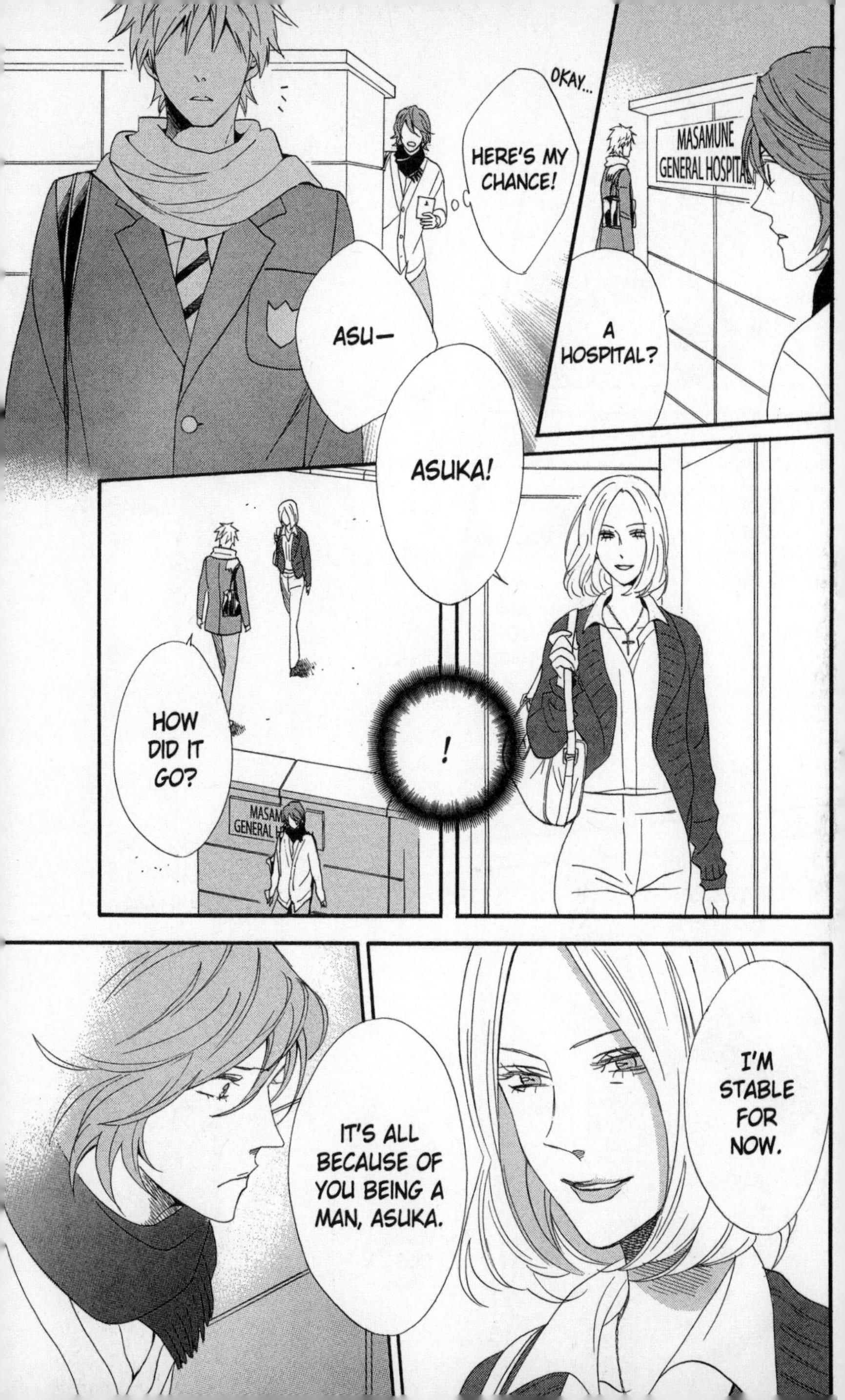
MASAMUNE GENERAL HOSPITAL
A HOSPITAL?
OKAY...
HERE'S MY CHANCE!
ASU—
ASUKA!
!
HOW DID IT GO?
I'M STABLE FOR NOW.
IT'S ALL BECAUSE OF YOU BEING A MAN, ASUKA.

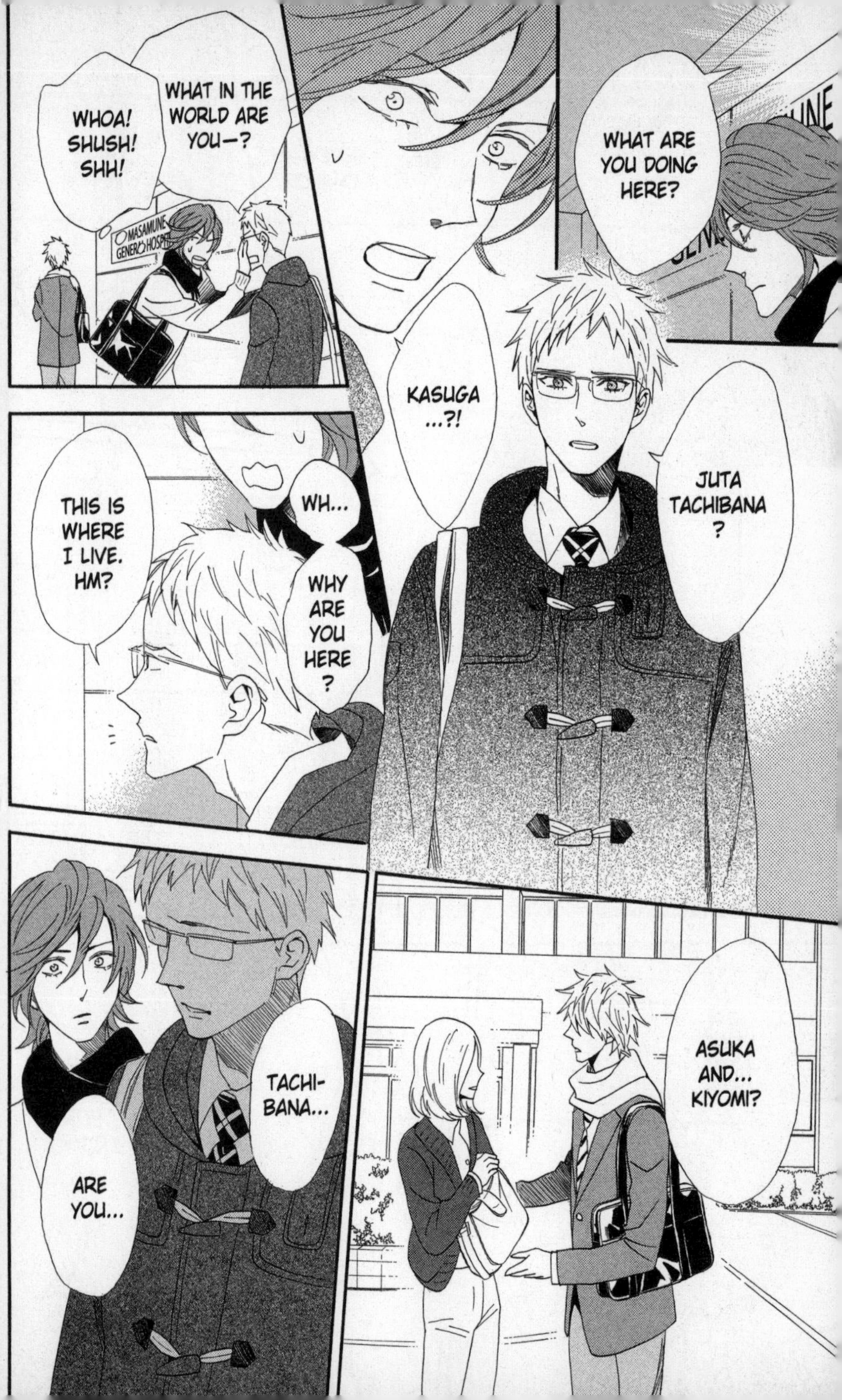
WHAT ARE YOU DOING HERE?
WHAT IN THE WORLD ARE YOU—?
WHOA! SHUSH! SHH!
MASAMUNE
JUTA TACHIBANA ?
KASUGA ...?!
WH...
WHY ARE YOU HERE ?
THIS IS WHERE I LIVE. HM?
ASUKA AND... KIYOMI?
TACHI-BANA...
ARE YOU...

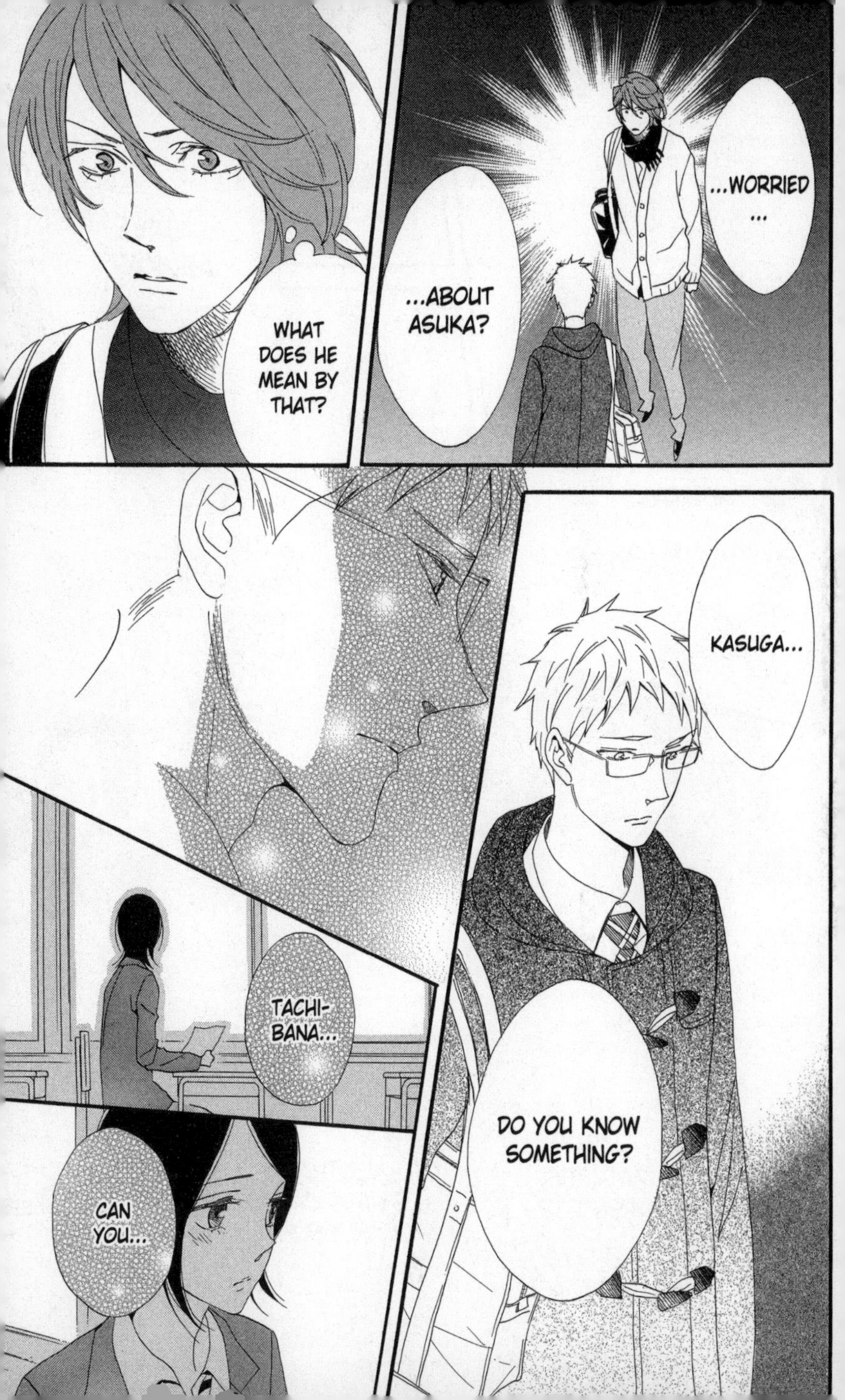
...WORRIED ...
...ABOUT ASUKA?
WHAT DOES HE MEAN BY THAT?
KASUGA...
DO YOU KNOW SOMETHING?
TACHI-BANA...
CAN YOU...

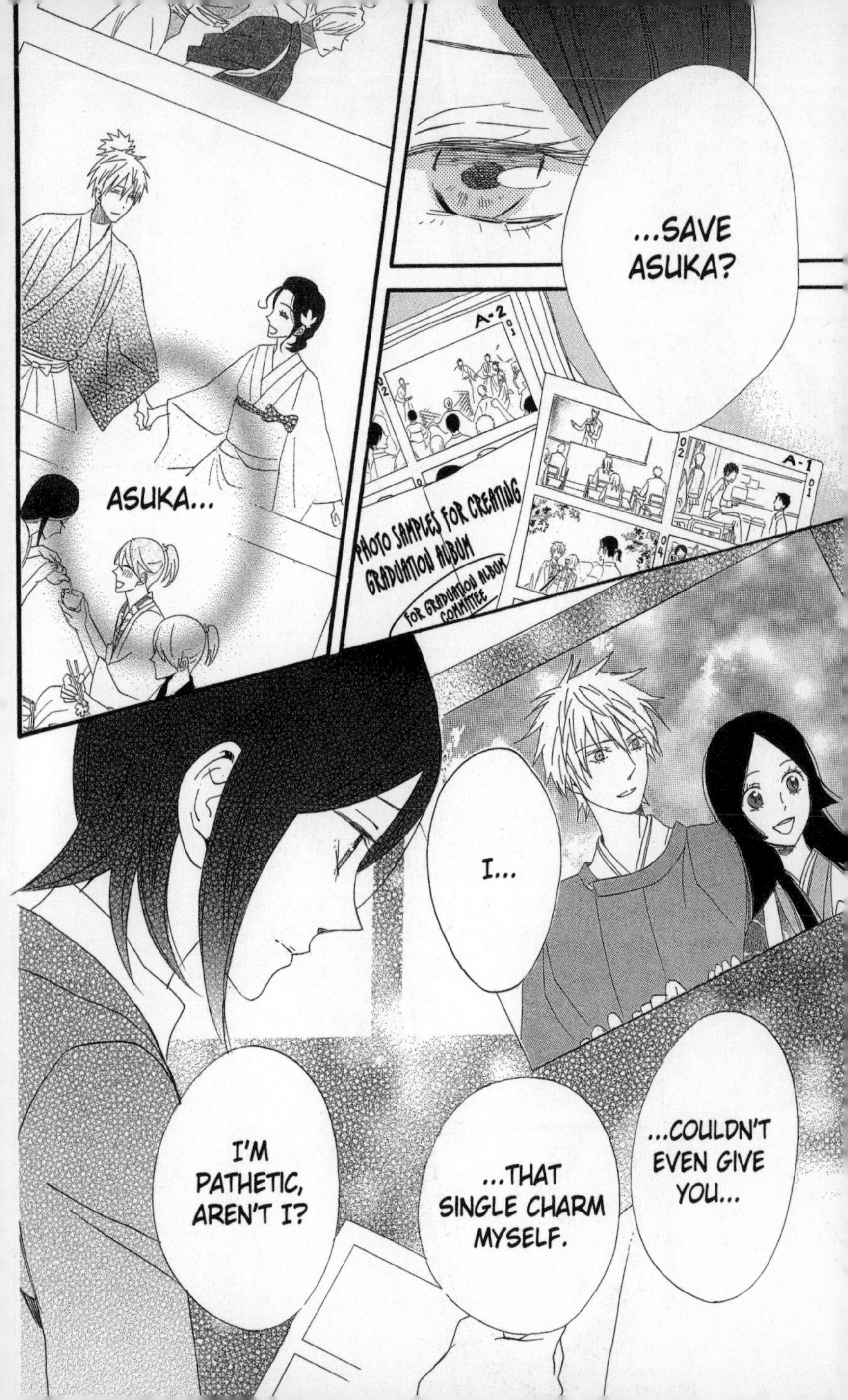
...SAVE ASUKA?
PHOTO SAMPLES FOR CREATING GRADUATION ALBUM
FOR GRADUATION ALBUM COMMITTEE
ASUKA...
I...
...COULDN'T EVEN GIVE YOU...
...THAT SINGLE CHARM MYSELF.
I'M PATHETIC, AREN'T I?

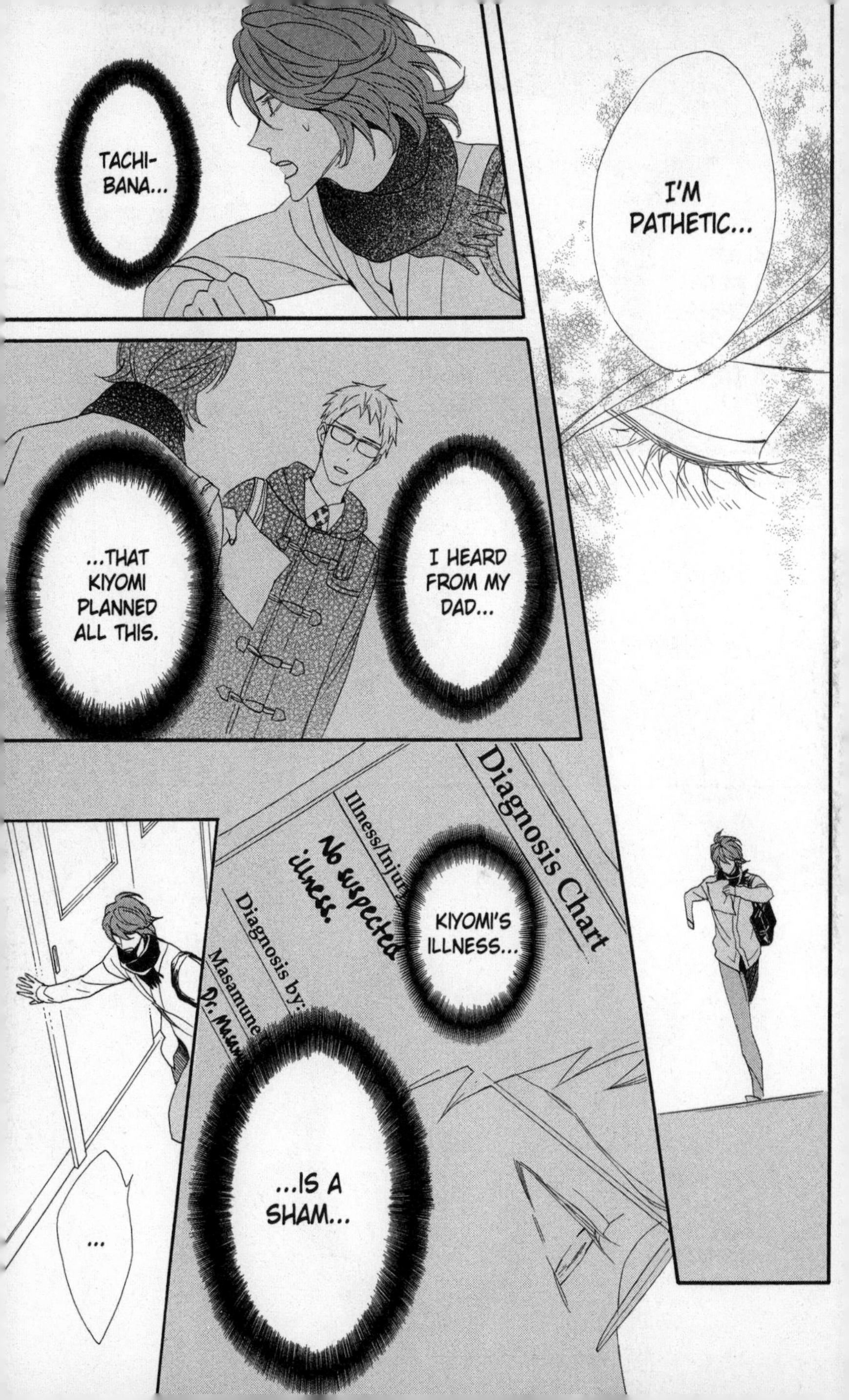
I'M PATHETIC...
TACHI-BANA...
I HEARD FROM MY DAD...
...THAT KIYOMI PLANNED ALL THIS.
Diagnosis Chart
Illness/Injur
No suspected illness.
Diagnosis by:
Masamune
KIYOMI'S ILLNESS...
...IS A SHAM...
...

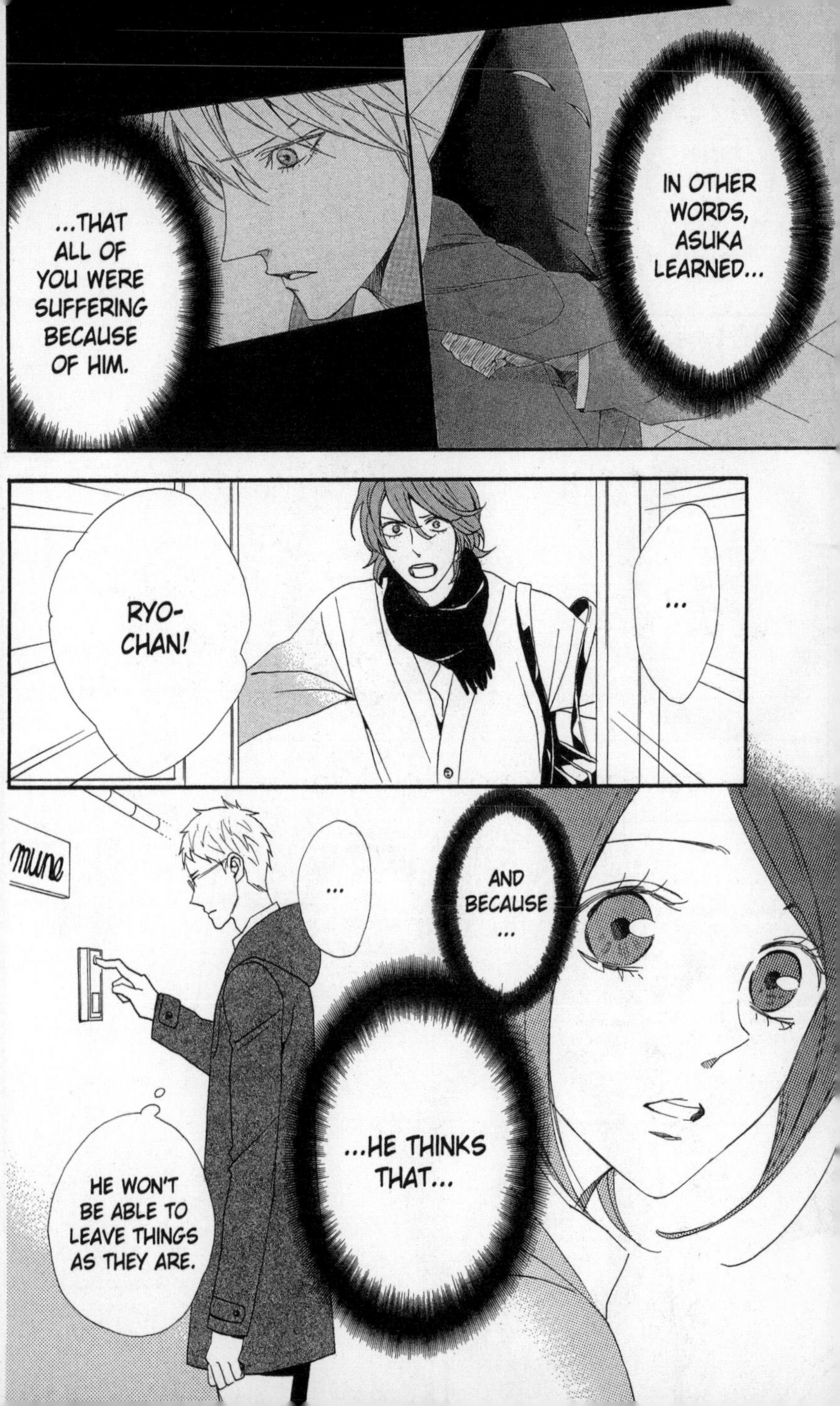
IN OTHER WORDS, ASUKA LEARNED...
...THAT ALL OF YOU WERE SUFFERING BECAUSE OF HIM.
...
RYO-CHAN!
AND BECAUSE ...
...HE THINKS THAT...
mune
...
HE WON'T BE ABLE TO LEAVE THINGS AS THEY ARE.

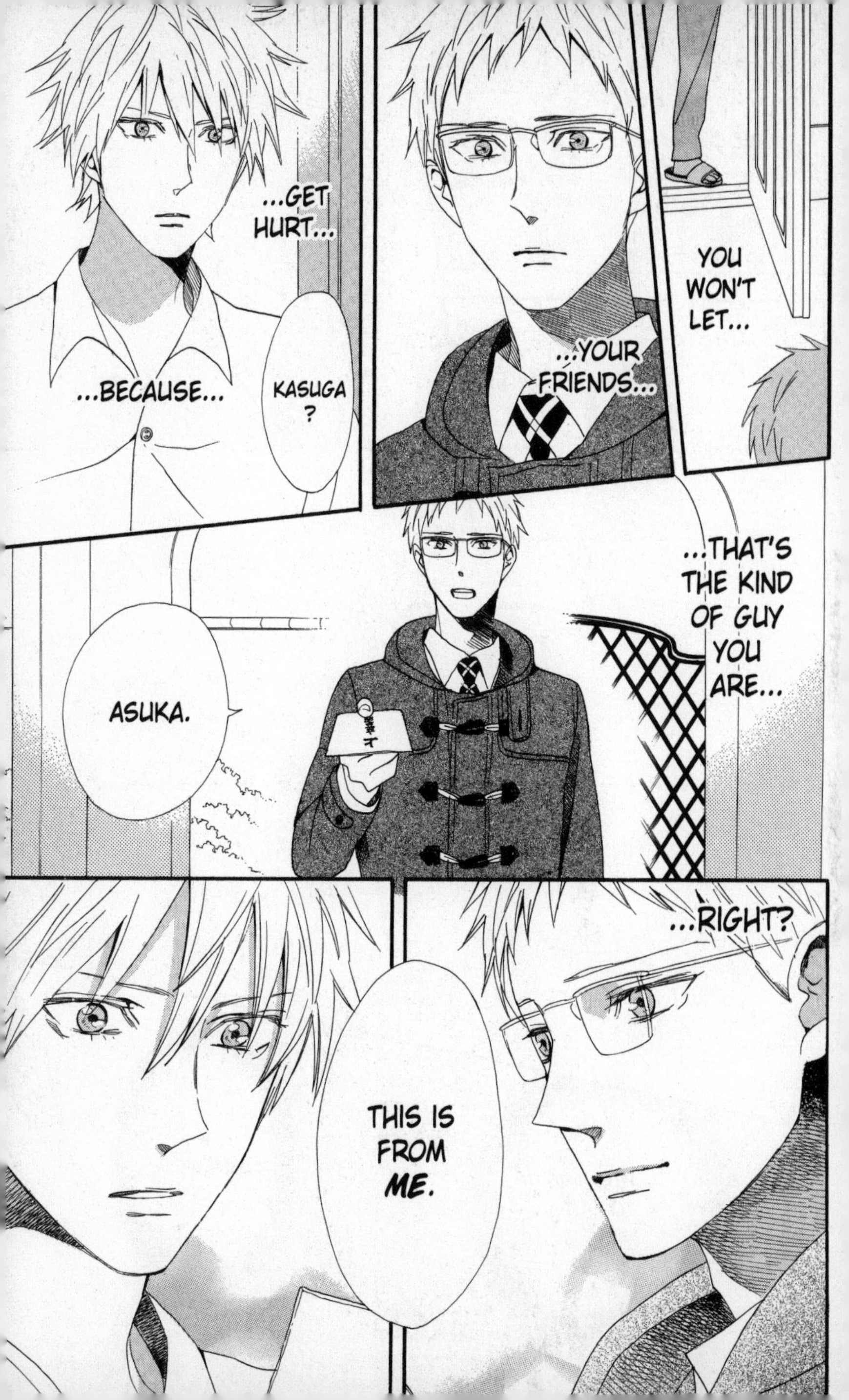
YOU WON'T LET...
...YOUR FRIENDS...
...GET HURT...
KASUGA ?
...BECAUSE...
...THAT'S THE KIND OF GUY YOU ARE...
ASUKA.
...RIGHT?
THIS IS FROM ME.

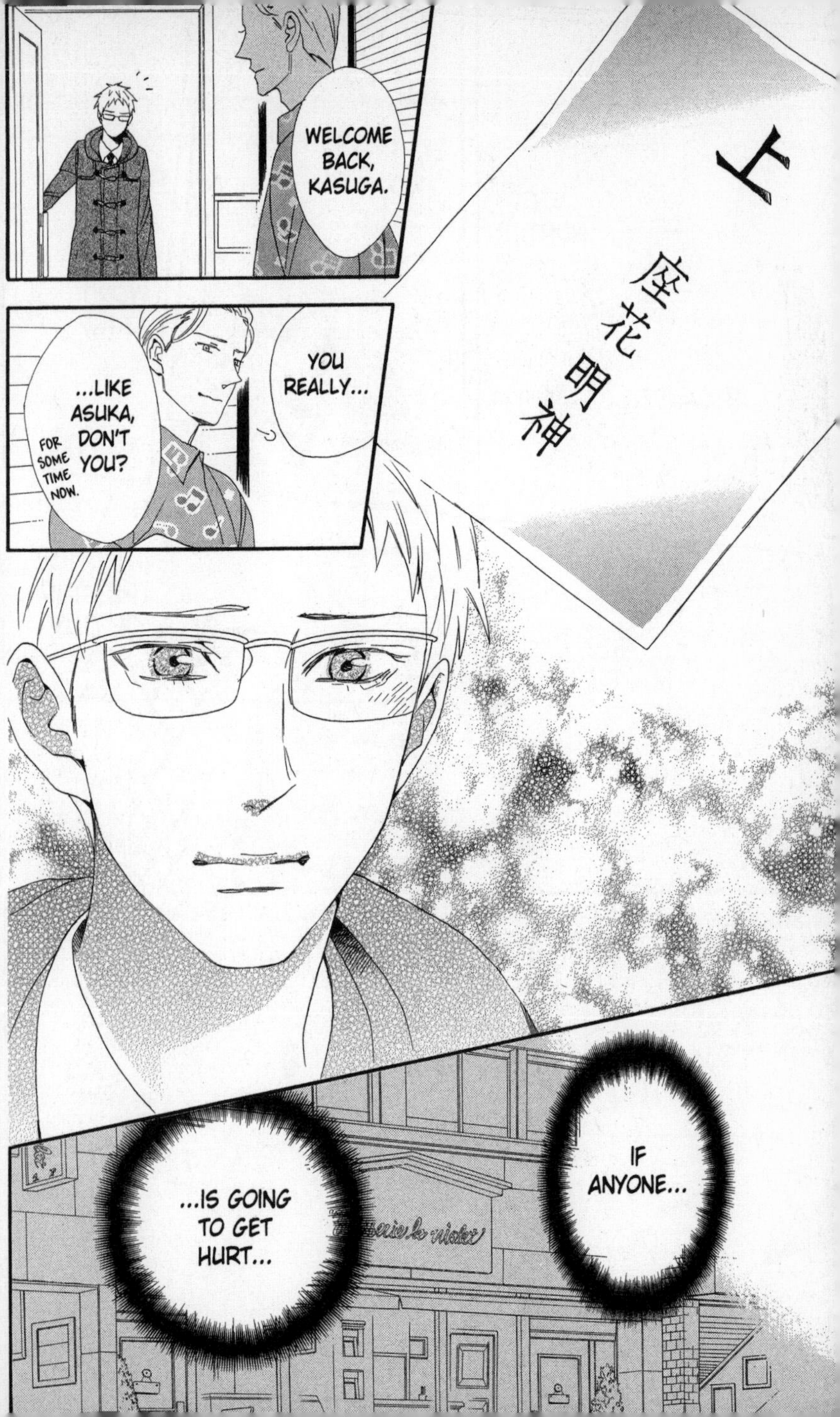
上
座花明神
WELCOME BACK, KASUGA.
YOU REALLY...
...LIKE ASUKA, DON'T YOU?
FOR SOME TIME NOW.
IF ANYONE...
...IS GOING TO GET HURT...

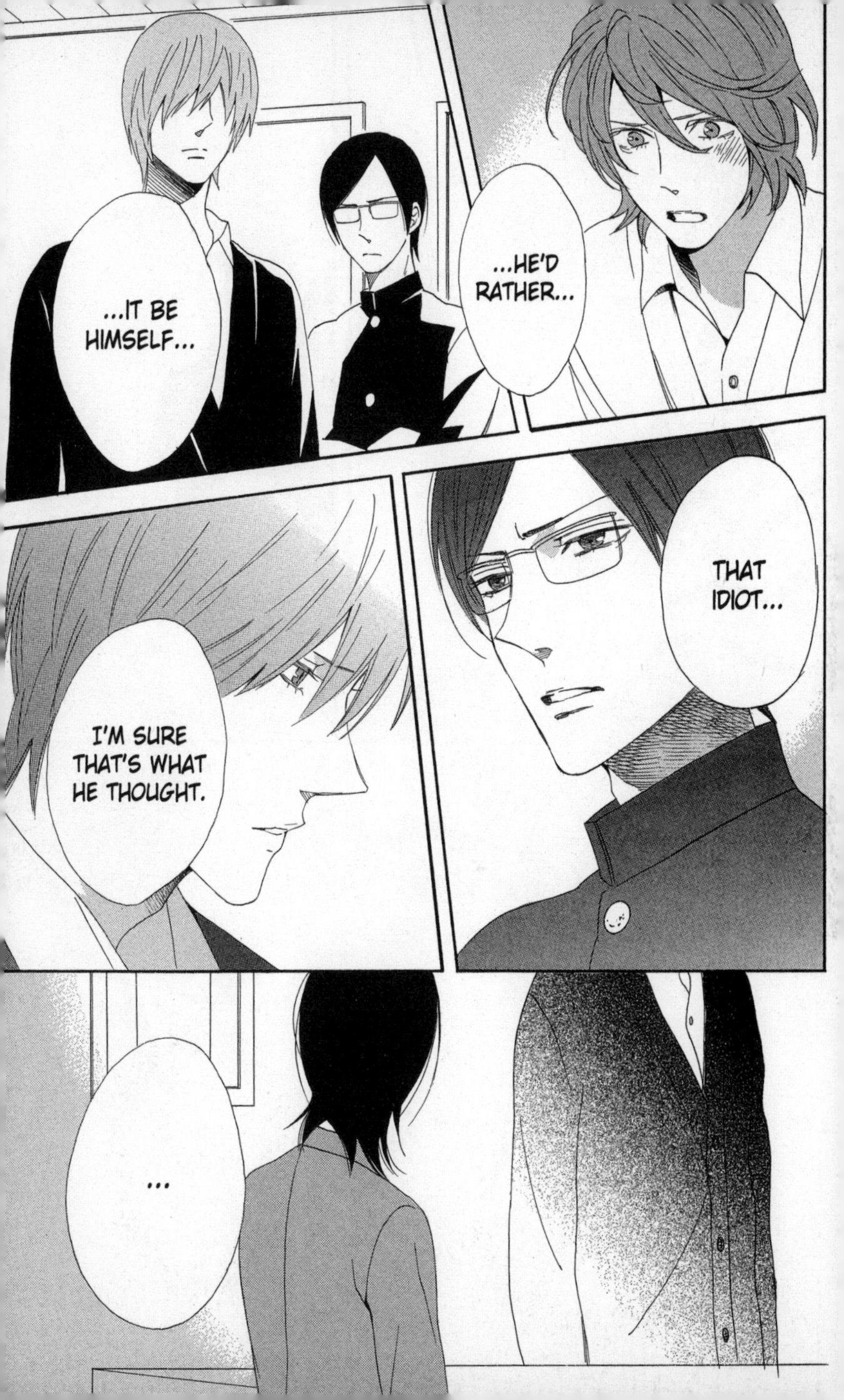
...HE'D RATHER...
...IT BE HIMSELF...
THAT IDIOT...
I'M SURE THAT'S WHAT HE THOUGHT.
...

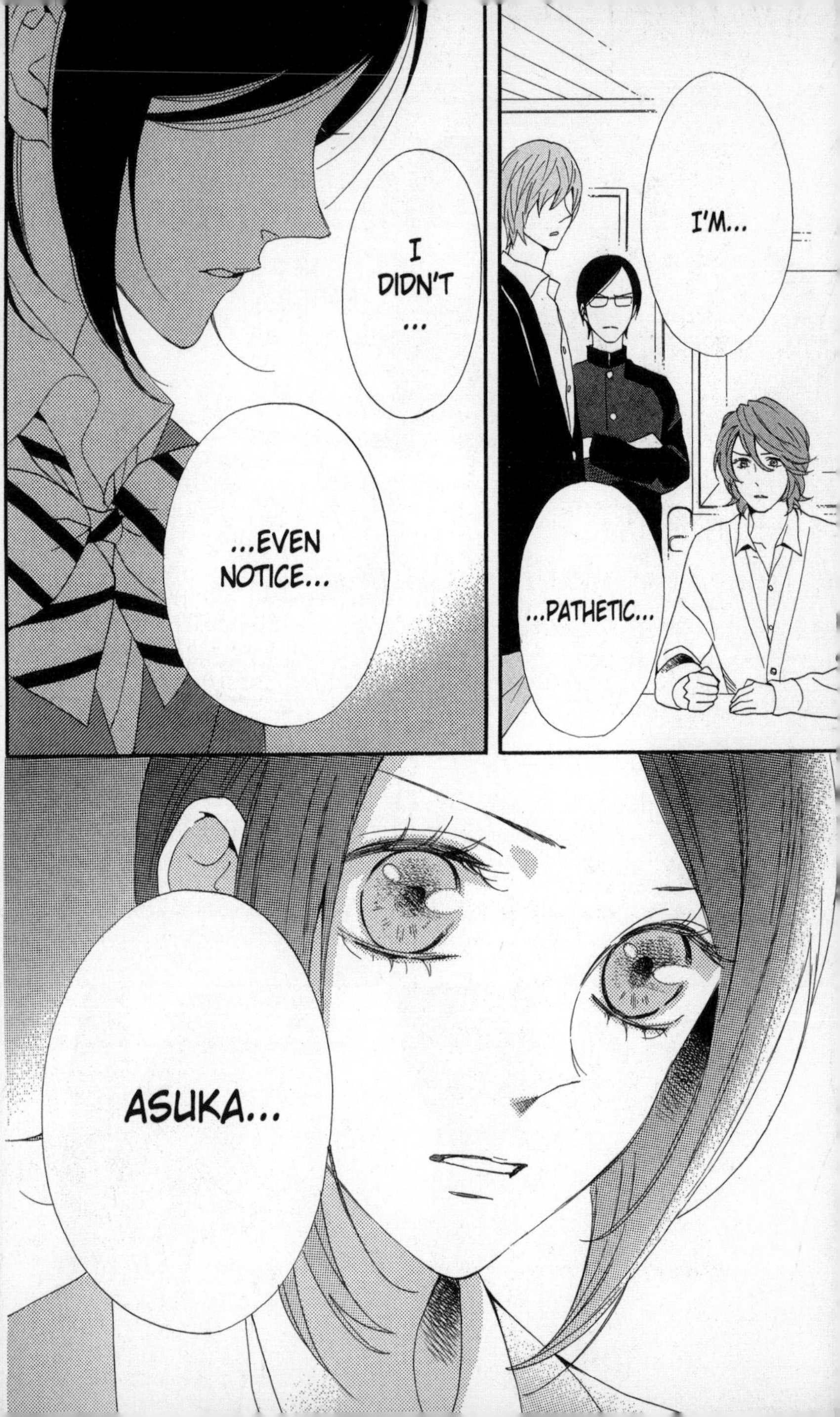
I'M...
...PATHETIC...
I DIDN'T ...
...EVEN NOTICE...
ASUKA...

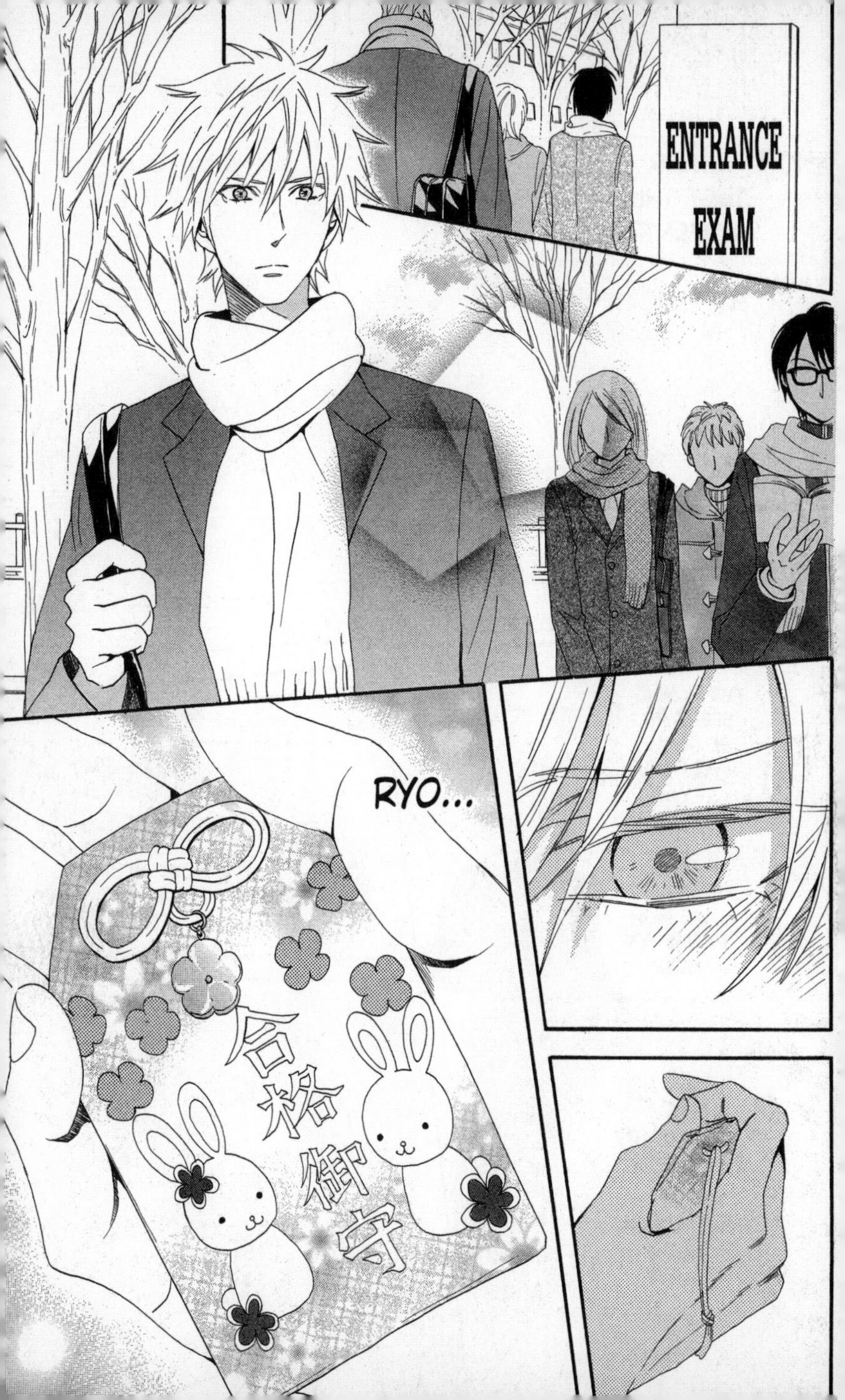
ENTRANCE EXAM
RYO...
合格御守

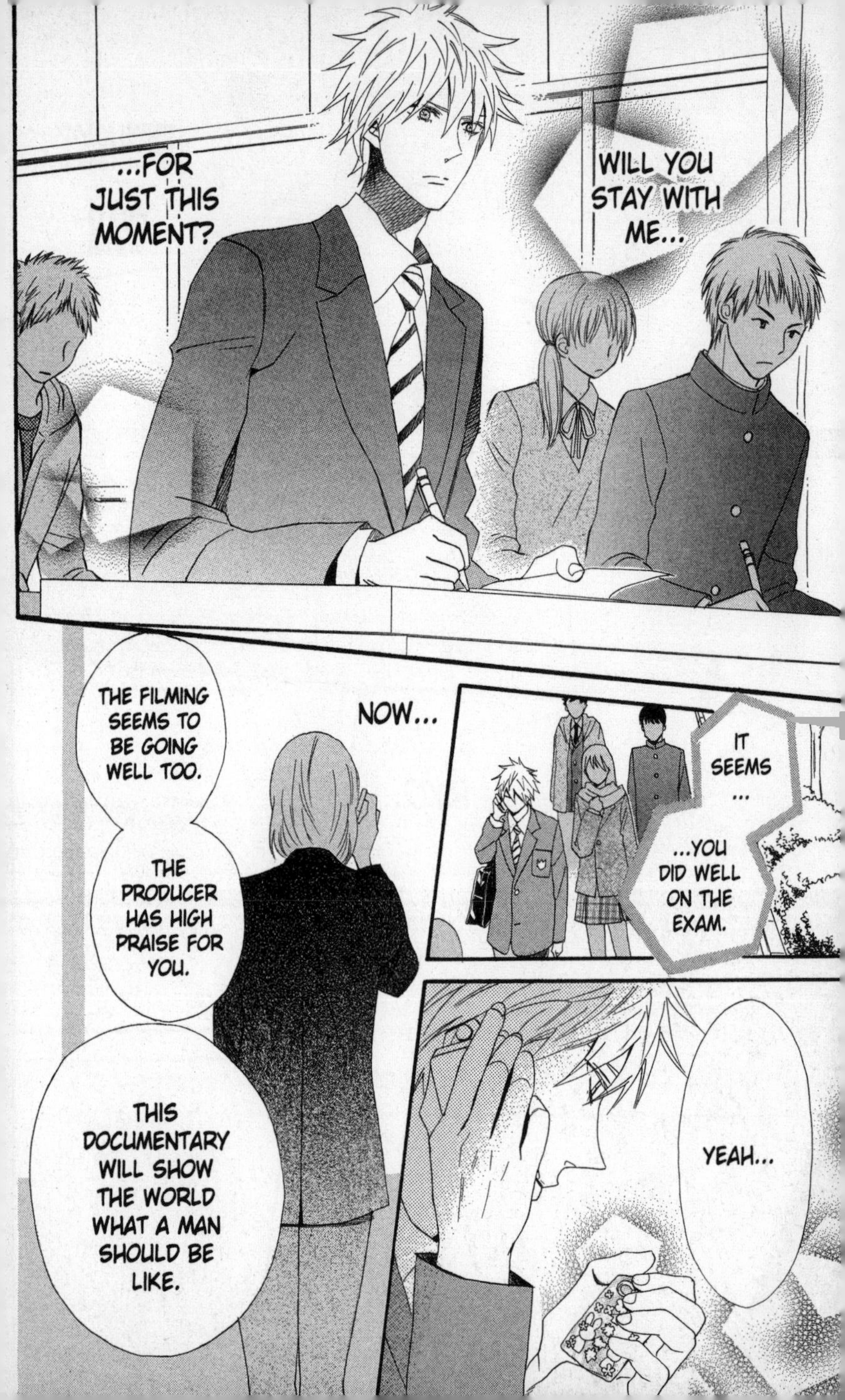
WILL YOU STAY WITH ME...
...FOR JUST THIS MOMENT?
NOW...
IT SEEMS ...
...YOU DID WELL ON THE EXAM.
YEAH...
THE FILMING SEEMS TO BE GOING WELL TOO.
THE PRODUCER HAS HIGH PRAISE FOR YOU.
THIS DOCUMENTARY WILL SHOW THE WORLD WHAT A MAN SHOULD BE LIKE.

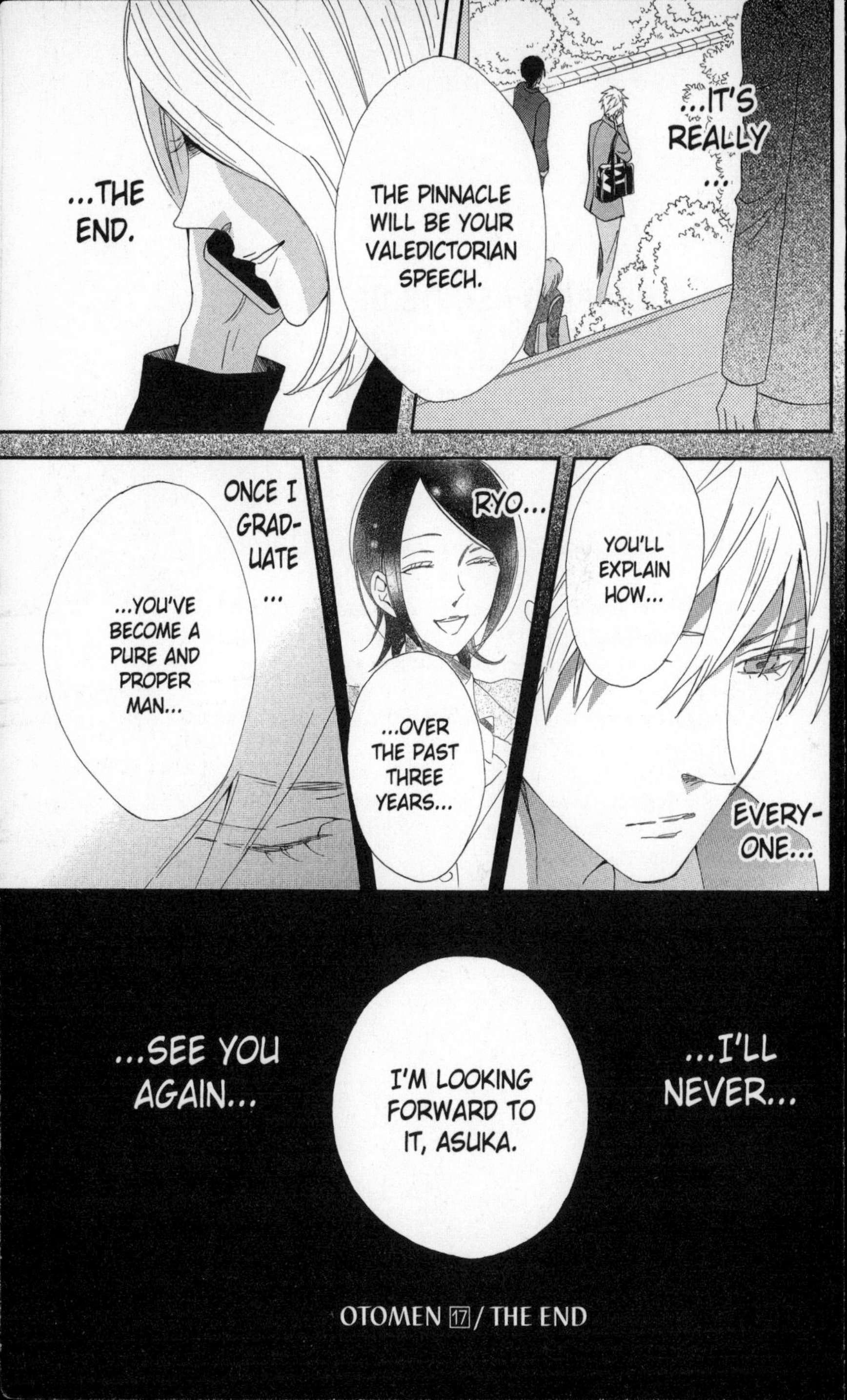
...IT'S REALLY ...
THE PINNACLE WILL BE YOUR VALEDICTORIAN SPEECH.
...THE END.
YOU'LL EXPLAIN HOW...
EVERY-ONE...
RYO...
...OVER THE PAST THREE YEARS...
ONCE I GRAD-UATE ...
...YOU'VE BECOME A PURE AND PROPER MAN...
...I'LL NEVER...
I'M LOOKING FORWARD TO IT, ASUKA.
...SEE YOU AGAIN...

OTOMEN 17 / THE END

# Confused by some of the terms, but too MANLY to ask for help?

Here are some **cultural notes** to assist you!

## HONORIFICS

**Chan** – an informal honorific used to address children and females. *Chan* can also be used toward animals, lovers, intimate friends and people whom one has known since childhood.

**San** – the most common honorific title. It is used to address people outside one's immediate family and close circle of friends.

**Senpai** – used to address one's senior colleagues or mentor figures; it is used when students refer to or address more senior students in their school.

**Sensei** – honorific title used to address teachers as well as professionals such as doctors, lawyers and artists.

# NOTES

*Page 3* | **Kotobuki**
The fan that Ryo is holding has the kanji for *kotobuki* (寿), which means "longevity" and "joy."

*Page 7, panel 1* | **Hana to Mame**
The name *Hana to Mame* (Flowers and Beans) is a play on the real shojo manga magazine *Hana to Yume* (Flowers and Dreams) published by Hakusensha.

*Page 13, panel 1* | **Mira Jonouchi**
A shojo manga artist who inspired Juta to become a shojo manga artist himself. For more information, see *Otomen* volume 5.

*Page 14, panel 3* | **Kokusensha**
Kokusensha is the fictional publisher of the *Love Chick* shojo manga series that Juta Tachibana draws secretly (under the pen name Jewel Sachihana).

*Page 18, panel 3* | **Bento**
A lunch box that may contain rice, meat, pickles and an assortment of side dishes. Sometimes the food is arranged in such a way as to resemble objects like animals, flowers, leaves and so forth.

*Page 111, panel 1* | **Hagakure**
Asuka is reading *Hagakure*, an 18th century book of writing intended to act as a guide on to how to live as a warrior.

*Page 160, panel 2* | **Charms**
The charms shown in this panel are for good health and success in exams. Ryo purchases one of the success-in-exams charms, shown on p.185, panel 5. The envelope that the charm comes in has the shrine's name on it (see p.166, panel 5).

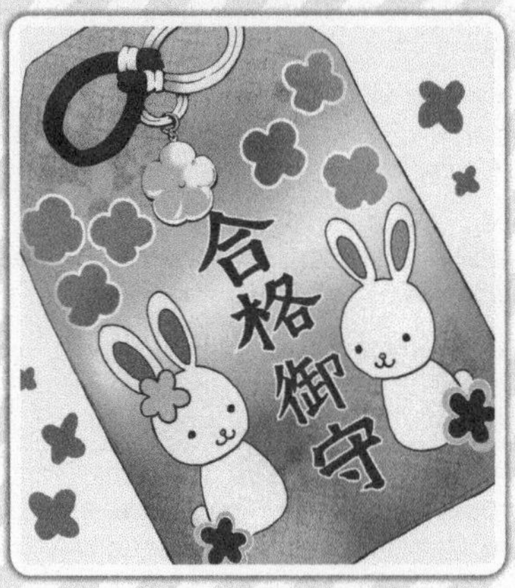
合格御守

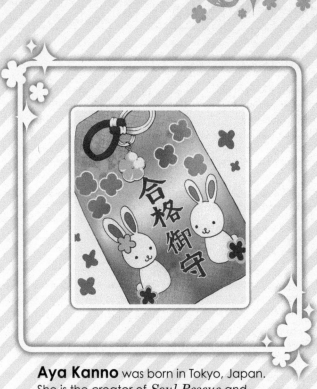

**Aya Kanno** was born in Tokyo, Japan. She is the creator of *Soul Rescue* and *Blank Slate* (originally published as *Akusaga* in Japan's *BetsuHana* magazine).

# OTOMEN

*Vol. 17*
Shojo Beat Edition

*Story and Art by* | **AYA KANNO**

*Translation & Adaptation* | **JN Productions**
*Touch-up Art & Lettering* | **Mark McMurray**
*Design* | **Fawn Lau**
*Editor* | **Amy Yu**

Otomen by Aya Kanno © Aya Kanno 2013
All rights reserved. First published in Japan in 2013 by HAKUSENSHA, Inc., Tokyo.
English language translation rights arranged with HAKUSENSHA, Inc., Tokyo.

The stories, characters and incidents mentioned
in this publication are entirely fictional.

Printed in the U.S.A.

Published by VIZ Media, LLC
P.O. Box 77010
San Francisco, CA 94107

10 9 8 7 6 5 4 3 2 1
First printing, January 2014

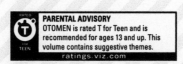

**PARENTAL ADVISORY**
OTOMEN is rated T for Teen and is
recommended for ages 13 and up. This
volume contains suggestive themes.
ratings.viz.com

www.viz.com

www.shojobeat.com

# SURPRISE!

## YOU MAY BE READING THE WRONG WAY!

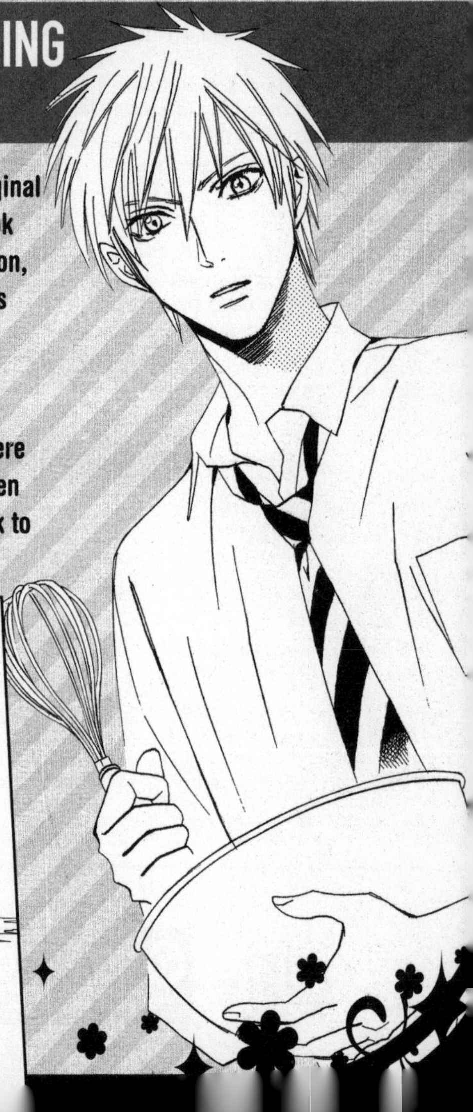

**It's true: In keeping with the original Japanese comic format, this book reads from right to left—so action, sound effects, and word balloons are completely reversed. This preserves the orientation of the original artwork—plus, it's fun! Check out the diagram shown here to get the hang of things, and then turn to the other side of the book to get started!**

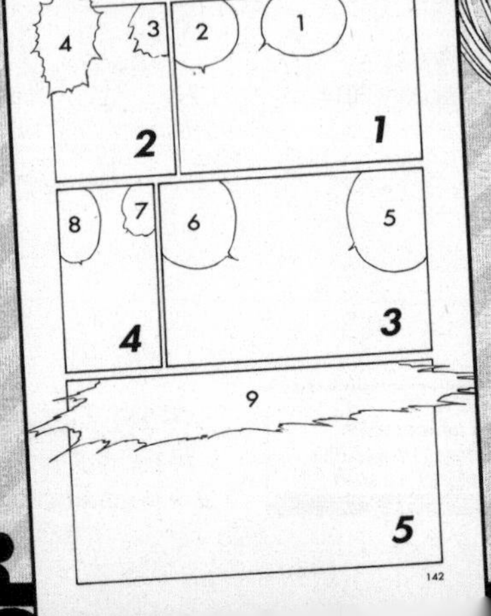
1
2
1
3
4
2
5
6
3
7
8
4
9
5
142